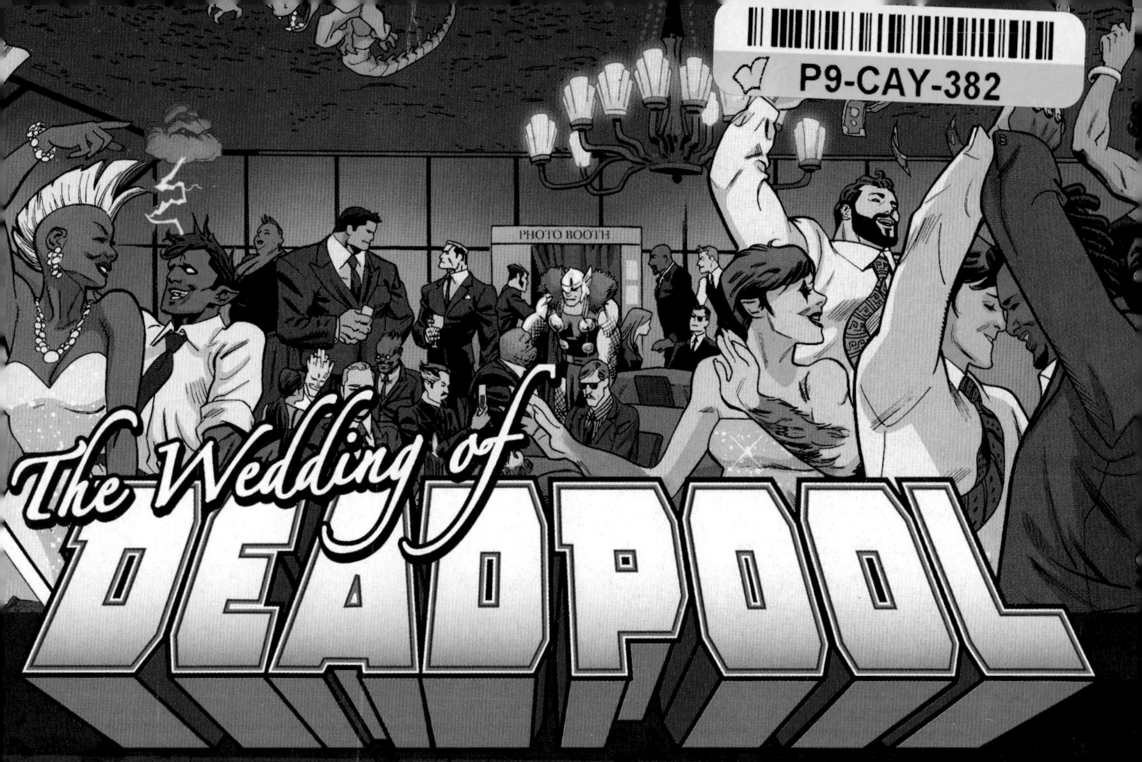
PHOTO BOOTH

The Wedding of DEADPOOL

WRITERS
GERRY DUGGAN & BRIAN POSEHN

ARTISTS
MIKE HAWTHORNE (#27) & SCOTT KOBLISH (#26 & #28)

COLORISTS
VAL STAPLES (#27) & JORDIE BELLAIRE (#26 & #28)

COVER ART
SCOTT KOBLISH & VAL STAPLES (#27), GURIHIRU (#28) AND PHIL NOTO (#26)

DEADPOOL ANNUAL #1

WRITERS
BEN ACKER & BEN BLACKER

ARTIST
EVAN "DOC" SHANER

COLORIST
VERONICA GANDINI

COVER ART
TRADD MOORE & JORDIE BELLAIRE

LETTERER
VC'S JOE SABINO

ASSISTANT EDITOR
FRANKIE JOHNSON

EDITOR
JORDAN D. WHITE

DEADPOOL CREATED BY ROB LIEFELD & FABIAN NICIEZA

Collection Editor: Jennifer Grünwald • Assistant Editor: Sarah Brunstad • Associate Managing Editor: Alex Starbuck
Editor, Special Projects: Mark D. Beazley • Senior Editor, Special Projects: Jeff Youngquist • SVP Print, Sales & Marketing: David Gabriel

Editor in Chief: Axel Alonso • Chief Creative Officer: Joe Quesada • Publisher: Dan Buckley • Executive Producer: Alan Fine

DPOOL VOL. 5: THE WEDDING OF DEADPOOL. Contains material originally published in magazine form as DEADPOOL #26-28 and DEADPOOL ANNUAL #1. Second printing 2015. ISBN# 978-0-7851-8933-6. Published by MARVEL RLDWIDE, INC., a subsidiary of MARVEL ENTERTAINMENT, LLC. OFFICE OF PUBLICATION: 135 West 50th Street, New York, NY 10020. Copyright © 2014 MARVEL No similarity between any of the names, characters, persons, and/or tutions in this magazine with those of any living or dead person or institution is intended, and any such similarity which may exist is purely coincidental. **Printed in the U.S.A.** ALAN FINE, President, Marvel Entertainment; DAN BUCKLEY, ident, TV, Publishing and Brand Management; JOE QUESADA, Chief Creative Officer; TOM BREVOORT, SVP of Publishing; DAVID BOGART, SVP of Operations & Procurement, Publishing; C.B. CEBULSKI, VP of International Development & d Management; DAVID GABRIEL, SVP Print, Sales & M… AN CRESPI, Editorial Operations Manager; ALEX MORALES, Publishing rations Manager; STAN LEE, Chairman Emeritus. For … Custom Solutions & Ad Sales, at jrheingold@marvel.com. For Marvel scription inquiries, please call 800-217-9158. **Manuf… IMFIELD, OH, USA.**

8765432

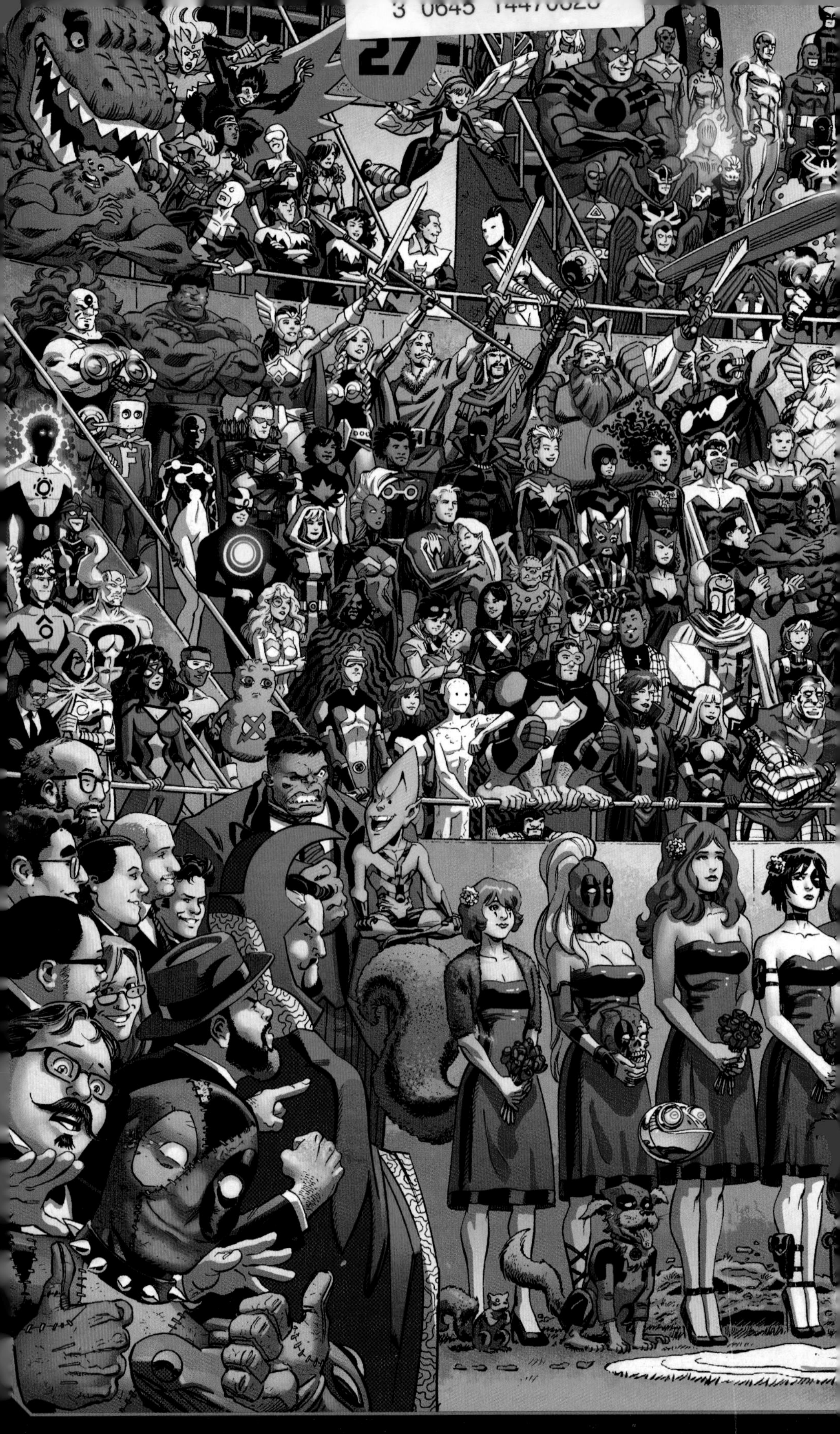
27

THE WEDDING OF DEADPOOL

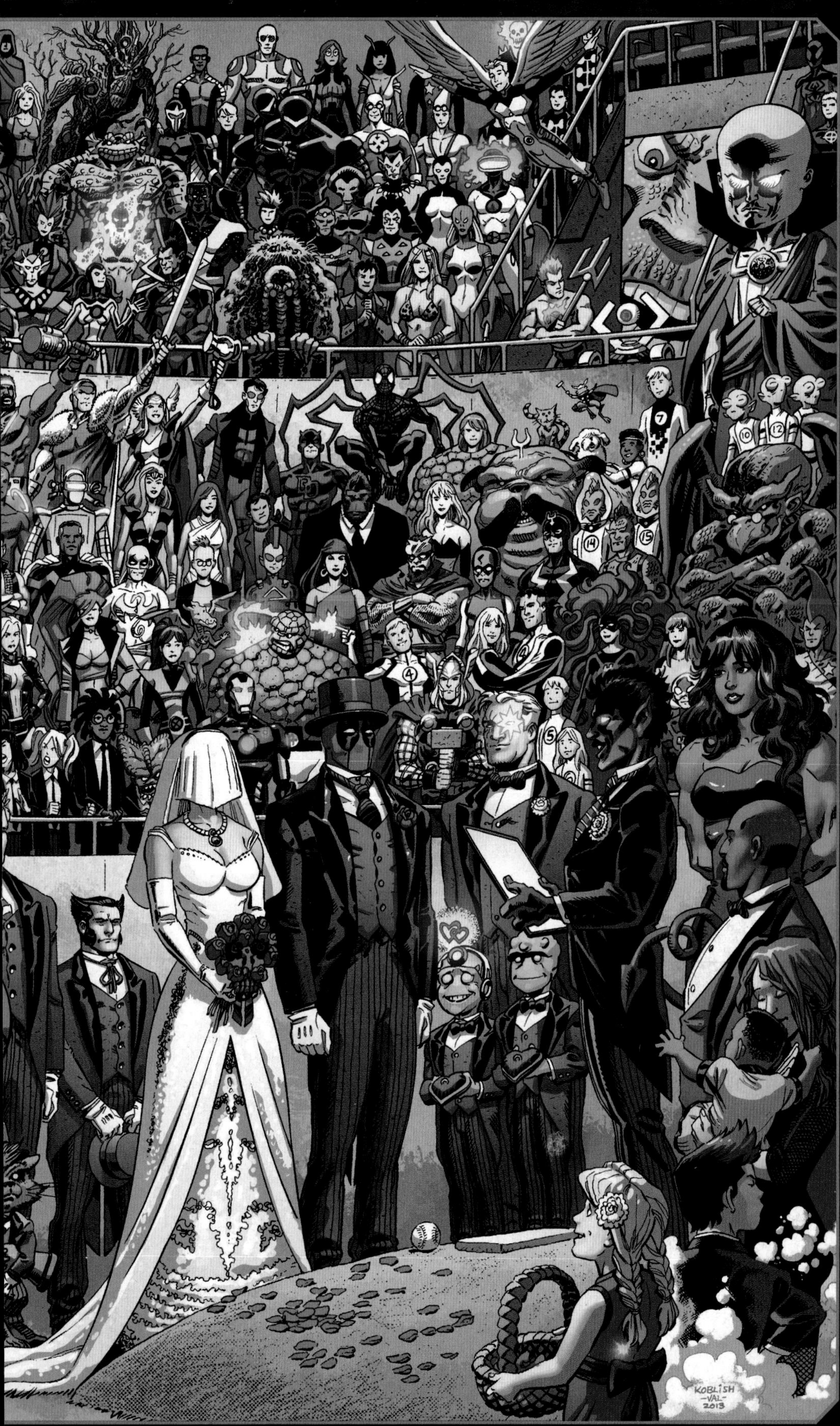
KOBLISH
-VAL-
2013

Possibly the world's most skilled mercenary, definitely the world's most annoying, Wade Wilson was chosen for a top-secret government program that gave him a healing factor allowing him to heal from any wound. Now, Wade makes his way as a gun for hire, shooting his prey's faces off while talking his friends' ears off. Call him the Merc with the Mouth...call him the Regeneratin' Degenerate...call him...

DEADPOOL

WELCOME, ONE AND ALL, TO THE WEDDING OF THE CENTURY!
THAT'S RIGHT--NOT A DREAM, NOT AN IMAGINARY STORY--I, DEADPOOL, THE MERC WITH THE MOUTH, THE REGENERATIN' DEGENERATE, AM GETTING MARRIED!
I KNOW WHAT YOU'RE THINKING.
"DEADPOOL! HOW CAN YOU BE GETTING MARRIED? LAST TIME WE SAW YOU, YOU WERE ALL AWASH WITH FEELS AFTER FINDING OUT YOU WERE MANIPULATED FOR MANY YEARS LONGER THAN YOU THOUGHT, YOU HAD A DAUGHTER WHO MIGHT BE DEAD, YOU SLAUGHTERED A WHOLE HELICARRIER FULL OF BADDIES, AND YOU FINALLY GOT AGENT PRESTON INTO HER OWN (NEW ROBOT) BODY! YOU WEREN'T EVEN DATING ANYONE!"
WHAT CAN I SAY? SOMETIMES THESE THINGS HAPPEN QUICKLY.
ANYWAY, IN CELEBRATION OF THE HAPPY OCCASION, CHECK OUT THE HUGE PACKAGE I'VE GOT FOR YOU! NOT ONLY DO YOU GET OUR MAIN STORY FEATURING MY IMPENDING NUPTIALS...I'VE LINED UP TWELVE BACKUP STORIES FEATURING THE RETURN OF SOME OLD FRIENDS!
AND DID I MENTION THAT THE COVER TO THIS ISSUE SET A WORLD RECORD? IT'S TRUE.
SO RAISE YOUR GLASSES AND TOAST TO ME AND MY BRIDE-TO-BE! WELCOME TO...

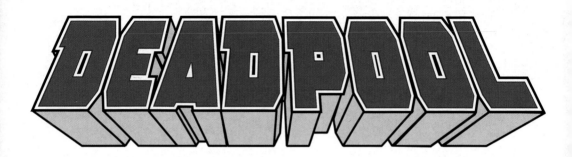

LI'L DEADPOOL ART BY
IRENE Y. LEE

THE WEDDING OF DEADPOOL

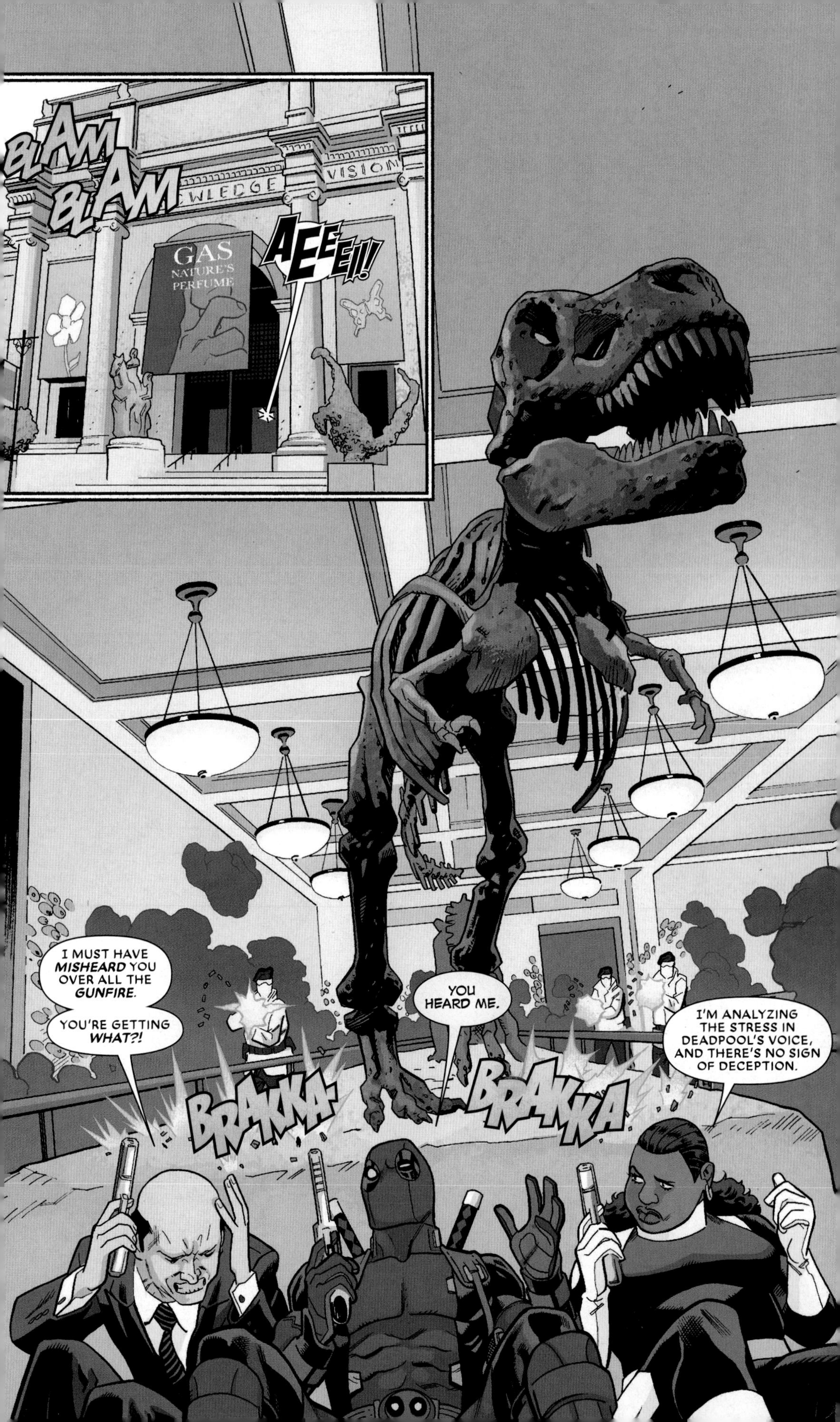
BLAM BLAM
WLEDGE
VISION
GAS
NATURE'S
PERFUME
AEEEII!
I MUST HAVE *MISHEARD* YOU OVER ALL THE *GUNFIRE*.
YOU'RE GETTING *WHAT?!*
YOU HEARD ME.
I'M ANALYZING THE STRESS IN DEADPOOL'S VOICE, AND THERE'S NO SIGN OF DECEPTION.
BRAKKA
BRAKKA

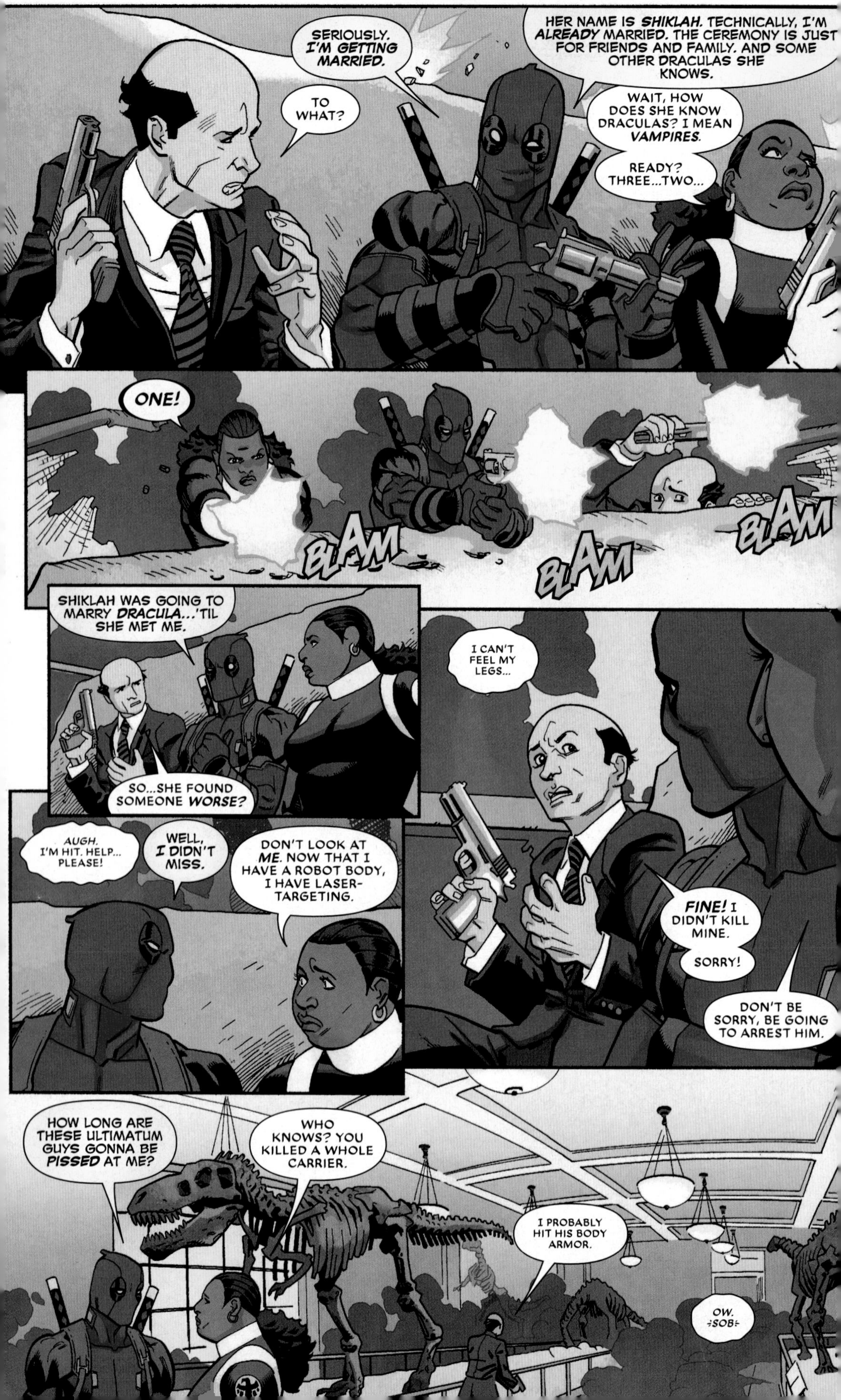

SERIOUSLY. I'M GETTING MARRIED.
TO WHAT?
HER NAME IS SHIKLAH. TECHNICALLY, I'M ALREADY MARRIED. THE CEREMONY IS JUST FOR FRIENDS AND FAMILY. AND SOME OTHER DRACULAS SHE KNOWS.
WAIT, HOW DOES SHE KNOW DRACULAS? I MEAN VAMPIRES.
READY? THREE...TWO...
ONE!
BLAM
BLAM
BLAM
SHIKLAH WAS GOING TO MARRY DRACULA...'TIL SHE MET ME.
SO...SHE FOUND SOMEONE WORSE?
I CAN'T FEEL MY LEGS...
AUGH. I'M HIT. HELP... PLEASE!
WELL, I DIDN'T MISS.
DON'T LOOK AT ME. NOW THAT I HAVE A ROBOT BODY, I HAVE LASER-TARGETING.
FINE! I DIDN'T KILL MINE.
SORRY!
DON'T BE SORRY, BE GOING TO ARREST HIM.
HOW LONG ARE THESE ULTIMATUM GUYS GONNA BE PISSED AT ME?
WHO KNOWS? YOU KILLED A WHOLE CARRIER.
I PROBABLY HIT HIS BODY ARMOR.
OW. ÷SOB÷

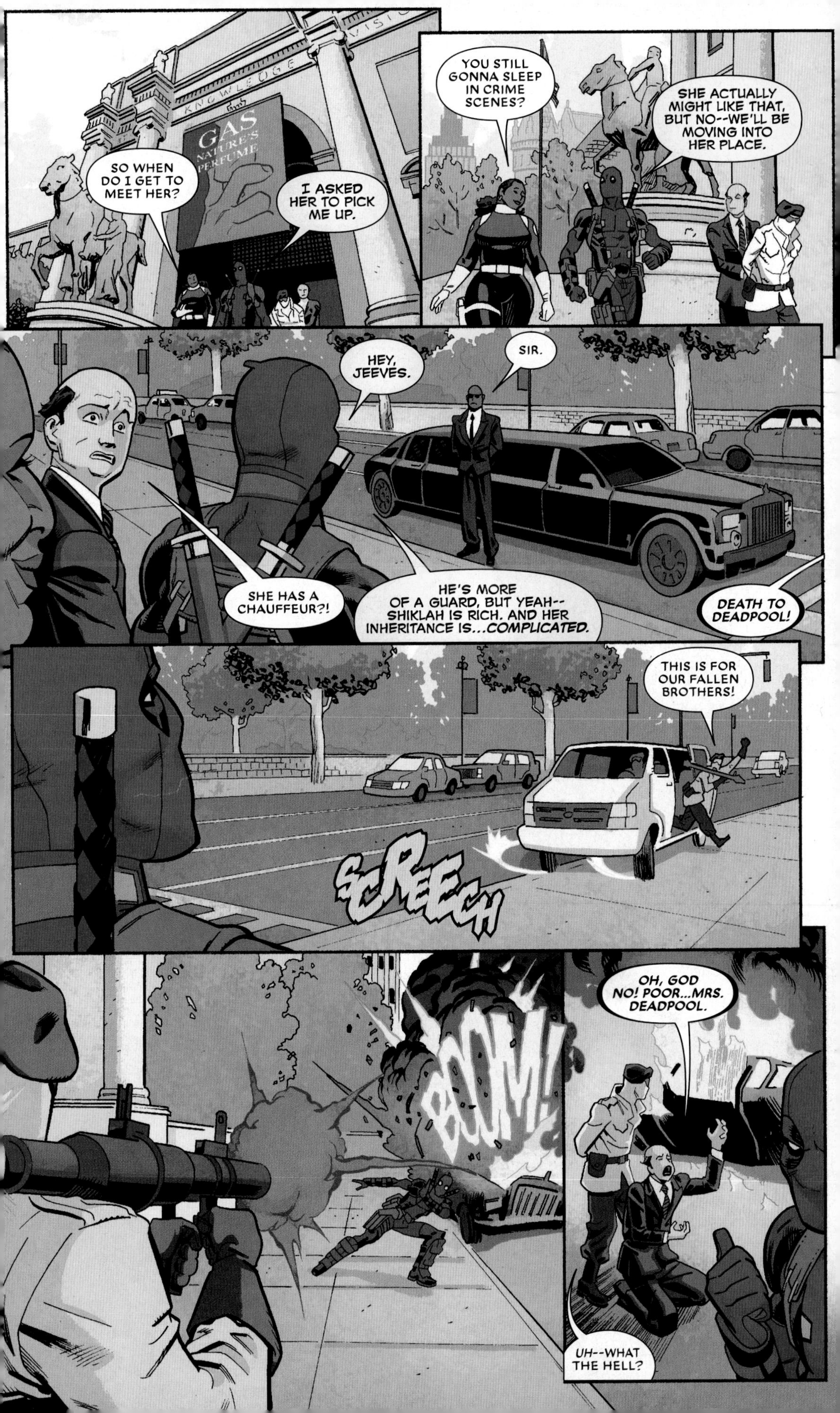
KNOWLEDGE
GAS
NATURE'S PERFUME
SO WHEN DO I GET TO MEET HER?
I ASKED HER TO PICK ME UP.
YOU STILL GONNA SLEEP IN CRIME SCENES?
SHE ACTUALLY MIGHT LIKE THAT, BUT NO--WE'LL BE MOVING INTO HER PLACE.
HEY, JEEVES.
SIR.
SHE HAS A CHAUFFEUR?!
HE'S MORE OF A GUARD, BUT YEAH--SHIKLAH IS RICH. AND HER INHERITANCE IS...COMPLICATED.
DEATH TO DEADPOOL!
THIS IS FOR OUR FALLEN BROTHERS!
SCREECH
BOOM!
OH, GOD NO! POOR...MRS. DEADPOOL.
UH--WHAT THE HELL?

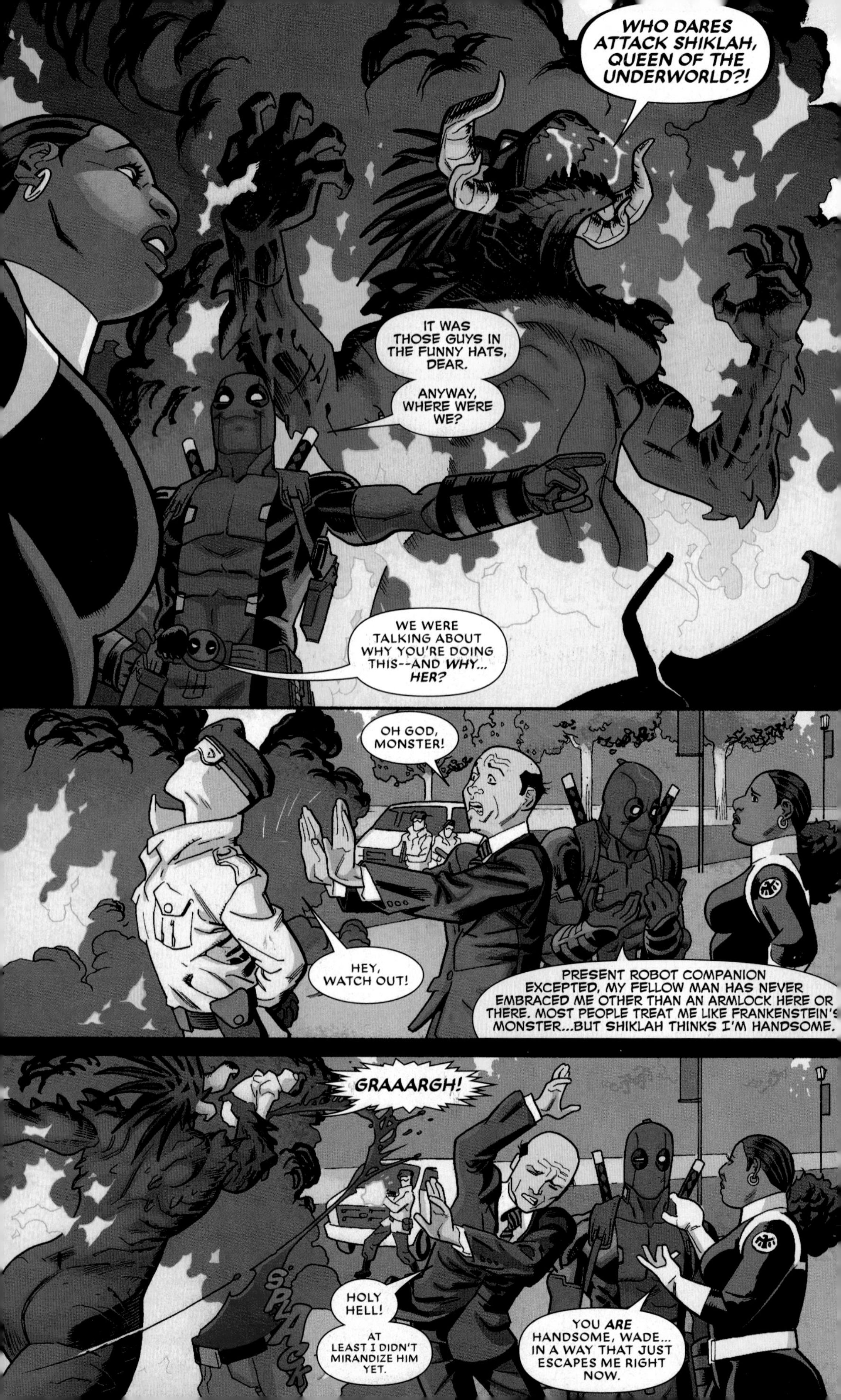
WHO DARES ATTACK SHIKLAH, QUEEN OF THE UNDERWORLD?!
IT WAS THOSE GUYS IN THE FUNNY HATS, DEAR.
ANYWAY, WHERE WERE WE?
WE WERE TALKING ABOUT WHY YOU'RE DOING THIS--AND WHY... HER?
OH GOD, MONSTER!
HEY, WATCH OUT!
PRESENT ROBOT COMPANION EXCEPTED, MY FELLOW MAN HAS NEVER EMBRACED ME OTHER THAN AN ARMLOCK HERE OR THERE. MOST PEOPLE TREAT ME LIKE FRANKENSTEIN'S MONSTER...BUT SHIKLAH THINKS I'M HANDSOME.
GRAAARGH!
SPLACK
HOLY HELL!
AT LEAST I DIDN'T MIRANDIZE HIM YET.
YOU ARE HANDSOME, WADE... IN A WAY THAT JUST ESCAPES ME RIGHT NOW.

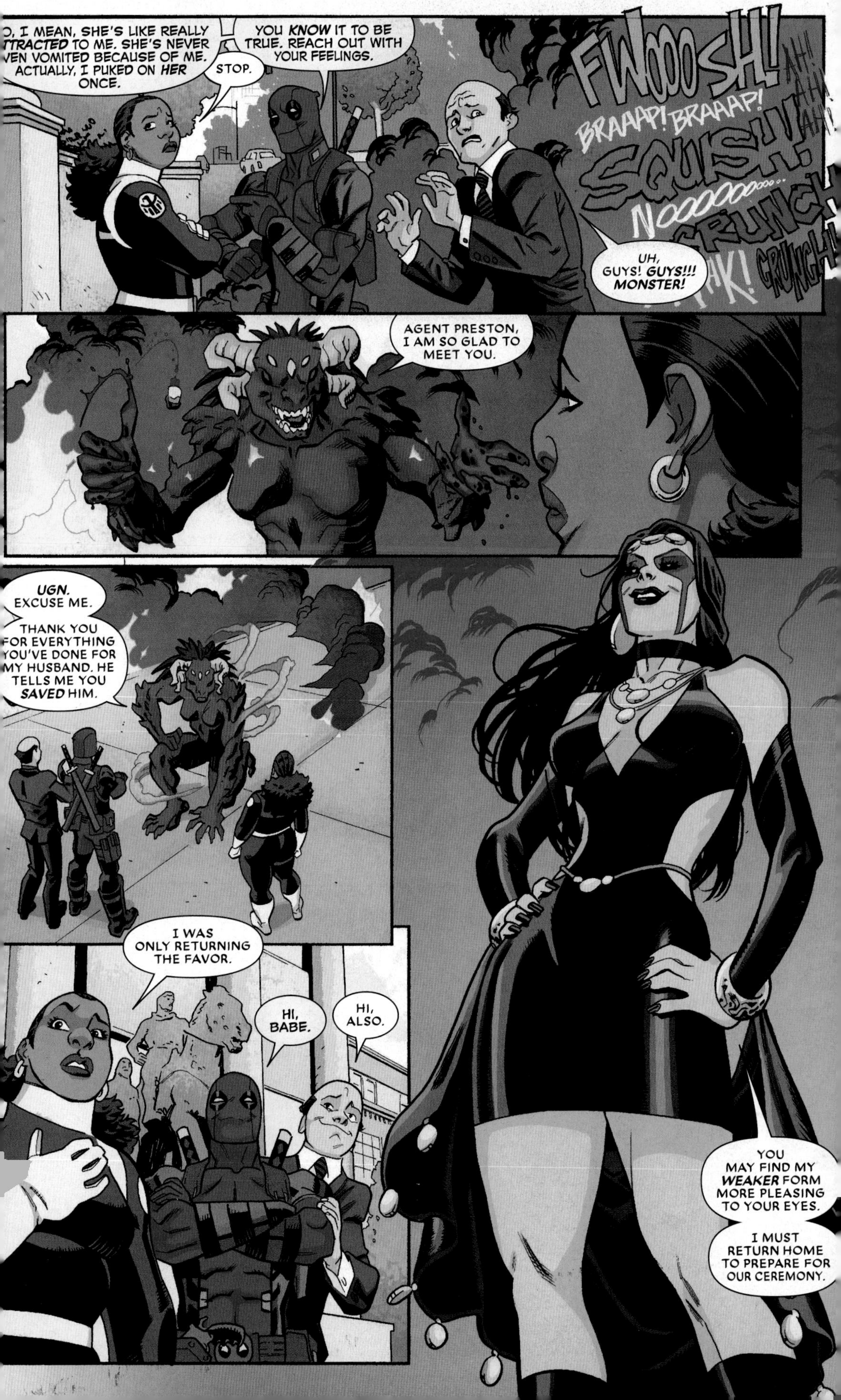

O, I MEAN, SHE'S LIKE REALLY ATTRACTED TO ME. SHE'S NEVER EVEN VOMITED BECAUSE OF ME. ACTUALLY, I PUKED ON HER ONCE.
STOP.
YOU KNOW IT TO BE TRUE. REACH OUT WITH YOUR FEELINGS.
FWOOOSH!
BRAAAP! BRAAAP!
SQUISH!
NOOOOOOOooo...
CRUNCH!
CRUNCH!
UH, GUYS! GUYS!!! MONSTER!
AGENT PRESTON, I AM SO GLAD TO MEET YOU.
UGN. EXCUSE ME.
THANK YOU FOR EVERYTHING YOU'VE DONE FOR MY HUSBAND. HE TELLS ME YOU SAVED HIM.
I WAS ONLY RETURNING THE FAVOR.
HI, BABE.
HI, ALSO.
YOU MAY FIND MY WEAKER FORM MORE PLEASING TO YOUR EYES.
I MUST RETURN HOME TO PREPARE FOR OUR CEREMONY.

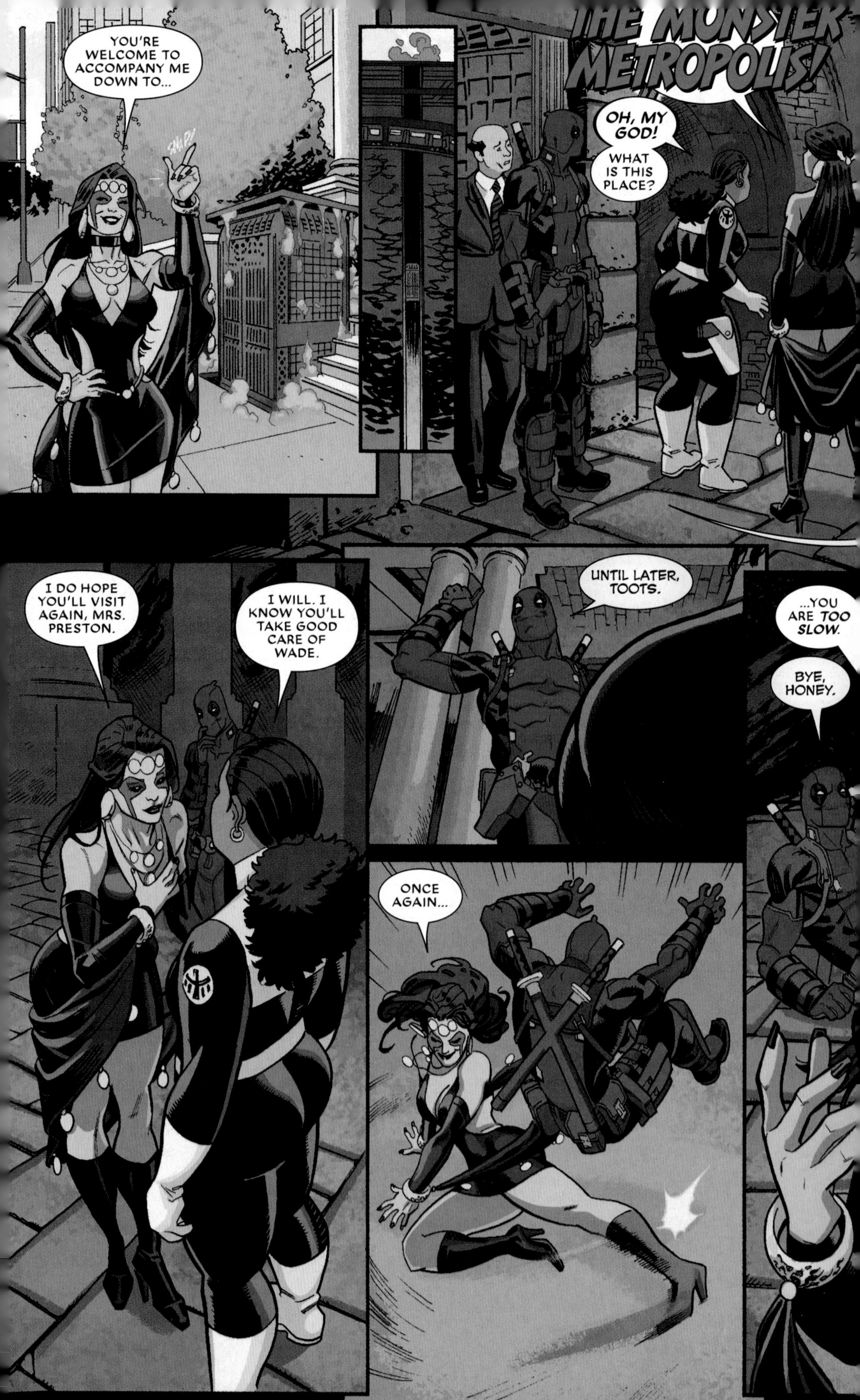
YOU'RE WELCOME TO ACCOMPANY ME DOWN TO...
SNAP!
THE MONSTER METROPOLIS!
OH, MY GOD!
WHAT IS THIS PLACE?
I DO HOPE YOU'LL VISIT AGAIN, MRS. PRESTON.
I WILL. I KNOW YOU'LL TAKE GOOD CARE OF WADE.
UNTIL LATER, TOOTS.
ONCE AGAIN...
...YOU ARE TOO SLOW.
BYE, HONEY.

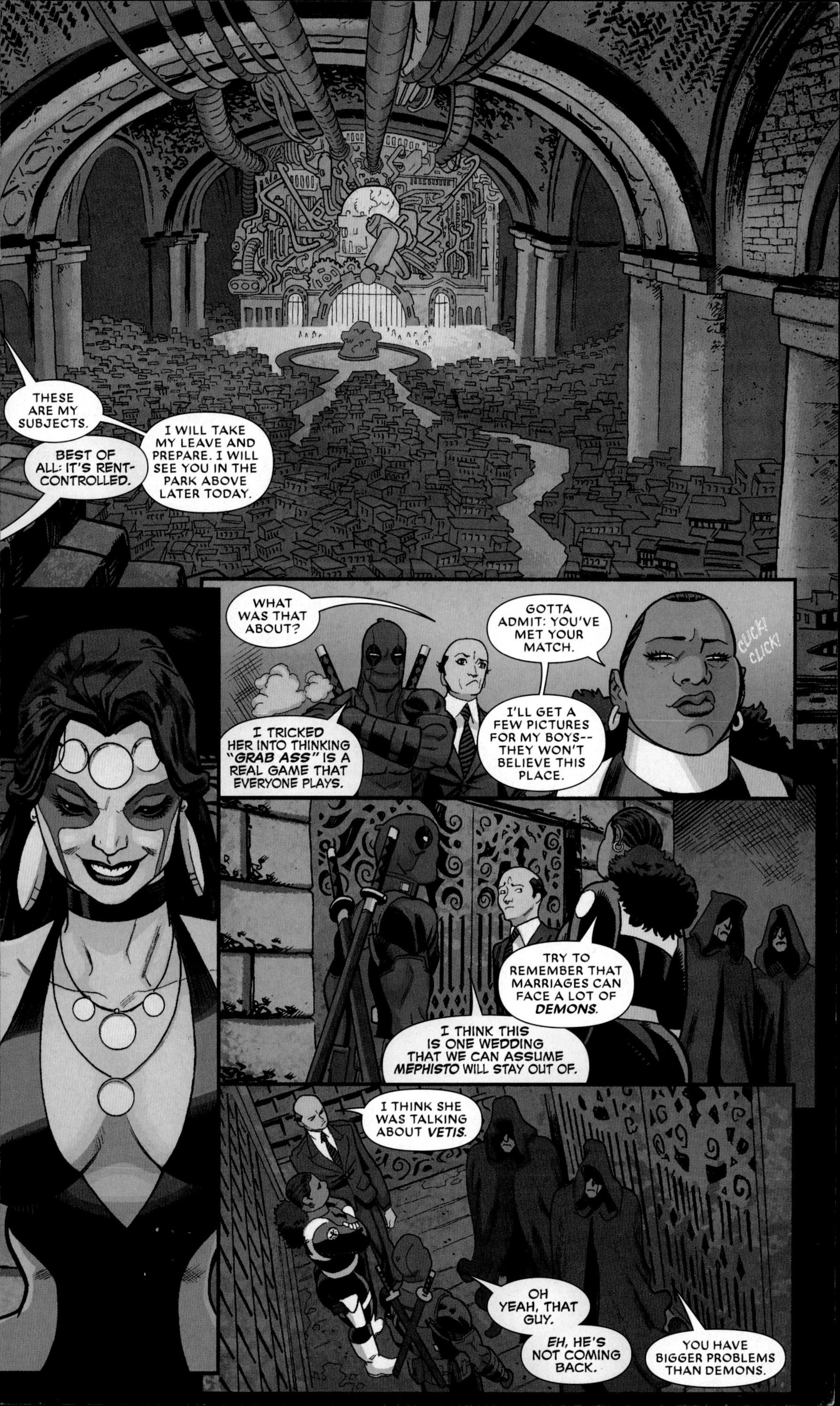

THESE ARE MY SUBJECTS.
BEST OF ALL: IT'S RENT-CONTROLLED.
I WILL TAKE MY LEAVE AND PREPARE. I WILL SEE YOU IN THE PARK ABOVE LATER TODAY.
WHAT WAS THAT ABOUT?
I TRICKED HER INTO THINKING "GRAB ASS" IS A REAL GAME THAT EVERYONE PLAYS.
GOTTA ADMIT: YOU'VE MET YOUR MATCH.
I'LL GET A FEW PICTURES FOR MY BOYS-- THEY WON'T BELIEVE THIS PLACE.
CLICK! CLICK!
TRY TO REMEMBER THAT MARRIAGES CAN FACE A LOT OF DEMONS.
I THINK THIS IS ONE WEDDING THAT WE CAN ASSUME MEPHISTO WILL STAY OUT OF.
I THINK SHE WAS TALKING ABOUT VETIS.
OH YEAH, THAT GUY.
EH, HE'S NOT COMING BACK.
YOU HAVE BIGGER PROBLEMS THAN DEMONS.

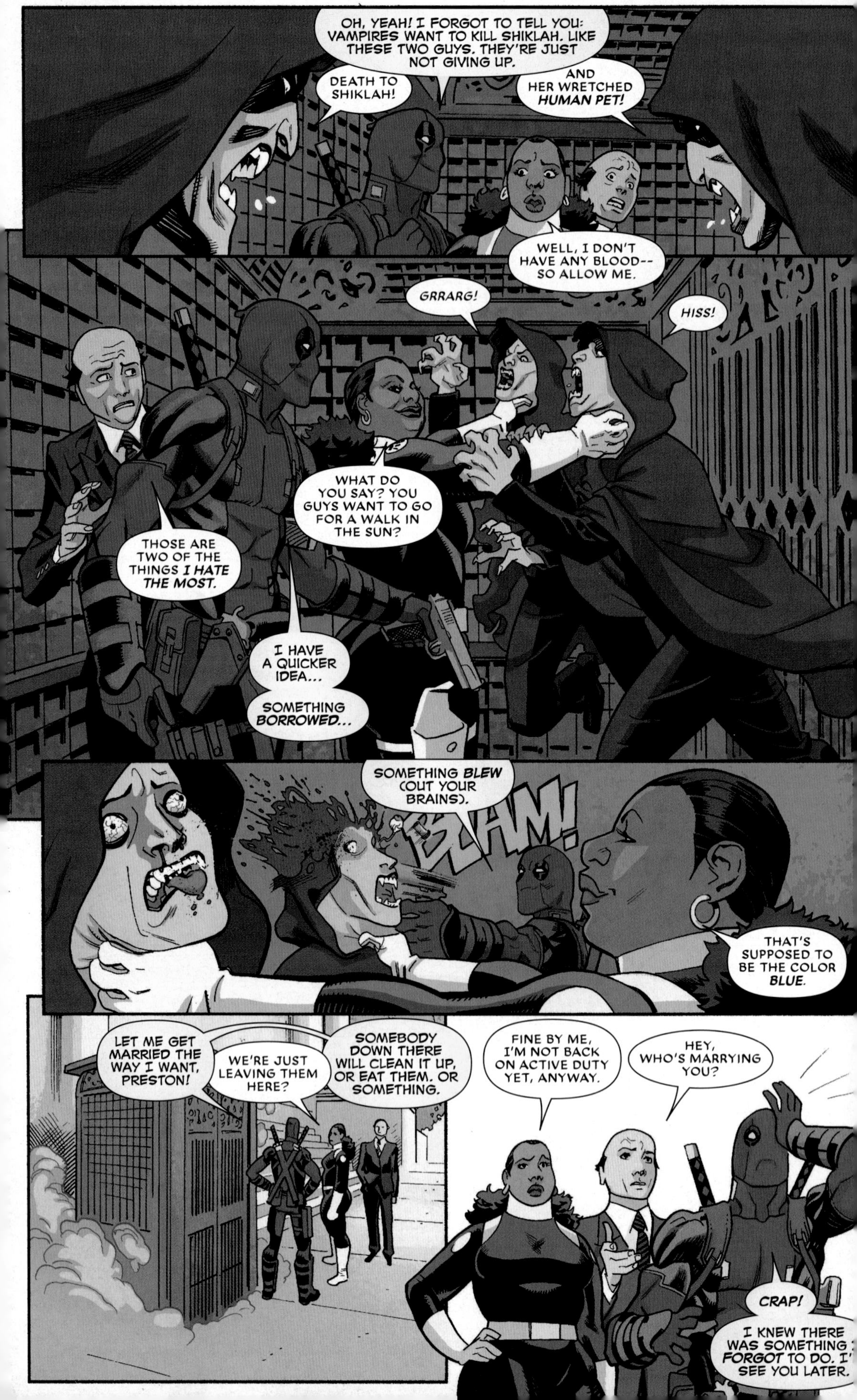

OH, YEAH! I FORGOT TO TELL YOU: VAMPIRES WANT TO KILL SHIKLAH. LIKE THESE TWO GUYS. THEY'RE JUST NOT GIVING UP.
DEATH TO SHIKLAH!
AND HER WRETCHED HUMAN PET!
WELL, I DON'T HAVE ANY BLOOD-- SO ALLOW ME.
GRRARG!
HISS!
WHAT DO YOU SAY? YOU GUYS WANT TO GO FOR A WALK IN THE SUN?
THOSE ARE TWO OF THE THINGS I HATE THE MOST.
I HAVE A QUICKER IDEA...
SOMETHING BORROWED...
SOMETHING BLEW (OUT YOUR BRAINS).
BLAM!
THAT'S SUPPOSED TO BE THE COLOR BLUE.
LET ME GET MARRIED THE WAY I WANT, PRESTON!
WE'RE JUST LEAVING THEM HERE?
SOMEBODY DOWN THERE WILL CLEAN IT UP, OR EAT THEM. OR SOMETHING.
FINE BY ME, I'M NOT BACK ON ACTIVE DUTY YET, ANYWAY.
HEY, WHO'S MARRYING YOU?
CRAP!
I KNEW THERE WAS SOMETHING I FORGOT TO DO. I' SEE YOU LATER.

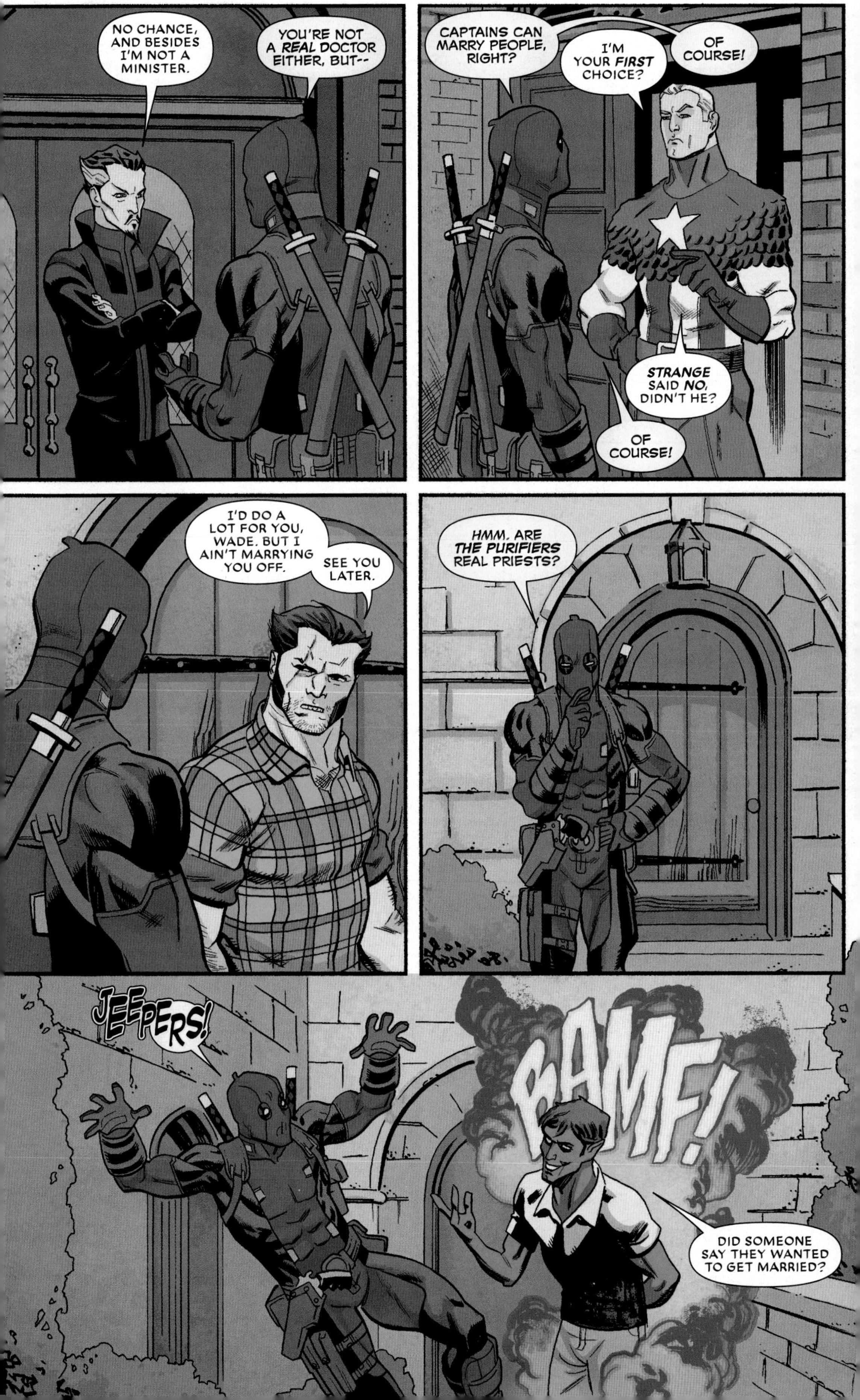

NO CHANCE, AND BESIDES I'M NOT A MINISTER.
YOU'RE NOT A REAL DOCTOR EITHER, BUT--
CAPTAINS CAN MARRY PEOPLE, RIGHT?
I'M YOUR FIRST CHOICE?
OF COURSE!
STRANGE SAID NO, DIDN'T HE?
OF COURSE!
I'D DO A LOT FOR YOU, WADE. BUT I AIN'T MARRYING YOU OFF.
SEE YOU LATER.
HMM. ARE THE PURIFIERS REAL PRIESTS?
JEEPERS!
BAMF!
DID SOMEONE SAY THEY WANTED TO GET MARRIED?

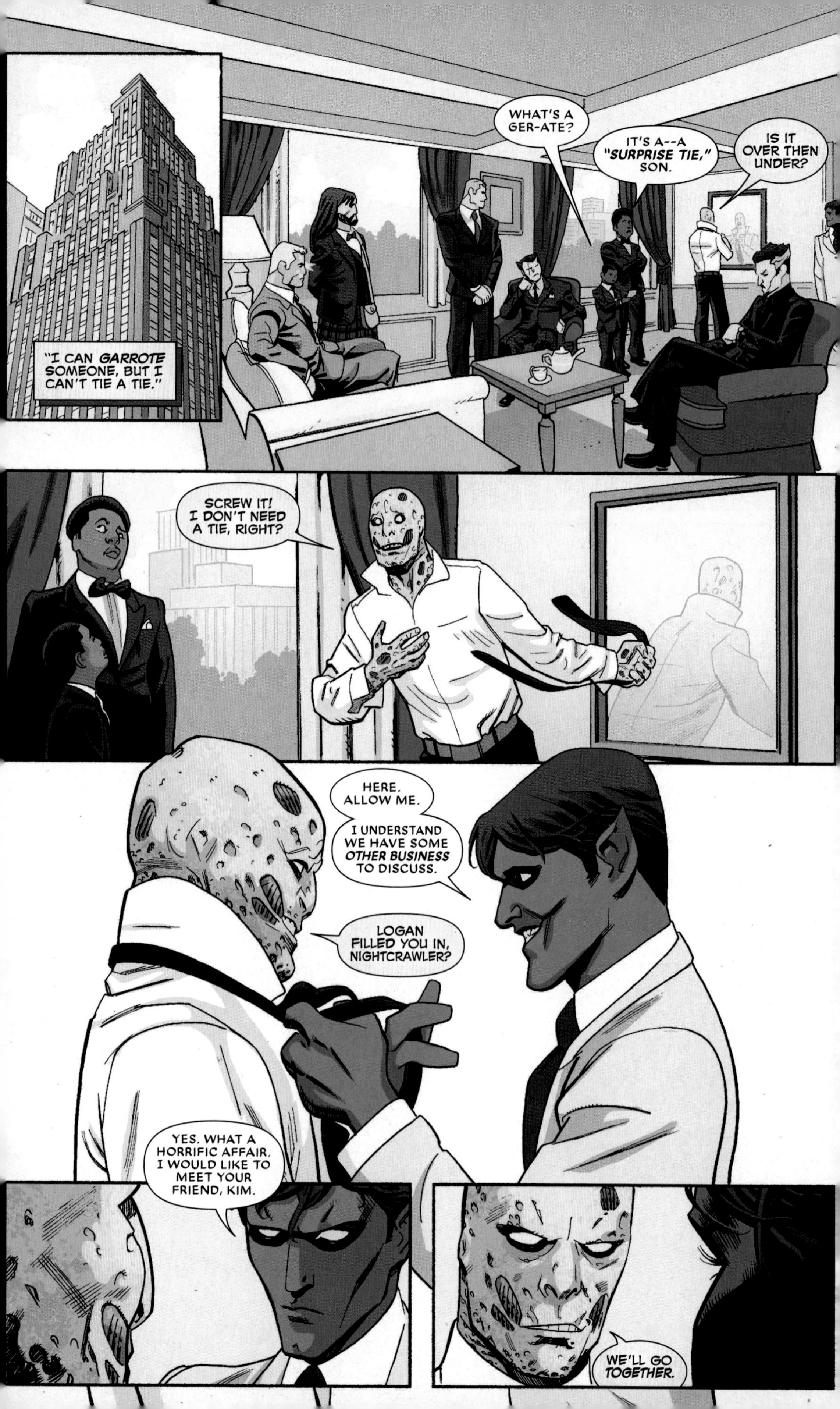

"I CAN GARROTE SOMEONE, BUT I CAN'T TIE A TIE."
WHAT'S A GER-ATE?
IT'S A--A "SURPRISE TIE," SON.
IS IT OVER THEN UNDER?
SCREW IT! I DON'T NEED A TIE, RIGHT?
HERE. ALLOW ME.
I UNDERSTAND WE HAVE SOME OTHER BUSINESS TO DISCUSS.
LOGAN FILLED YOU IN, NIGHTCRAWLER?
YES. WHAT A HORRIFIC AFFAIR. I WOULD LIKE TO MEET YOUR FRIEND, KIM.
WE'LL GO TOGETHER.

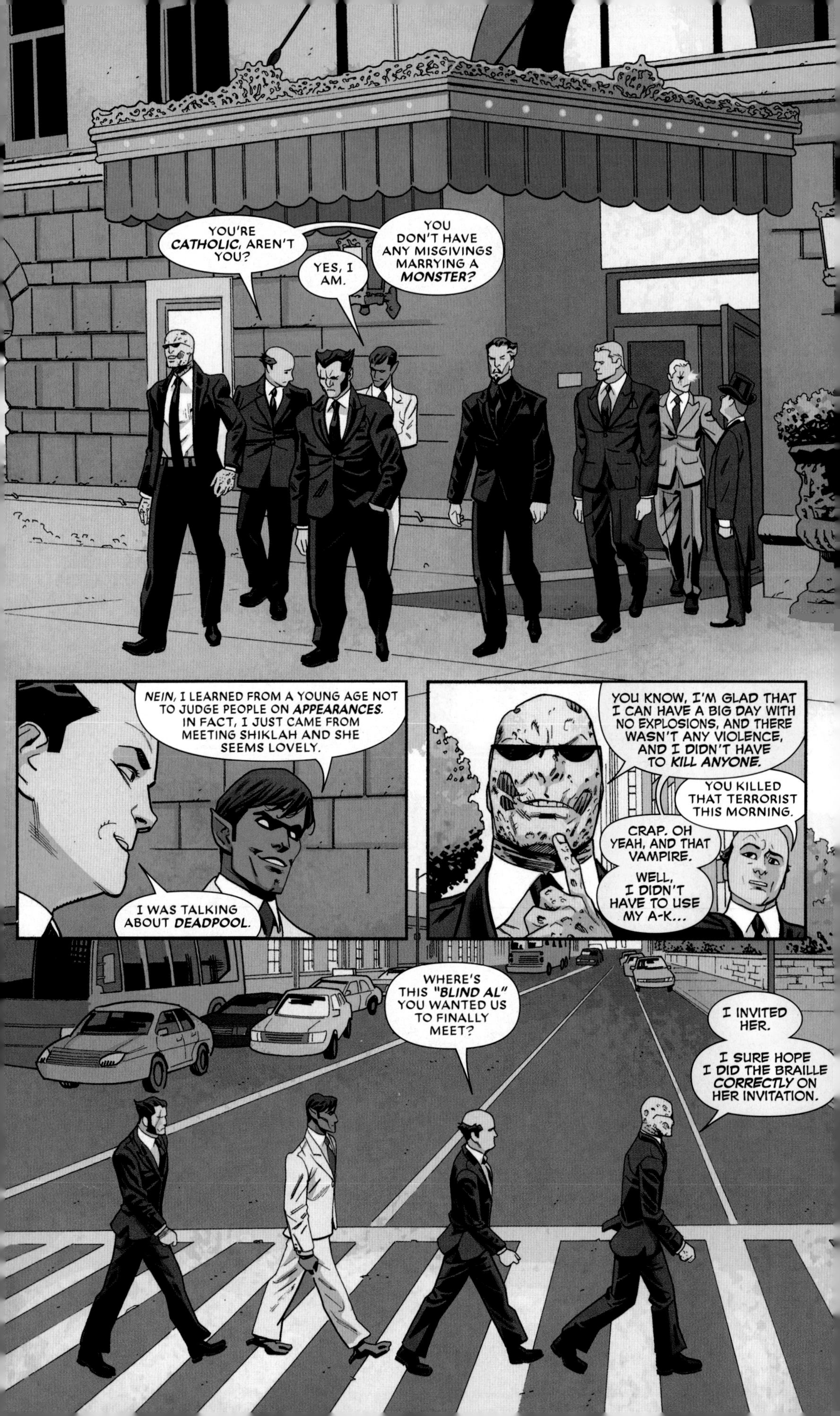

YOU'RE CATHOLIC, AREN'T YOU?
YOU DON'T HAVE ANY MISGIVINGS MARRYING A MONSTER?
YES, I AM.
NEIN, I LEARNED FROM A YOUNG AGE NOT TO JUDGE PEOPLE ON APPEARANCES. IN FACT, I JUST CAME FROM MEETING SHIKLAH AND SHE SEEMS LOVELY.
I WAS TALKING ABOUT DEADPOOL.
YOU KNOW, I'M GLAD THAT I CAN HAVE A BIG DAY WITH NO EXPLOSIONS, AND THERE WASN'T ANY VIOLENCE, AND I DIDN'T HAVE TO KILL ANYONE.
YOU KILLED THAT TERRORIST THIS MORNING.
CRAP. OH YEAH, AND THAT VAMPIRE.
WELL, I DIDN'T HAVE TO USE MY A-K...
WHERE'S THIS "BLIND AL" YOU WANTED US TO FINALLY MEET?
I INVITED HER.
I SURE HOPE I DID THE BRAILLE CORRECTLY ON HER INVITATION.

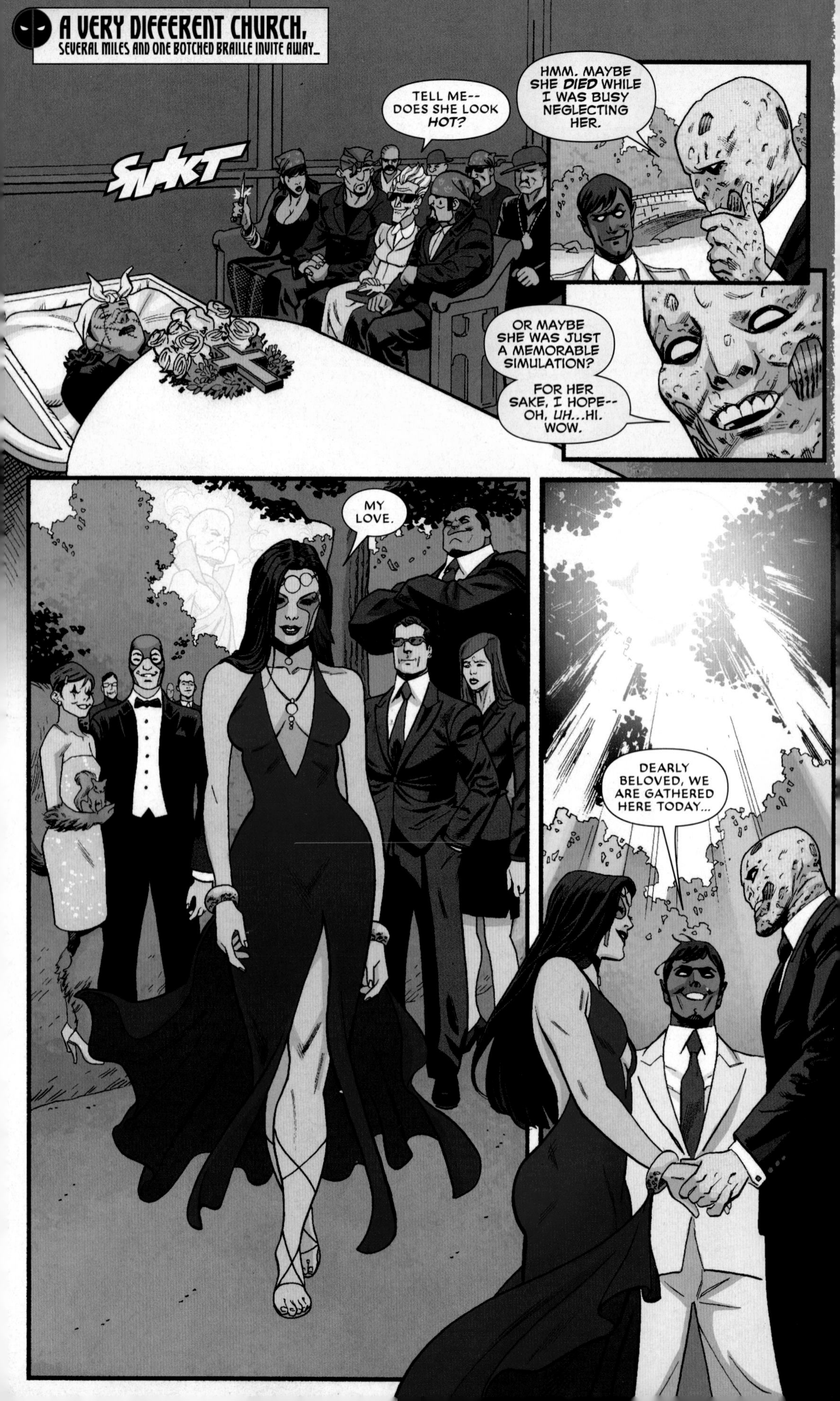
A VERY DIFFERENT CHURCH,
SEVERAL MILES AND ONE BOTCHED BRAILLE INVITE AWAY...
TELL ME-- DOES SHE LOOK HOT?
HMM. MAYBE SHE DIED WHILE I WAS BUSY NEGLECTING HER.
SNIKT
OR MAYBE SHE WAS JUST A MEMORABLE SIMULATION?
FOR HER SAKE, I HOPE-- OH, UH...HI. WOW.
MY LOVE.
DEARLY BELOVED, WE ARE GATHERED HERE TODAY...

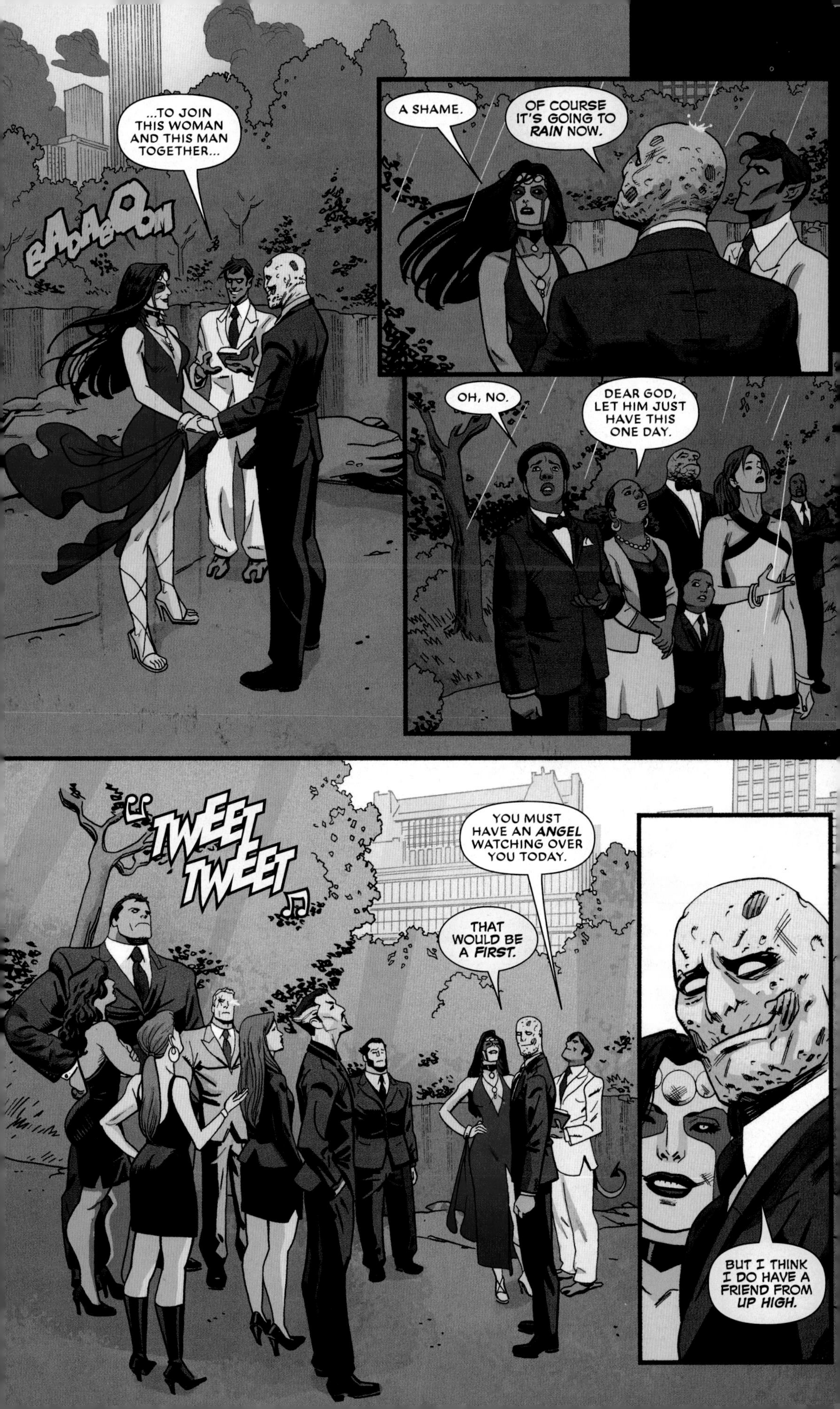
...TO JOIN THIS WOMAN AND THIS MAN TOGETHER...
BADABOOM
A SHAME.
OF COURSE IT'S GOING TO RAIN NOW.
OH, NO.
DEAR GOD, LET HIM JUST HAVE THIS ONE DAY.
TWEET TWEET
YOU MUST HAVE AN ANGEL WATCHING OVER YOU TODAY.
THAT WOULD BE A FIRST.
BUT I THINK I DO HAVE A FRIEND FROM UP HIGH.

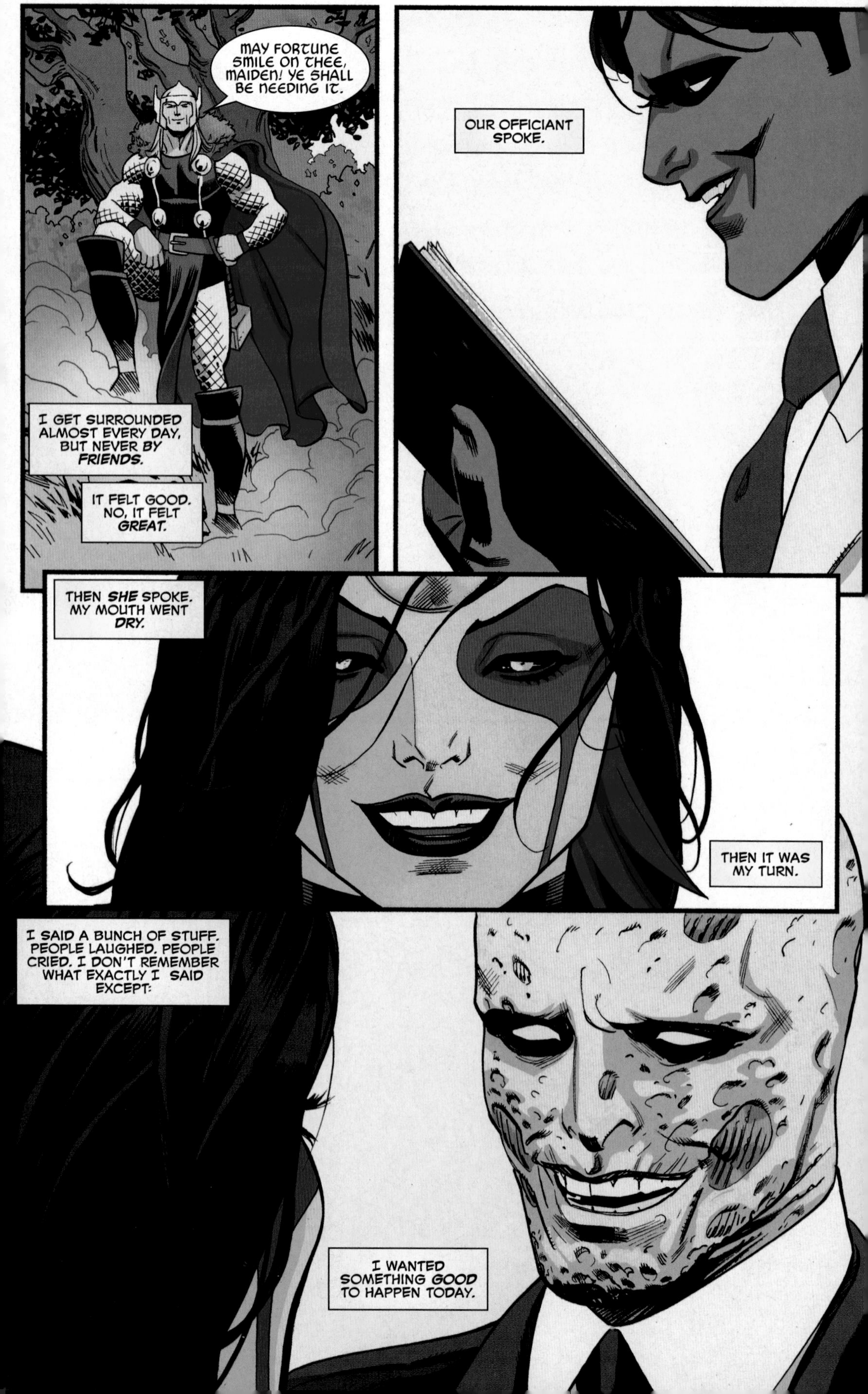

MAY FORTUNE SMILE ON THEE, MAIDEN! YE SHALL BE NEEDING IT.
I GET SURROUNDED ALMOST EVERY DAY, BUT NEVER BY FRIENDS.
IT FELT GOOD. NO, IT FELT GREAT.
OUR OFFICIANT SPOKE.
THEN SHE SPOKE. MY MOUTH WENT DRY.
THEN IT WAS MY TURN.
I SAID A BUNCH OF STUFF. PEOPLE LAUGHED. PEOPLE CRIED. I DON'T REMEMBER WHAT EXACTLY I SAID EXCEPT:
I WANTED SOMETHING GOOD TO HAPPEN TODAY.

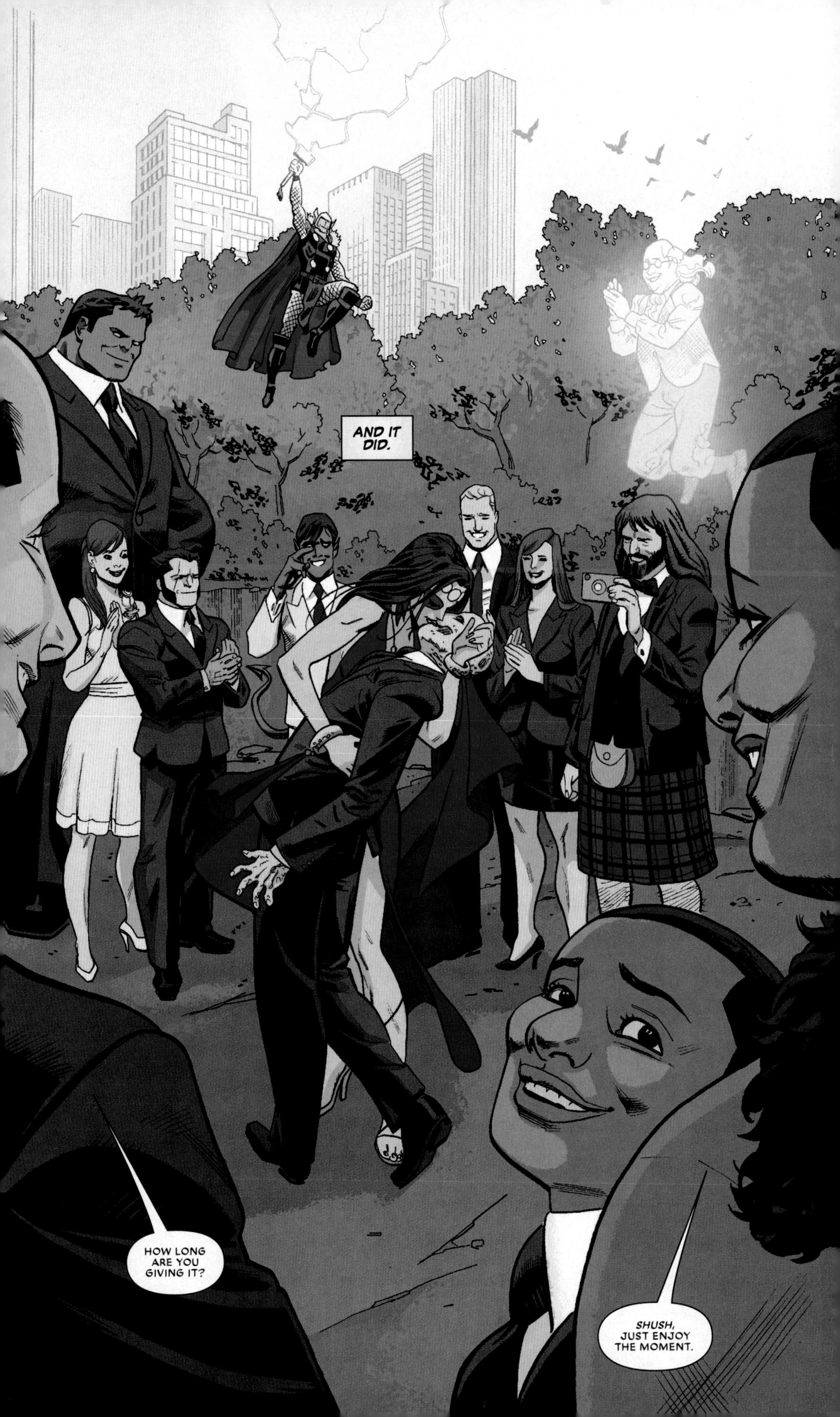
AND IT DID.
HOW LONG ARE YOU GIVING IT?
SHUSH, JUST ENJOY THE MOMENT.

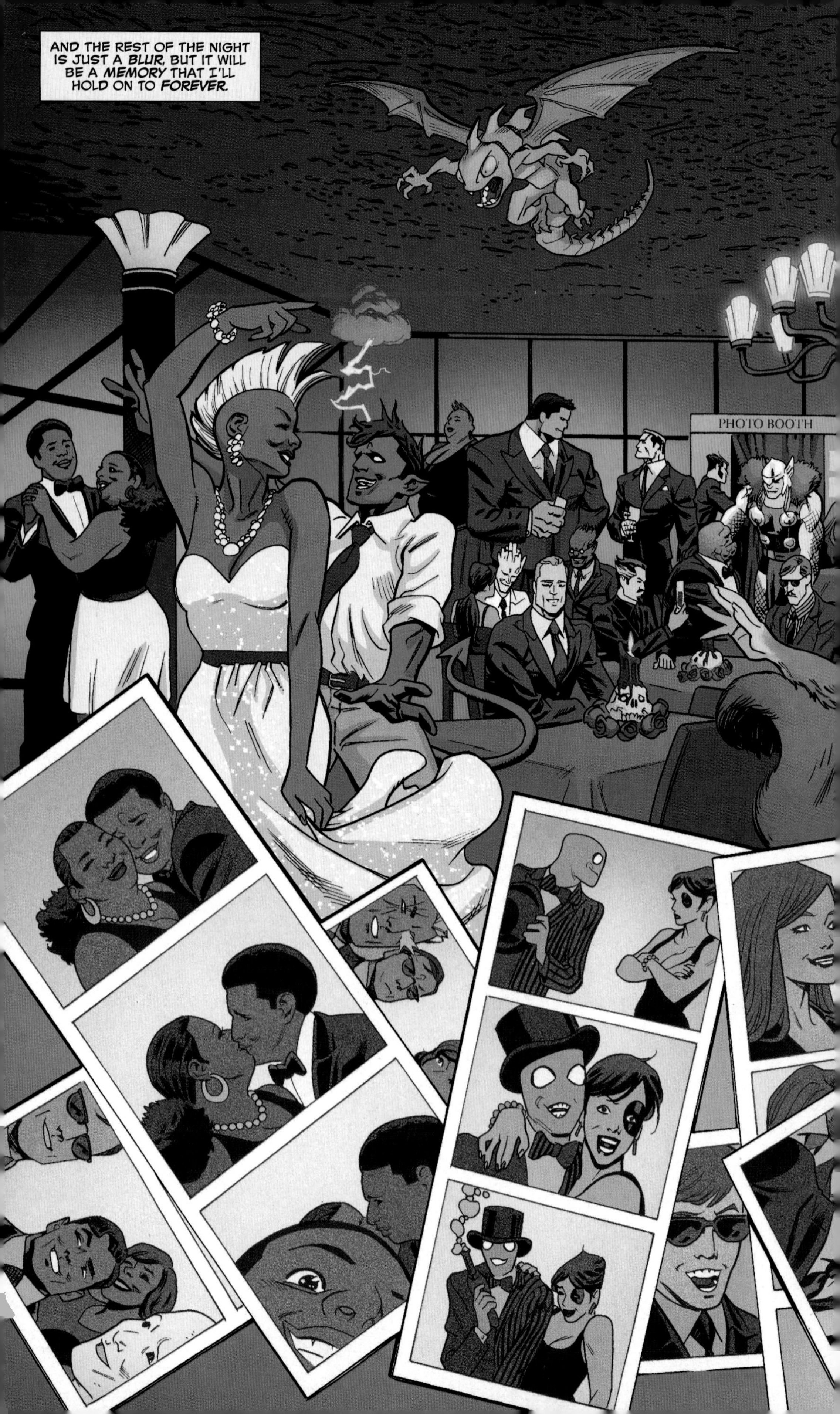

AND THE REST OF THE NIGHT IS JUST A *BLUR*, BUT IT WILL BE A *MEMORY* THAT I'LL HOLD ON TO *FOREVER*.
PHOTO BOOTH

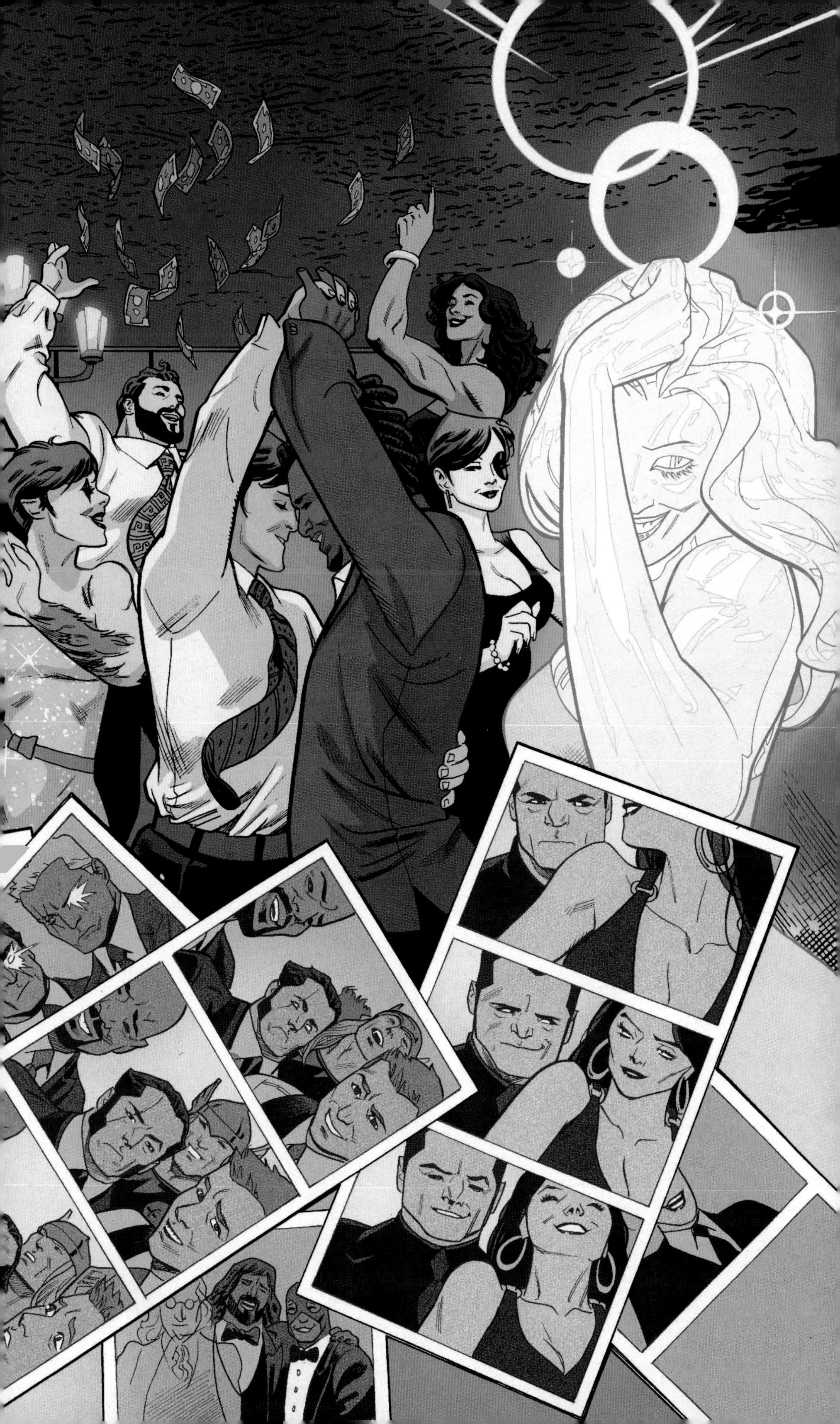

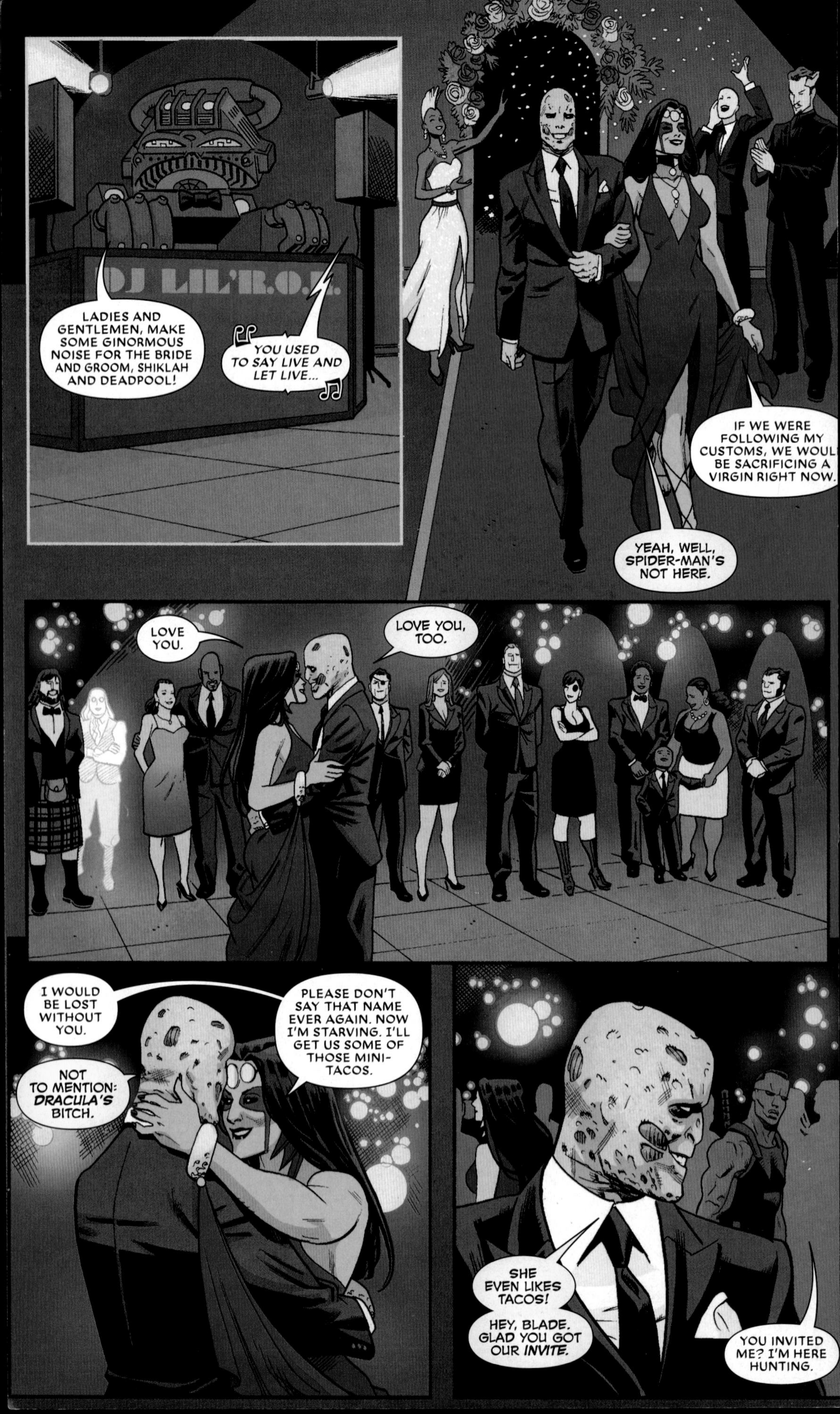
LADIES AND GENTLEMEN, MAKE SOME GINORMOUS NOISE FOR THE BRIDE AND GROOM, SHIKLAH AND DEADPOOL!
YOU USED TO SAY LIVE AND LET LIVE...
IF WE WERE FOLLOWING MY CUSTOMS, WE WOUL BE SACRIFICING A VIRGIN RIGHT NOW.
YEAH, WELL, SPIDER-MAN'S NOT HERE.
LOVE YOU.
LOVE YOU, TOO.
I WOULD BE LOST WITHOUT YOU.
NOT TO MENTION: *DRACULA'S* BITCH.
PLEASE DON'T SAY THAT NAME EVER AGAIN. NOW I'M STARVING. I'LL GET US SOME OF THOSE MINI-TACOS.
SHE EVEN LIKES TACOS!
HEY, BLADE. GLAD YOU GOT OUR *INVITE*.
YOU INVITED ME? I'M HERE HUNTING.

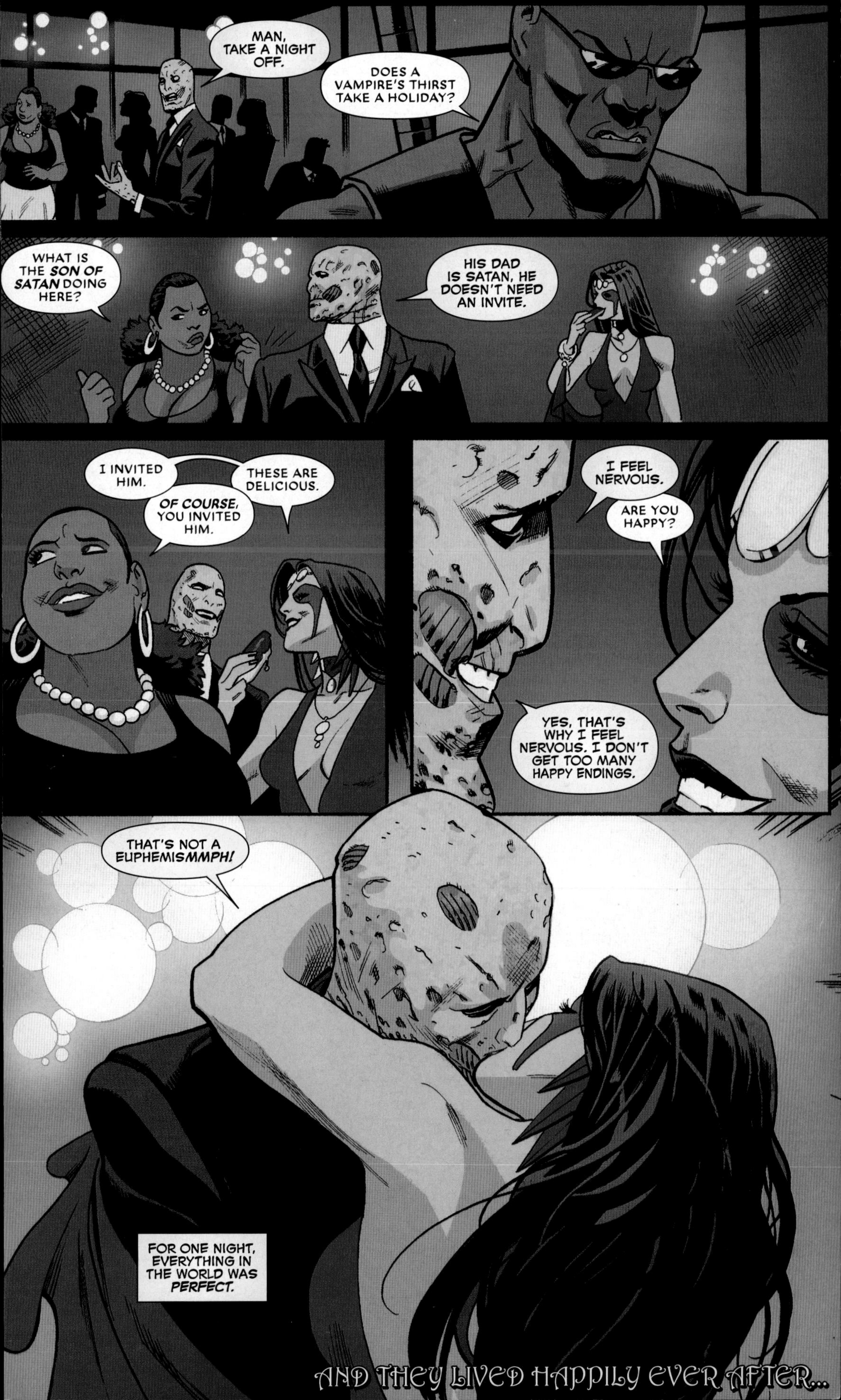
MAN, TAKE A NIGHT OFF.
DOES A VAMPIRE'S THIRST TAKE A HOLIDAY?
WHAT IS THE SON OF SATAN DOING HERE?
HIS DAD IS SATAN, HE DOESN'T NEED AN INVITE.
I INVITED HIM.
OF COURSE, YOU INVITED HIM.
THESE ARE DELICIOUS.
I FEEL NERVOUS.
ARE YOU HAPPY?
YES, THAT'S WHY I FEEL NERVOUS. I DON'T GET TOO MANY HAPPY ENDINGS.
THAT'S NOT A EUPHEMISMMPH!
FOR ONE NIGHT, EVERYTHING IN THE WORLD WAS PERFECT.
AND THEY LIVED HAPPILY EVER AFTER...

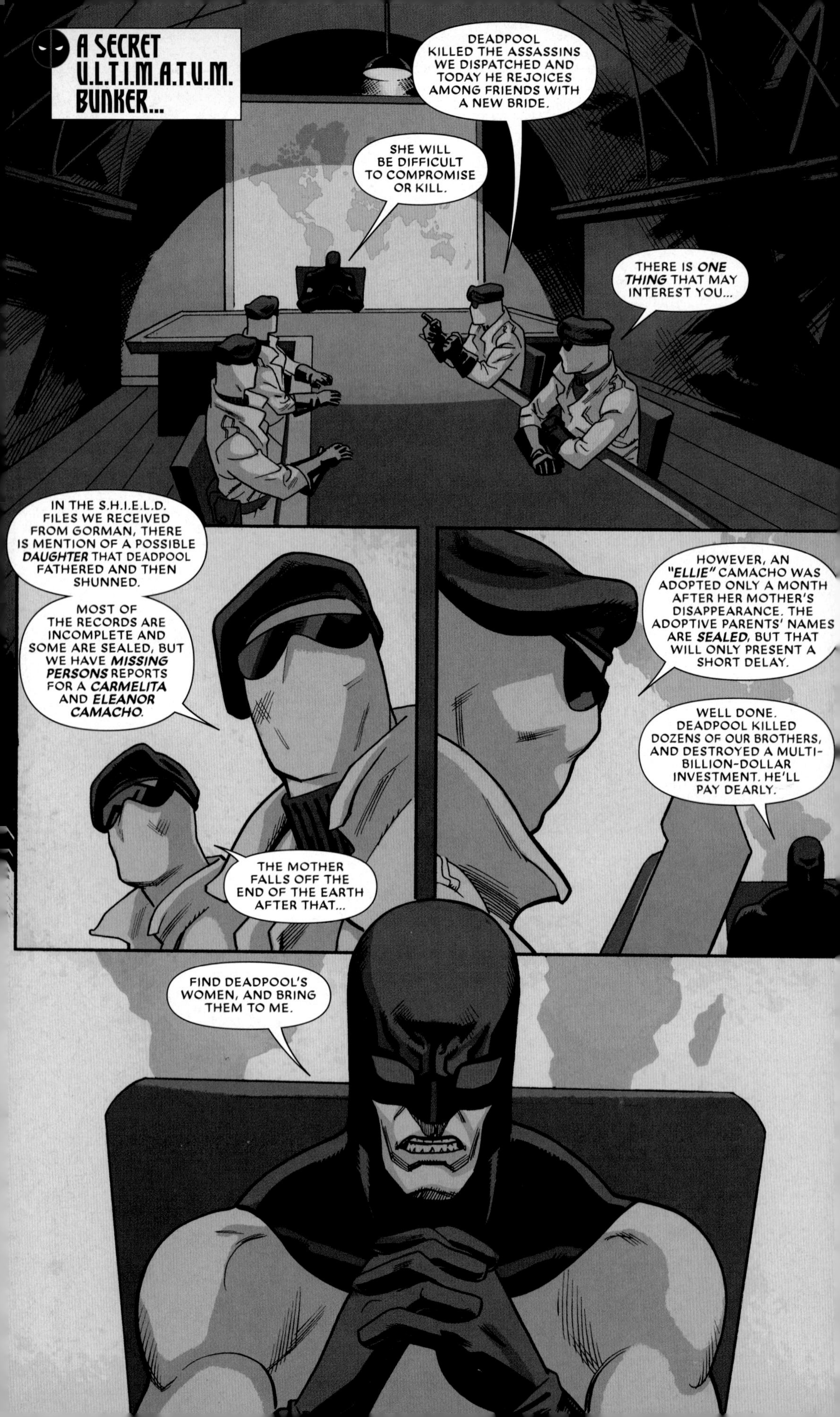
A SECRET U.L.T.I.M.A.T.U.M. BUNKER...
DEADPOOL KILLED THE ASSASSINS WE DISPATCHED AND TODAY HE REJOICES AMONG FRIENDS WITH A NEW BRIDE.
SHE WILL BE DIFFICULT TO COMPROMISE OR KILL.
THERE IS ONE THING THAT MAY INTEREST YOU...
IN THE S.H.I.E.L.D. FILES WE RECEIVED FROM GORMAN, THERE IS MENTION OF A POSSIBLE DAUGHTER THAT DEADPOOL FATHERED AND THEN SHUNNED.
MOST OF THE RECORDS ARE INCOMPLETE AND SOME ARE SEALED, BUT WE HAVE MISSING PERSONS REPORTS FOR A CARMELITA AND ELEANOR CAMACHO.
THE MOTHER FALLS OFF THE END OF THE EARTH AFTER THAT...
HOWEVER, AN "ELLIE" CAMACHO WAS ADOPTED ONLY A MONTH AFTER HER MOTHER'S DISAPPEARANCE. THE ADOPTIVE PARENTS' NAMES ARE SEALED, BUT THAT WILL ONLY PRESENT A SHORT DELAY.
WELL DONE. DEADPOOL KILLED DOZENS OF OUR BROTHERS, AND DESTROYED A MULTI-BILLION-DOLLAR INVESTMENT. HE'LL PAY DEARLY.
FIND DEADPOOL'S WOMEN, AND BRING THEM TO ME.

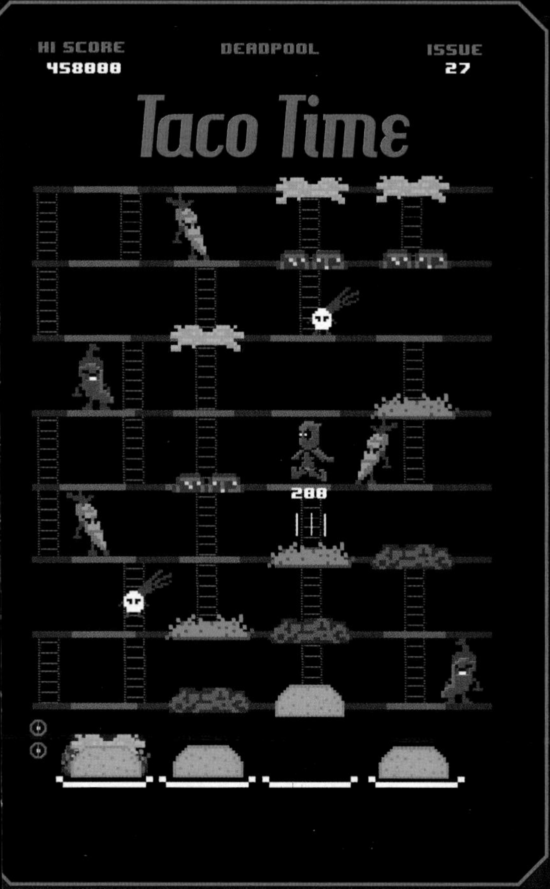
HI SCORE
458000
DEADPOOL
ISSUE
27
Taco Time
200

#27 VARIANT
BY MATTHEW WAITE

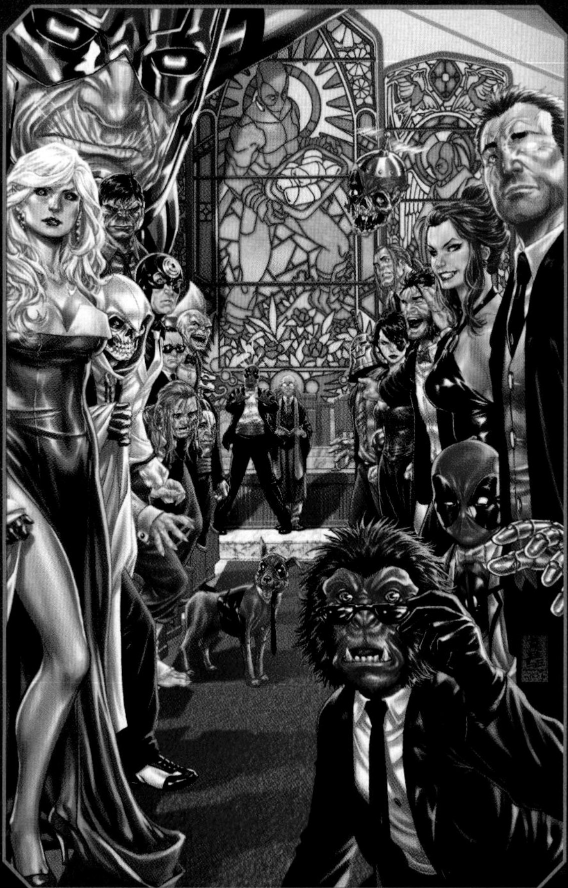

#27 VARIANT
BY MARK BROOKS

In celebration of the wedding of Deadpool in this, the most important issue #27 in the history of comics, we've rounded up an all-star assemblage of the writers who have guided Wade's destiny since his first appearance way back in 1991. Please join us in welcoming back some of the best writers in the comic book industry...and Gerry and Brian.

Operation Ballerina Drop

Written by Gerry Duggan
Art by Scott Koblish
Colors by Val Staples

#$%@-Faced in Vegas

Written by Brian Posehn
Art by Scott Koblish
Colors by Val Staples

With This Hand, I Thee Wed

Written by Fabian Nicieza
Art by Scott Hepburn
Colors by Val Staples

Continuity Spontinuity

Written by Mark Waid
Art by John McCrea
Colors by Andrew Elder

The Niagara Bride

Written by Joe Kelly
Pencils by Paco Medina
Inks by Juan Velasco
Colors by David Curiel

Fanged

Written by Christopher Priest
Art by Niko Henrichon

Quickie

Written by Jimmy Palmiotti
Art by John Timms
Colors by Veronica Gandini

So Deadpool Walks into a Bar...

Written by Frank Tieri
Art by Dexter Soy
Colors by Veronica Gandini

Eulogy for a Winkie

Written by Gail Simone
Art by Alvin Lee
Colors by Veronica Gandini

There Will Be No Honeymoon

Written by Fabian Nicieza
Art by Shawn Crystal
Colors by Veronica Gandini

Savage Land: The Other Niagara Falls

Written by Victor Gischler
Art by Bong Dazo
Colors by Veronica Gandini

The Space Racist

Written by Daniel Way
Art by Carlo Barberi
Colors by Val Staples

All stories lettered by VC's Joe Sabino
Wedding invitations designed by Irene Y. Lee

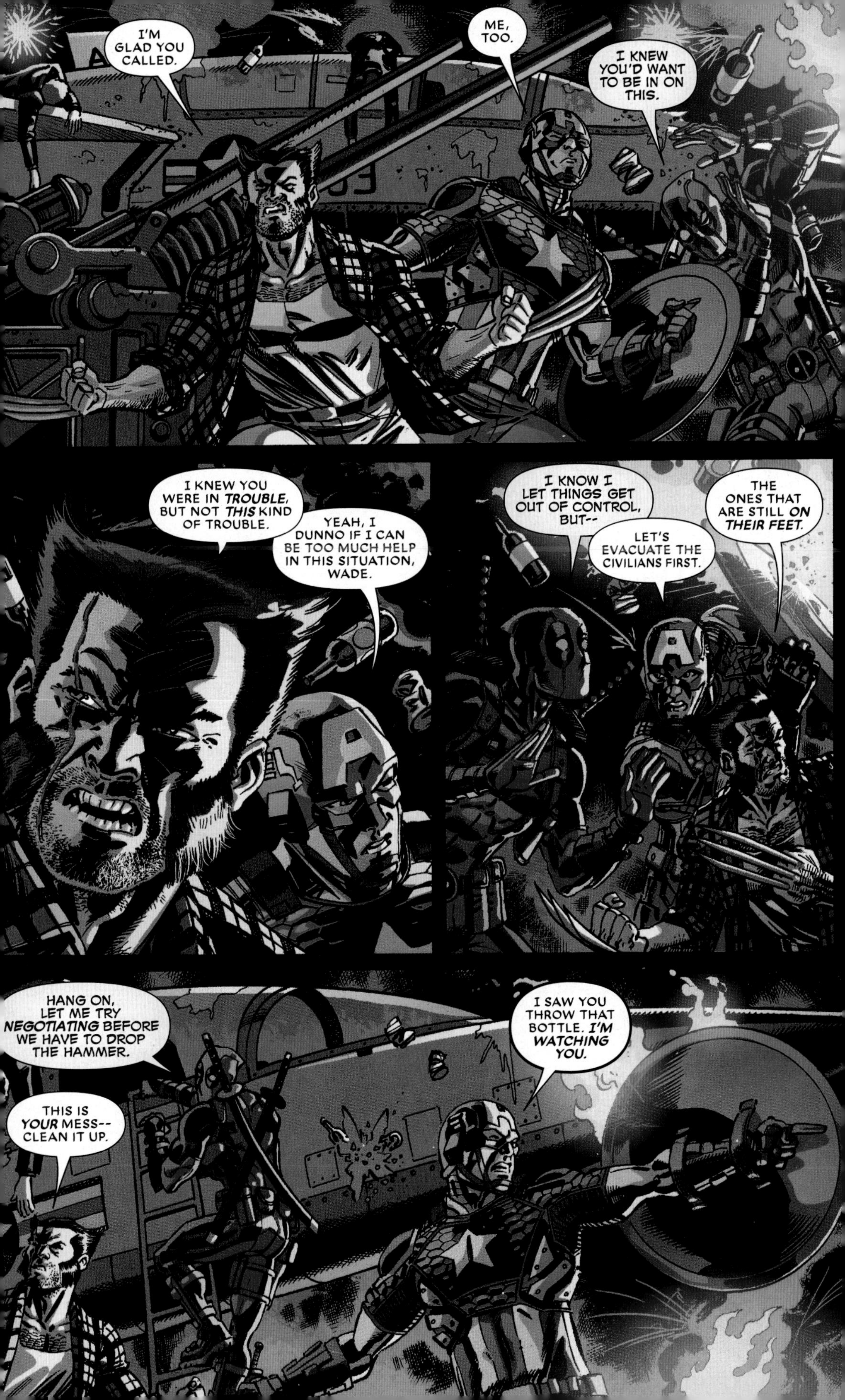
I'M GLAD YOU CALLED.
ME, TOO.
I KNEW YOU'D WANT TO BE IN ON THIS.
I KNEW YOU WERE IN *TROUBLE*, BUT NOT *THIS* KIND OF TROUBLE.
YEAH, I DUNNO IF I CAN BE TOO MUCH HELP IN THIS SITUATION, WADE.
I KNOW I LET THINGS GET OUT OF CONTROL, BUT--
LET'S EVACUATE THE CIVILIANS FIRST.
THE ONES THAT ARE STILL *ON THEIR FEET*.
HANG ON, LET ME TRY *NEGOTIATING* BEFORE WE HAVE TO DROP THE HAMMER.
THIS IS *YOUR* MESS-- CLEAN IT UP.
I SAW YOU THROW THAT BOTTLE. *I'M WATCHING YOU.*

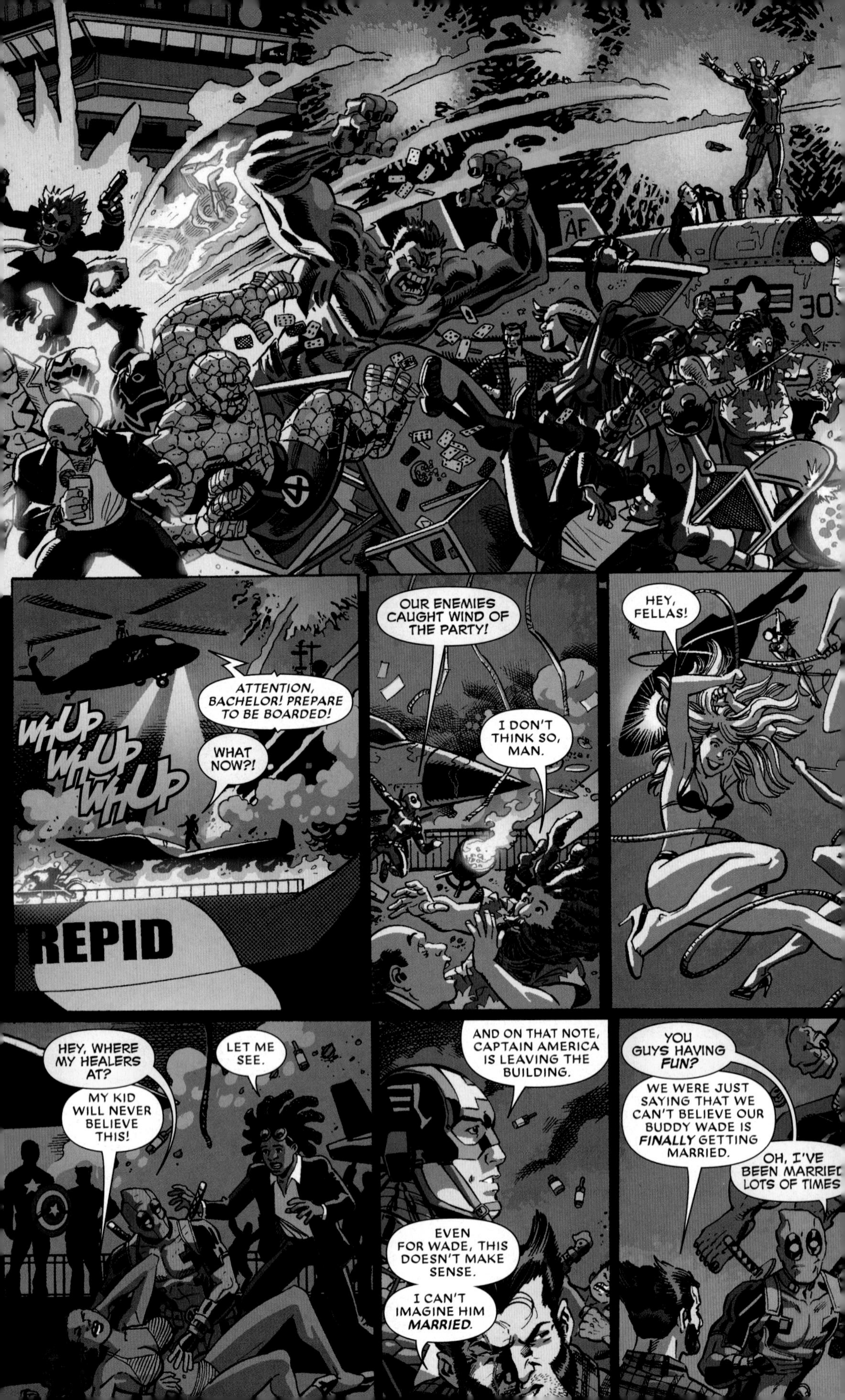
AF
30
WHUP WHUP WHUP
ATTENTION, BACHELOR! PREPARE TO BE BOARDED!
WHAT NOW?!
REPID
OUR ENEMIES CAUGHT WIND OF THE PARTY!
I DON'T THINK SO, MAN.
HEY, FELLAS!
HEY, WHERE MY HEALERS AT?
MY KID WILL NEVER BELIEVE THIS!
LET ME SEE.
AND ON THAT NOTE, CAPTAIN AMERICA IS LEAVING THE BUILDING.
EVEN FOR WADE, THIS DOESN'T MAKE SENSE.
I CAN'T IMAGINE HIM MARRIED.
YOU GUYS HAVING FUN?
WE WERE JUST SAYING THAT WE CAN'T BELIEVE OUR BUDDY WADE IS FINALLY GETTING MARRIED.
OH, I'VE BEEN MARRIED LOTS OF TIMES

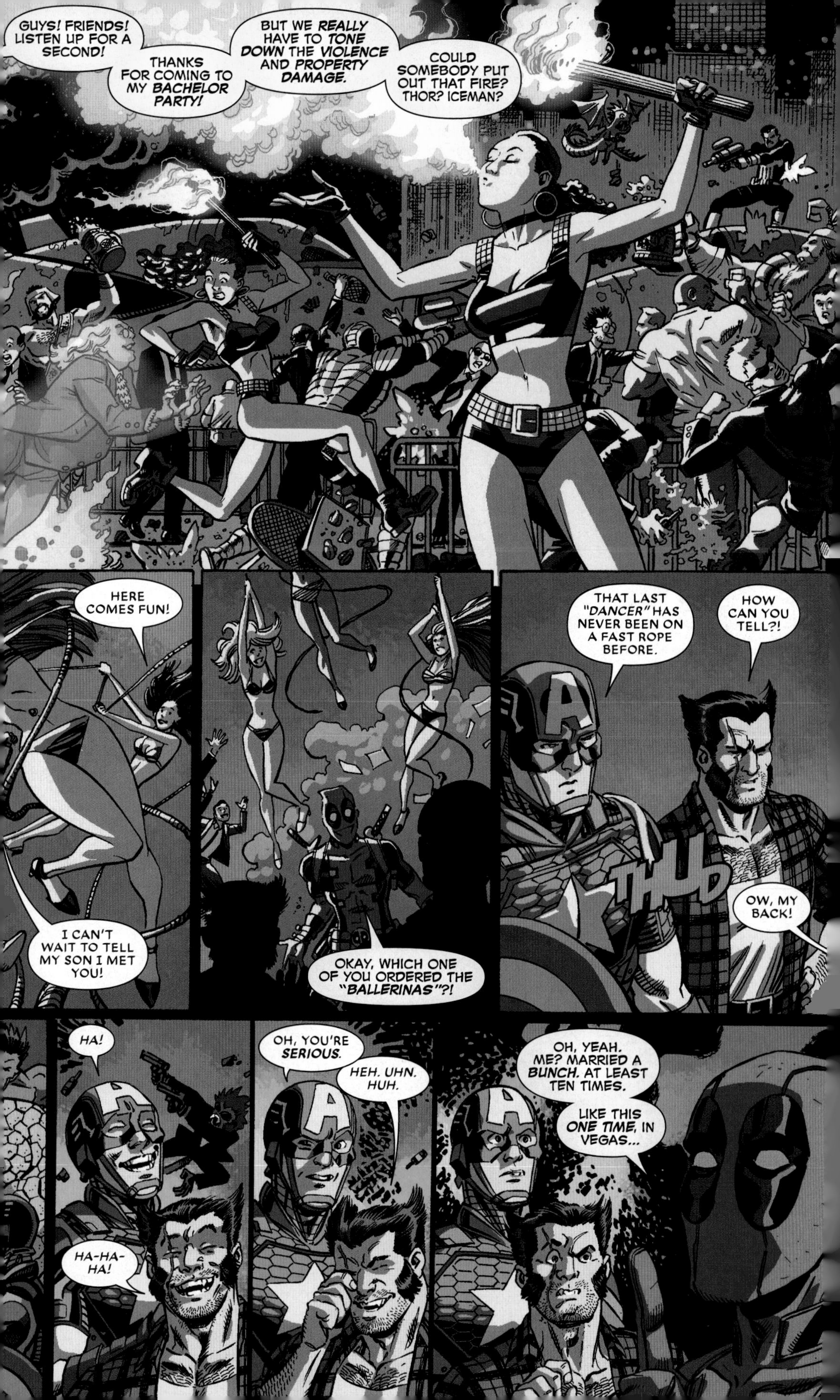
GUYS! FRIENDS! LISTEN UP FOR A SECOND!
THANKS FOR COMING TO MY BACHELOR PARTY!
BUT WE REALLY HAVE TO TONE DOWN THE VIOLENCE AND PROPERTY DAMAGE.
COULD SOMEBODY PUT OUT THAT FIRE? THOR? ICEMAN?
HERE COMES FUN!
I CAN'T WAIT TO TELL MY SON I MET YOU!
OKAY, WHICH ONE OF YOU ORDERED THE "BALLERINAS"?!
THAT LAST "DANCER" HAS NEVER BEEN ON A FAST ROPE BEFORE.
HOW CAN YOU TELL?!
THUD
OW, MY BACK!
HA!
HA-HA-HA!
OH, YOU'RE SERIOUS.
HEH. UHN. HUH.
OH, YEAH. ME? MARRIED A BUNCH. AT LEAST TEN TIMES.
LIKE THIS ONE TIME, IN VEGAS...

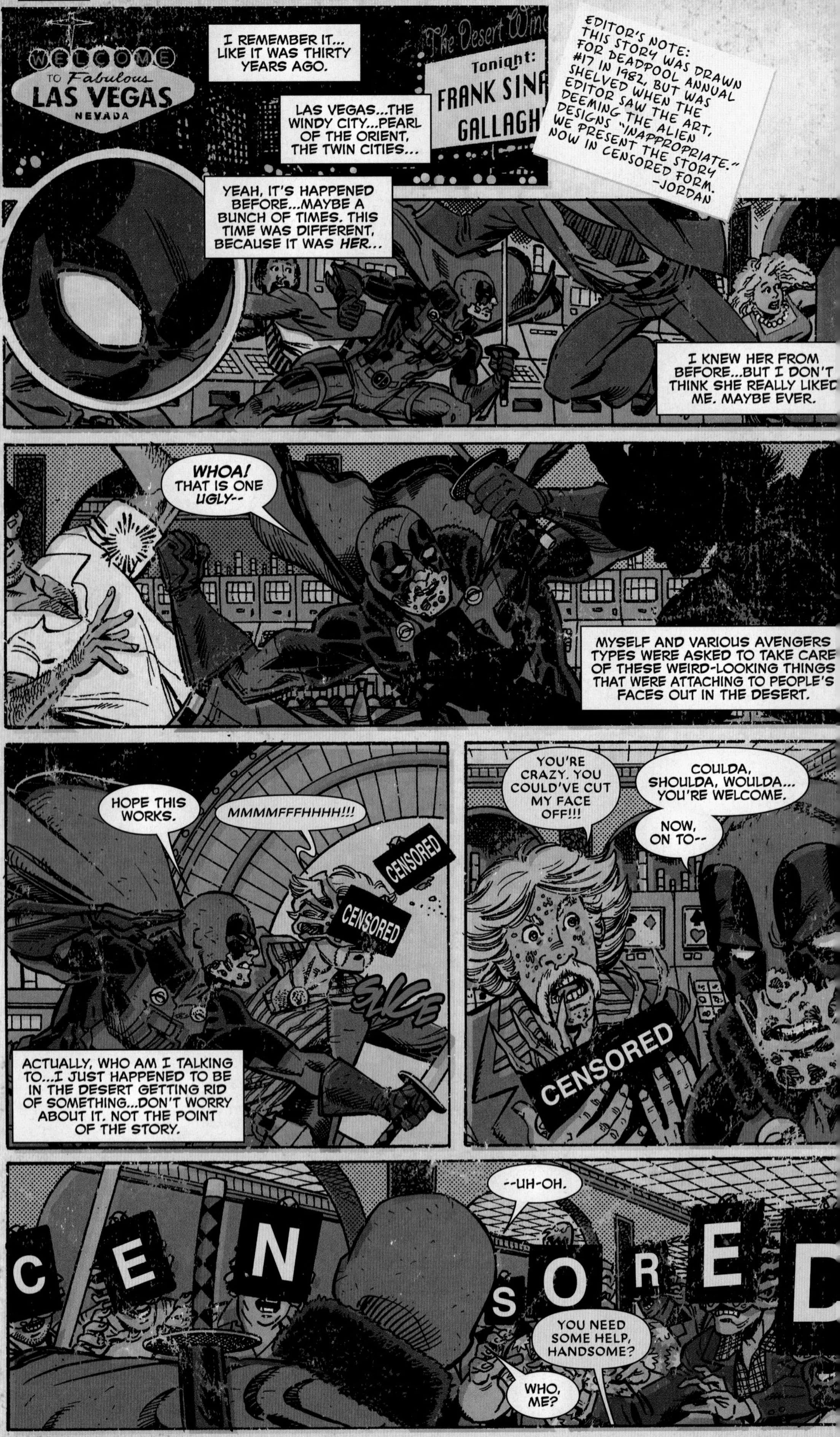
WELCOME TO Fabulous LAS VEGAS NEVADA
I REMEMBER IT... LIKE IT WAS THIRTY YEARS AGO.
LAS VEGAS...THE WINDY CITY...PEARL OF THE ORIENT, THE TWIN CITIES...
Tonight: FRANK SINA GALLAGH
EDITOR'S NOTE: THIS STORY WAS DRAWN FOR DEADPOOL ANNUAL #17 IN 1982, BUT WAS SHELVED WHEN THE EDITOR SAW THE ART, DEEMING THE ALIEN DESIGNS "INAPPROPRIATE." WE PRESENT THE STORY NOW IN CENSORED FORM. -JORDAN
YEAH, IT'S HAPPENED BEFORE...MAYBE A BUNCH OF TIMES. THIS TIME WAS DIFFERENT, BECAUSE IT WAS HER...
I KNEW HER FROM BEFORE...BUT I DON'T THINK SHE REALLY LIKED ME. MAYBE EVER.
WHOA! THAT IS ONE UGLY--
MYSELF AND VARIOUS AVENGERS TYPES WERE ASKED TO TAKE CARE OF THESE WEIRD-LOOKING THINGS THAT WERE ATTACHING TO PEOPLE'S FACES OUT IN THE DESERT.
HOPE THIS WORKS.
MMMMFFFHHHH!!!
CENSORED
CENSORED
SLICE
ACTUALLY, WHO AM I TALKING TO...I JUST HAPPENED TO BE IN THE DESERT GETTING RID OF SOMETHING...DON'T WORRY ABOUT IT. NOT THE POINT OF THE STORY.
YOU'RE CRAZY. YOU COULD'VE CUT MY FACE OFF!!!
COULDA, SHOULDA, WOULDA... YOU'RE WELCOME.
NOW, ON TO--
CENSORED
--UH-OH.
C E N S O R E D
YOU NEED SOME HELP, HANDSOME?
WHO, ME?

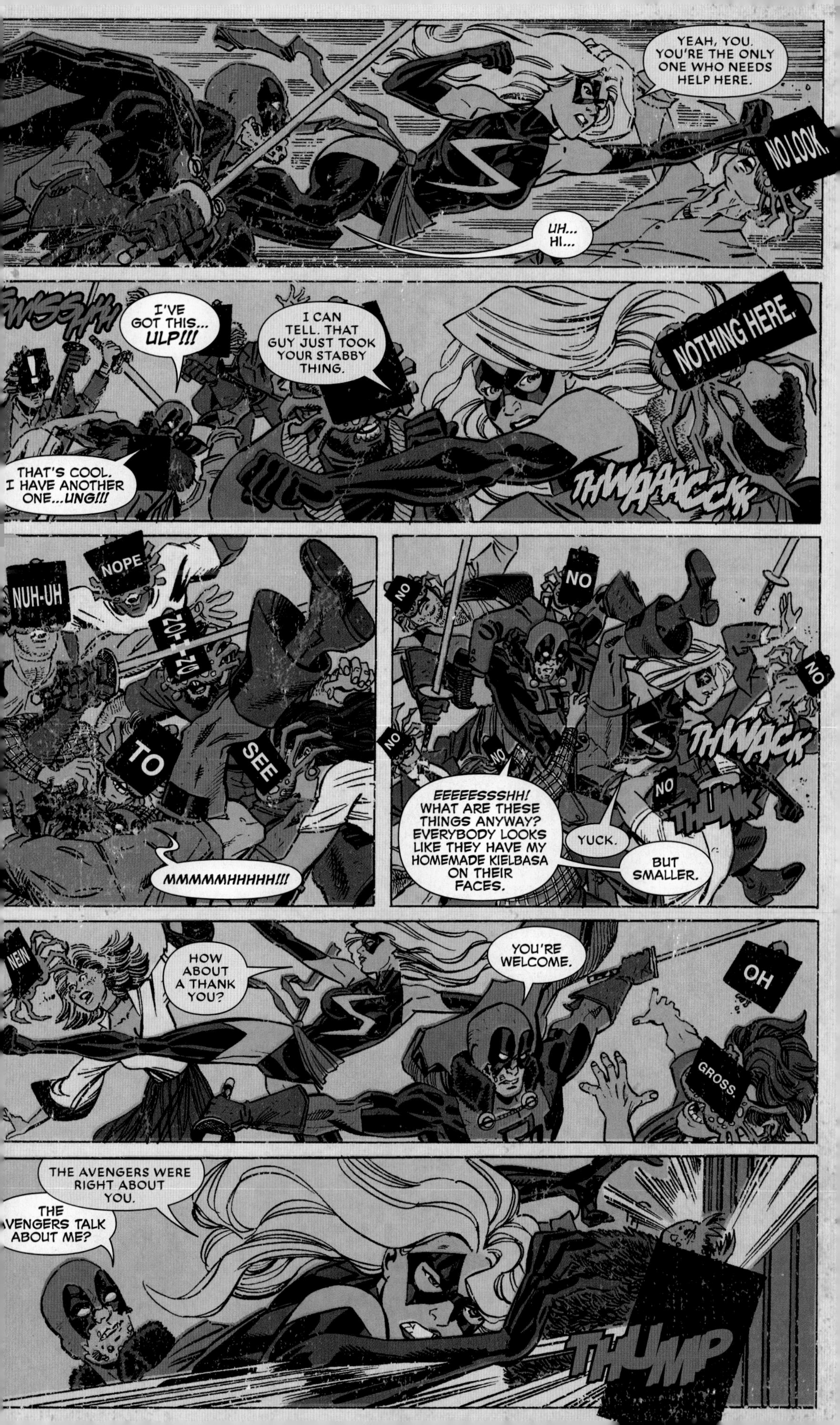

YEAH, YOU. YOU'RE THE ONLY ONE WHO NEEDS HELP HERE.
NO LOOK.
UH... HI...
FWSSHH
I'VE GOT THIS... ULP!!!
I CAN TELL. THAT GUY JUST TOOK YOUR STABBY THING.
NOTHING HERE.
!
THAT'S COOL. I HAVE ANOTHER ONE...UNG!!!
THWAAACCKK
NUH-UH
NOPE
TO
SEE
MMMMMHHHHH!!!
NO
NO
NO
NO
NO
NO
THWACK
THUNK
EEEEESSSHH! WHAT ARE THESE THINGS ANYWAY? EVERYBODY LOOKS LIKE THEY HAVE MY HOMEMADE KIELBASA ON THEIR FACES.
YUCK.
BUT SMALLER.
NEIN
HOW ABOUT A THANK YOU?
YOU'RE WELCOME.
OH
GROSS.
THE AVENGERS WERE RIGHT ABOUT YOU.
THE AVENGERS TALK ABOUT ME?
THUMP

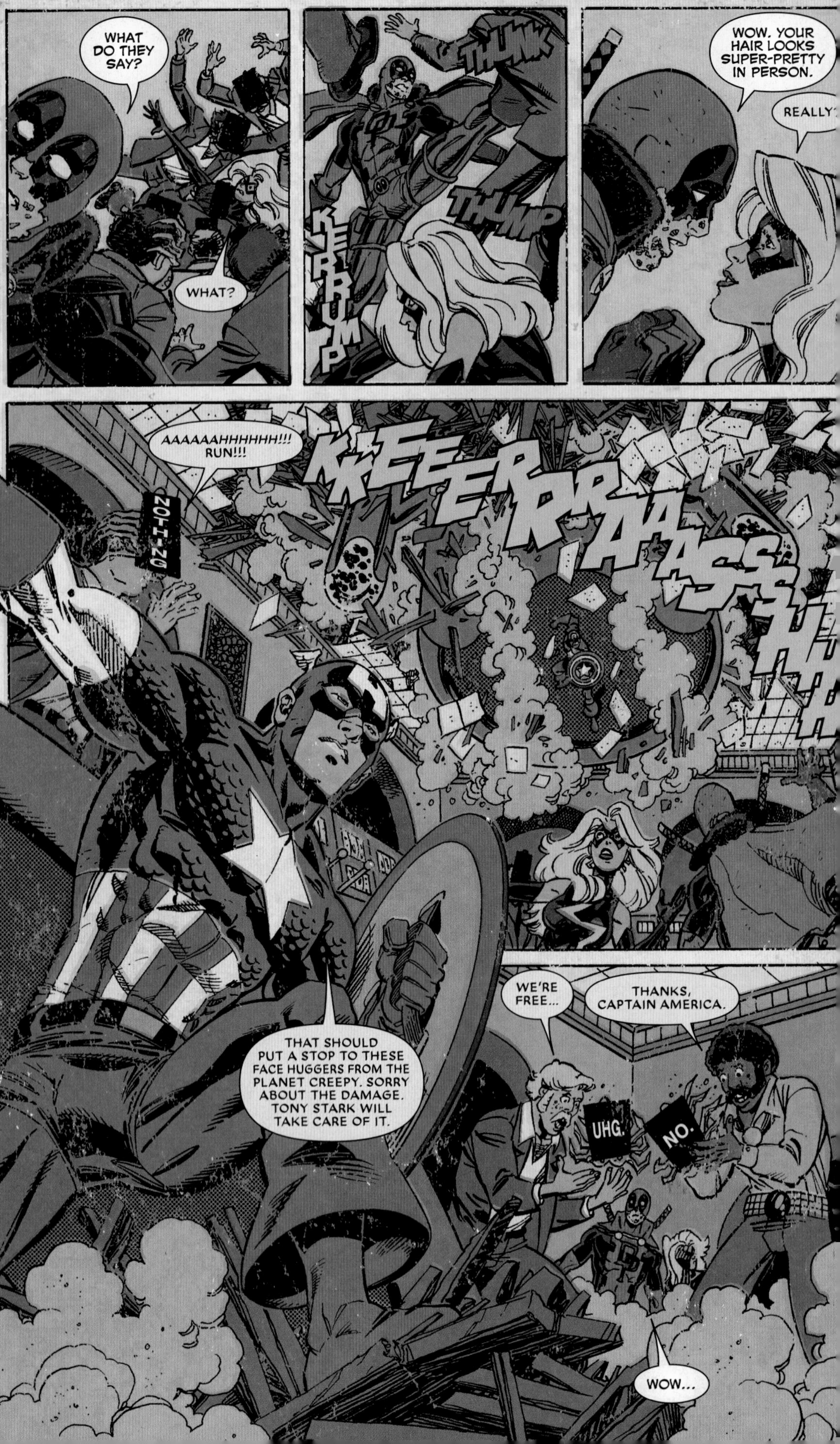
WHAT DO THEY SAY?
WHAT?
THUNK
KERRUMP
THUMP
WOW. YOUR HAIR LOOKS SUPER-PRETTY IN PERSON.
REALLY?
AAAAAAHHHHHH!!! RUN!!!
NOTHING
KKEERRAASSHH
WE'RE FREE...
THANKS, CAPTAIN AMERICA.
THAT SHOULD PUT A STOP TO THESE FACE HUGGERS FROM THE PLANET CREEPY. SORRY ABOUT THE DAMAGE. TONY STARK WILL TAKE CARE OF IT.
UHG.
NO.
WOW...

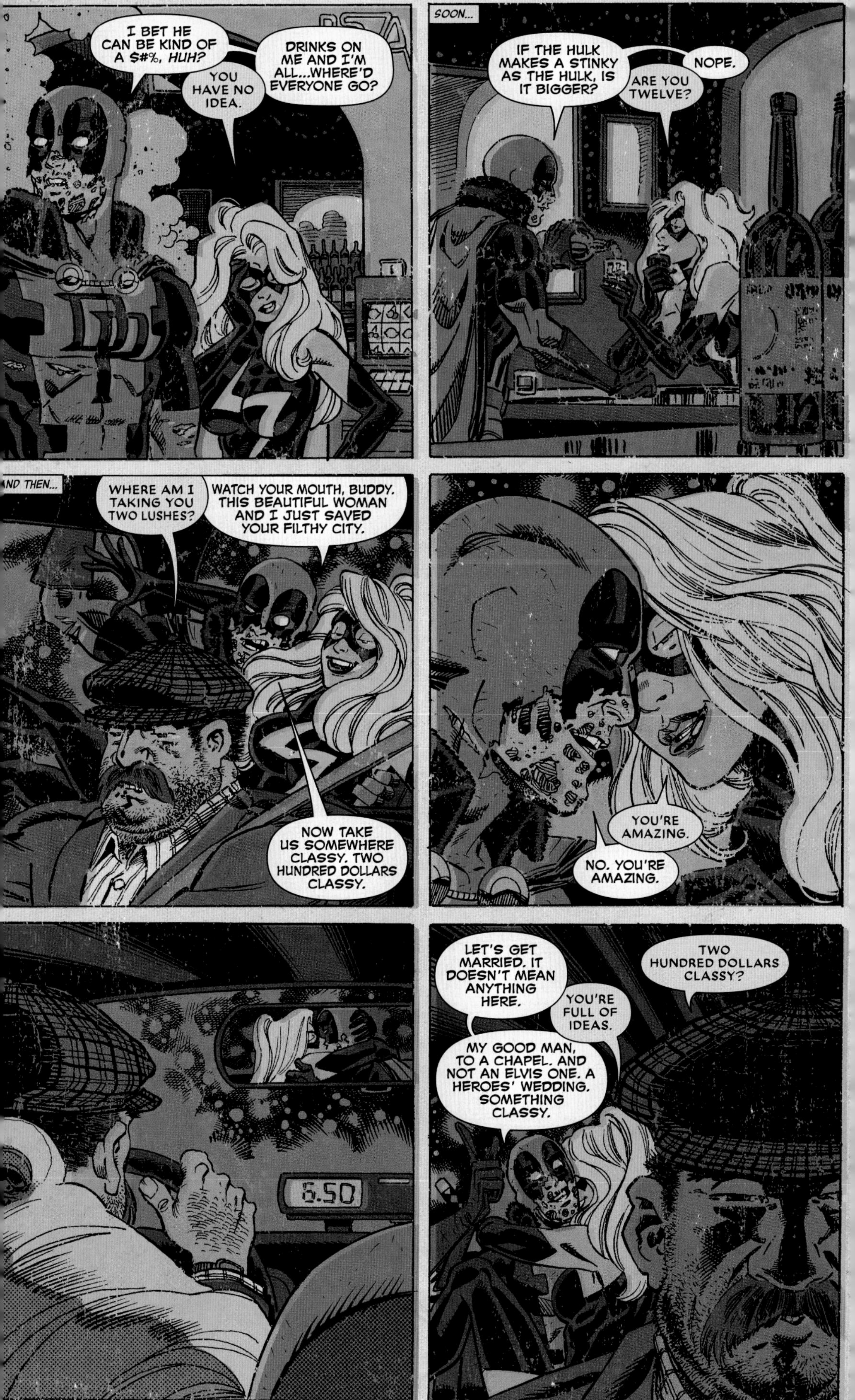

I BET HE CAN BE KIND OF A $#%, HUH?
DRINKS ON ME AND I'M ALL...WHERE'D EVERYONE GO?
YOU HAVE NO IDEA.
SOON...
IF THE HULK MAKES A STINKY AS THE HULK, IS IT BIGGER?
NOPE.
ARE YOU TWELVE?
ND THEN...
WHERE AM I TAKING YOU TWO LUSHES?
WATCH YOUR MOUTH, BUDDY. THIS BEAUTIFUL WOMAN AND I JUST SAVED YOUR FILTHY CITY.
NOW TAKE US SOMEWHERE CLASSY. TWO HUNDRED DOLLARS CLASSY.
YOU'RE AMAZING.
NO. YOU'RE AMAZING.
6.50
LET'S GET MARRIED. IT DOESN'T MEAN ANYTHING HERE.
TWO HUNDRED DOLLARS CLASSY?
YOU'RE FULL OF IDEAS.
MY GOOD MAN, TO A CHAPEL. AND NOT AN ELVIS ONE. A HEROES' WEDDING. SOMETHING CLASSY.

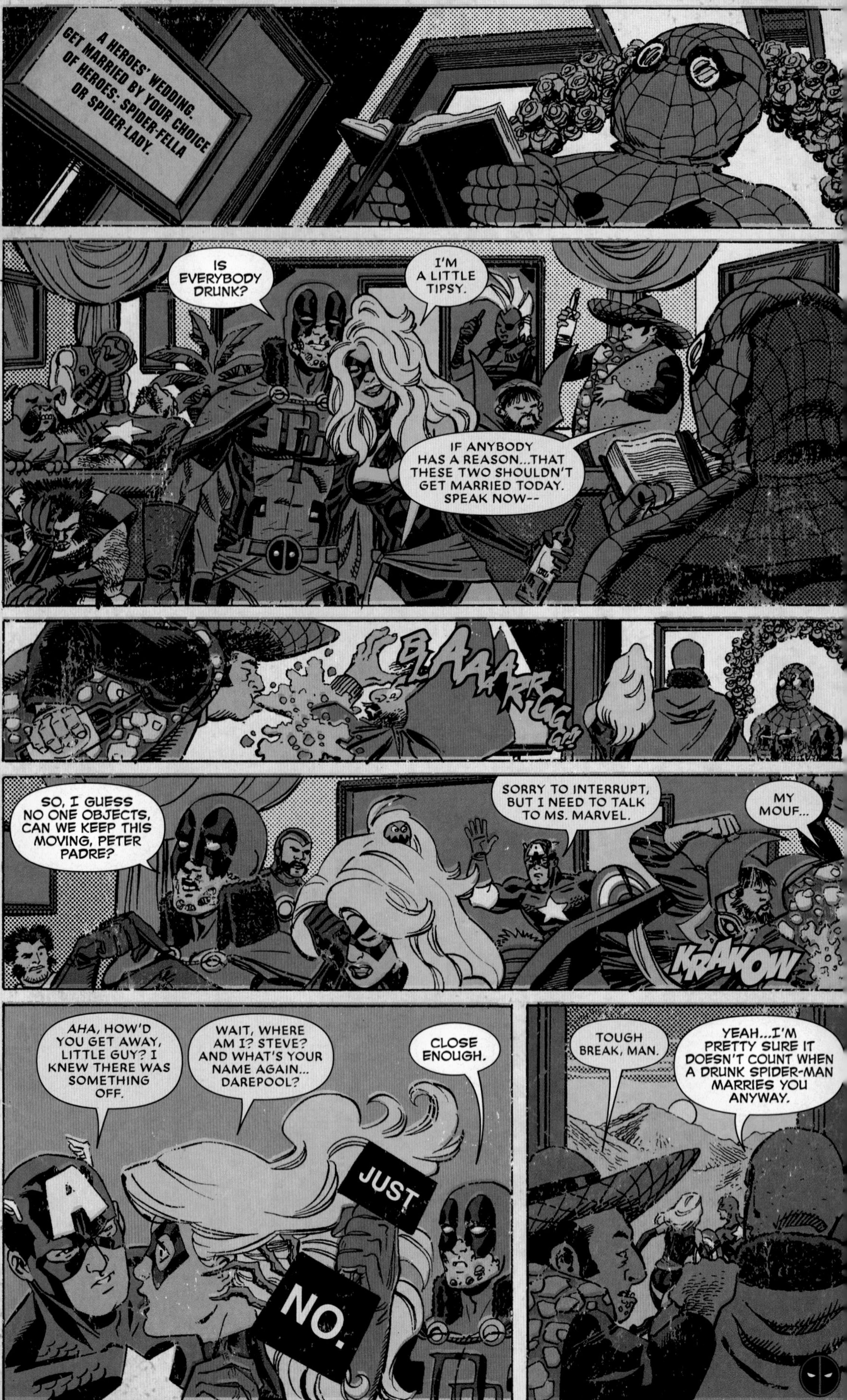

A HEROES' WEDDING. GET MARRIED BY YOUR CHOICE OF HEROES: SPIDER-FELLA OR SPIDER-LADY.
IS EVERYBODY DRUNK?
I'M A LITTLE TIPSY.
IF ANYBODY HAS A REASON...THAT THESE TWO SHOULDN'T GET MARRIED TODAY. SPEAK NOW--
BLAAARRGG!
SO, I GUESS NO ONE OBJECTS, CAN WE KEEP THIS MOVING, PETER PADRE?
SORRY TO INTERRUPT, BUT I NEED TO TALK TO MS. MARVEL.
MY MOUF...
KRAKOW
AHA, HOW'D YOU GET AWAY, LITTLE GUY? I KNEW THERE WAS SOMETHING OFF.
WAIT, WHERE AM I? STEVE? AND WHAT'S YOUR NAME AGAIN... DAREPOOL?
CLOSE ENOUGH.
JUST
NO.
TOUGH BREAK, MAN.
YEAH...I'M PRETTY SURE IT DOESN'T COUNT WHEN A DRUNK SPIDER-MAN MARRIES YOU ANYWAY.

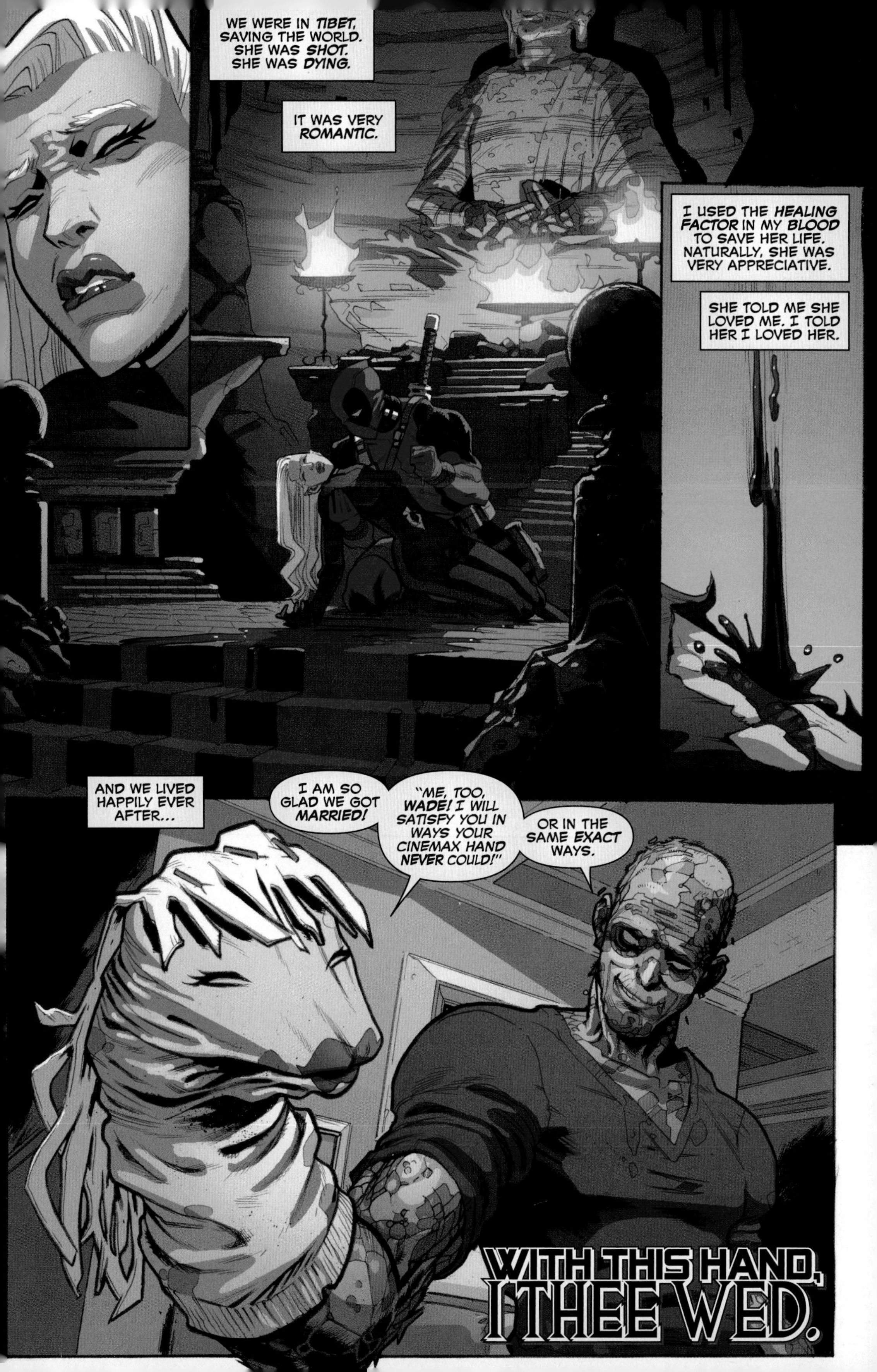

WE WERE IN TIBET, SAVING THE WORLD. SHE WAS SHOT. SHE WAS DYING.
IT WAS VERY ROMANTIC.
I USED THE HEALING FACTOR IN MY BLOOD TO SAVE HER LIFE. NATURALLY, SHE WAS VERY APPRECIATIVE.
SHE TOLD ME SHE LOVED ME. I TOLD HER I LOVED HER.
AND WE LIVED HAPPILY EVER AFTER...
I AM SO GLAD WE GOT MARRIED!
"ME, TOO, WADE! I WILL SATISFY YOU IN WAYS YOUR CINEMAX HAND NEVER COULD!"
OR IN THE SAME EXACT WAYS.
WITH THIS HAND, I THEE WED.

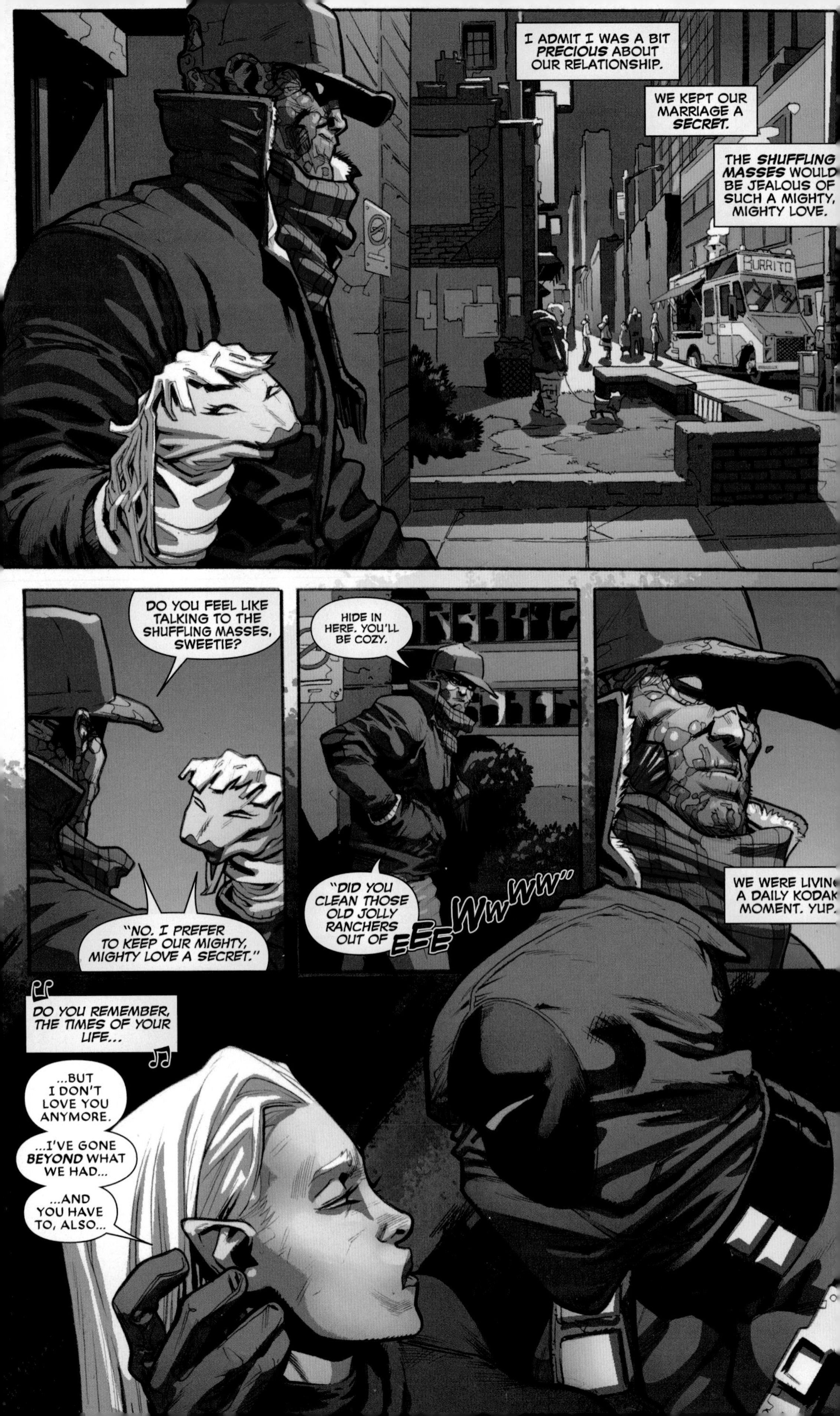
I ADMIT I WAS A BIT *PRECIOUS* ABOUT OUR RELATIONSHIP.
WE KEPT OUR MARRIAGE A *SECRET.*
THE *SHUFFLING MASSES* WOULD BE JEALOUS OF SUCH A MIGHTY, MIGHTY LOVE.
BURRITO
DO YOU FEEL LIKE TALKING TO THE SHUFFLING MASSES, SWEETIE?
"NO. I PREFER TO KEEP OUR MIGHTY, MIGHTY LOVE A SECRET."
HIDE IN HERE. YOU'LL BE COZY.
"DID YOU CLEAN THOSE OLD JOLLY RANCHERS OUT OF
EEEWWWW"
WE WERE LIVIN A DAILY KODAK MOMENT. YUP.
DO YOU REMEMBER, THE TIMES OF YOUR LIFE...
...BUT I DON'T LOVE YOU ANYMORE.
...I'VE GONE *BEYOND* WHAT WE HAD...
...AND YOU HAVE TO, ALSO...

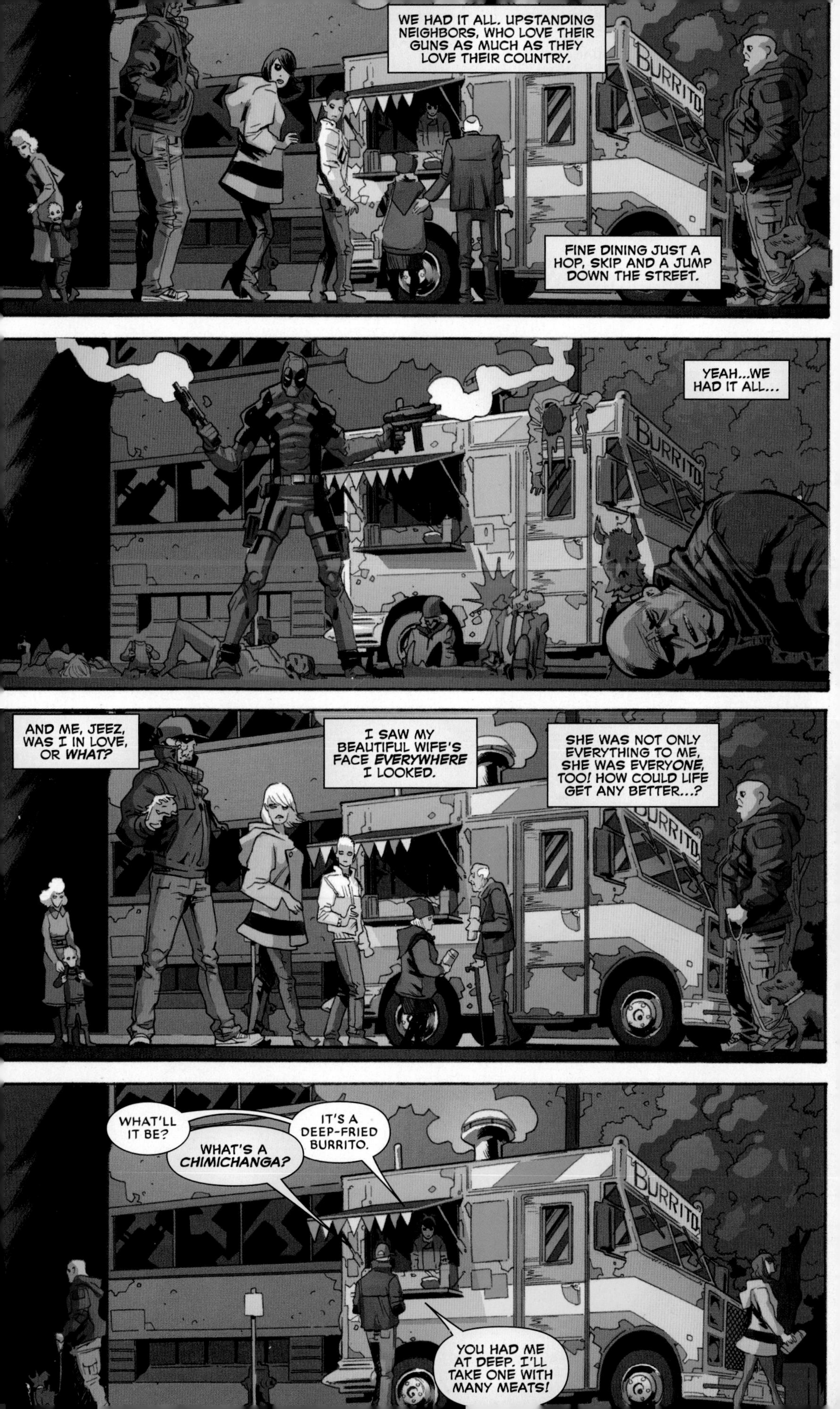
WE HAD IT ALL. UPSTANDING NEIGHBORS, WHO LOVE THEIR GUNS AS MUCH AS THEY LOVE THEIR COUNTRY.
BURRITO
FINE DINING JUST A HOP, SKIP AND A JUMP DOWN THE STREET.
YEAH...WE HAD IT ALL...
BURRITO
AND ME, JEEZ, WAS I IN LOVE, OR WHAT?
I SAW MY BEAUTIFUL WIFE'S FACE EVERYWHERE I LOOKED.
SHE WAS NOT ONLY EVERYTHING TO ME, SHE WAS EVERYONE, TOO! HOW COULD LIFE GET ANY BETTER...?
BURRITO
WHAT'LL IT BE?
WHAT'S A CHIMICHANGA?
IT'S A DEEP-FRIED BURRITO.
BURRITO
YOU HAD ME AT DEEP. I'LL TAKE ONE WITH MANY MEATS!

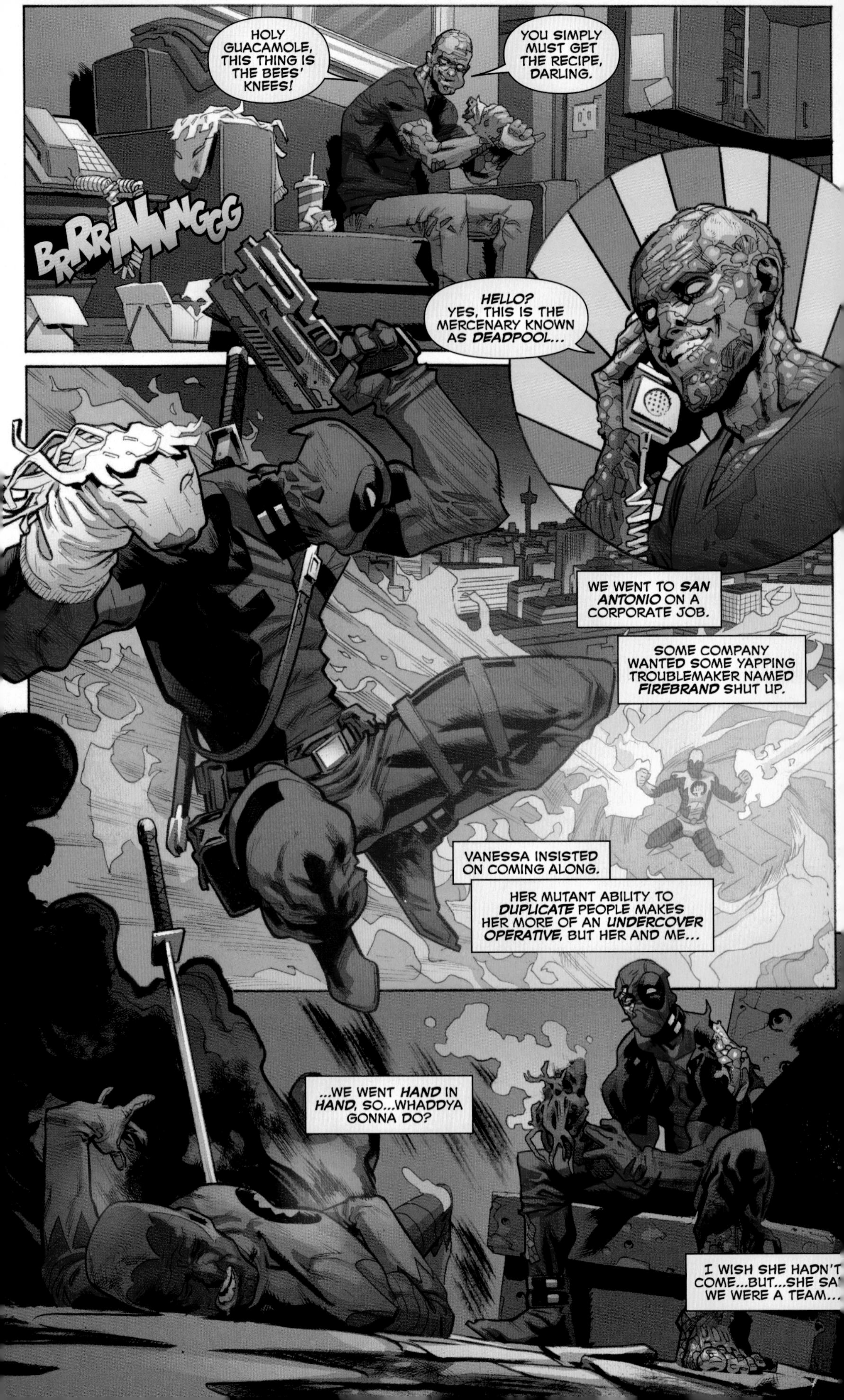
HOLY GUACAMOLE, THIS THING IS THE BEES' KNEES!
YOU SIMPLY MUST GET THE RECIPE, DARLING.
BRRRINNNGGG
HELLO? YES, THIS IS THE MERCENARY KNOWN AS DEADPOOL...
WE WENT TO SAN ANTONIO ON A CORPORATE JOB.
SOME COMPANY WANTED SOME YAPPING TROUBLEMAKER NAMED FIREBRAND SHUT UP.
VANESSA INSISTED ON COMING ALONG.
HER MUTANT ABILITY TO DUPLICATE PEOPLE MAKES HER MORE OF AN UNDERCOVER OPERATIVE, BUT HER AND ME...
...WE WENT HAND IN HAND, SO...WHADDYA GONNA DO?
I WISH SHE HADN'T COME...BUT...SHE SA
WE WERE A TEAM...

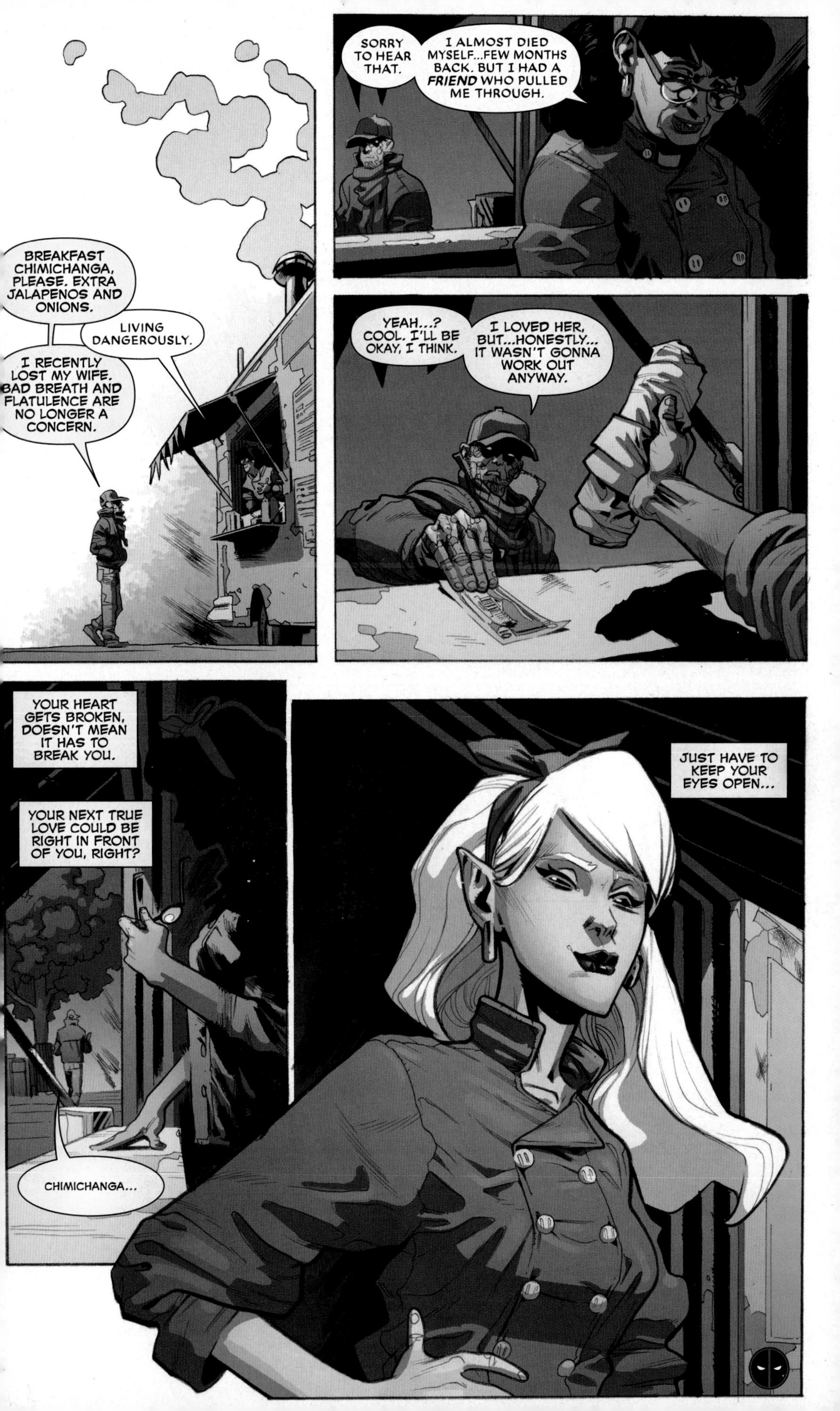
BREAKFAST CHIMICHANGA, PLEASE. EXTRA JALAPENOS AND ONIONS.
LIVING DANGEROUSLY.
I RECENTLY LOST MY WIFE. BAD BREATH AND FLATULENCE ARE NO LONGER A CONCERN.
SORRY TO HEAR THAT.
I ALMOST DIED MYSELF...FEW MONTHS BACK. BUT I HAD A FRIEND WHO PULLED ME THROUGH.
YEAH...? COOL. I'LL BE OKAY, I THINK.
I LOVED HER, BUT...HONESTLY... IT WASN'T GONNA WORK OUT ANYWAY.
YOUR HEART GETS BROKEN, DOESN'T MEAN IT HAS TO BREAK YOU.
YOUR NEXT TRUE LOVE COULD BE RIGHT IN FRONT OF YOU, RIGHT?
CHIMICHANGA...
JUST HAVE TO KEEP YOUR EYES OPEN...

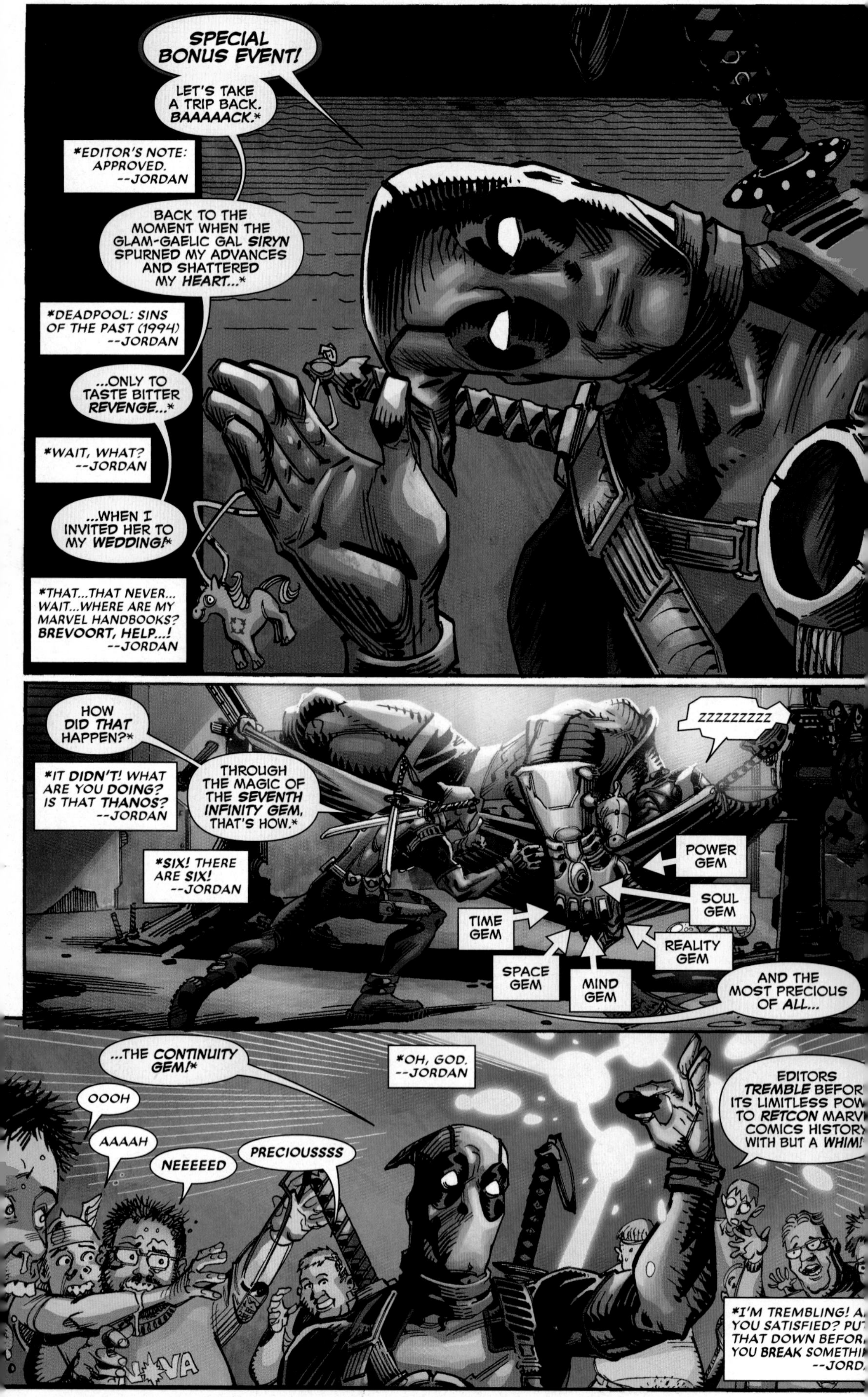

SPECIAL BONUS EVENT!
LET'S TAKE A TRIP BACK. BAAAAACK.*
*EDITOR'S NOTE: APPROVED. --JORDAN
BACK TO THE MOMENT WHEN THE GLAM-GAELIC GAL SIRYN SPURNED MY ADVANCES AND SHATTERED MY HEART...*
*DEADPOOL: SINS OF THE PAST (1994) --JORDAN
...ONLY TO TASTE BITTER REVENGE...*
*WAIT, WHAT? --JORDAN
...WHEN I INVITED HER TO MY WEDDING!*
*THAT...THAT NEVER... WAIT...WHERE ARE MY MARVEL HANDBOOKS? BREVOORT, HELP...! --JORDAN
HOW DID THAT HAPPEN?*
*IT DIDN'T! WHAT ARE YOU DOING? IS THAT THANOS? --JORDAN
THROUGH THE MAGIC OF THE SEVENTH INFINITY GEM, THAT'S HOW.*
ZZZZZZZZZ
*SIX! THERE ARE SIX! --JORDAN
POWER GEM
SOUL GEM
TIME GEM
REALITY GEM
SPACE GEM
MIND GEM
AND THE MOST PRECIOUS OF ALL...
...THE CONTINUITY GEM!*
*OH, GOD. --JORDAN
OOOH
AAAAH
NEEEEED
PRECIOUSSSS
EDITORS TREMBLE BEFOR ITS LIMITLESS POW TO RETCON MARV COMICS HISTORY WITH BUT A WHIM!
VIVA
*I'M TREMBLING! A YOU SATISFIED? PU THAT DOWN BEFOR YOU BREAK SOMETHI --JORD

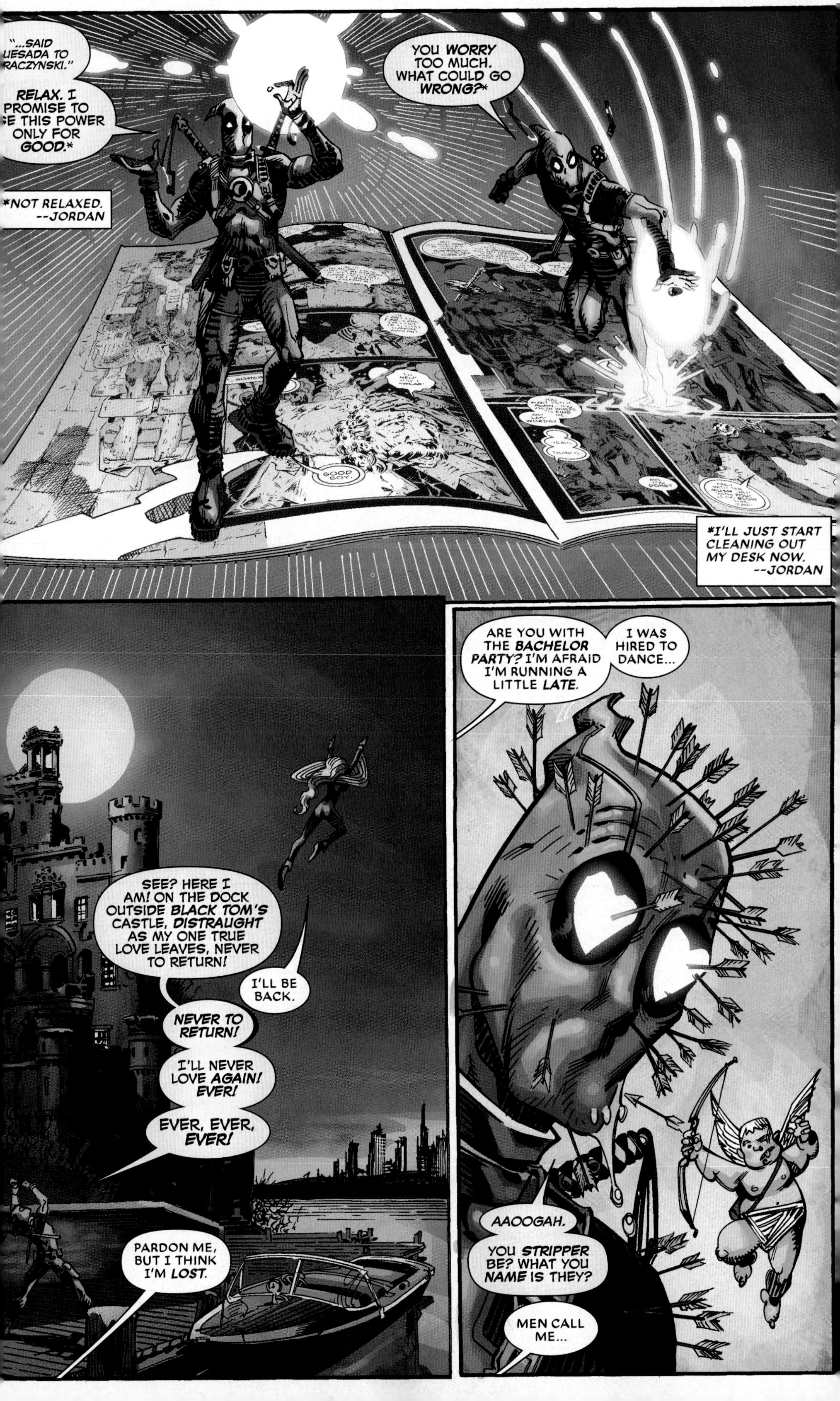
"...SAID
UESADA TO
RACZYNSKI."
RELAX. I PROMISE TO
E THIS POWER ONLY FOR GOOD.*
*NOT RELAXED. --JORDAN
YOU WORRY TOO MUCH. WHAT COULD GO WRONG?*
*I'LL JUST START CLEANING OUT MY DESK NOW. --JORDAN
GOOD BOY.
SEE? HERE I AM! ON THE DOCK OUTSIDE BLACK TOM'S CASTLE, DISTRAUGHT AS MY ONE TRUE LOVE LEAVES, NEVER TO RETURN!
I'LL BE BACK.
NEVER TO RETURN!
I'LL NEVER LOVE AGAIN! EVER!
EVER, EVER, EVER!
PARDON ME, BUT I THINK I'M LOST.
ARE YOU WITH THE BACHELOR PARTY? I'M AFRAID I'M RUNNING A LITTLE LATE.
I WAS HIRED TO DANCE...
AAOOGAH.
YOU STRIPPER BE? WHAT YOU NAME IS THEY?
MEN CALL ME...

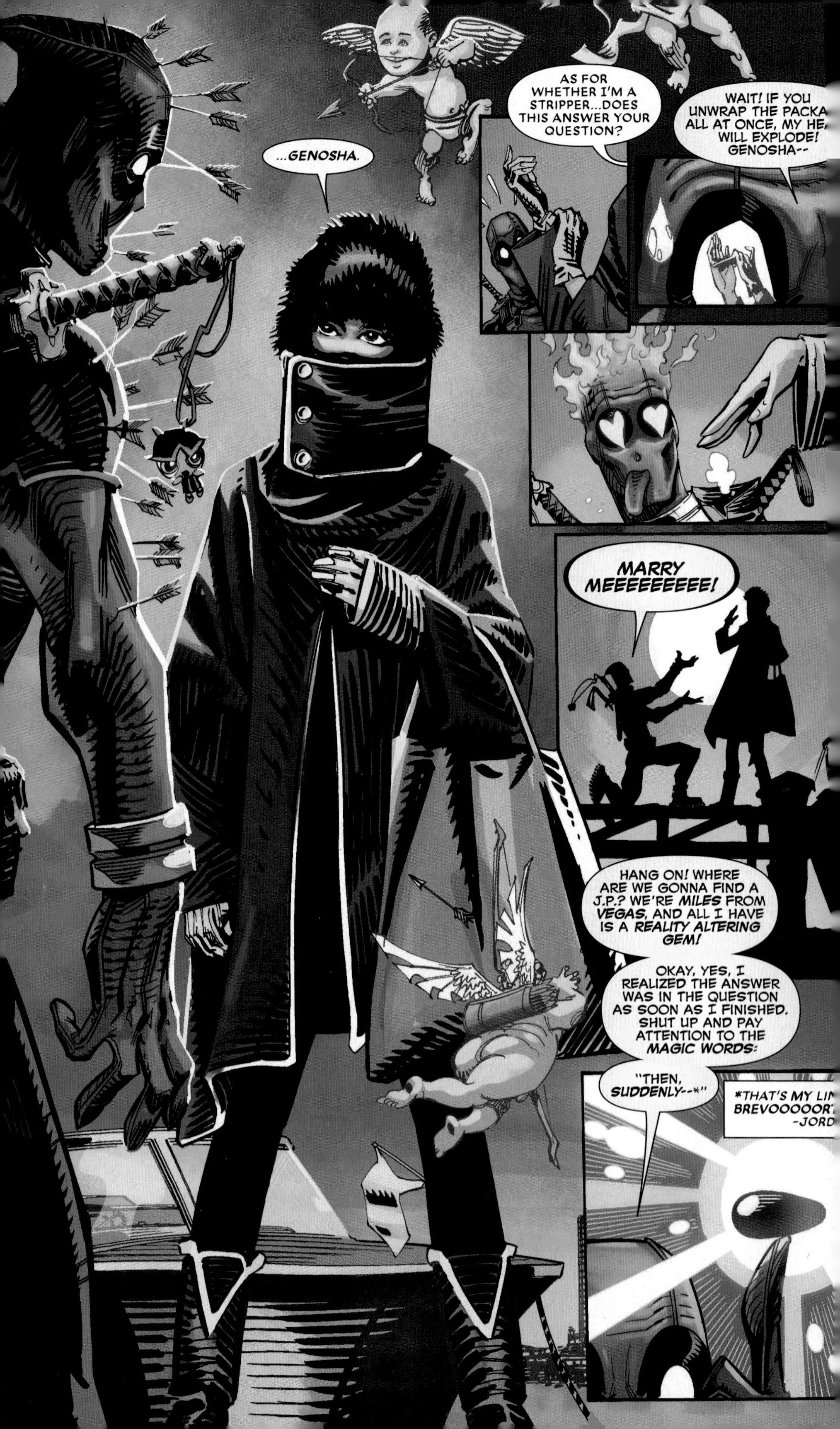
...GENOSHA.
AS FOR WHETHER I'M A STRIPPER...DOES THIS ANSWER YOUR QUESTION?
WAIT! IF YOU UNWRAP THE PACKA ALL AT ONCE, MY HE WILL EXPLODE! GENOSHA--
MARRY MEEEEEEEEE!
HANG ON! WHERE ARE WE GONNA FIND A J.P.? WE'RE MILES FROM VEGAS, AND ALL I HAVE IS A REALITY ALTERING GEM!
OKAY, YES, I REALIZED THE ANSWER WAS IN THE QUESTION AS SOON AS I FINISHED. SHUT UP AND PAY ATTENTION TO THE MAGIC WORDS:
"THEN, SUDDENLY--*"
*THAT'S MY LIN BREVOOOOOR -JORD

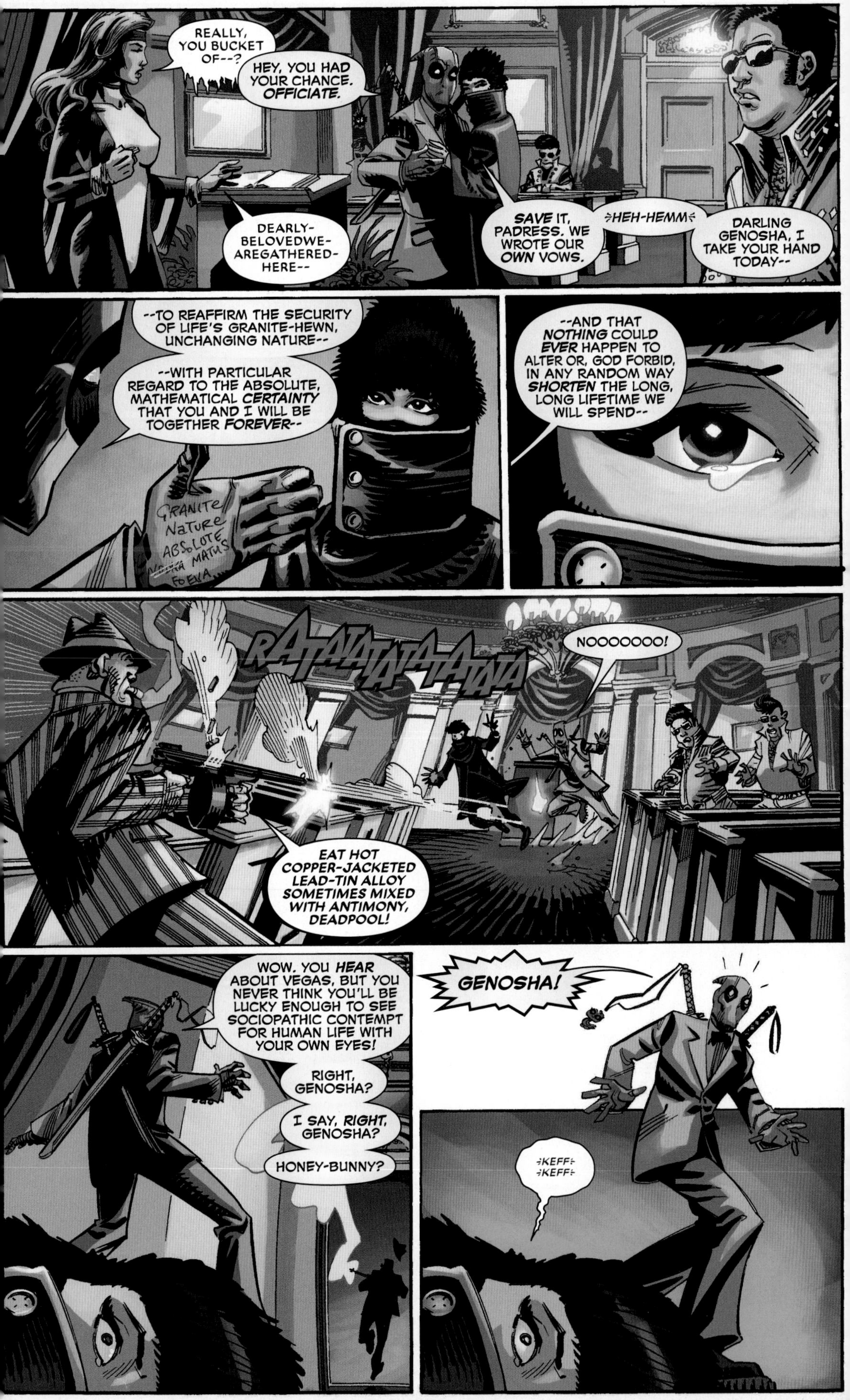
REALLY, YOU BUCKET OF--?
HEY, YOU HAD YOUR CHANCE. *OFFICIATE.*
DEARLY-BELOVEDWE-AREGATHERED-HERE--
SAVE IT, PADRESS. WE WROTE OUR *OWN* VOWS.
HEH-HEMM
DARLING GENOSHA, I TAKE YOUR HAND TODAY--
--TO REAFFIRM THE SECURITY OF LIFE'S GRANITE-HEWN, UNCHANGING NATURE--
--WITH PARTICULAR REGARD TO THE ABSOLUTE, MATHEMATICAL *CERTAINTY* THAT YOU AND I WILL BE TOGETHER *FOREVER*--
GRANITE
NATURE
ABSOLUTE
MATHS
FOEVA
--AND THAT *NOTHING* COULD *EVER* HAPPEN TO ALTER OR, GOD FORBID, IN ANY RANDOM WAY *SHORTEN* THE LONG, LONG LIFETIME WE WILL SPEND--
RATATATATATATATATATA
NOOOOOOO!
EAT HOT COPPER-JACKETED LEAD-TIN ALLOY SOMETIMES MIXED WITH ANTIMONY, DEADPOOL!
WOW. YOU *HEAR* ABOUT VEGAS, BUT YOU NEVER THINK YOU'LL BE LUCKY ENOUGH TO SEE SOCIOPATHIC CONTEMPT FOR HUMAN LIFE WITH YOUR OWN EYES!
RIGHT, GENOSHA?
I SAY, *RIGHT,* GENOSHA?
HONEY-BUNNY?
GENOSHA!
KEFF
KEFF

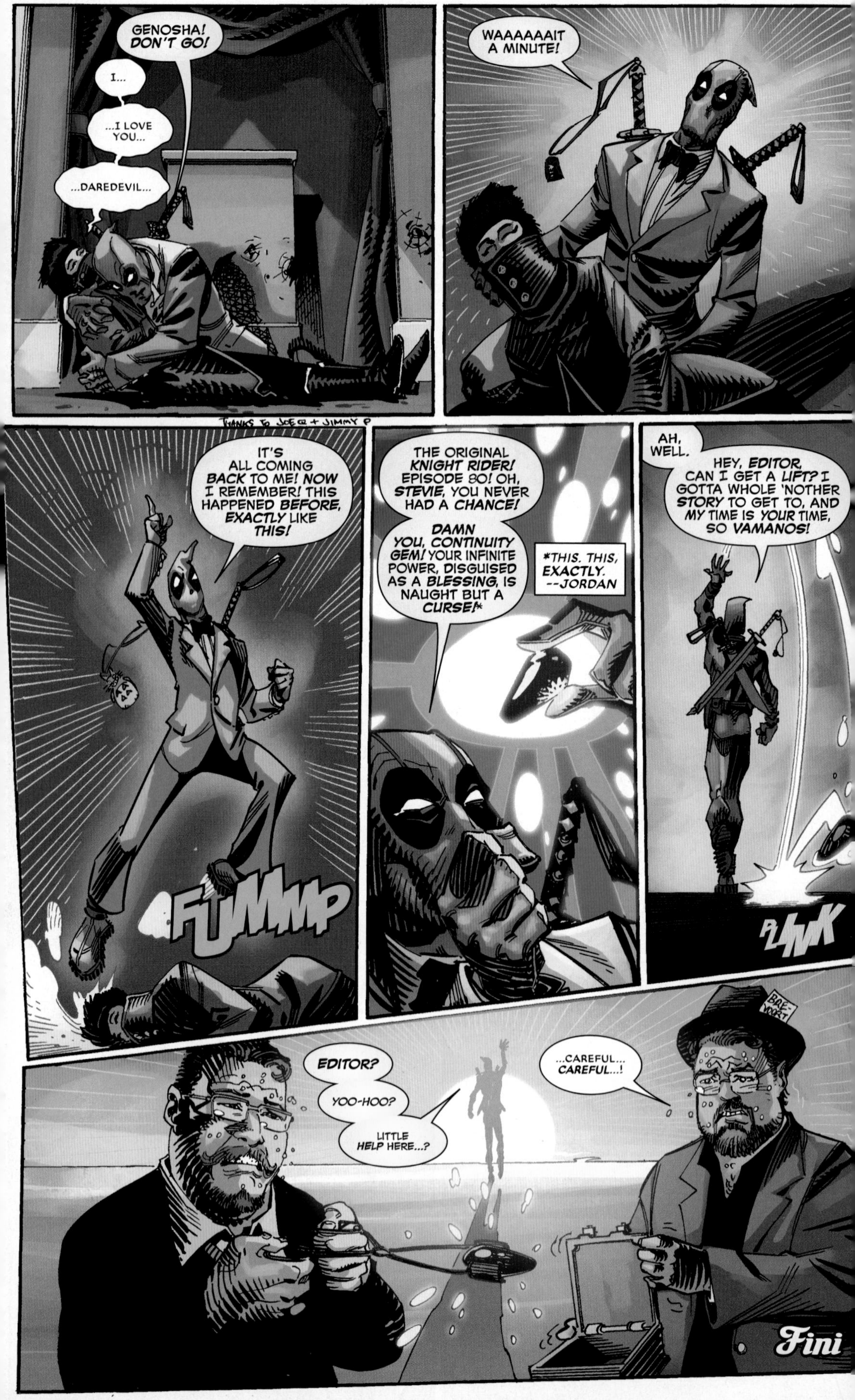
GENOSHA! DON'T GO!
I...
...I LOVE YOU...
...DAREDEVIL...
WAAAAAAIT A MINUTE!
THANKS TO JOE Q + JIMMY P
IT'S ALL COMING BACK TO ME! NOW I REMEMBER! THIS HAPPENED BEFORE, EXACTLY LIKE THIS!
FUMMMP
THE ORIGINAL KNIGHT RIDER! EPISODE 80! OH, STEVIE, YOU NEVER HAD A CHANCE!
DAMN YOU, CONTINUITY GEM! YOUR INFINITE POWER, DISGUISED AS A BLESSING, IS NAUGHT BUT A CURSE!*
*THIS. THIS, EXACTLY. --JORDAN
AH, WELL.
HEY, EDITOR, CAN I GET A LIFT? I GOTTA WHOLE 'NOTHER STORY TO GET TO, AND MY TIME IS YOUR TIME, SO VAMANOS!
PLINK
BRE-VOORT
EDITOR?
YOO-HOO?
LITTLE HELP HERE...?
...CAREFUL... CAREFUL...!
Fini

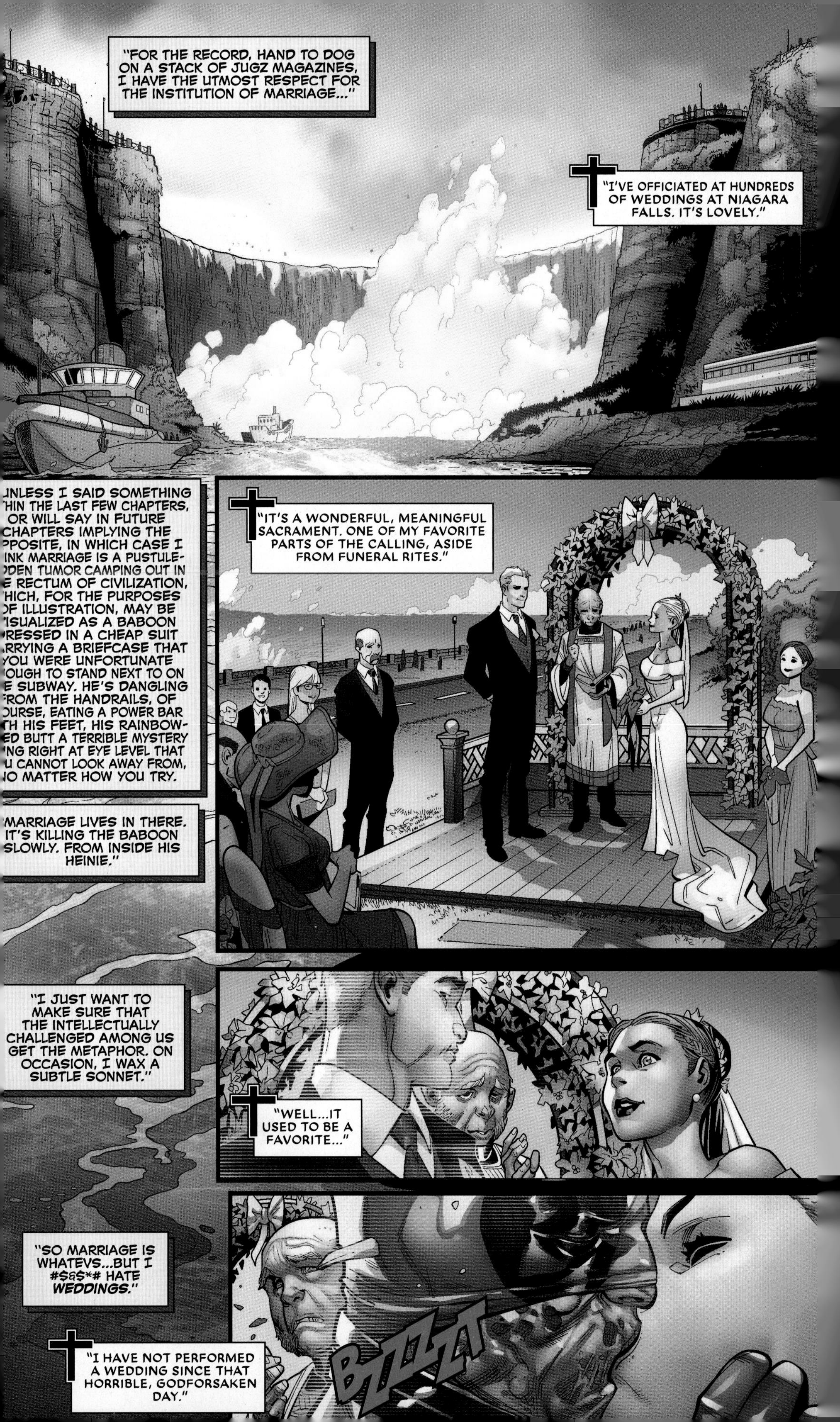

"FOR THE RECORD, HAND TO DOG ON A STACK OF JUGZ MAGAZINES, I HAVE THE UTMOST RESPECT FOR THE INSTITUTION OF MARRIAGE..."
"I'VE OFFICIATED AT HUNDREDS OF WEDDINGS AT NIAGARA FALLS. IT'S LOVELY."
JNLESS I SAID SOMETHING THIN THE LAST FEW CHAPTERS, OR WILL SAY IN FUTURE CHAPTERS IMPLYING THE PPOSITE, IN WHICH CASE I INK MARRIAGE IS A PUSTULE-DDEN TUMOR CAMPING OUT IN E RECTUM OF CIVILIZATION, HICH, FOR THE PURPOSES OF ILLUSTRATION, MAY BE ISUALIZED AS A BABOON RESSED IN A CHEAP SUIT RRYING A BRIEFCASE THAT YOU WERE UNFORTUNATE OUGH TO STAND NEXT TO ON E SUBWAY. HE'S DANGLING FROM THE HANDRAILS, OF OURSE, EATING A POWER BAR TH HIS FEET, HIS RAINBOW-ED BUTT A TERRIBLE MYSTERY NG RIGHT AT EYE LEVEL THAT U CANNOT LOOK AWAY FROM, O MATTER HOW YOU TRY.
"IT'S A WONDERFUL, MEANINGFUL SACRAMENT. ONE OF MY FAVORITE PARTS OF THE CALLING, ASIDE FROM FUNERAL RITES."
MARRIAGE LIVES IN THERE. IT'S KILLING THE BABOON SLOWLY. FROM INSIDE HIS HEINIE."
"I JUST WANT TO MAKE SURE THAT THE INTELLECTUALLY CHALLENGED AMONG US GET THE METAPHOR. ON OCCASION, I WAX A SUBTLE SONNET."
"WELL...IT USED TO BE A FAVORITE..."
"SO MARRIAGE IS WHATEVS...BUT I #$&$*# HATE WEDDINGS."
"I HAVE NOT PERFORMED A WEDDING SINCE THAT HORRIBLE, GODFORSAKEN DAY."
BZZZT

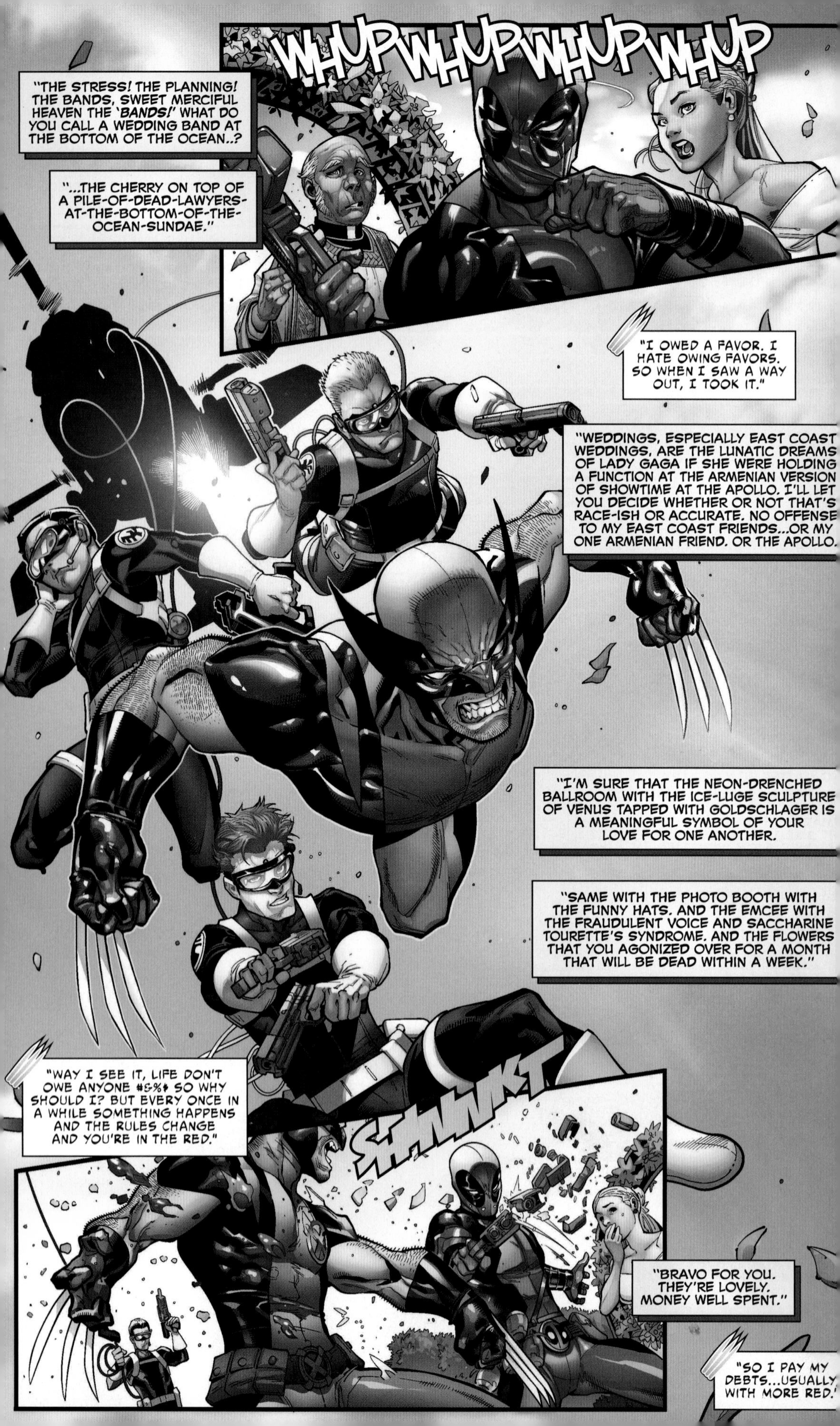
WHUP WHUP WHUP WHUP
"THE STRESS! THE PLANNING! THE BANDS, SWEET MERCIFUL HEAVEN THE 'BANDS!' WHAT DO YOU CALL A WEDDING BAND AT THE BOTTOM OF THE OCEAN..?
"...THE CHERRY ON TOP OF A PILE-OF-DEAD-LAWYERS-AT-THE-BOTTOM-OF-THE-OCEAN-SUNDAE."
"I OWED A FAVOR. I HATE OWING FAVORS. SO WHEN I SAW A WAY OUT, I TOOK IT."
"WEDDINGS, ESPECIALLY EAST COAST WEDDINGS, ARE THE LUNATIC DREAMS OF LADY GAGA IF SHE WERE HOLDING A FUNCTION AT THE ARMENIAN VERSION OF SHOWTIME AT THE APOLLO. I'LL LET YOU DECIDE WHETHER OR NOT THAT'S RACE-ISH OR ACCURATE. NO OFFENSE TO MY EAST COAST FRIENDS...OR MY ONE ARMENIAN FRIEND. OR THE APOLLO.
"I'M SURE THAT THE NEON-DRENCHED BALLROOM WITH THE ICE-LUGE SCULPTURE OF VENUS TAPPED WITH GOLDSCHLAGER IS A MEANINGFUL SYMBOL OF YOUR LOVE FOR ONE ANOTHER.
"SAME WITH THE PHOTO BOOTH WITH THE FUNNY HATS. AND THE EMCEE WITH THE FRAUDULENT VOICE AND SACCHARINE TOURETTE'S SYNDROME. AND THE FLOWERS THAT YOU AGONIZED OVER FOR A MONTH THAT WILL BE DEAD WITHIN A WEEK."
"WAY I SEE IT, LIFE DON'T OWE ANYONE #&%$ SO WHY SHOULD I? BUT EVERY ONCE IN A WHILE SOMETHING HAPPENS AND THE RULES CHANGE AND YOU'RE IN THE RED."
SHNNKT
"BRAVO FOR YOU. THEY'RE LOVELY. MONEY WELL SPENT."
"SO I PAY MY DEBTS...USUALLY WITH MORE RED."

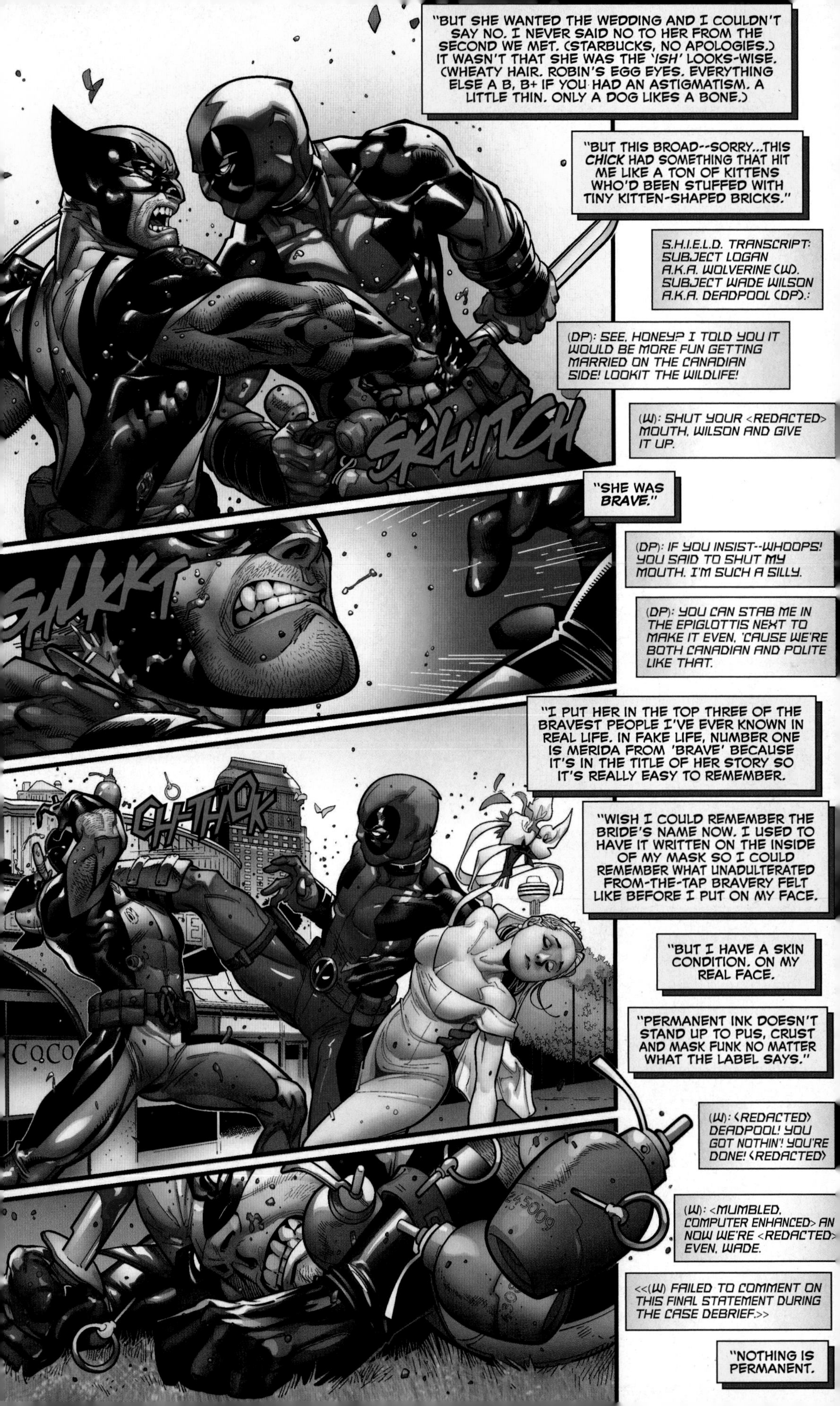

"BUT SHE WANTED THE WEDDING AND I COULDN'T SAY NO. I NEVER SAID NO TO HER FROM THE SECOND WE MET. (STARBUCKS, NO APOLOGIES.) IT WASN'T THAT SHE WAS THE 'ISH' LOOKS-WISE. (WHEATY HAIR. ROBIN'S EGG EYES. EVERYTHING ELSE A B, B+ IF YOU HAD AN ASTIGMATISM. A LITTLE THIN. ONLY A DOG LIKES A BONE.)
"BUT THIS BROAD--SORRY...THIS CHICK HAD SOMETHING THAT HIT ME LIKE A TON OF KITTENS WHO'D BEEN STUFFED WITH TINY KITTEN-SHAPED BRICKS."
S.H.I.E.L.D. TRANSCRIPT: SUBJECT LOGAN A.K.A. WOLVERINE (W). SUBJECT WADE WILSON A.K.A. DEADPOOL (DP).:
(DP): SEE, HONEY? I TOLD YOU IT WOULD BE MORE FUN GETTING MARRIED ON THE CANADIAN SIDE! LOOKIT THE WILDLIFE!
(W): SHUT YOUR <REDACTED> MOUTH, WILSON AND GIVE IT UP.
SKLUTCH
"SHE WAS BRAVE."
SHUKKT
(DP): IF YOU INSIST--WHOOPS! YOU SAID TO SHUT MY MOUTH. I'M SUCH A SILLY.
(DP): YOU CAN STAB ME IN THE EPIGLOTTIS NEXT TO MAKE IT EVEN, 'CAUSE WE'RE BOTH CANADIAN AND POLITE LIKE THAT.
"I PUT HER IN THE TOP THREE OF THE BRAVEST PEOPLE I'VE EVER KNOWN IN REAL LIFE. IN FAKE LIFE, NUMBER ONE IS MERIDA FROM 'BRAVE' BECAUSE IT'S IN THE TITLE OF HER STORY SO IT'S REALLY EASY TO REMEMBER.
CH-THOK
"WISH I COULD REMEMBER THE BRIDE'S NAME NOW. I USED TO HAVE IT WRITTEN ON THE INSIDE OF MY MASK SO I COULD REMEMBER WHAT UNADULTERATED FROM-THE-TAP BRAVERY FELT LIKE BEFORE I PUT ON MY FACE.
"BUT I HAVE A SKIN CONDITION. ON MY REAL FACE.
"PERMANENT INK DOESN'T STAND UP TO PUS, CRUST AND MASK FUNK NO MATTER WHAT THE LABEL SAYS."
COCO
(W): <REDACTED> DEADPOOL! YOU GOT NOTHIN'! YOU'RE DONE! <REDACTED>
(W): <MUMBLED, COMPUTER ENHANCED> AN NOW WE'RE <REDACTED> EVEN, WADE.
<<(W) FAILED TO COMMENT ON THIS FINAL STATEMENT DURING THE CASE DEBRIEF.>>
"NOTHING IS PERMANENT.

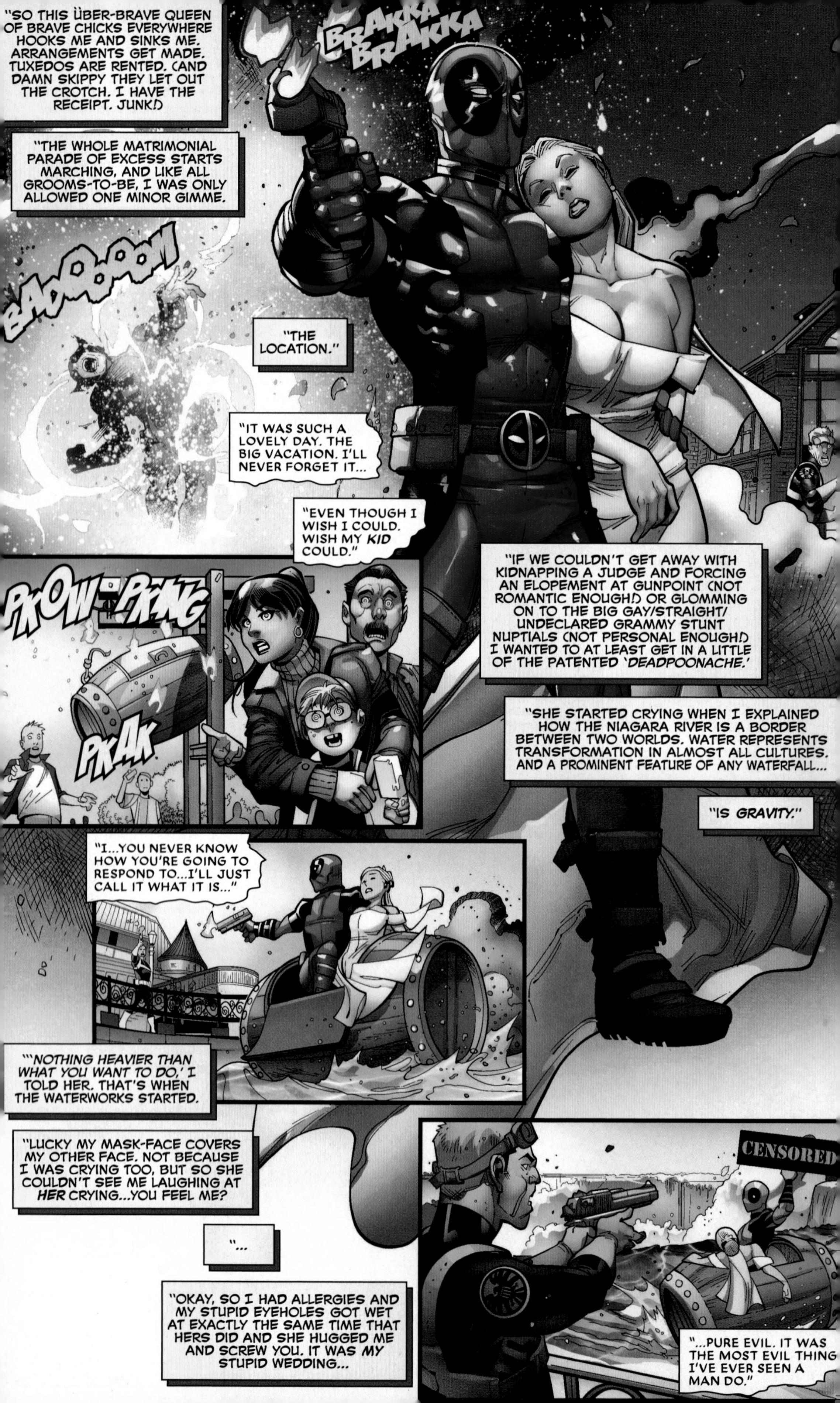
"SO THIS ÜBER-BRAVE QUEEN OF BRAVE CHICKS EVERYWHERE HOOKS ME AND SINKS ME. ARRANGEMENTS GET MADE. TUXEDOS ARE RENTED. (AND DAMN SKIPPY THEY LET OUT THE CROTCH. I HAVE THE RECEIPT. JUNK!)
BRAKKA BRAKKA
"THE WHOLE MATRIMONIAL PARADE OF EXCESS STARTS MARCHING, AND LIKE ALL GROOMS-TO-BE, I WAS ONLY ALLOWED ONE MINOR GIMME.
BADOOOOM
"THE LOCATION."
"IT WAS SUCH A LOVELY DAY. THE BIG VACATION. I'LL NEVER FORGET IT...
"EVEN THOUGH I WISH I COULD. WISH MY *KID* COULD."
PKOW-PKING
PKAK
"IF WE COULDN'T GET AWAY WITH KIDNAPPING A JUDGE AND FORCING AN ELOPEMENT AT GUNPOINT (NOT ROMANTIC ENOUGH!) OR GLOMMING ON TO THE BIG GAY/STRAIGHT/ UNDECLARED GRAMMY STUNT NUPTIALS (NOT PERSONAL ENOUGH!) I WANTED TO AT LEAST GET IN A LITTLE OF THE PATENTED '*DEADPOONACHE.*'
"SHE STARTED CRYING WHEN I EXPLAINED HOW THE NIAGARA RIVER IS A BORDER BETWEEN TWO WORLDS. WATER REPRESENTS TRANSFORMATION IN ALMOST ALL CULTURES. AND A PROMINENT FEATURE OF ANY WATERFALL...
"IS *GRAVITY.*"
"I...YOU NEVER KNOW HOW YOU'RE GOING TO RESPOND TO...I'LL JUST CALL IT WHAT IT IS..."
"'*NOTHING HEAVIER THAN WHAT YOU WANT TO DO,*' I TOLD HER. THAT'S WHEN THE WATERWORKS STARTED.
"LUCKY MY MASK-FACE COVERS MY OTHER FACE. NOT BECAUSE I WAS CRYING TOO, BUT SO SHE COULDN'T SEE ME LAUGHING AT *HER* CRYING...YOU FEEL ME?
"...
"OKAY, SO I HAD ALLERGIES AND MY STUPID EYEHOLES GOT WET AT EXACTLY THE SAME TIME THAT HERS DID AND SHE HUGGED ME AND SCREW YOU. IT WAS *MY* STUPID WEDDING...
CENSORED
"...PURE EVIL. IT WAS THE MOST EVIL THING I'VE EVER SEEN A MAN DO."

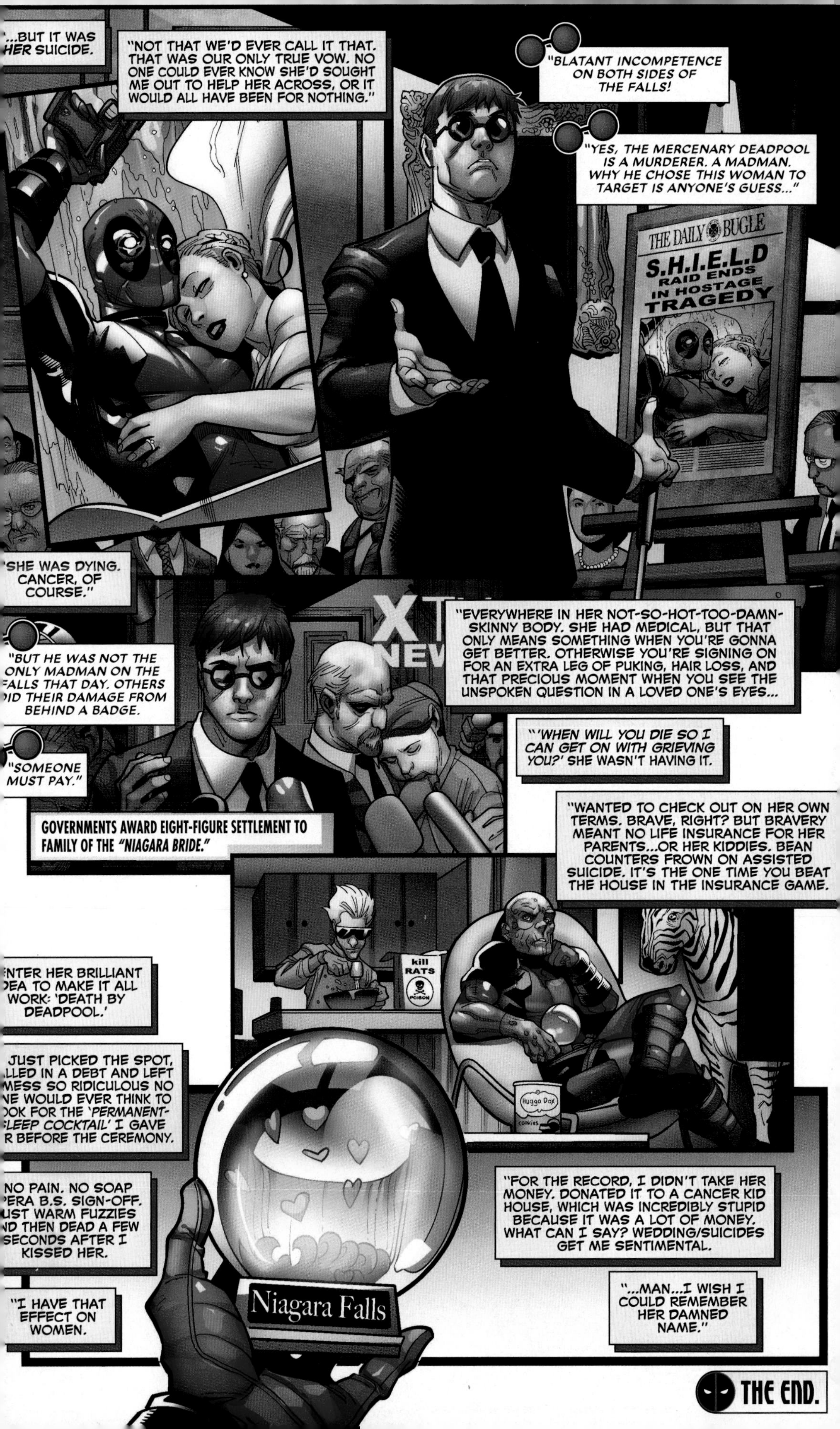

"...BUT IT WAS HER SUICIDE.
"NOT THAT WE'D EVER CALL IT THAT. THAT WAS OUR ONLY TRUE VOW. NO ONE COULD EVER KNOW SHE'D SOUGHT ME OUT TO HELP HER ACROSS, OR IT WOULD ALL HAVE BEEN FOR NOTHING."
"BLATANT INCOMPETENCE ON BOTH SIDES OF THE FALLS!
"YES, THE MERCENARY DEADPOOL IS A MURDERER. A MADMAN. WHY HE CHOSE THIS WOMAN TO TARGET IS ANYONE'S GUESS..."
THE DAILY BUGLE
S.H.I.E.L.D RAID ENDS IN HOSTAGE TRAGEDY
"SHE WAS DYING. CANCER, OF COURSE."
"EVERYWHERE IN HER NOT-SO-HOT-TOO-DAMN-SKINNY BODY. SHE HAD MEDICAL, BUT THAT ONLY MEANS SOMETHING WHEN YOU'RE GONNA GET BETTER. OTHERWISE YOU'RE SIGNING ON FOR AN EXTRA LEG OF PUKING, HAIR LOSS, AND THAT PRECIOUS MOMENT WHEN YOU SEE THE UNSPOKEN QUESTION IN A LOVED ONE'S EYES...
"BUT HE WAS NOT THE ONLY MADMAN ON THE FALLS THAT DAY. OTHERS DID THEIR DAMAGE FROM BEHIND A BADGE.
"'WHEN WILL YOU DIE SO I CAN GET ON WITH GRIEVING YOU?' SHE WASN'T HAVING IT.
"SOMEONE MUST PAY."
GOVERNMENTS AWARD EIGHT-FIGURE SETTLEMENT TO FAMILY OF THE "NIAGARA BRIDE."
"WANTED TO CHECK OUT ON HER OWN TERMS. BRAVE, RIGHT? BUT BRAVERY MEANT NO LIFE INSURANCE FOR HER PARENTS...OR HER KIDDIES. BEAN COUNTERS FROWN ON ASSISTED SUICIDE. IT'S THE ONE TIME YOU BEAT THE HOUSE IN THE INSURANCE GAME.
ENTER HER BRILLIANT IDEA TO MAKE IT ALL WORK: 'DEATH BY DEADPOOL.'
kill RATS POISON
I JUST PICKED THE SPOT, CALLED IN A DEBT AND LEFT A MESS SO RIDICULOUS NO ONE WOULD EVER THINK TO LOOK FOR THE 'PERMANENT-SLEEP COCKTAIL' I GAVE HER BEFORE THE CEREMONY.
Huggo Dox cookies
NO PAIN. NO SOAP OPERA B.S. SIGN-OFF. JUST WARM FUZZIES AND THEN DEAD A FEW SECONDS AFTER I KISSED HER.
"FOR THE RECORD, I DIDN'T TAKE HER MONEY. DONATED IT TO A CANCER KID HOUSE, WHICH WAS INCREDIBLY STUPID BECAUSE IT WAS A LOT OF MONEY. WHAT CAN I SAY? WEDDING/SUICIDES GET ME SENTIMENTAL.
"I HAVE THAT EFFECT ON WOMEN.
Niagara Falls
"...MAN...I WISH I COULD REMEMBER HER DAMNED NAME."
THE END.

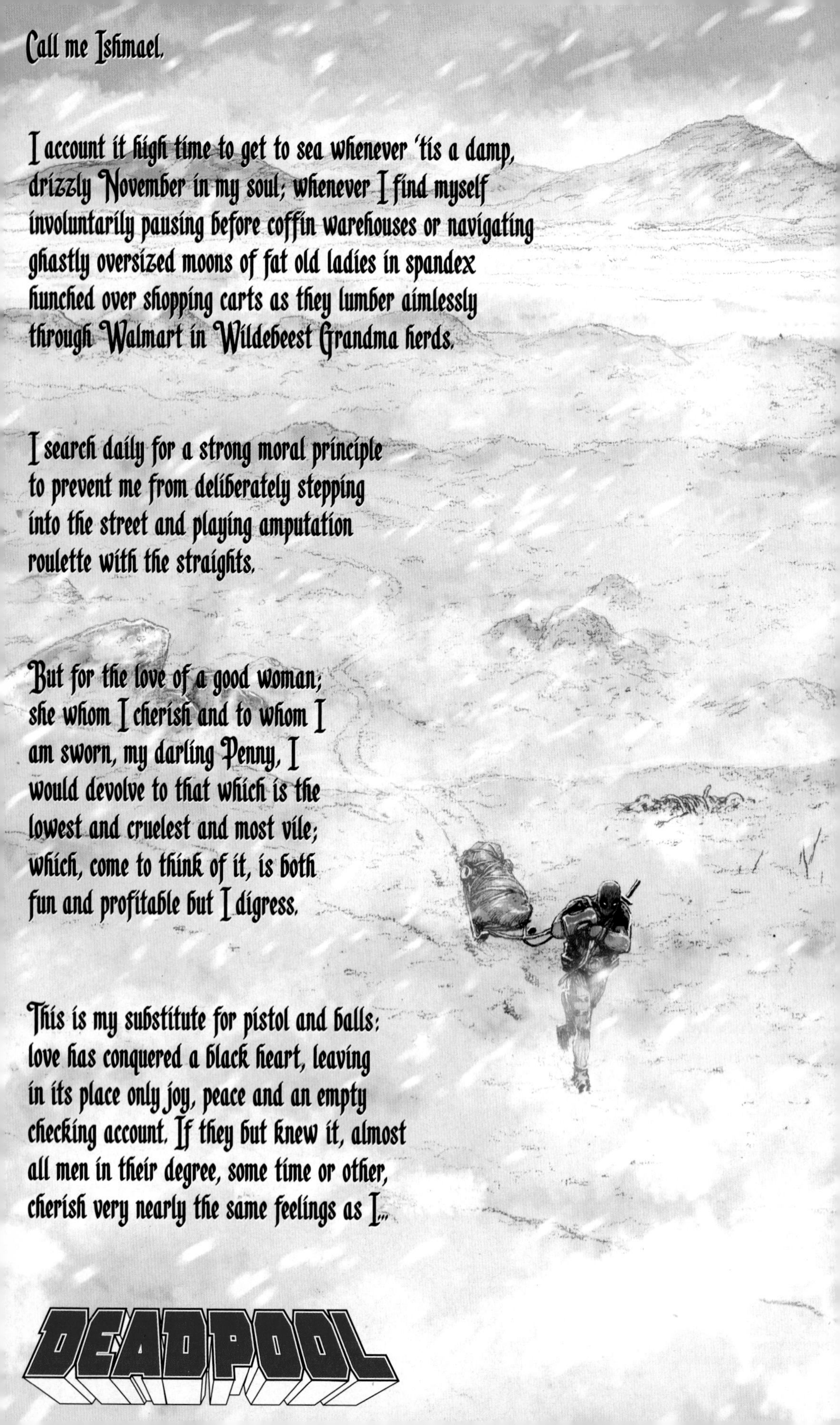
Call me Ishmael.
I account it high time to get to sea whenever 'tis a damp, drizzly November in my soul; whenever I find myself involuntarily pausing before coffin warehouses or navigating ghastly oversized moons of fat old ladies in spandex hunched over shopping carts as they lumber aimlessly through Walmart in Wildebeest Grandma herds.
I search daily for a strong moral principle to prevent me from deliberately stepping into the street and playing amputation roulette with the straights.
But for the love of a good woman; she whom I cherish and to whom I am sworn, my darling Penny, I would devolve to that which is the lowest and cruelest and most vile; which, come to think of it, is both fun and profitable but I digress.
This is my substitute for pistol and balls: love has conquered a black heart, leaving in its place only joy, peace and an empty checking account. If they but knew it, almost all men in their degree, some time or other, cherish very nearly the same feelings as I...
DEADPOOL

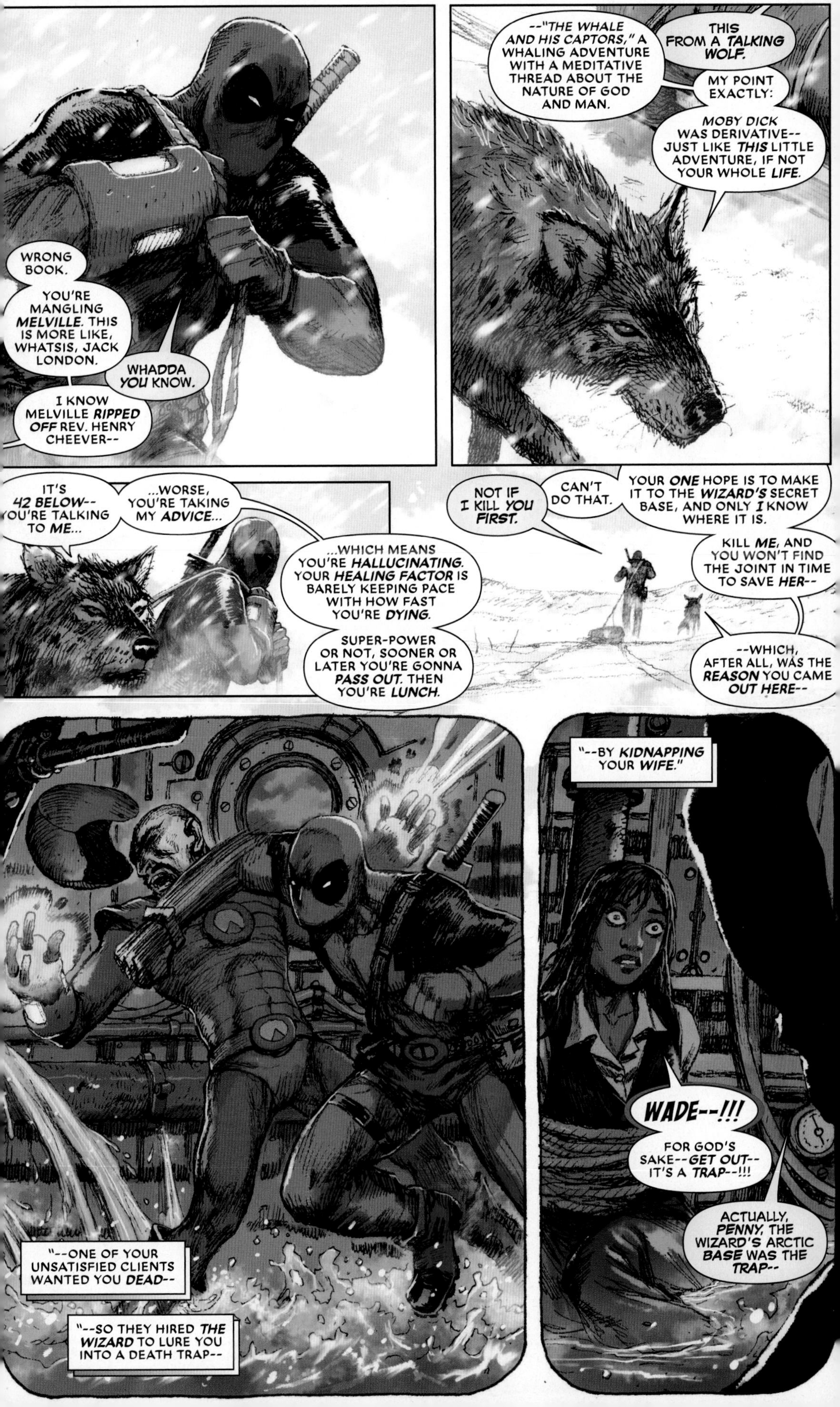
--"THE WHALE AND HIS CAPTORS," A WHALING ADVENTURE WITH A MEDITATIVE THREAD ABOUT THE NATURE OF GOD AND MAN.
THIS FROM A TALKING WOLF.
MY POINT EXACTLY:
MOBY DICK WAS DERIVATIVE-- JUST LIKE THIS LITTLE ADVENTURE, IF NOT YOUR WHOLE LIFE.
WRONG BOOK.
YOU'RE MANGLING MELVILLE. THIS IS MORE LIKE, WHATSIS, JACK LONDON.
WHADDA YOU KNOW.
I KNOW MELVILLE RIPPED OFF REV. HENRY CHEEVER--
IT'S 42 BELOW-- YOU'RE TALKING TO ME...
...WORSE, YOU'RE TAKING MY ADVICE...
...WHICH MEANS YOU'RE HALLUCINATING. YOUR HEALING FACTOR IS BARELY KEEPING PACE WITH HOW FAST YOU'RE DYING.
SUPER-POWER OR NOT, SOONER OR LATER YOU'RE GONNA PASS OUT. THEN YOU'RE LUNCH.
NOT IF I KILL YOU FIRST.
CAN'T DO THAT.
YOUR ONE HOPE IS TO MAKE IT TO THE WIZARD'S SECRET BASE, AND ONLY I KNOW WHERE IT IS.
KILL ME, AND YOU WON'T FIND THE JOINT IN TIME TO SAVE HER--
--WHICH, AFTER ALL, WAS THE REASON YOU CAME OUT HERE--
"--ONE OF YOUR UNSATISFIED CLIENTS WANTED YOU DEAD--
"--SO THEY HIRED THE WIZARD TO LURE YOU INTO A DEATH TRAP--
"--BY KIDNAPPING YOUR WIFE."
WADE--!!!
FOR GOD'S SAKE--GET OUT-- IT'S A TRAP--!!!
ACTUALLY, PENNY, THE WIZARD'S ARCTIC BASE WAS THE TRAP--

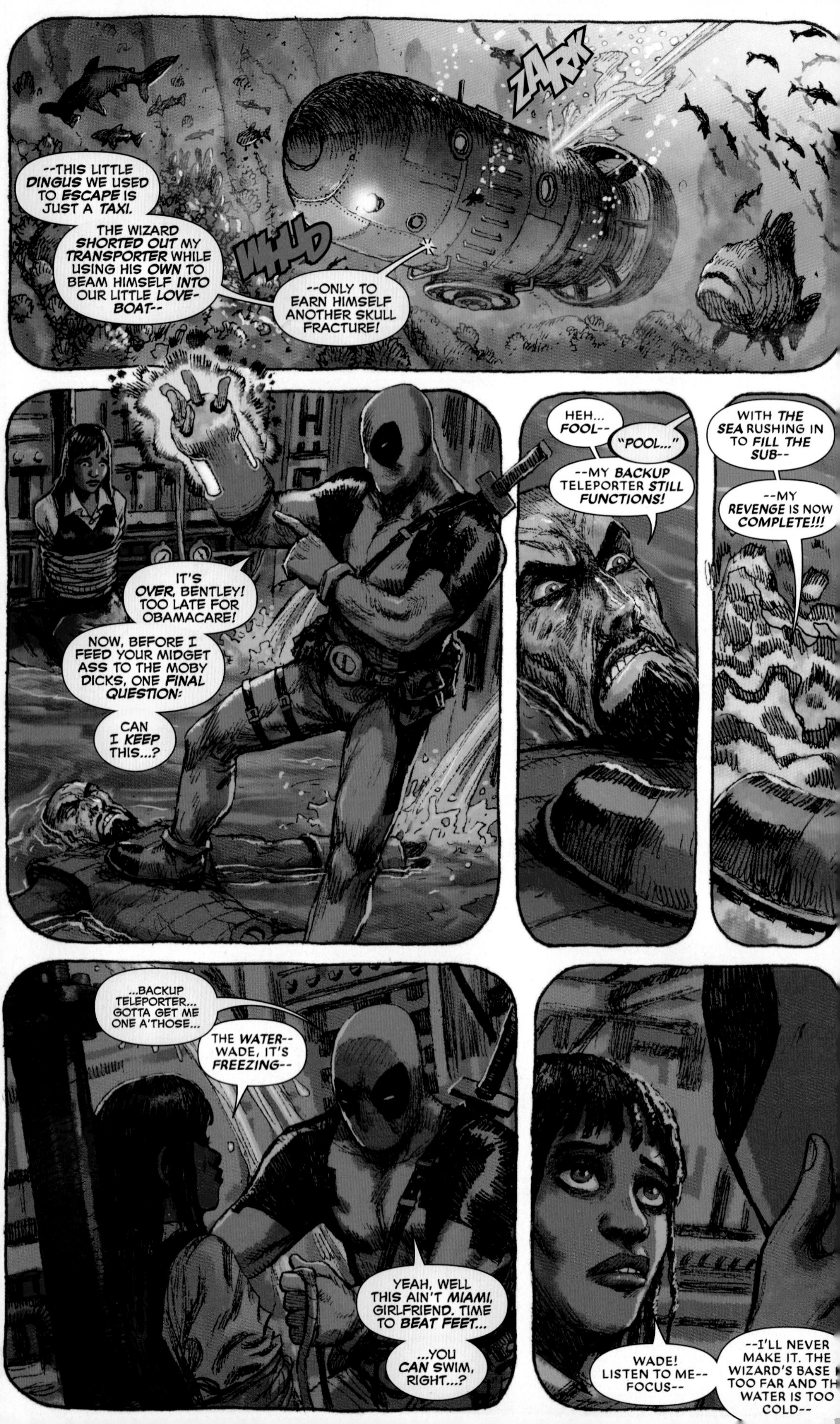

ZARK
--THIS LITTLE DINGUS WE USED TO ESCAPE IS JUST A TAXI.
THE WIZARD SHORTED OUT MY TRANSPORTER WHILE USING HIS OWN TO BEAM HIMSELF INTO OUR LITTLE LOVE-BOAT--
WHUD
--ONLY TO EARN HIMSELF ANOTHER SKULL FRACTURE!
IT'S OVER, BENTLEY! TOO LATE FOR OBAMACARE!
NOW, BEFORE I FEED YOUR MIDGET ASS TO THE MOBY DICKS, ONE FINAL QUESTION:
CAN I KEEP THIS...?
HEH... FOOL--
"POOL..."
--MY BACKUP TELEPORTER STILL FUNCTIONS!
WITH THE SEA RUSHING IN TO FILL THE SUB--
--MY REVENGE IS NOW COMPLETE!!!
...BACKUP TELEPORTER... GOTTA GET ME ONE A'THOSE...
THE WATER-- WADE, IT'S FREEZING--
YEAH, WELL THIS AIN'T MIAMI, GIRLFRIEND. TIME TO BEAT FEET...
...YOU CAN SWIM, RIGHT...?
WADE! LISTEN TO ME-- FOCUS--
--I'LL NEVER MAKE IT. THE WIZARD'S BASE TOO FAR AND TH WATER IS TOO COLD--

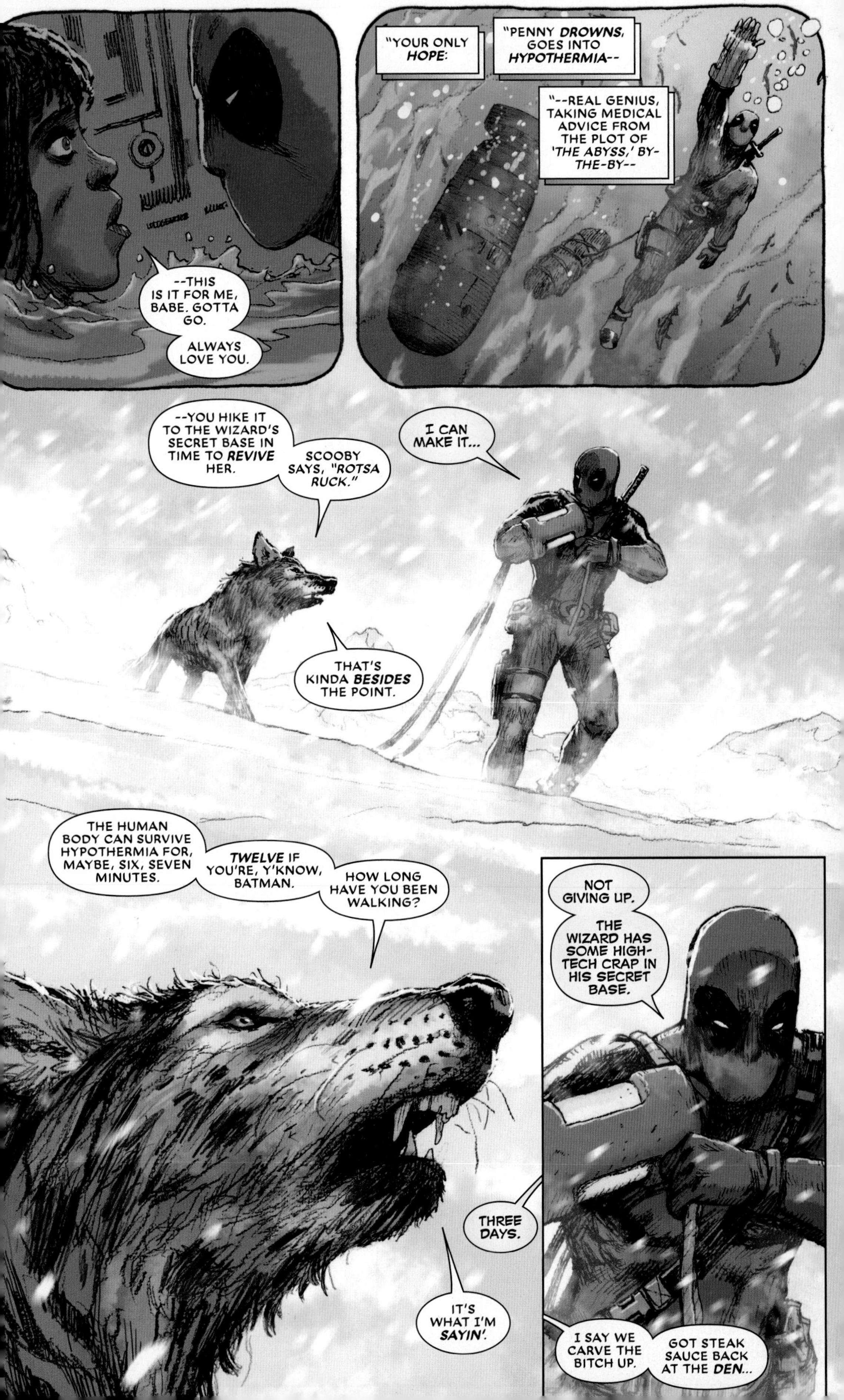
--THIS IS IT FOR ME, BABE. GOTTA GO.
ALWAYS LOVE YOU.
"YOUR ONLY HOPE:
"PENNY DROWNS, GOES INTO HYPOTHERMIA--
"--REAL GENIUS, TAKING MEDICAL ADVICE FROM THE PLOT OF 'THE ABYSS,' BY-THE-BY--
--YOU HIKE IT TO THE WIZARD'S SECRET BASE IN TIME TO REVIVE HER.
SCOOBY SAYS, "ROTSA RUCK."
I CAN MAKE IT...
THAT'S KINDA BESIDES THE POINT.
THE HUMAN BODY CAN SURVIVE HYPOTHERMIA FOR, MAYBE, SIX, SEVEN MINUTES.
TWELVE IF YOU'RE, Y'KNOW, BATMAN.
HOW LONG HAVE YOU BEEN WALKING?
NOT GIVING UP.
THE WIZARD HAS SOME HIGH-TECH CRAP IN HIS SECRET BASE.
THREE DAYS.
IT'S WHAT I'M SAYIN'.
I SAY WE CARVE THE BITCH UP.
GOT STEAK SAUCE BACK AT THE DEN...

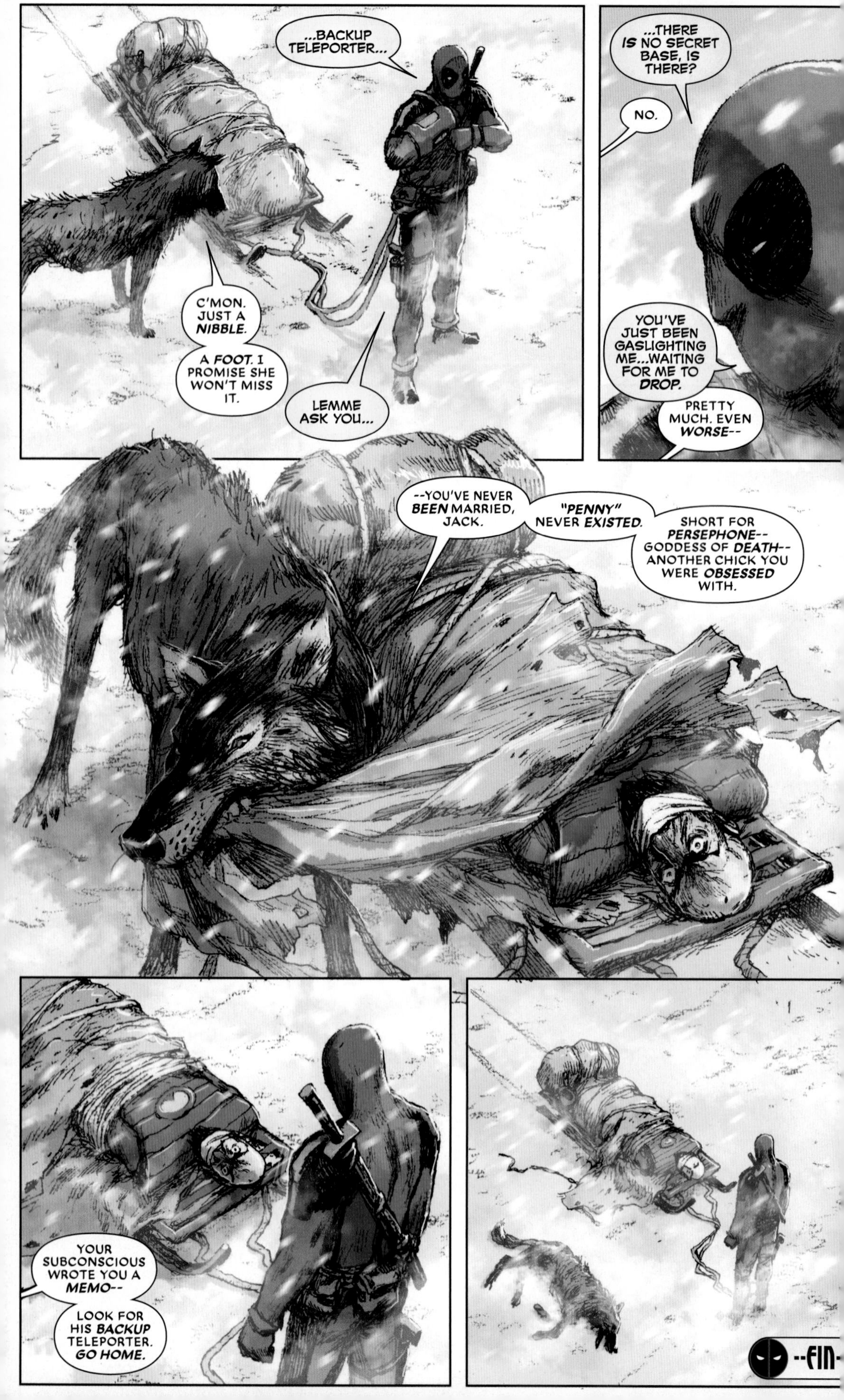
...BACKUP TELEPORTER...
C'MON. JUST A NIBBLE.
A FOOT. I PROMISE SHE WON'T MISS IT.
LEMME ASK YOU...
...THERE IS NO SECRET BASE, IS THERE?
NO.
YOU'VE JUST BEEN GASLIGHTING ME...WAITING FOR ME TO DROP.
PRETTY MUCH. EVEN WORSE--
--YOU'VE NEVER BEEN MARRIED, JACK.
"PENNY" NEVER EXISTED.
SHORT FOR PERSEPHONE--GODDESS OF DEATH--ANOTHER CHICK YOU WERE OBSESSED WITH.
YOUR SUBCONSCIOUS WROTE YOU A MEMO--
LOOK FOR HIS BACKUP TELEPORTER. GO HOME.
--FIN-

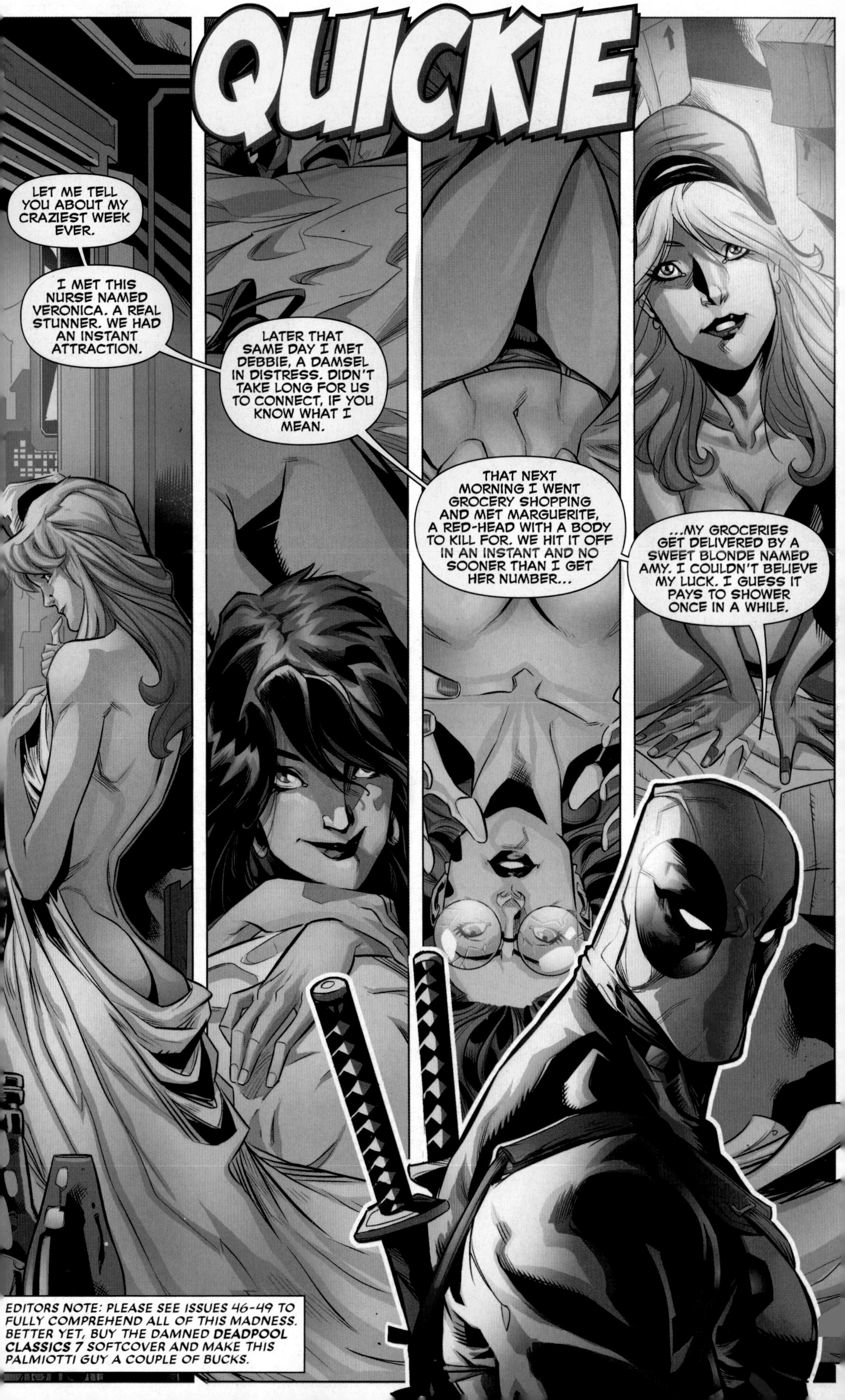
QUICKIE
LET ME TELL YOU ABOUT MY CRAZIEST WEEK EVER.
I MET THIS NURSE NAMED VERONICA. A REAL STUNNER. WE HAD AN INSTANT ATTRACTION.
LATER THAT SAME DAY I MET DEBBIE, A DAMSEL IN DISTRESS. DIDN'T TAKE LONG FOR US TO CONNECT, IF YOU KNOW WHAT I MEAN.
THAT NEXT MORNING I WENT GROCERY SHOPPING AND MET MARGUERITE, A RED-HEAD WITH A BODY TO KILL FOR. WE HIT IT OFF IN AN INSTANT AND NO SOONER THAN I GET HER NUMBER...
...MY GROCERIES GET DELIVERED BY A SWEET BLONDE NAMED AMY. I COULDN'T BELIEVE MY LUCK. I GUESS IT PAYS TO SHOWER ONCE IN A WHILE.
EDITORS NOTE: PLEASE SEE ISSUES 46-49 TO FULLY COMPREHEND ALL OF THIS MADNESS. BETTER YET, BUY THE DAMNED DEADPOOL CLASSICS 7 SOFTCOVER AND MAKE THIS PALMIOTTI GUY A COUPLE OF BUCKS.

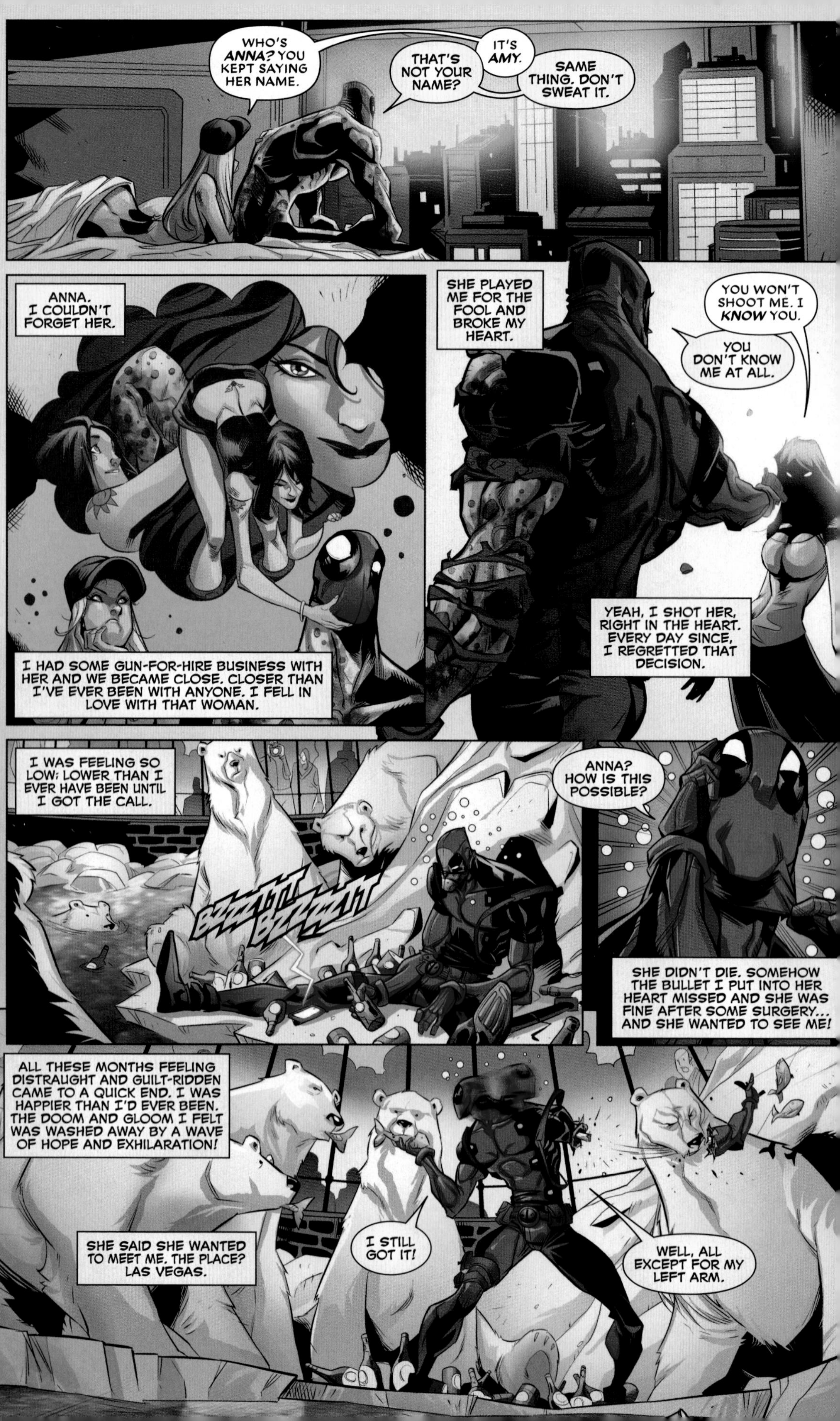
WHO'S ANNA? YOU KEPT SAYING HER NAME.
IT'S AMY.
THAT'S NOT YOUR NAME?
SAME THING. DON'T SWEAT IT.
ANNA. I COULDN'T FORGET HER.
I HAD SOME GUN-FOR-HIRE BUSINESS WITH HER AND WE BECAME CLOSE. CLOSER THAN I'VE EVER BEEN WITH ANYONE. I FELL IN LOVE WITH THAT WOMAN.
SHE PLAYED ME FOR THE FOOL AND BROKE MY HEART.
YOU WON'T SHOOT ME. I KNOW YOU.
YOU DON'T KNOW ME AT ALL.
YEAH, I SHOT HER, RIGHT IN THE HEART. EVERY DAY SINCE, I REGRETTED THAT DECISION.
I WAS FEELING SO LOW; LOWER THAN I EVER HAVE BEEN UNTIL I GOT THE CALL.
BZZZTTT BZZZTTT
ANNA? HOW IS THIS POSSIBLE?
SHE DIDN'T DIE. SOMEHOW THE BULLET I PUT INTO HER HEART MISSED AND SHE WAS FINE AFTER SOME SURGERY... AND SHE WANTED TO SEE ME!
ALL THESE MONTHS FEELING DISTRAUGHT AND GUILT-RIDDEN CAME TO A QUICK END. I WAS HAPPIER THAN I'D EVER BEEN. THE DOOM AND GLOOM I FELT WAS WASHED AWAY BY A WAVE OF HOPE AND EXHILARATION!
SHE SAID SHE WANTED TO MEET ME. THE PLACE? LAS VEGAS.
I STILL GOT IT!
WELL, ALL EXCEPT FOR MY LEFT ARM.

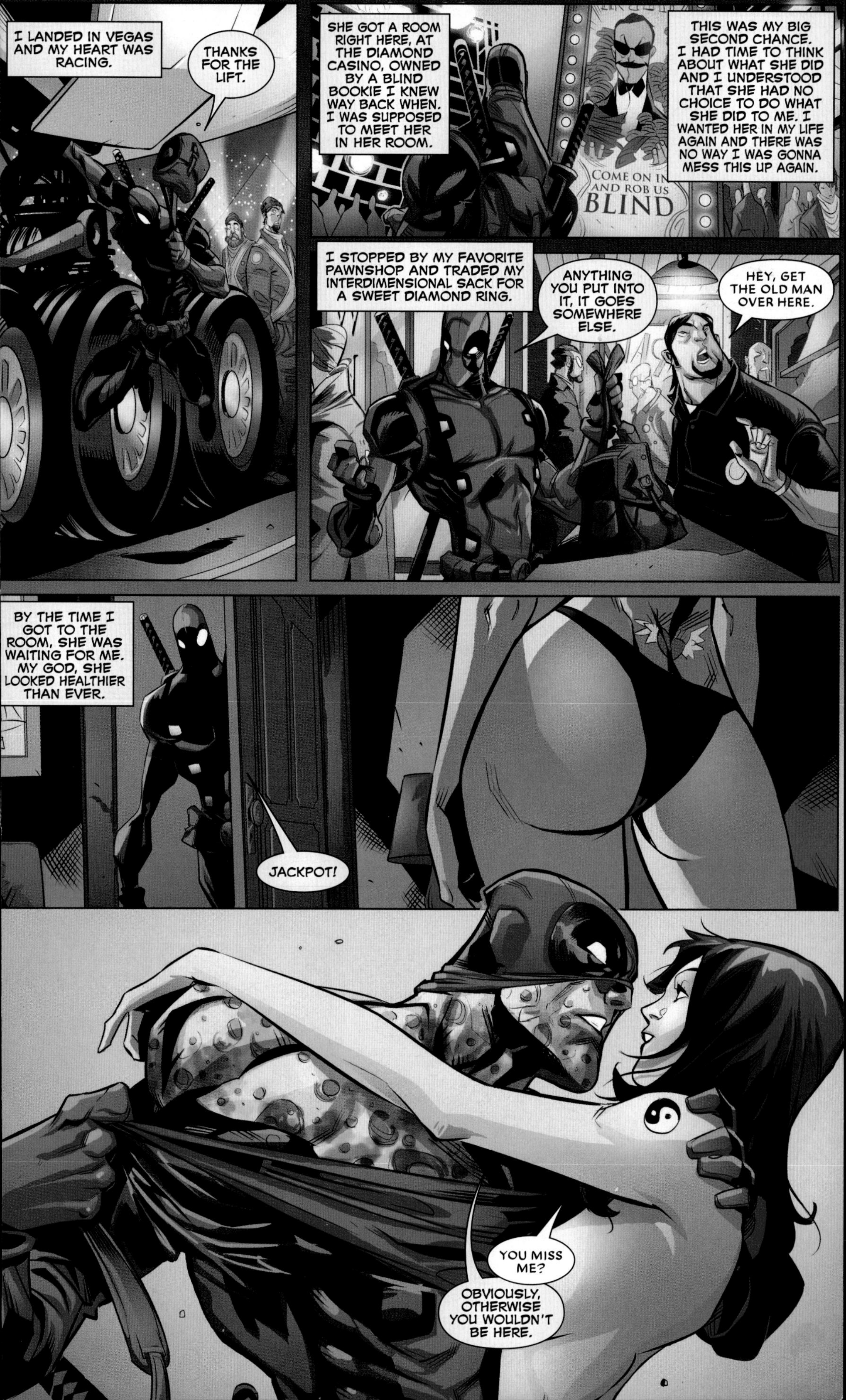
I LANDED IN VEGAS AND MY HEART WAS RACING.
THANKS FOR THE LIFT.
SHE GOT A ROOM RIGHT HERE, AT THE DIAMOND CASINO, OWNED BY A BLIND BOOKIE I KNEW WAY BACK WHEN. I WAS SUPPOSED TO MEET HER IN HER ROOM.
COME ON IN AND ROB US BLIND
THIS WAS MY BIG SECOND CHANCE. I HAD TIME TO THINK ABOUT WHAT SHE DID AND I UNDERSTOOD THAT SHE HAD NO CHOICE TO DO WHAT SHE DID TO ME. I WANTED HER IN MY LIFE AGAIN AND THERE WAS NO WAY I WAS GONNA MESS THIS UP AGAIN.
I STOPPED BY MY FAVORITE PAWNSHOP AND TRADED MY INTERDIMENSIONAL SACK FOR A SWEET DIAMOND RING.
ANYTHING YOU PUT INTO IT, IT GOES SOMEWHERE ELSE.
HEY, GET THE OLD MAN OVER HERE.
BY THE TIME I GOT TO THE ROOM, SHE WAS WAITING FOR ME. MY GOD, SHE LOOKED HEALTHIER THAN EVER.
JACKPOT!
YOU MISS ME?
OBVIOUSLY, OTHERWISE YOU WOULDN'T BE HERE.

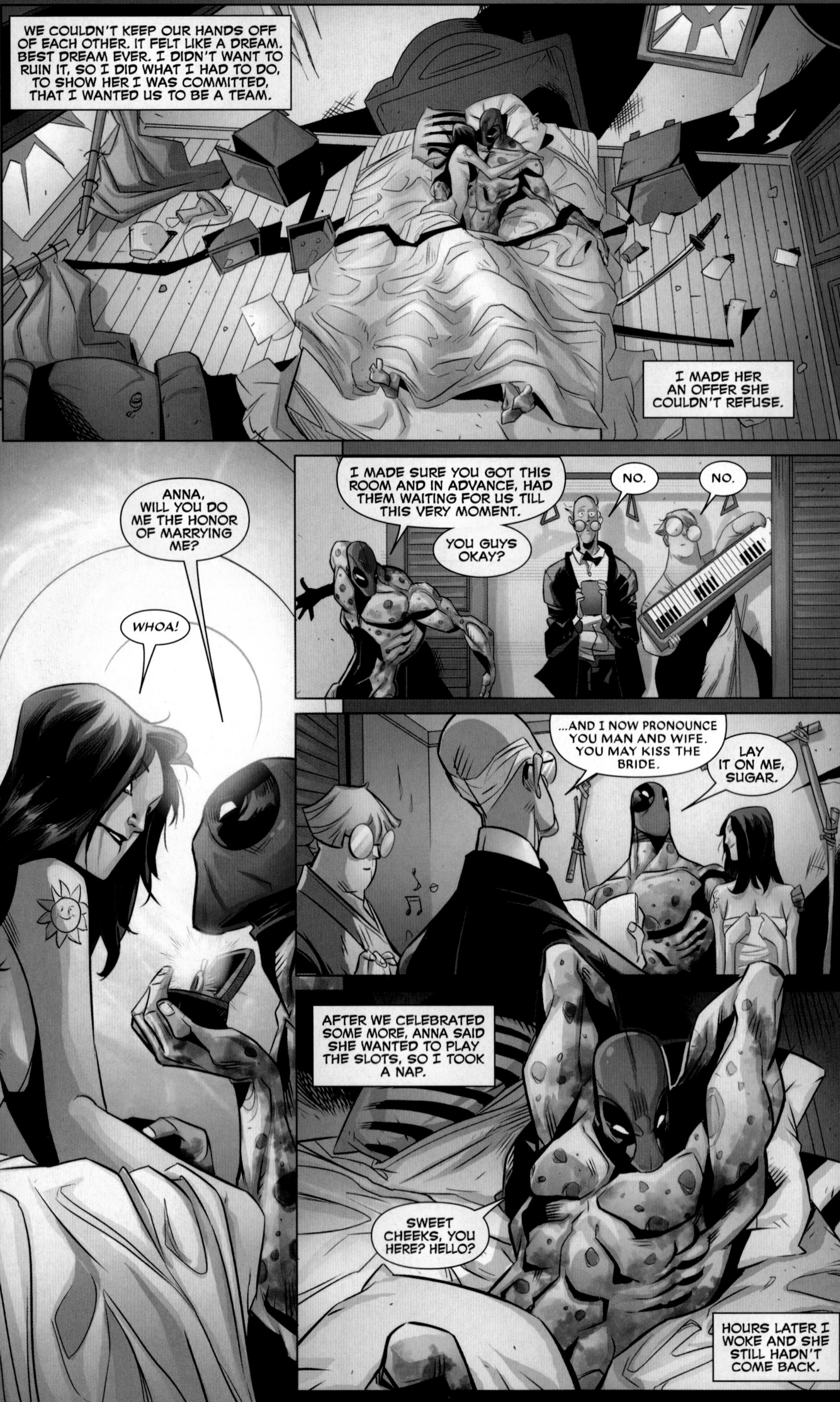
WE COULDN'T KEEP OUR HANDS OFF OF EACH OTHER. IT FELT LIKE A DREAM. BEST DREAM EVER. I DIDN'T WANT TO RUIN IT, SO I DID WHAT I HAD TO DO, TO SHOW HER I WAS COMMITTED, THAT I WANTED US TO BE A TEAM.
I MADE HER AN OFFER SHE COULDN'T REFUSE.
ANNA, WILL YOU DO ME THE HONOR OF MARRYING ME?
WHOA!
I MADE SURE YOU GOT THIS ROOM AND IN ADVANCE, HAD THEM WAITING FOR US TILL THIS VERY MOMENT.
YOU GUYS OKAY?
NO.
NO.
...AND I NOW PRONOUNCE YOU MAN AND WIFE. YOU MAY KISS THE BRIDE.
LAY IT ON ME, SUGAR.
AFTER WE CELEBRATED SOME MORE, ANNA SAID SHE WANTED TO PLAY THE SLOTS, SO I TOOK A NAP.
SWEET CHEEKS, YOU HERE? HELLO?
HOURS LATER I WOKE AND SHE STILL HADN'T COME BACK.

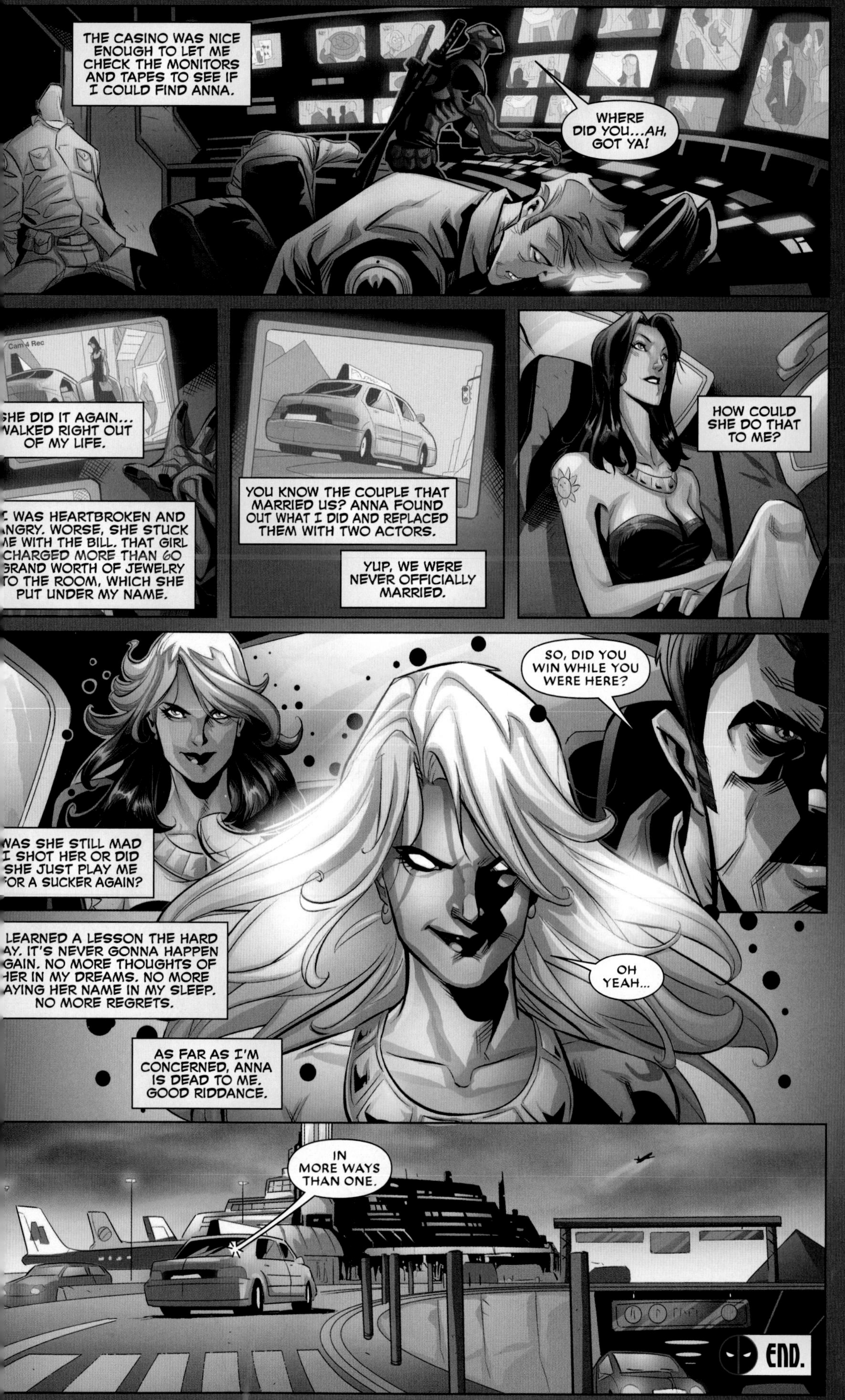

THE CASINO WAS NICE ENOUGH TO LET ME CHECK THE MONITORS AND TAPES TO SEE IF I COULD FIND ANNA.
WHERE DID YOU...AH, GOT YA!
Cam 4 Rec
SHE DID IT AGAIN... WALKED RIGHT OUT OF MY LIFE.
I WAS HEARTBROKEN AND ANGRY. WORSE, SHE STUCK ME WITH THE BILL. THAT GIRL CHARGED MORE THAN 60 GRAND WORTH OF JEWELRY TO THE ROOM, WHICH SHE PUT UNDER MY NAME.
YOU KNOW THE COUPLE THAT MARRIED US? ANNA FOUND OUT WHAT I DID AND REPLACED THEM WITH TWO ACTORS.
YUP, WE WERE NEVER OFFICIALLY MARRIED.
HOW COULD SHE DO THAT TO ME?
SO, DID YOU WIN WHILE YOU WERE HERE?
WAS SHE STILL MAD I SHOT HER OR DID SHE JUST PLAY ME FOR A SUCKER AGAIN?
I LEARNED A LESSON THE HARD WAY. IT'S NEVER GONNA HAPPEN AGAIN. NO MORE THOUGHTS OF HER IN MY DREAMS. NO MORE SAYING HER NAME IN MY SLEEP. NO MORE REGRETS.
OH YEAH...
AS FAR AS I'M CONCERNED, ANNA IS DEAD TO ME. GOOD RIDDANCE.
IN MORE WAYS THAN ONE.
END.

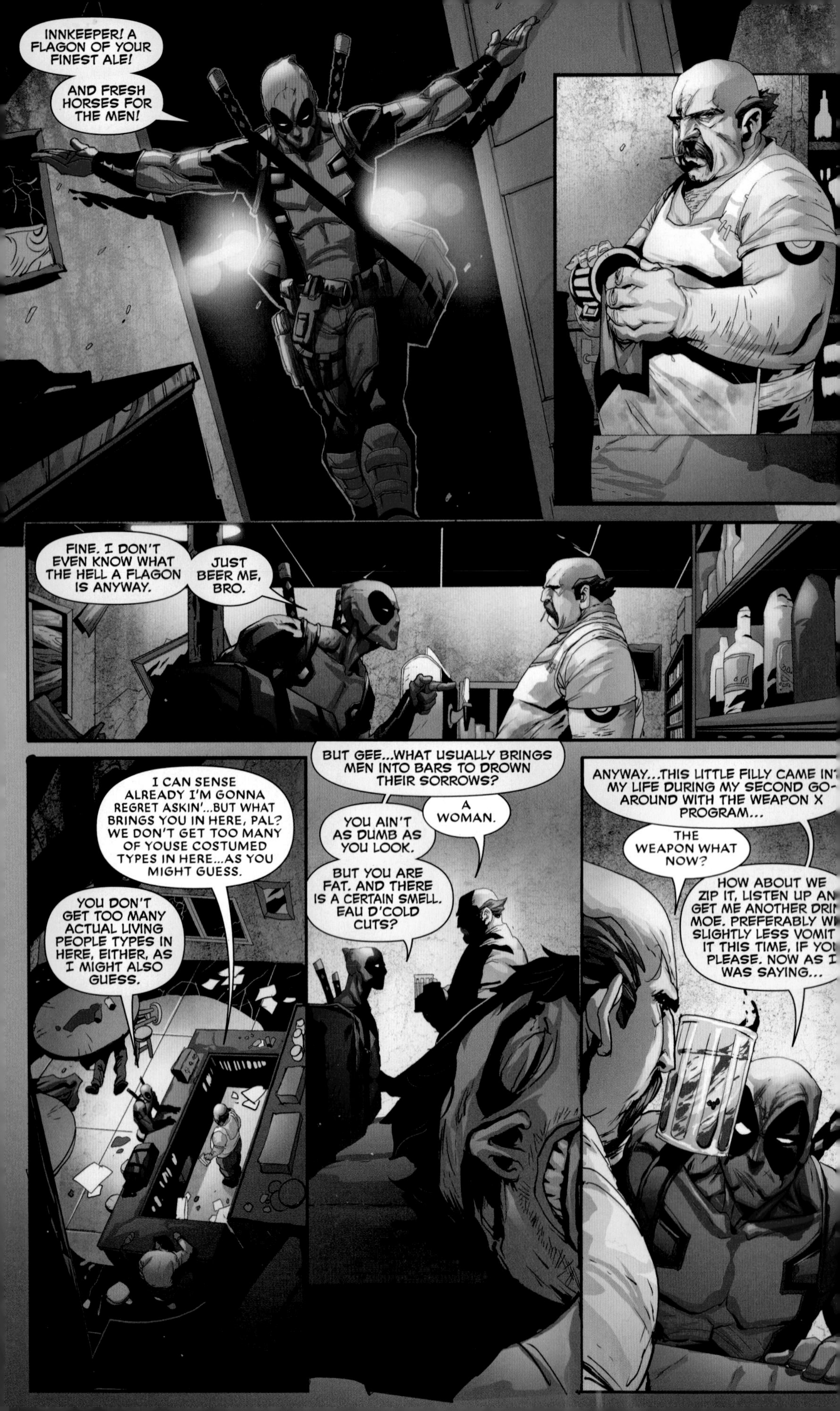
INNKEEPER! A FLAGON OF YOUR FINEST ALE!
AND FRESH HORSES FOR THE MEN!
FINE. I DON'T EVEN KNOW WHAT THE HELL A FLAGON IS ANYWAY.
JUST BEER ME, BRO.
I CAN SENSE ALREADY I'M GONNA REGRET ASKIN'...BUT WHAT BRINGS YOU IN HERE, PAL? WE DON'T GET TOO MANY OF YOUSE COSTUMED TYPES IN HERE...AS YOU MIGHT GUESS.
YOU DON'T GET TOO MANY ACTUAL LIVING PEOPLE TYPES IN HERE, EITHER, AS I MIGHT ALSO GUESS.
BUT GEE...WHAT USUALLY BRINGS MEN INTO BARS TO DROWN THEIR SORROWS?
A WOMAN.
YOU AIN'T AS DUMB AS YOU LOOK.
BUT YOU ARE FAT. AND THERE IS A CERTAIN SMELL. EAU D'COLD CUTS?
ANYWAY...THIS LITTLE FILLY CAME IN MY LIFE DURING MY SECOND GO-AROUND WITH THE WEAPON X PROGRAM...
THE WEAPON WHAT NOW?
HOW ABOUT WE ZIP IT, LISTEN UP AN GET ME ANOTHER DRI MOE. PREFERABLY W SLIGHTLY LESS VOMIT IT THIS TIME, IF YO PLEASE. NOW AS I WAS SAYING...

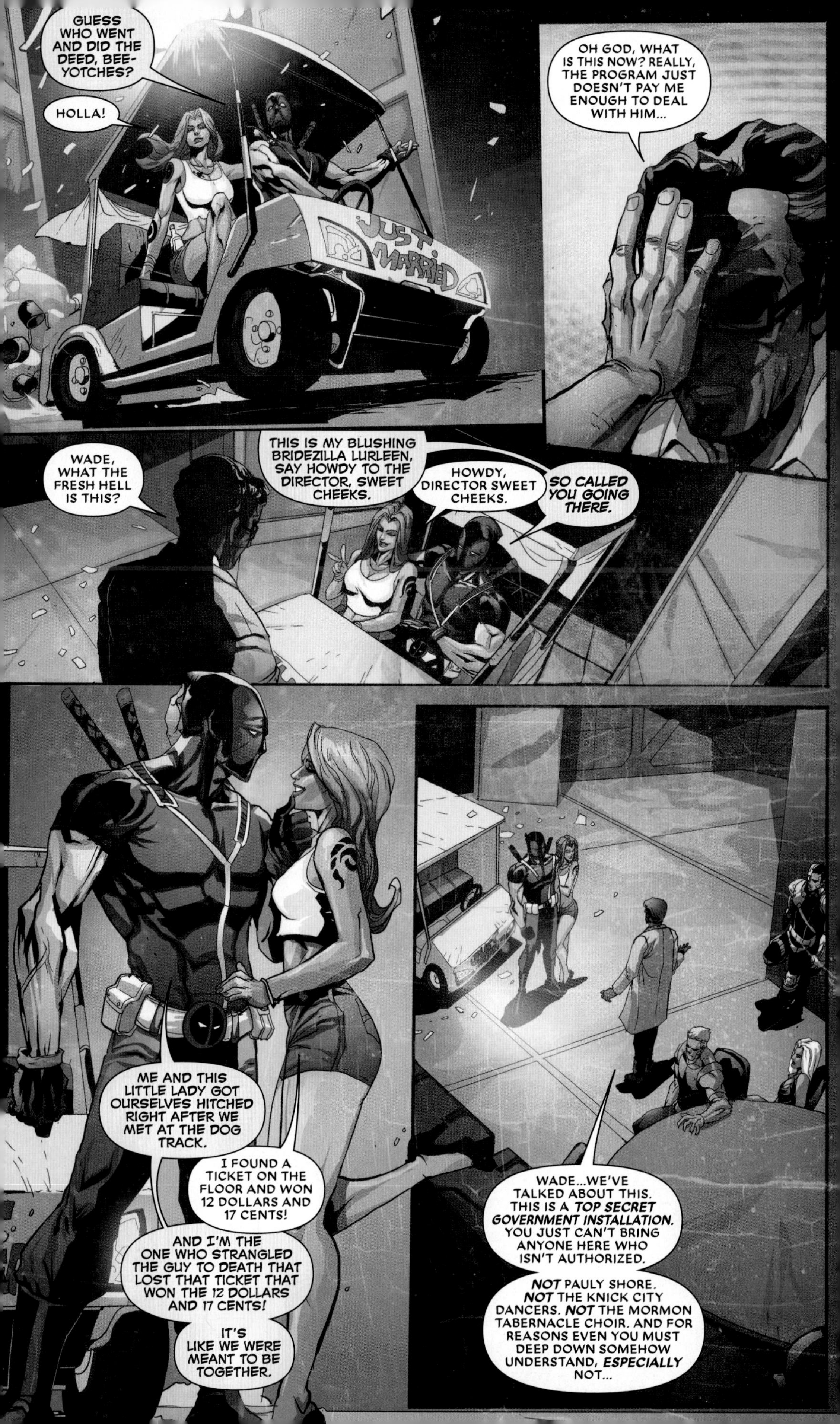
GUESS WHO WENT AND DID THE DEED, BEE-YOTCHES?
HOLLA!
JUST MARRIED
OH GOD, WHAT IS THIS NOW? REALLY, THE PROGRAM JUST DOESN'T PAY ME ENOUGH TO DEAL WITH HIM...
WADE, WHAT THE FRESH HELL IS THIS?
THIS IS MY BLUSHING BRIDEZILLA LURLEEN, SAY HOWDY TO THE DIRECTOR, SWEET CHEEKS.
HOWDY, DIRECTOR SWEET CHEEKS.
SO CALLED YOU GOING THERE.
ME AND THIS LITTLE LADY GOT OURSELVES HITCHED RIGHT AFTER WE MET AT THE DOG TRACK.
I FOUND A TICKET ON THE FLOOR AND WON 12 DOLLARS AND 17 CENTS!
AND I'M THE ONE WHO STRANGLED THE GUY TO DEATH THAT LOST THAT TICKET THAT WON THE 12 DOLLARS AND 17 CENTS!
IT'S LIKE WE WERE MEANT TO BE TOGETHER.
WADE...WE'VE TALKED ABOUT THIS. THIS IS A TOP SECRET GOVERNMENT INSTALLATION. YOU JUST CAN'T BRING ANYONE HERE WHO ISN'T AUTHORIZED.
NOT PAULY SHORE. NOT THE KNICK CITY DANCERS. NOT THE MORMON TABERNACLE CHOIR. AND FOR REASONS EVEN YOU MUST DEEP DOWN SOMEHOW UNDERSTAND, ESPECIALLY NOT...

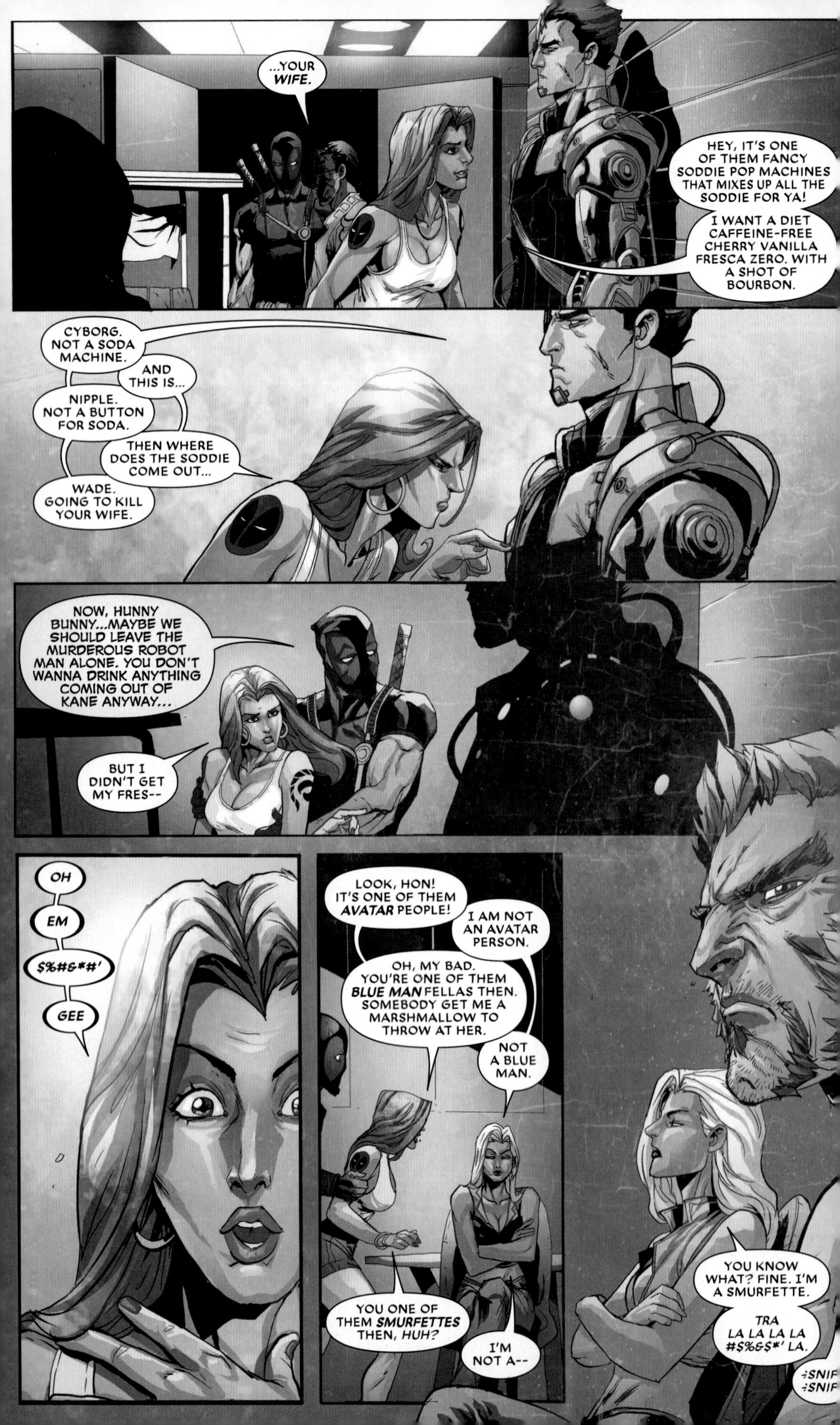

...YOUR WIFE.
HEY, IT'S ONE OF THEM FANCY SODDIE POP MACHINES THAT MIXES UP ALL THE SODDIE FOR YA!
I WANT A DIET CAFFEINE-FREE CHERRY VANILLA FRESCA ZERO. WITH A SHOT OF BOURBON.
CYBORG. NOT A SODA MACHINE.
AND THIS IS...
NIPPLE. NOT A BUTTON FOR SODA.
THEN WHERE DOES THE SODDIE COME OUT...
WADE. GOING TO KILL YOUR WIFE.
NOW, HUNNY BUNNY...MAYBE WE SHOULD LEAVE THE MURDEROUS ROBOT MAN ALONE. YOU DON'T WANNA DRINK ANYTHING COMING OUT OF KANE ANYWAY...
BUT I DIDN'T GET MY FRES--
OH
EM
$%#&*#'
GEE
LOOK, HON! IT'S ONE OF THEM AVATAR PEOPLE!
I AM NOT AN AVATAR PERSON.
OH, MY BAD. YOU'RE ONE OF THEM BLUE MAN FELLAS THEN. SOMEBODY GET ME A MARSHMALLOW TO THROW AT HER.
NOT A BLUE MAN.
YOU ONE OF THEM SMURFETTES THEN, HUH?
I'M NOT A--
YOU KNOW WHAT? FINE. I'M A SMURFETTE.
TRA LA LA LA LA #$%&$*' LA.

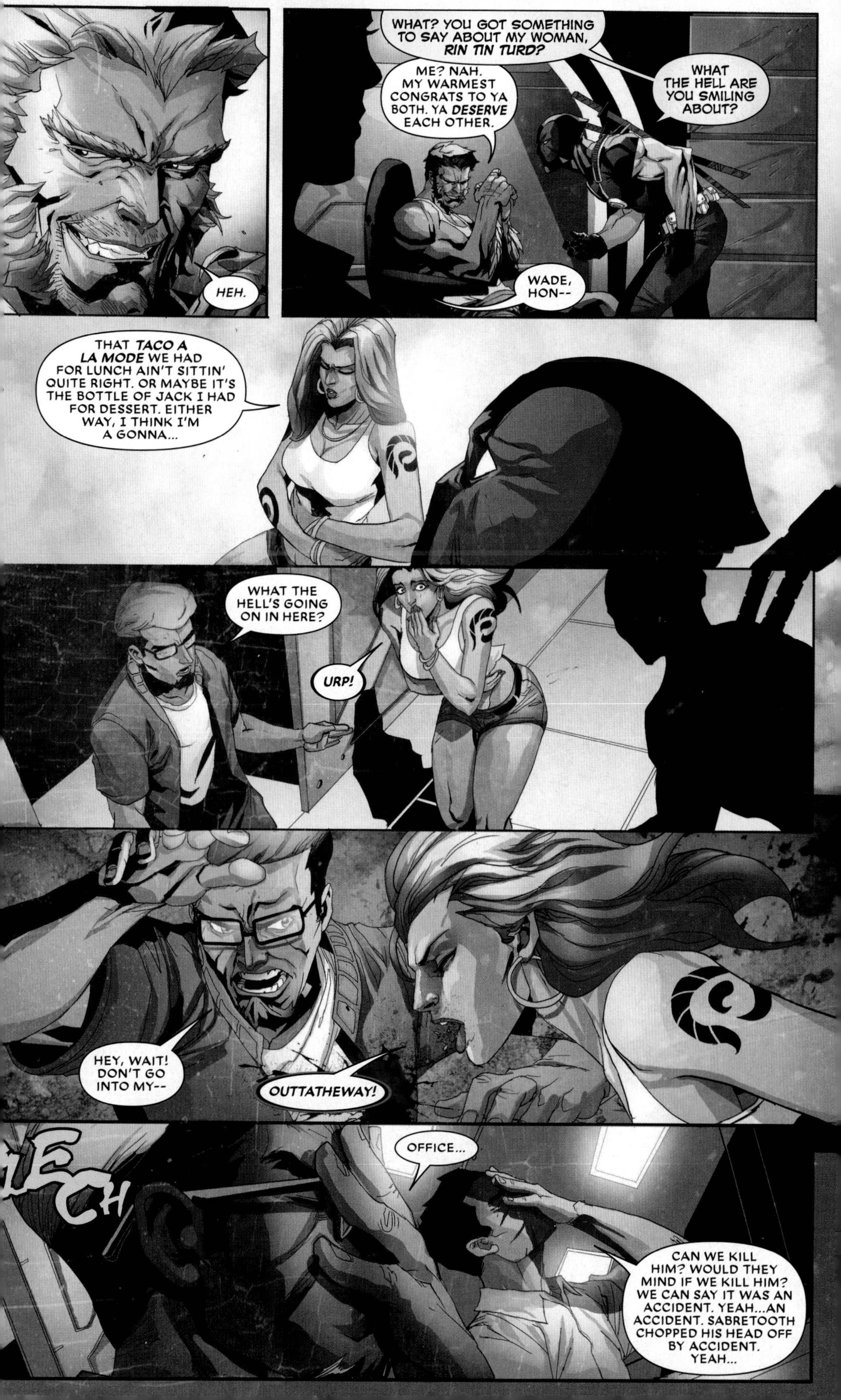
HEH.
WHAT? YOU GOT SOMETHING TO SAY ABOUT MY WOMAN, *RIN TIN TURD?*
ME? NAH. MY WARMEST CONGRATS TO YA BOTH. YA *DESERVE* EACH OTHER.
WHAT THE HELL ARE YOU SMILING ABOUT?
WADE, HON--
THAT *TACO A LA MODE* WE HAD FOR LUNCH AIN'T SITTIN' QUITE RIGHT. OR MAYBE IT'S THE BOTTLE OF JACK I HAD FOR DESSERT. EITHER WAY, I THINK I'M A GONNA...
WHAT THE HELL'S GOING ON IN HERE?
URP!
HEY, WAIT! DON'T GO INTO MY--
OUTTATHEWAY!
OFFICE...
CAN WE KILL HIM? WOULD THEY MIND IF WE KILL HIM? WE CAN SAY IT WAS AN ACCIDENT. YEAH...AN ACCIDENT. SABRETOOTH CHOPPED HIS HEAD OFF BY ACCIDENT. YEAH...

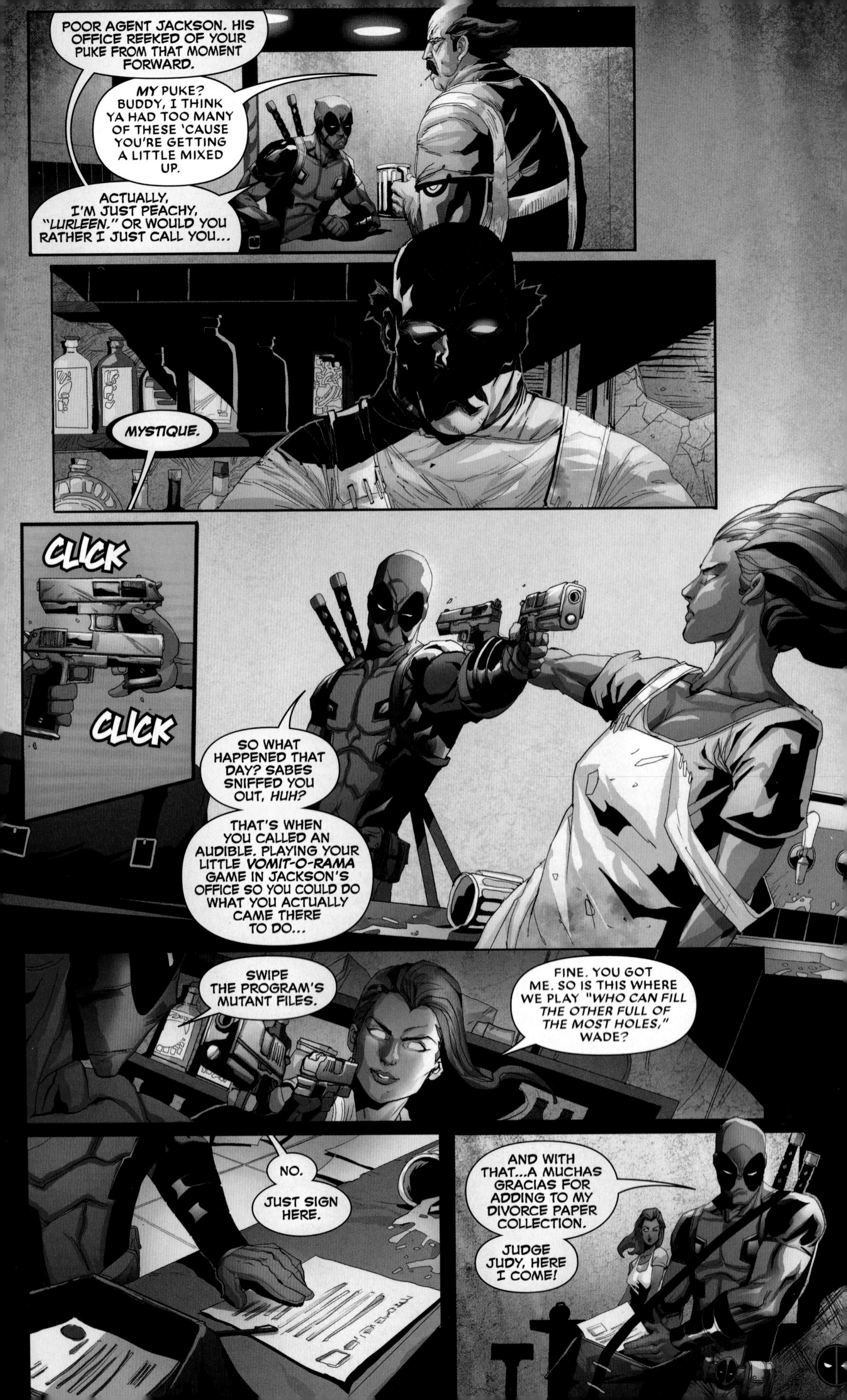
POOR AGENT JACKSON. HIS OFFICE REEKED OF YOUR PUKE FROM THAT MOMENT FORWARD.
MY PUKE? BUDDY, I THINK YA HAD TOO MANY OF THESE 'CAUSE YOU'RE GETTING A LITTLE MIXED UP.
ACTUALLY, I'M JUST PEACHY, "LURLEEN." OR WOULD YOU RATHER I JUST CALL YOU...
MYSTIQUE.
CLICK
CLICK
SO WHAT HAPPENED THAT DAY? SABES SNIFFED YOU OUT, HUH?
THAT'S WHEN YOU CALLED AN AUDIBLE. PLAYING YOUR LITTLE VOMIT-O-RAMA GAME IN JACKSON'S OFFICE SO YOU COULD DO WHAT YOU ACTUALLY CAME THERE TO DO...
SWIPE THE PROGRAM'S MUTANT FILES.
FINE. YOU GOT ME. SO IS THIS WHERE WE PLAY "WHO CAN FILL THE OTHER FULL OF THE MOST HOLES," WADE?
NO.
JUST SIGN HERE.
AND WITH THAT...A MUCHAS GRACIAS FOR ADDING TO MY DIVORCE PAPER COLLECTION.
JUDGE JUDY, HERE I COME!

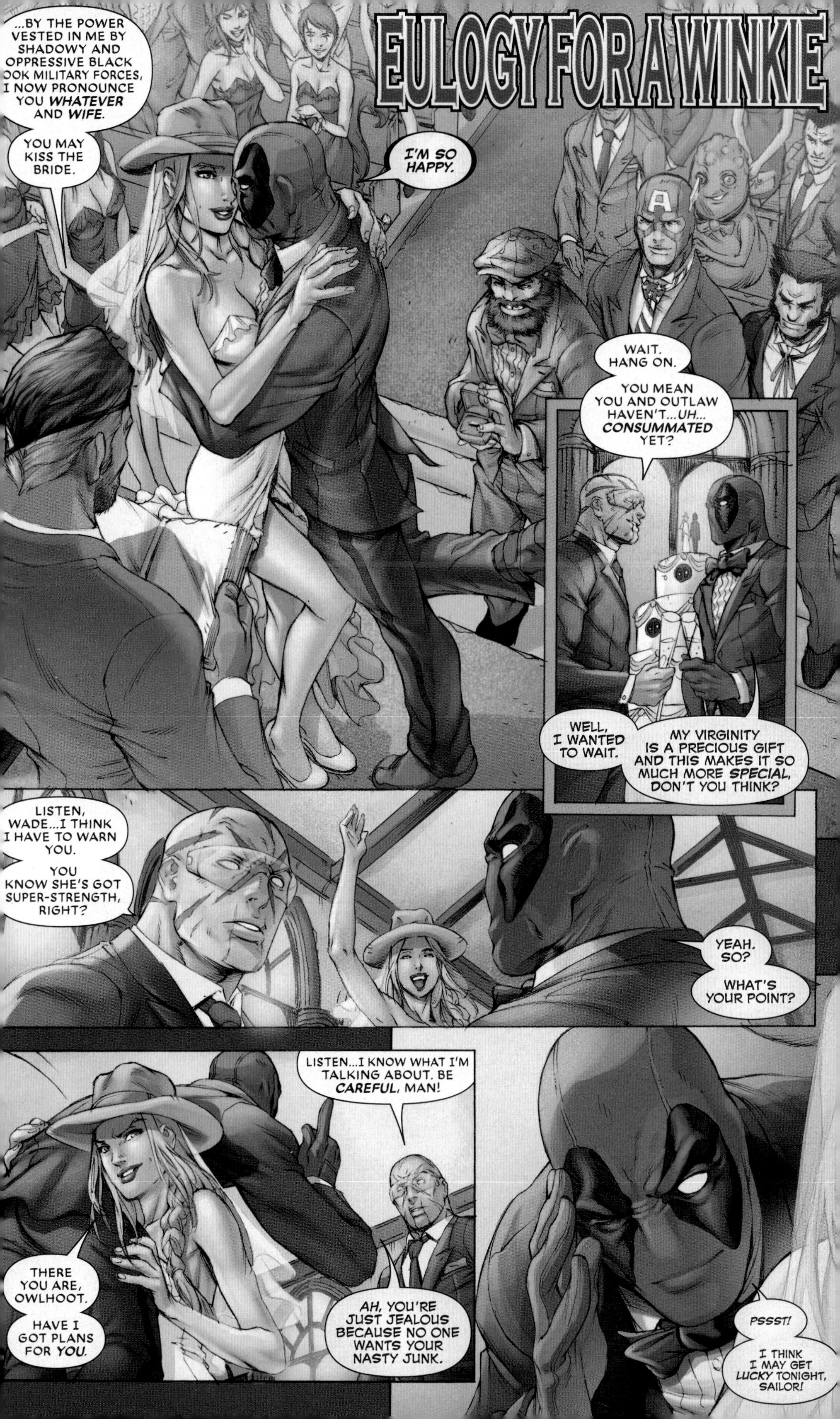

EULOGY FOR A WINKIE
...BY THE POWER VESTED IN ME BY SHADOWY AND OPPRESSIVE BLACK BOOK MILITARY FORCES, I NOW PRONOUNCE YOU WHATEVER AND WIFE.
YOU MAY KISS THE BRIDE.
I'M SO HAPPY.
WAIT. HANG ON.
YOU MEAN YOU AND OUTLAW HAVEN'T...UH... CONSUMMATED YET?
WELL, I WANTED TO WAIT.
MY VIRGINITY IS A PRECIOUS GIFT AND THIS MAKES IT SO MUCH MORE SPECIAL, DON'T YOU THINK?
LISTEN, WADE...I THINK I HAVE TO WARN YOU.
YOU KNOW SHE'S GOT SUPER-STRENGTH, RIGHT?
YEAH. SO?
WHAT'S YOUR POINT?
LISTEN...I KNOW WHAT I'M TALKING ABOUT. BE CAREFUL, MAN!
THERE YOU ARE, OWLHOOT.
HAVE I GOT PLANS FOR YOU.
AH, YOU'RE JUST JEALOUS BECAUSE NO ONE WANTS YOUR NASTY JUNK.
PSSST!
I THINK I MAY GET LUCKY TONIGHT, SAILOR!

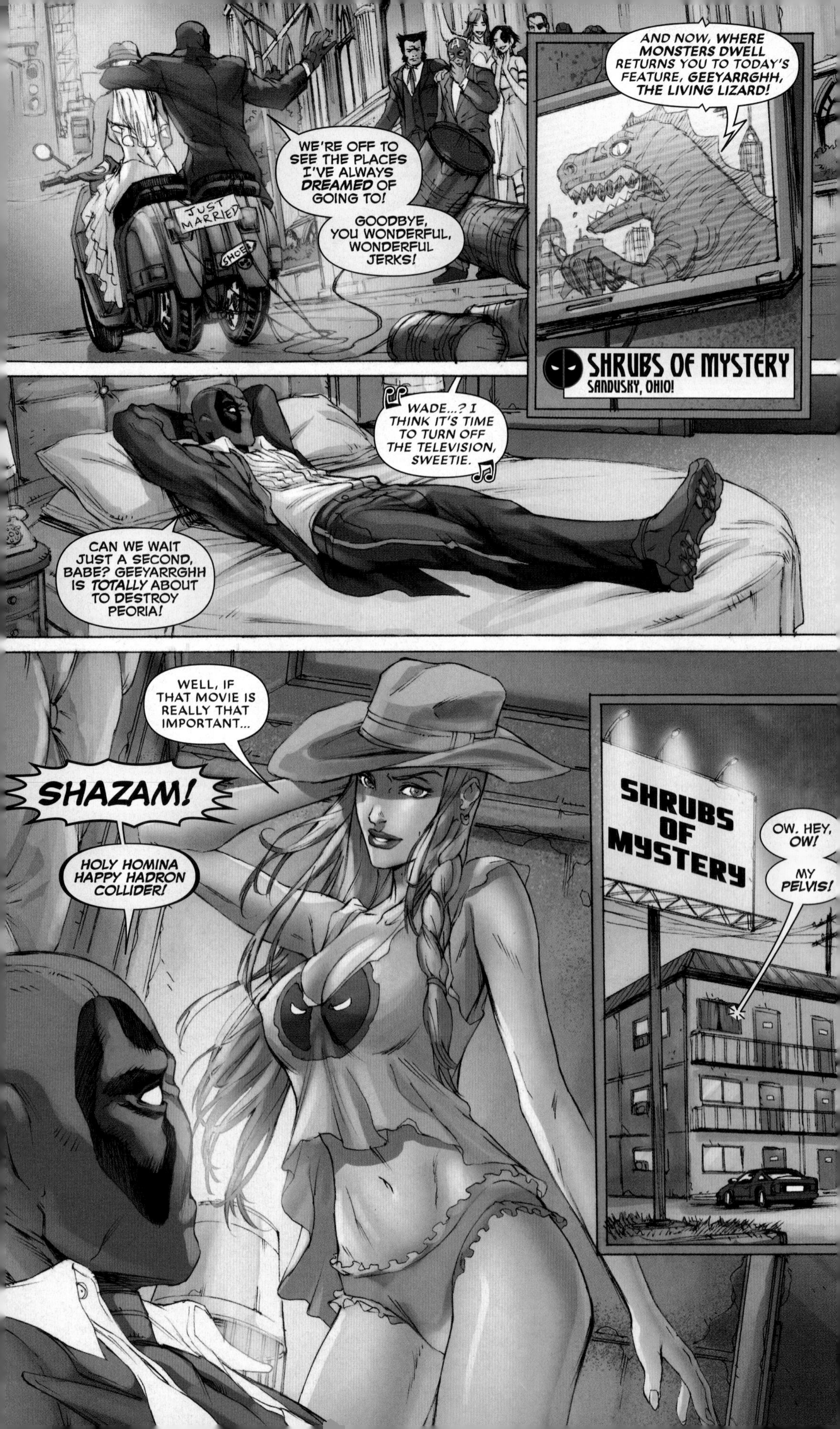
JUST MARRIED
SHOE
WE'RE OFF TO SEE THE PLACES I'VE ALWAYS DREAMED OF GOING TO!
GOODBYE, YOU WONDERFUL, WONDERFUL JERKS!
AND NOW, WHERE MONSTERS DWELL RETURNS YOU TO TODAY'S FEATURE, GEEYARRGHH, THE LIVING LIZARD!
SHRUBS OF MYSTERY
SANDUSKY, OHIO!
WADE...? I THINK IT'S TIME TO TURN OFF THE TELEVISION, SWEETIE.
CAN WE WAIT JUST A SECOND, BABE? GEEYARRGHH IS TOTALLY ABOUT TO DESTROY PEORIA!
WELL, IF THAT MOVIE IS REALLY THAT IMPORTANT...
SHAZAM!
HOLY HOMINA HAPPY HADRON COLLIDER!
SHRUBS OF MYSTERY
OW. HEY, OW!
MY PELVIS!

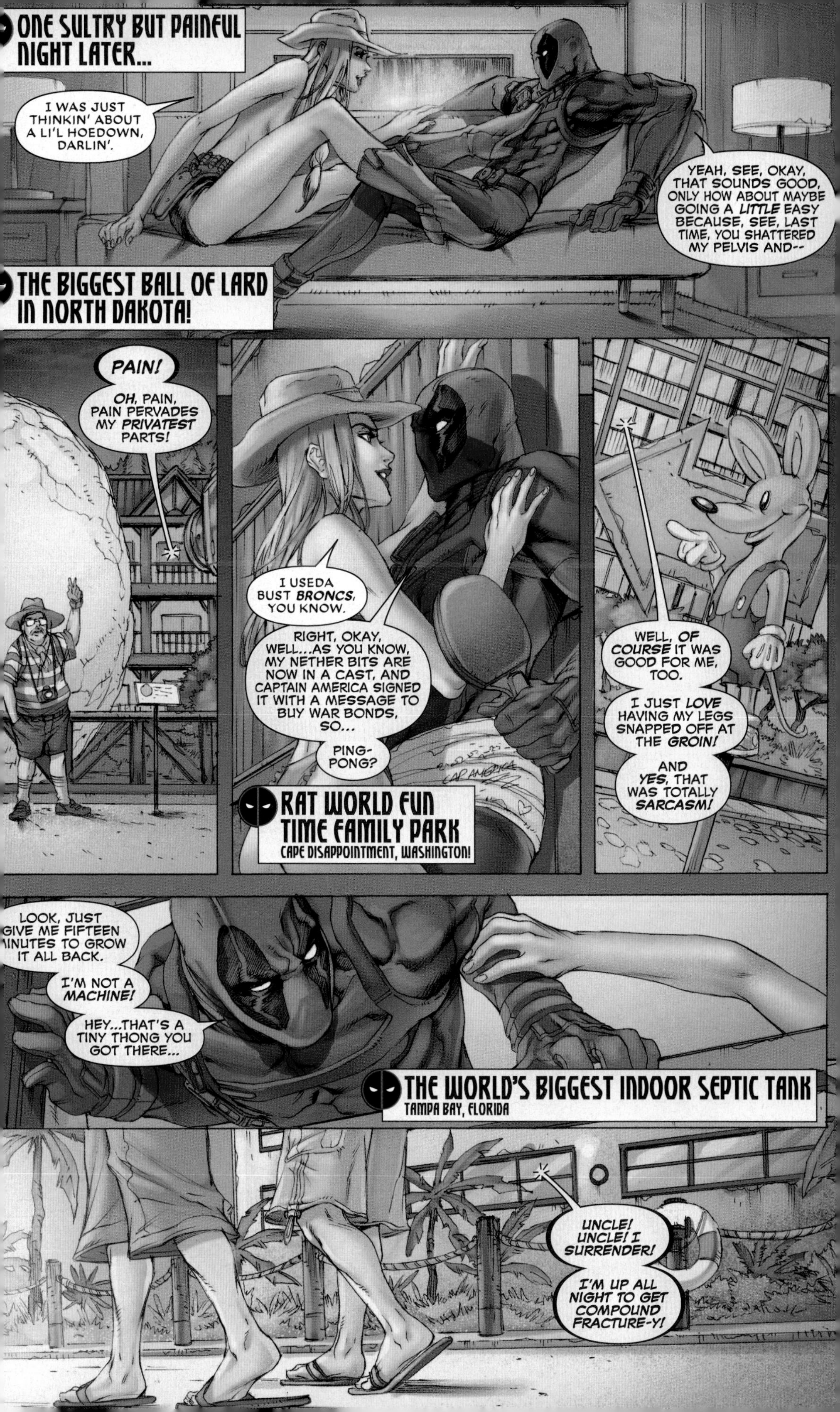

ONE SULTRY BUT PAINFUL NIGHT LATER...
I WAS JUST THINKIN' ABOUT A LI'L HOEDOWN, DARLIN'.
YEAH, SEE, OKAY, THAT SOUNDS GOOD, ONLY HOW ABOUT MAYBE GOING A LITTLE EASY BECAUSE, SEE, LAST TIME, YOU SHATTERED MY PELVIS AND--
THE BIGGEST BALL OF LARD IN NORTH DAKOTA!
PAIN!
OH, PAIN, PAIN PERVADES MY PRIVATEST PARTS!
I USEDA BUST BRONCS, YOU KNOW.
RIGHT, OKAY, WELL...AS YOU KNOW, MY NETHER BITS ARE NOW IN A CAST, AND CAPTAIN AMERICA SIGNED IT WITH A MESSAGE TO BUY WAR BONDS, SO...
PING-PONG?
CAP AMERICA
RAT WORLD FUN TIME FAMILY PARK
CAPE DISAPPOINTMENT, WASHINGTON!
WELL, OF COURSE IT WAS GOOD FOR ME, TOO.
I JUST LOVE HAVING MY LEGS SNAPPED OFF AT THE GROIN!
AND YES, THAT WAS TOTALLY SARCASM!
LOOK, JUST GIVE ME FIFTEEN MINUTES TO GROW IT ALL BACK.
I'M NOT A MACHINE!
HEY...THAT'S A TINY THONG YOU GOT THERE...
THE WORLD'S BIGGEST INDOOR SEPTIC TANK
TAMPA BAY, FLORIDA
UNCLE! UNCLE! I SURRENDER!
I'M UP ALL NIGHT TO GET COMPOUND FRACTURE-Y!

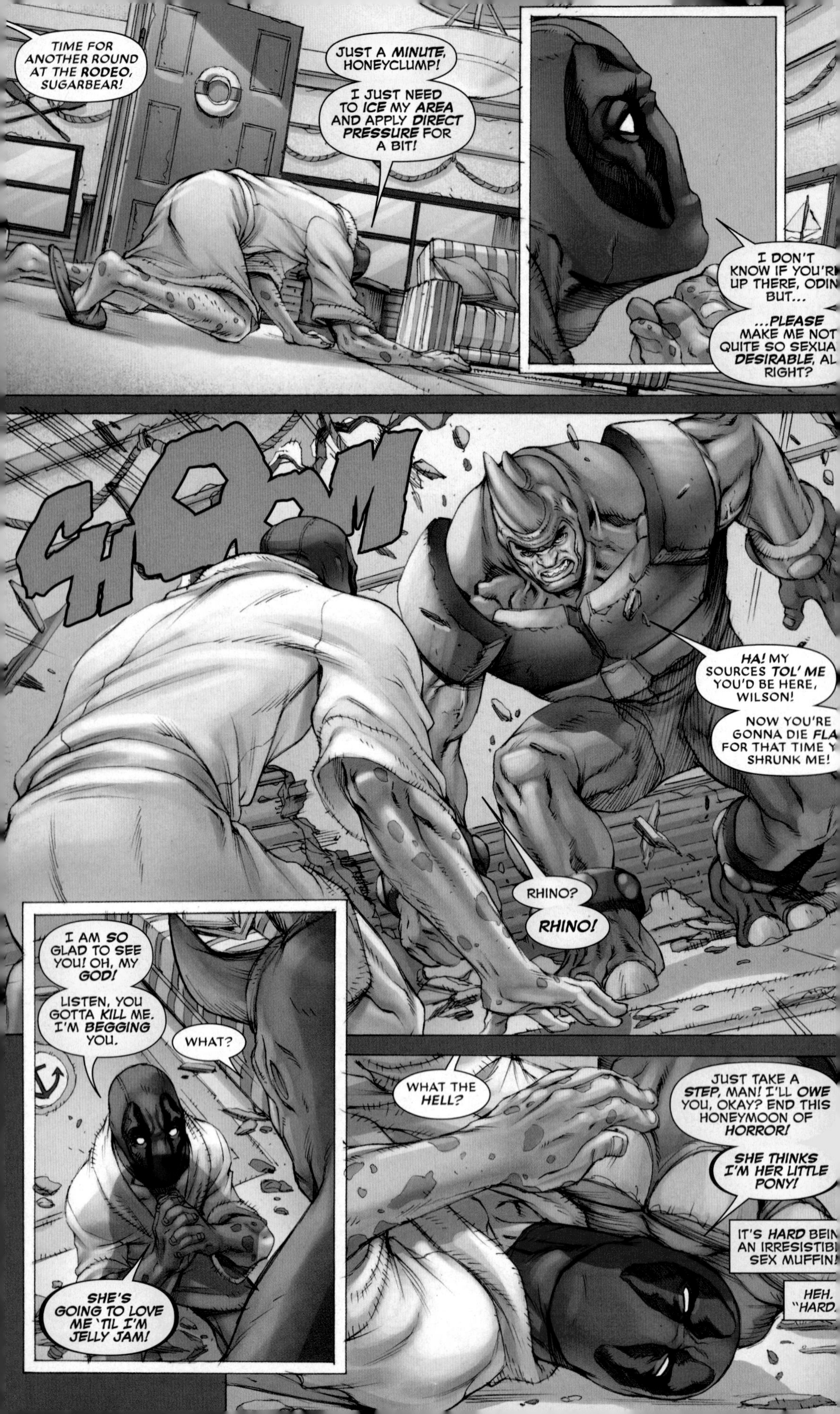

TIME FOR ANOTHER ROUND AT THE RODEO, SUGARBEAR!
JUST A MINUTE, HONEYCLUMP!
I JUST NEED TO ICE MY AREA AND APPLY DIRECT PRESSURE FOR A BIT!
I DON'T KNOW IF YOU'R UP THERE, ODIN BUT...
...PLEASE MAKE ME NOT QUITE SO SEXUA DESIRABLE, AL RIGHT?
SHOOM
HA! MY SOURCES TOL' ME YOU'D BE HERE, WILSON!
NOW YOU'RE GONNA DIE FLA FOR THAT TIME Y SHRUNK ME!
RHINO?
RHINO!
I AM SO GLAD TO SEE YOU! OH, MY GOD!
LISTEN, YOU GOTTA KILL ME. I'M BEGGING YOU.
WHAT?
SHE'S GOING TO LOVE ME 'TIL I'M JELLY JAM!
WHAT THE HELL?
JUST TAKE A STEP, MAN! I'LL OWE YOU, OKAY? END THIS HONEYMOON OF HORROR!
SHE THINKS I'M HER LITTLE PONY!
IT'S HARD BEIN AN IRRESISTIBI SEX MUFFIN!
HEH. "HARD.

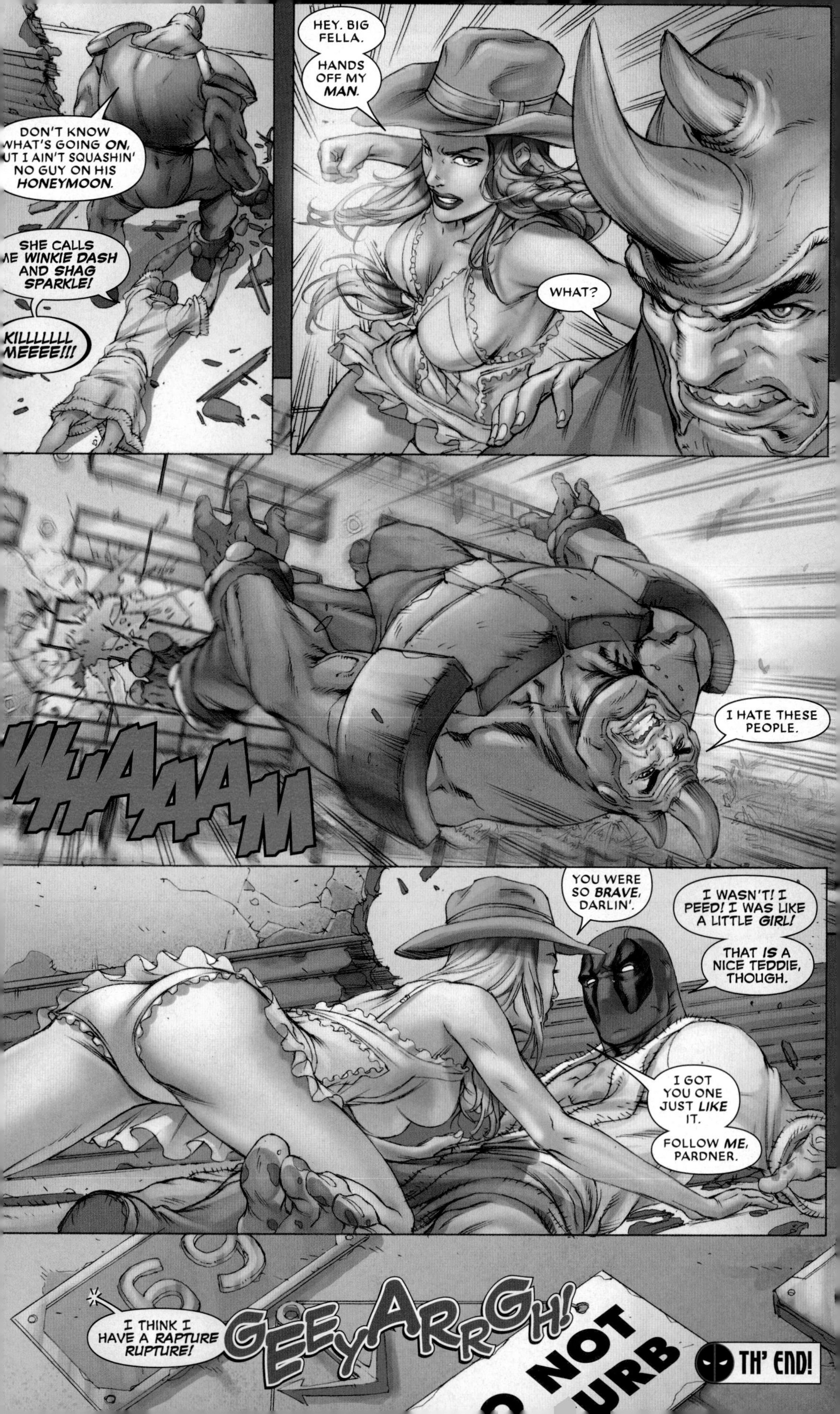
DON'T KNOW WHAT'S GOING *ON*, BUT I AIN'T SQUASHIN' NO GUY ON HIS *HONEYMOON*.
SHE CALLS ME *WINKIE DASH* AND *SHAG SPARKLE!*
KILLLLLLL MEEEE!!!
HEY. BIG FELLA.
HANDS OFF MY *MAN*.
WHAT?
WHAAAM
I HATE THESE PEOPLE.
YOU WERE SO *BRAVE*, DARLIN'.
I WASN'T! I PEED! I WAS LIKE A LITTLE *GIRL!*
THAT *IS* A NICE TEDDIE, THOUGH.
I GOT YOU ONE JUST *LIKE* IT.
FOLLOW *ME*, PARDNER.
I THINK I HAVE A *RAPTURE RUPTURE!*
GEEEyARRRGH!
NOT
URB
TH' END!

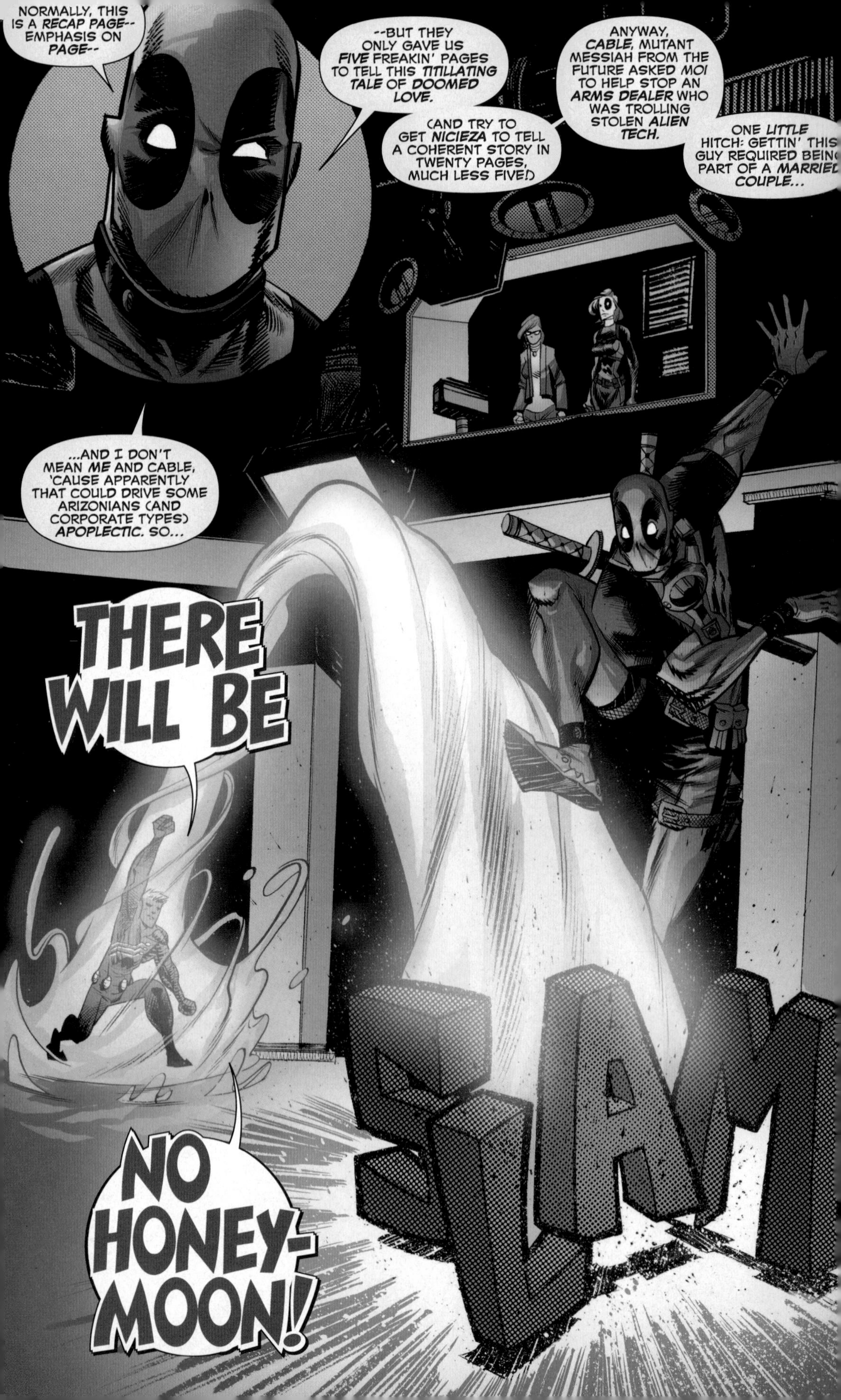
NORMALLY, THIS IS A RECAP PAGE-- EMPHASIS ON PAGE--
--BUT THEY ONLY GAVE US FIVE FREAKIN' PAGES TO TELL THIS TITILLATING TALE OF DOOMED LOVE.
(AND TRY TO GET NICIEZA TO TELL A COHERENT STORY IN TWENTY PAGES, MUCH LESS FIVE!)
ANYWAY, CABLE, MUTANT MESSIAH FROM THE FUTURE ASKED MOI TO HELP STOP AN ARMS DEALER WHO WAS TROLLING STOLEN ALIEN TECH.
ONE LITTLE HITCH: GETTIN' THIS GUY REQUIRED BEING PART OF A MARRIED COUPLE...
...AND I DON'T MEAN ME AND CABLE, 'CAUSE APPARENTLY THAT COULD DRIVE SOME ARIZONIANS (AND CORPORATE TYPES) APOPLECTIC. SO...
THERE WILL BE
NO HONEY-MOON!
SLAM

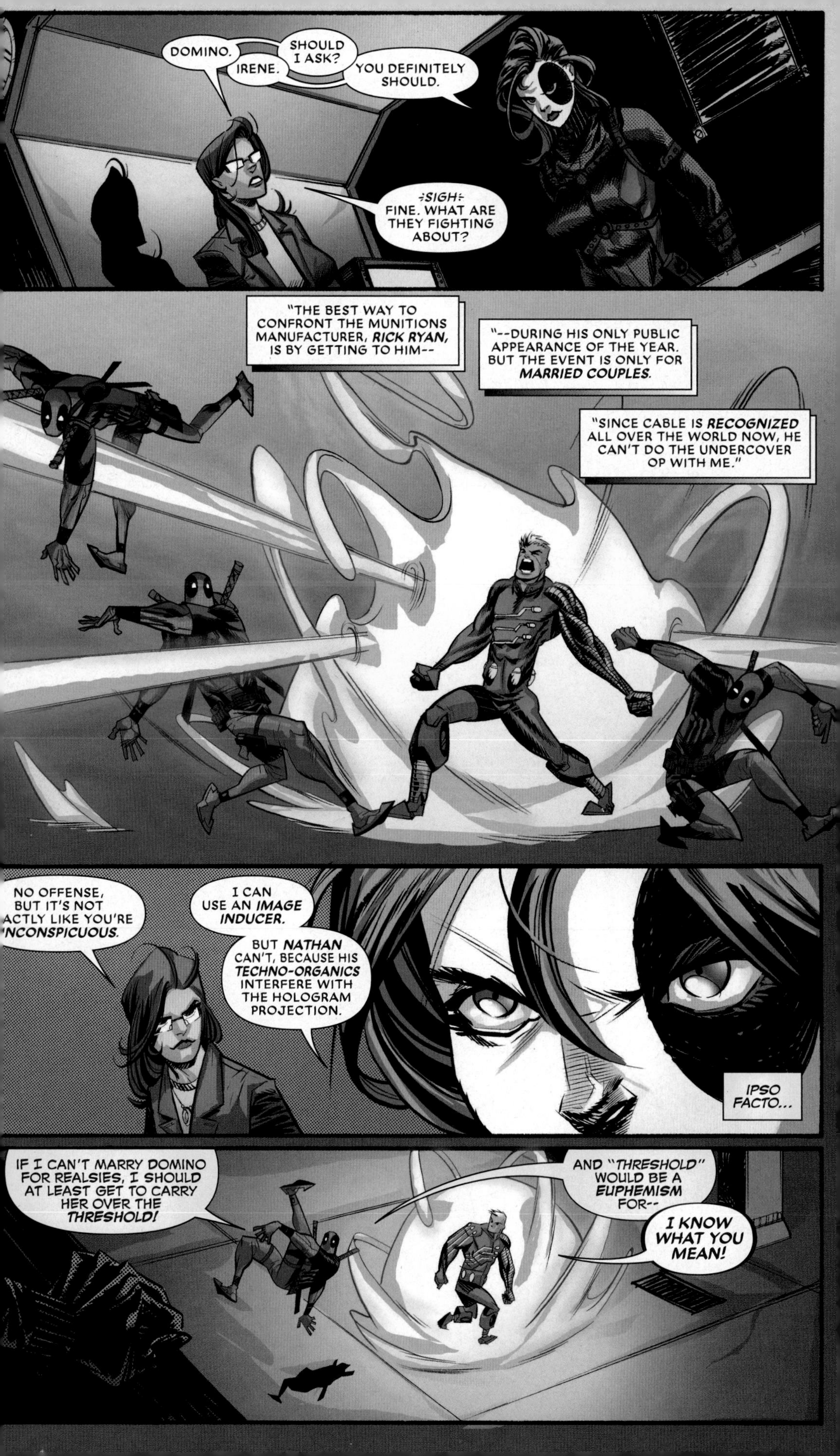
DOMINO.
IRENE.
SHOULD I ASK?
YOU DEFINITELY SHOULD.
=SIGH= FINE. WHAT ARE THEY FIGHTING ABOUT?
"THE BEST WAY TO CONFRONT THE MUNITIONS MANUFACTURER, RICK RYAN, IS BY GETTING TO HIM--
"--DURING HIS ONLY PUBLIC APPEARANCE OF THE YEAR. BUT THE EVENT IS ONLY FOR MARRIED COUPLES.
"SINCE CABLE IS RECOGNIZED ALL OVER THE WORLD NOW, HE CAN'T DO THE UNDERCOVER OP WITH ME."
NO OFFENSE, BUT IT'S NOT ACTLY LIKE YOU'RE NCONSPICUOUS.
I CAN USE AN IMAGE INDUCER.
BUT NATHAN CAN'T, BECAUSE HIS TECHNO-ORGANICS INTERFERE WITH THE HOLOGRAM PROJECTION.
IPSO FACTO...
IF I CAN'T MARRY DOMINO FOR REALSIES, I SHOULD AT LEAST GET TO CARRY HER OVER THE THRESHOLD!
AND "THRESHOLD" WOULD BE A EUPHEMISM FOR--
I KNOW WHAT YOU MEAN!

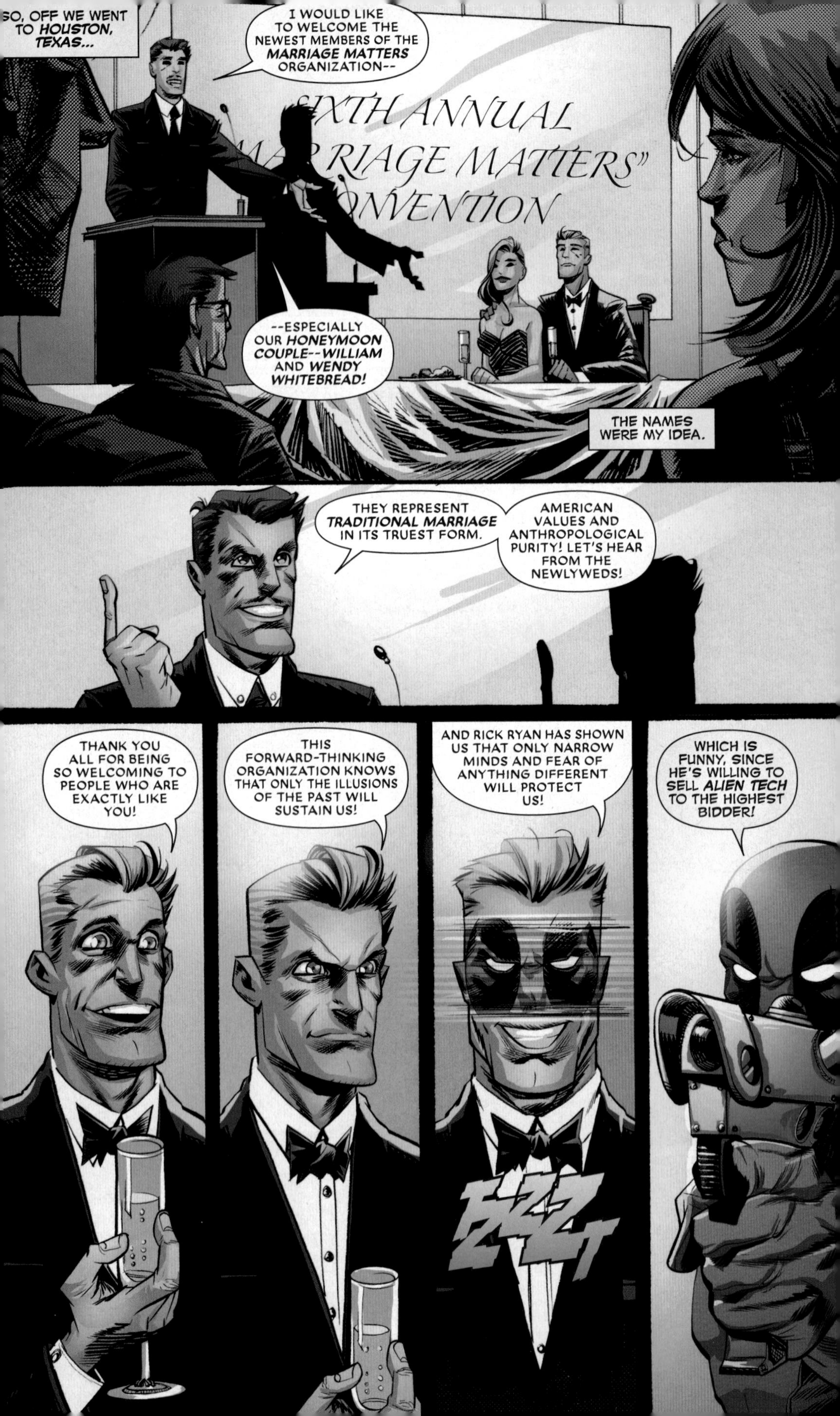
SO, OFF WE WENT TO HOUSTON, TEXAS...
I WOULD LIKE TO WELCOME THE NEWEST MEMBERS OF THE MARRIAGE MATTERS ORGANIZATION--
SIXTH ANNUAL "MARRIAGE MATTERS" CONVENTION
--ESPECIALLY OUR HONEYMOON COUPLE--WILLIAM AND WENDY WHITEBREAD!
THE NAMES WERE MY IDEA.
THEY REPRESENT TRADITIONAL MARRIAGE IN ITS TRUEST FORM.
AMERICAN VALUES AND ANTHROPOLOGICAL PURITY! LET'S HEAR FROM THE NEWLYWEDS!
THANK YOU ALL FOR BEING SO WELCOMING TO PEOPLE WHO ARE EXACTLY LIKE YOU!
THIS FORWARD-THINKING ORGANIZATION KNOWS THAT ONLY THE ILLUSIONS OF THE PAST WILL SUSTAIN US!
AND RICK RYAN HAS SHOWN US THAT ONLY NARROW MINDS AND FEAR OF ANYTHING DIFFERENT WILL PROTECT US!
ZZZT
WHICH IS FUNNY, SINCE HE'S WILLING TO SELL ALIEN TECH TO THE HIGHEST BIDDER!

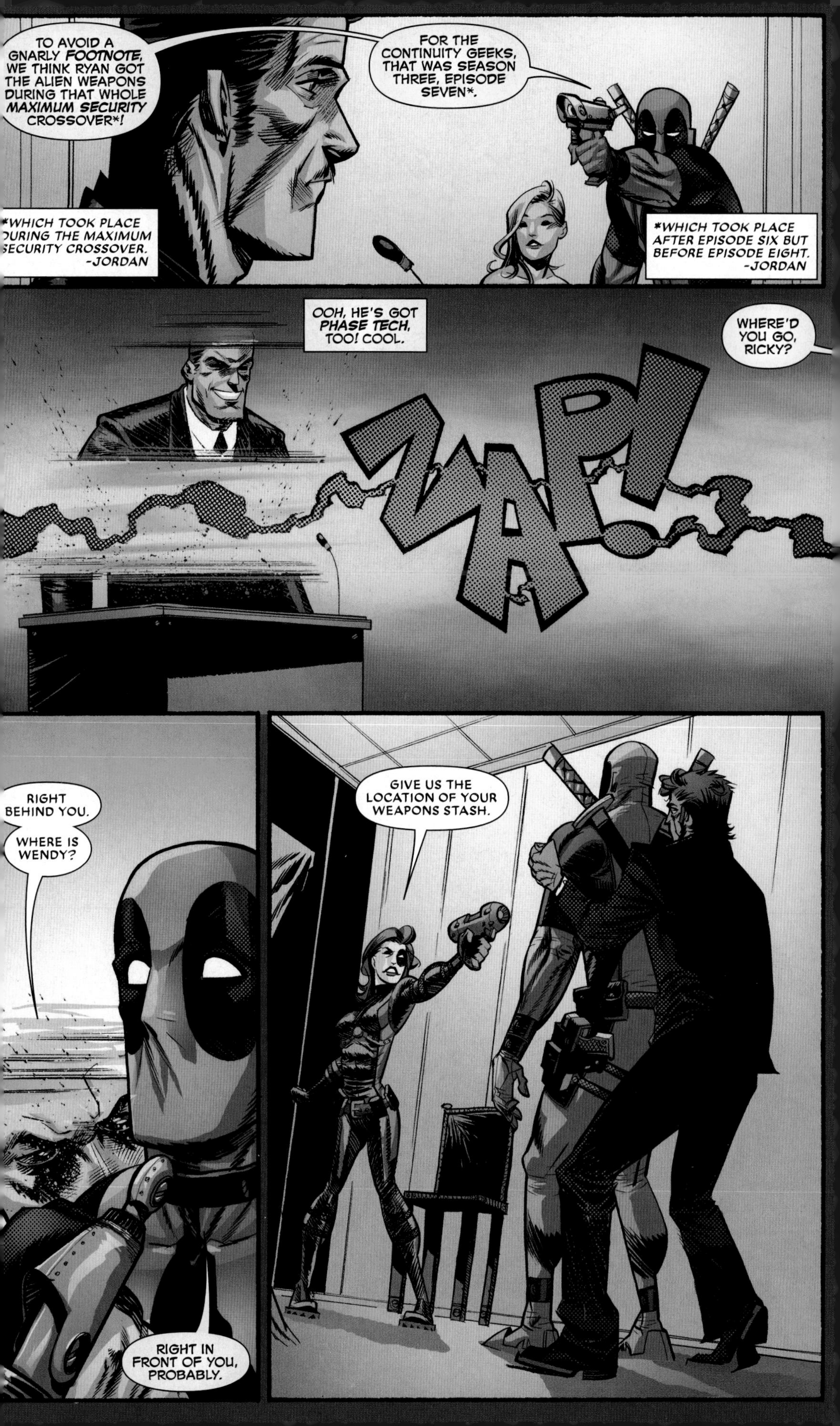
TO AVOID A GNARLY FOOTNOTE, WE THINK RYAN GOT THE ALIEN WEAPONS DURING THAT WHOLE MAXIMUM SECURITY CROSSOVER*!
FOR THE CONTINUITY GEEKS, THAT WAS SEASON THREE, EPISODE SEVEN*.
*WHICH TOOK PLACE DURING THE MAXIMUM SECURITY CROSSOVER. -JORDAN
*WHICH TOOK PLACE AFTER EPISODE SIX BUT BEFORE EPISODE EIGHT. -JORDAN
OOH, HE'S GOT PHASE TECH, TOO! COOL.
WHERE'D YOU GO, RICKY?
ZAP!
RIGHT BEHIND YOU.
WHERE IS WENDY?
RIGHT IN FRONT OF YOU, PROBABLY.
GIVE US THE LOCATION OF YOUR WEAPONS STASH.

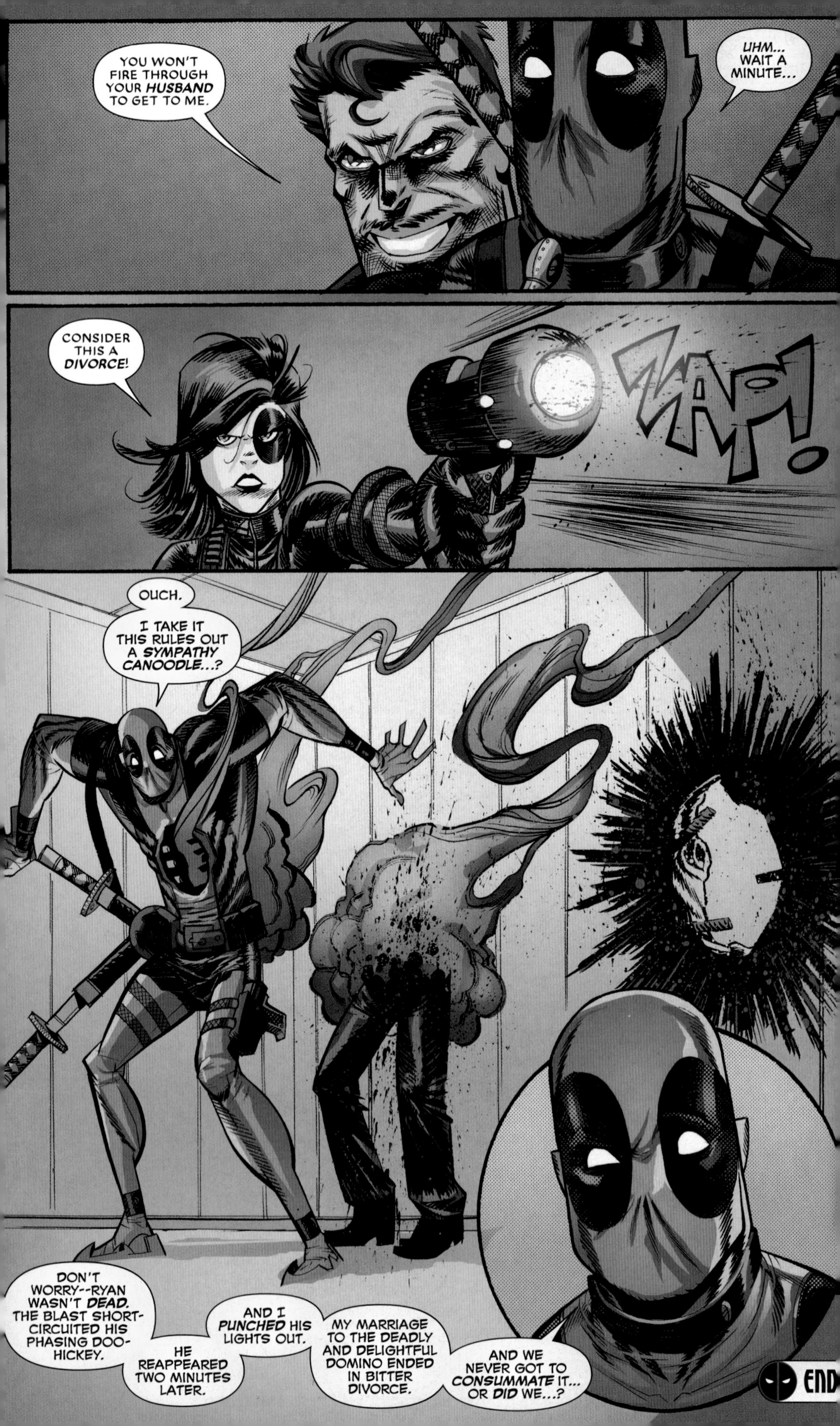
YOU WON'T FIRE THROUGH YOUR HUSBAND TO GET TO ME.
UHM... WAIT A MINUTE...
CONSIDER THIS A DIVORCE!
ZAP!
OUCH.
I TAKE IT THIS RULES OUT A SYMPATHY CANOODLE...?
DON'T WORRY--RYAN WASN'T DEAD. THE BLAST SHORT-CIRCUITED HIS PHASING DOO-HICKEY.
HE REAPPEARED TWO MINUTES LATER.
AND I PUNCHED HIS LIGHTS OUT.
MY MARRIAGE TO THE DEADLY AND DELIGHTFUL DOMINO ENDED IN BITTER DIVORCE.
AND WE NEVER GOT TO CONSUMMATE IT... OR DID WE...?
END

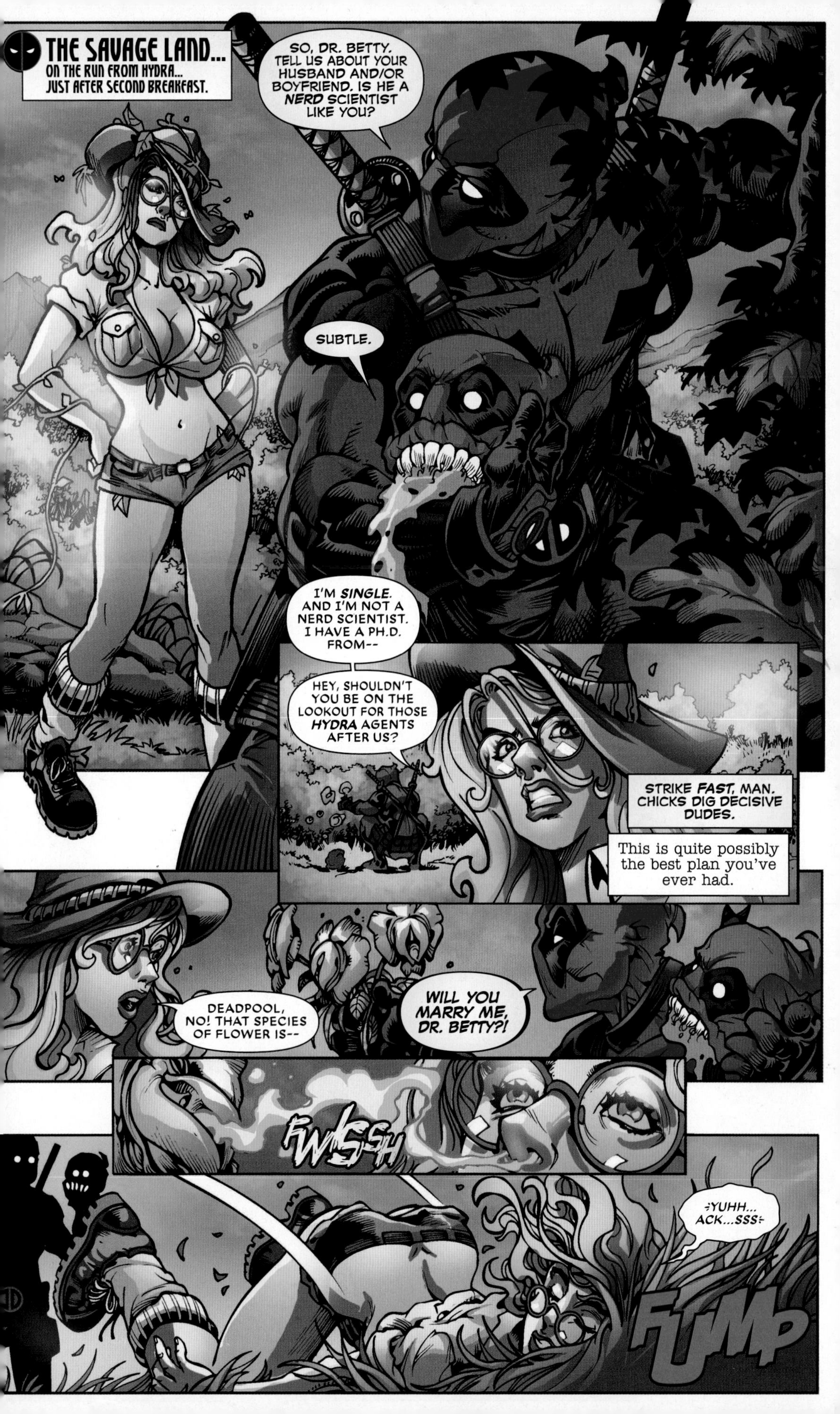
THE SAVAGE LAND... ON THE RUN FROM HYDRA... JUST AFTER SECOND BREAKFAST.
SO, DR. BETTY. TELL US ABOUT YOUR HUSBAND AND/OR BOYFRIEND. IS HE A NERD SCIENTIST LIKE YOU?
SUBTLE.
I'M SINGLE. AND I'M NOT A NERD SCIENTIST. I HAVE A PH.D. FROM--
HEY, SHOULDN'T YOU BE ON THE LOOKOUT FOR THOSE HYDRA AGENTS AFTER US?
STRIKE FAST, MAN. CHICKS DIG DECISIVE DUDES.
This is quite possibly the best plan you've ever had.
DEADPOOL, NO! THAT SPECIES OF FLOWER IS--
WILL YOU MARRY ME, DR. BETTY?!
FWISSH
YUHH... ACK...SSS
FUMP

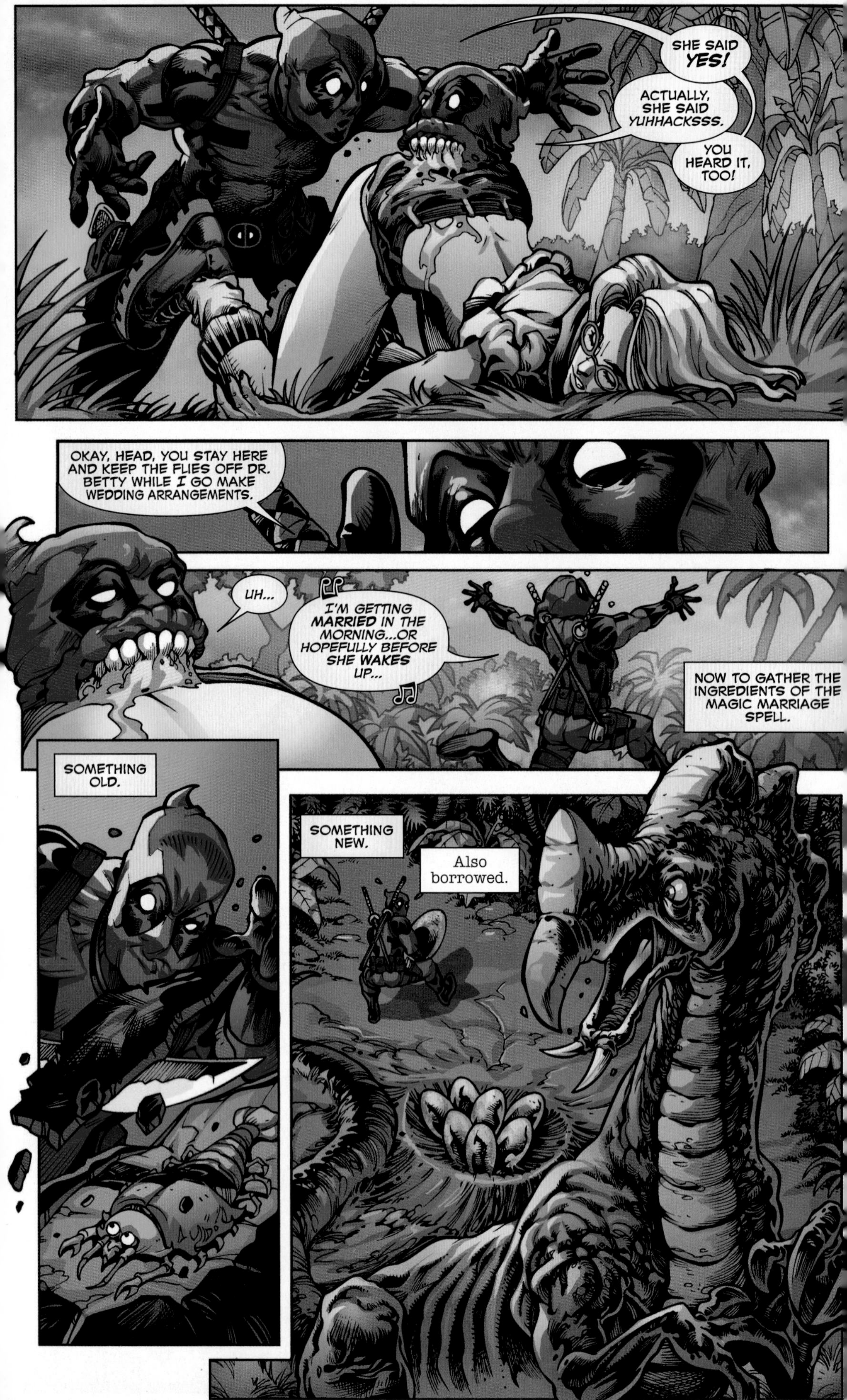
SHE SAID YES!
ACTUALLY, SHE SAID YUHHACKSSS.
YOU HEARD IT, TOO!
OKAY, HEAD, YOU STAY HERE AND KEEP THE FLIES OFF DR. BETTY WHILE I GO MAKE WEDDING ARRANGEMENTS.
UH...
I'M GETTING MARRIED IN THE MORNING...OR HOPEFULLY BEFORE SHE WAKES UP...
NOW TO GATHER THE INGREDIENTS OF THE MAGIC MARRIAGE SPELL.
SOMETHING OLD.
SOMETHING NEW.
Also borrowed.

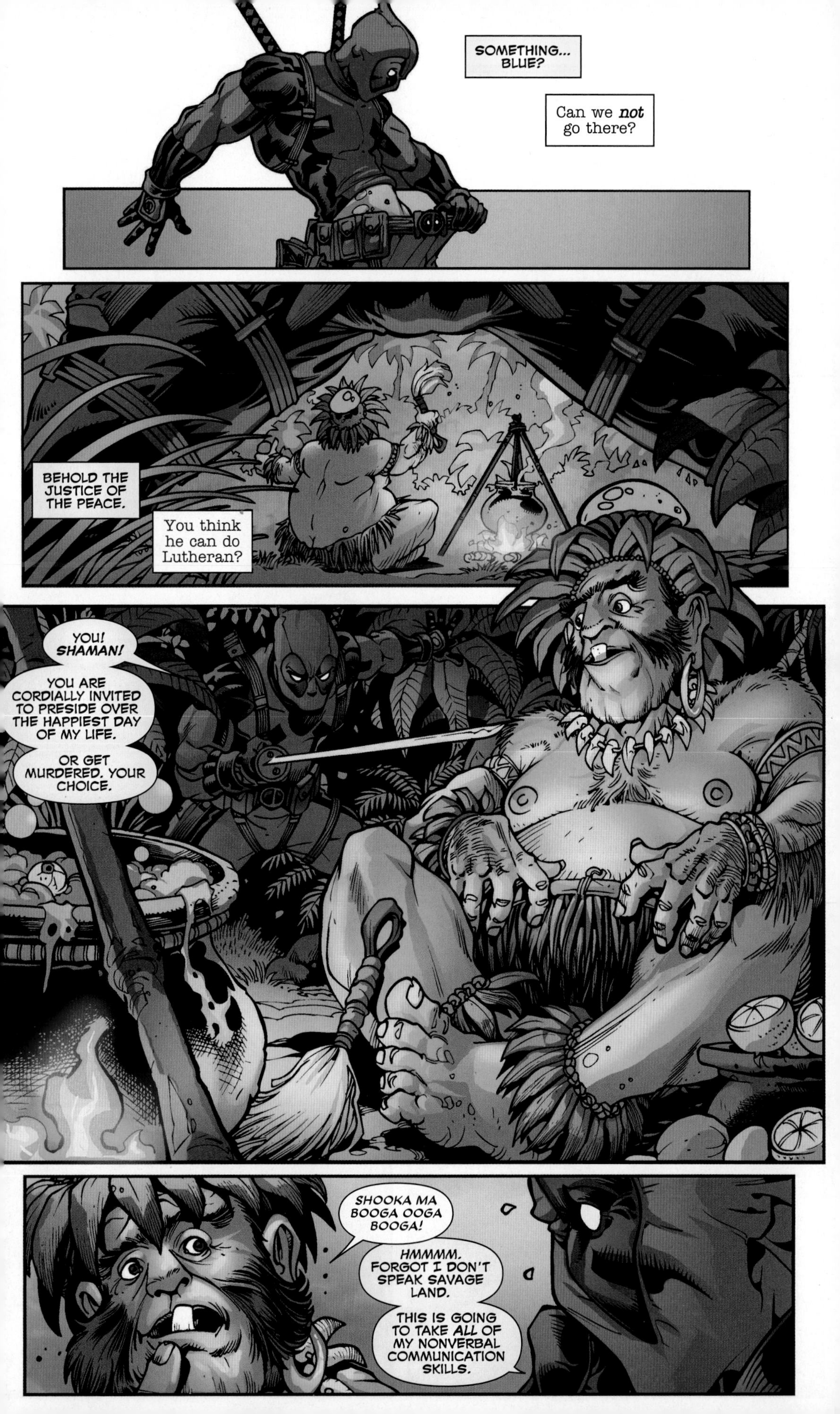
SOMETHING... BLUE?
Can we *not* go there?
BEHOLD THE JUSTICE OF THE PEACE.
You think he can do Lutheran?
YOU! *SHAMAN!*
YOU ARE CORDIALLY INVITED TO PRESIDE OVER THE HAPPIEST DAY OF MY LIFE.
OR GET MURDERED. YOUR CHOICE.
SHOOKA MA BOOGA OOGA BOOGA!
HMMMM. FORGOT I DON'T SPEAK SAVAGE LAND.
THIS IS GOING TO TAKE *ALL* OF MY NONVERBAL COMMUNICATION SKILLS.

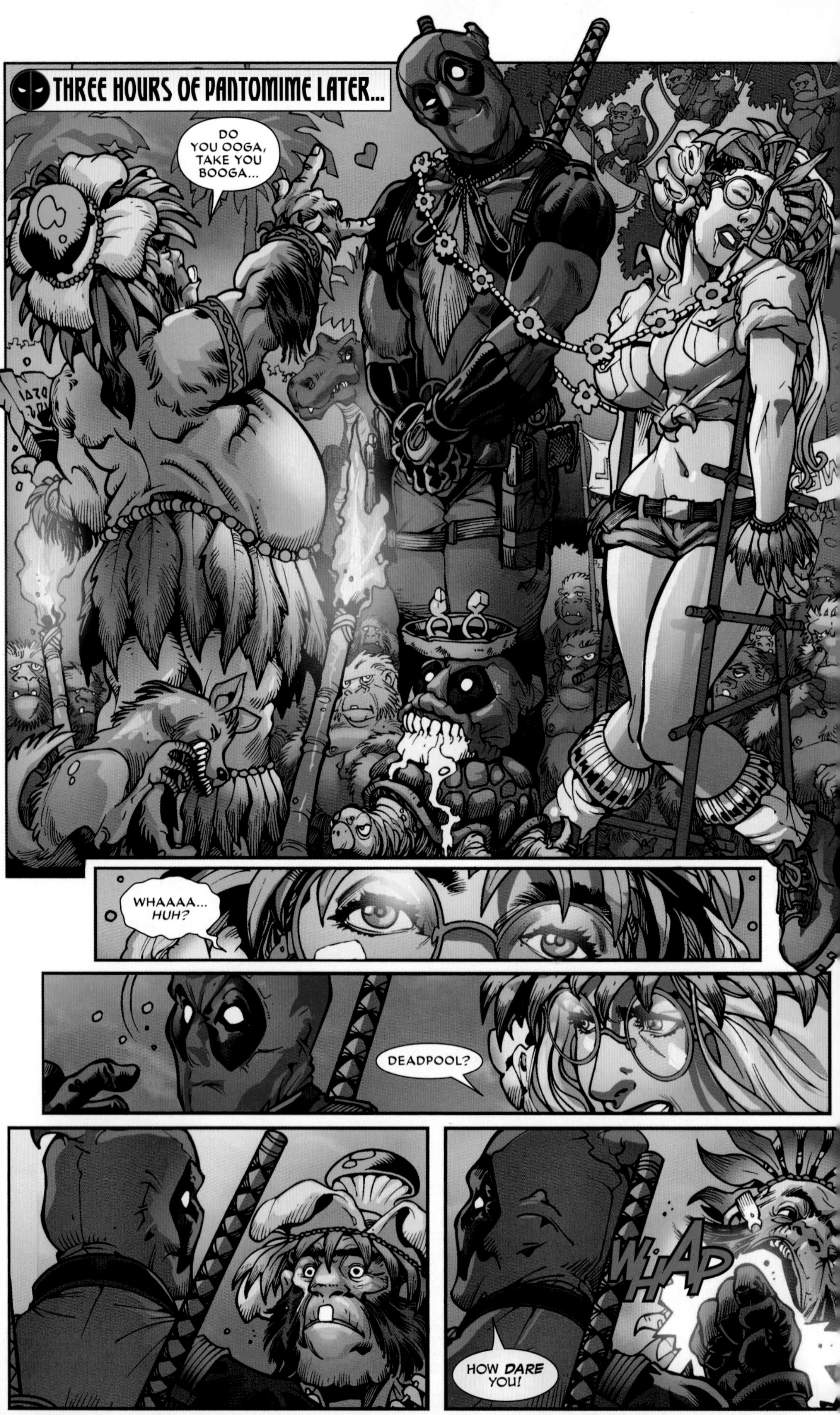
THREE HOURS OF PANTOMIME LATER...
DO YOU OOGA, TAKE YOU BOOGA...
WHAAAA... HUH?
DEADPOOL?
WHAP
HOW DARE YOU!

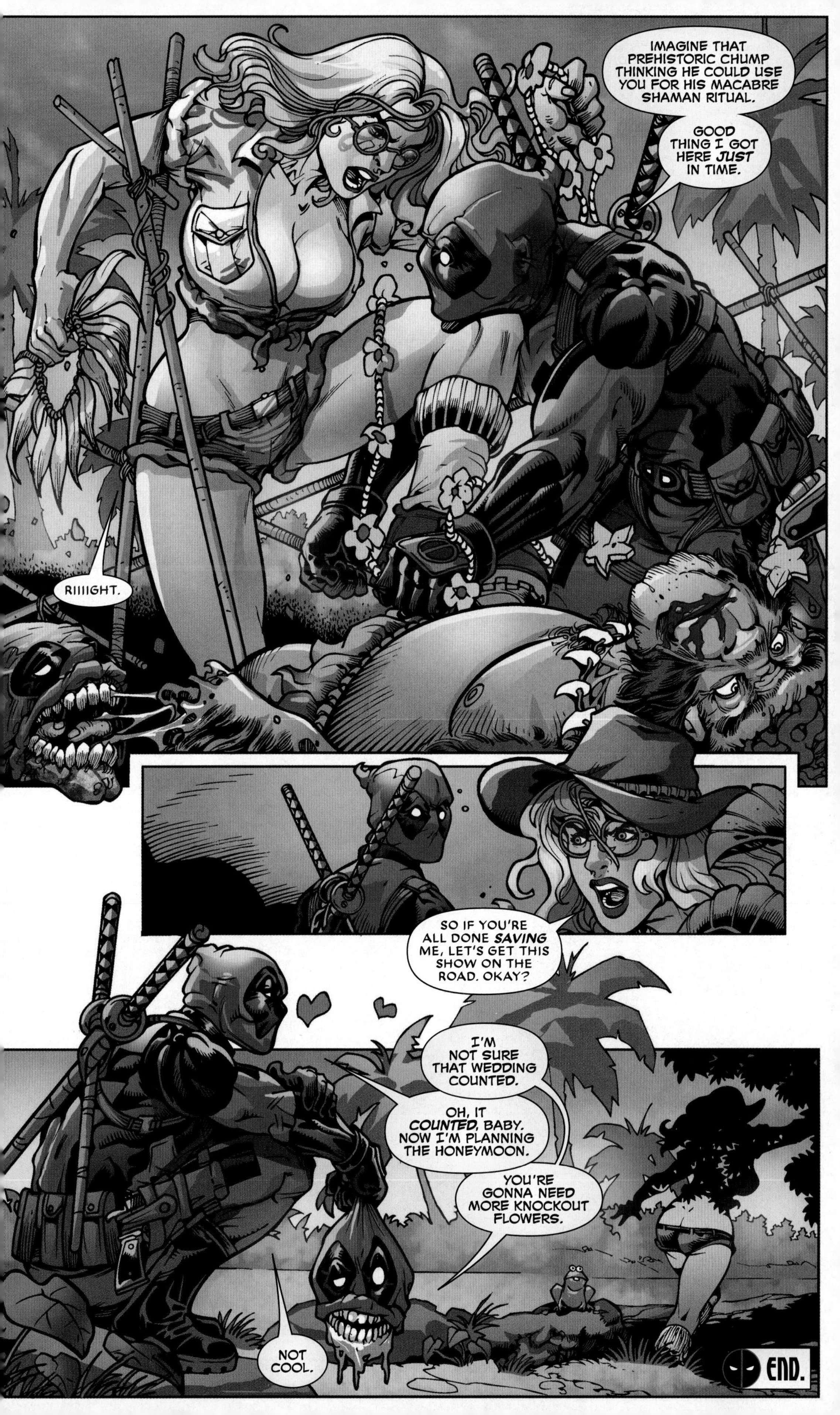
IMAGINE THAT PREHISTORIC CHUMP THINKING HE COULD USE YOU FOR HIS MACABRE SHAMAN RITUAL.
GOOD THING I GOT HERE JUST IN TIME.
RIIIIGHT.
SO IF YOU'RE ALL DONE SAVING ME, LET'S GET THIS SHOW ON THE ROAD. OKAY?
I'M NOT SURE THAT WEDDING COUNTED.
OH, IT COUNTED, BABY. NOW I'M PLANNING THE HONEYMOON.
YOU'RE GONNA NEED MORE KNOCKOUT FLOWERS.
NOT COOL.
END.

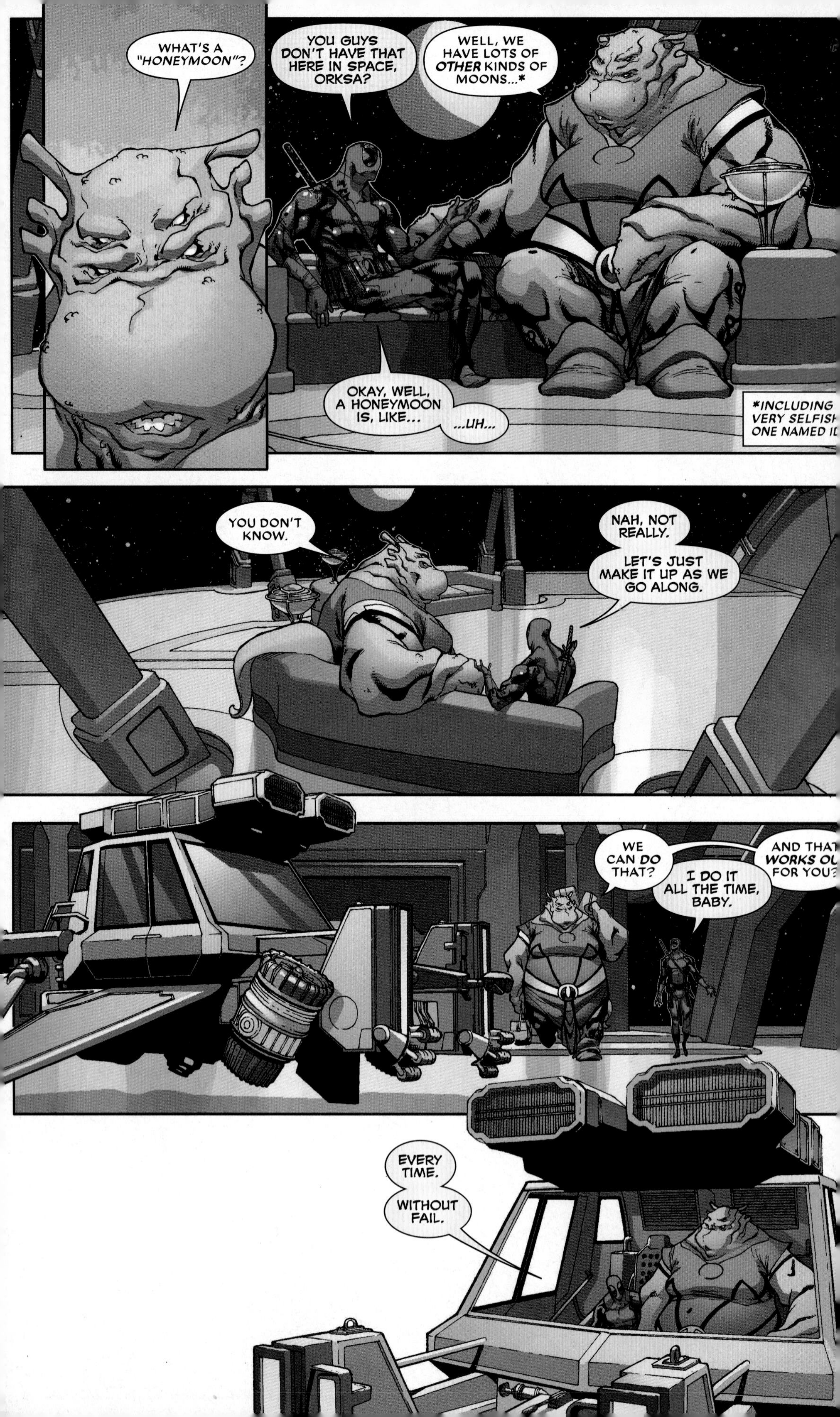
WHAT'S A "HONEYMOON"?
YOU GUYS DON'T HAVE THAT HERE IN SPACE, ORKSA?
WELL, WE HAVE LOTS OF OTHER KINDS OF MOONS...*
OKAY, WELL, A HONEYMOON IS, LIKE...
...UH...
YOU DON'T KNOW.
NAH, NOT REALLY.
LET'S JUST MAKE IT UP AS WE GO ALONG.
WE CAN DO THAT?
I DO IT ALL THE TIME, BABY.
EVERY TIME.
WITHOUT FAIL.

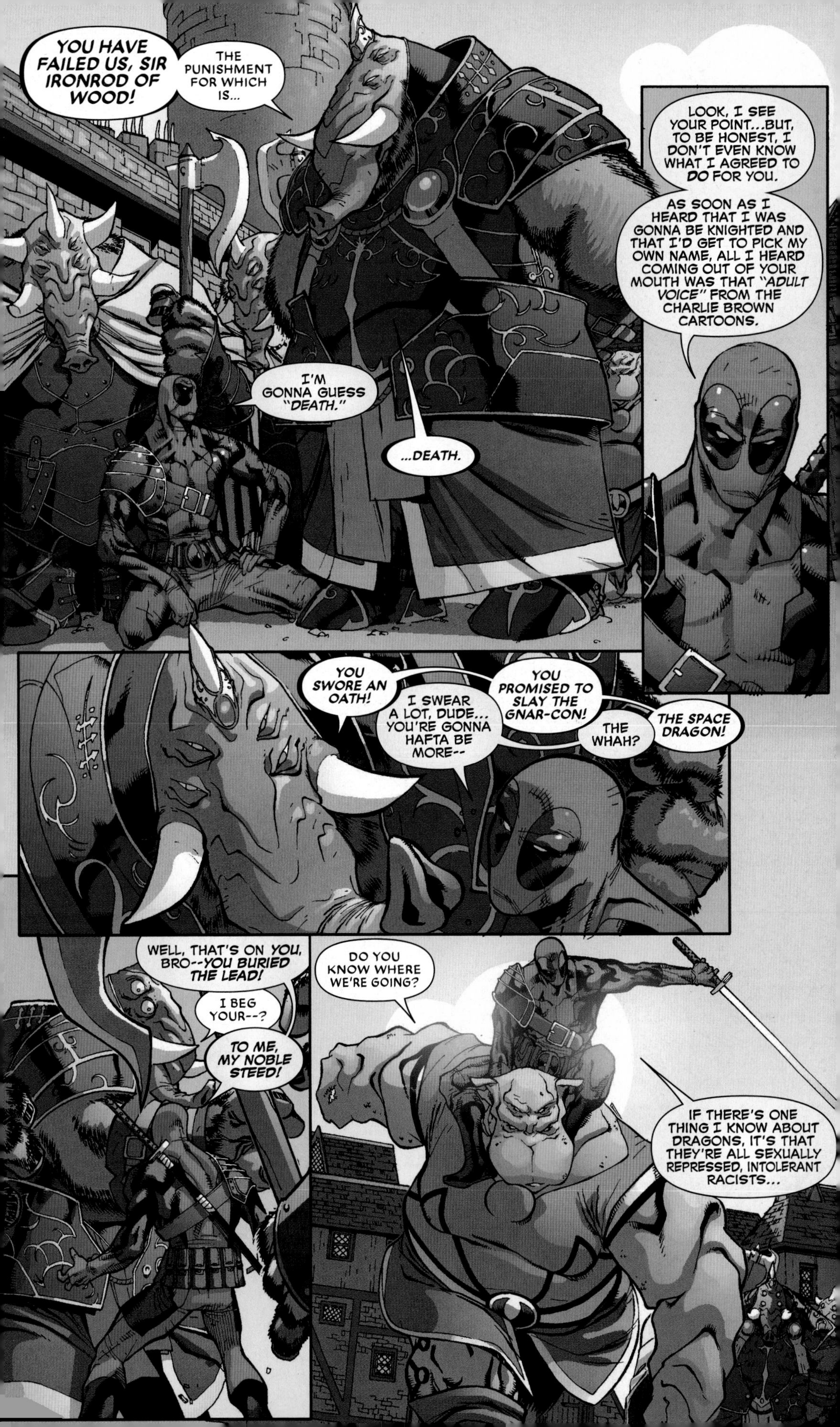
YOU HAVE FAILED US, SIR IRONROD OF WOOD!
THE PUNISHMENT FOR WHICH IS...
I'M GONNA GUESS "DEATH."
...DEATH.
LOOK, I SEE YOUR POINT...BUT, TO BE HONEST, I DON'T EVEN KNOW WHAT I AGREED TO DO FOR YOU.
AS SOON AS I HEARD THAT I WAS GONNA BE KNIGHTED AND THAT I'D GET TO PICK MY OWN NAME, ALL I HEARD COMING OUT OF YOUR MOUTH WAS THAT "ADULT VOICE" FROM THE CHARLIE BROWN CARTOONS.
YOU SWORE AN OATH!
I SWEAR A LOT, DUDE... YOU'RE GONNA HAFTA BE MORE--
YOU PROMISED TO SLAY THE GNAR-CON!
THE WHAH?
THE SPACE DRAGON!
WELL, THAT'S ON YOU, BRO--YOU BURIED THE LEAD!
I BEG YOUR--?
TO ME, MY NOBLE STEED!
DO YOU KNOW WHERE WE'RE GOING?
IF THERE'S ONE THING I KNOW ABOUT DRAGONS, IT'S THAT THEY'RE ALL SEXUALLY REPRESSED, INTOLERANT RACISTS...

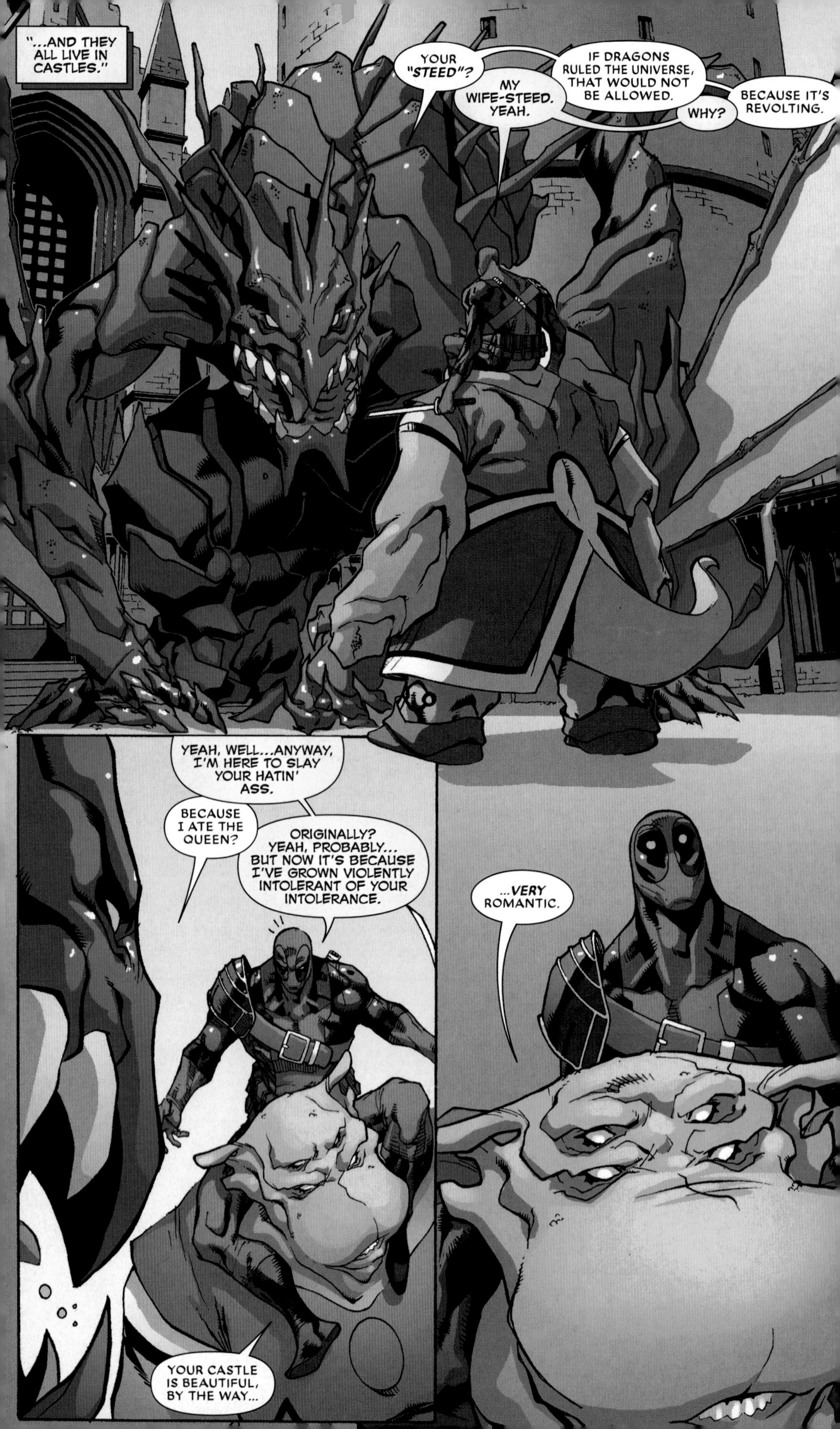
"...AND THEY ALL LIVE IN CASTLES."
YOUR "STEED"?
MY WIFE-STEED. YEAH.
IF DRAGONS RULED THE UNIVERSE, THAT WOULD NOT BE ALLOWED.
WHY?
BECAUSE IT'S REVOLTING.
YEAH, WELL...ANYWAY, I'M HERE TO SLAY YOUR HATIN' ASS.
BECAUSE I ATE THE QUEEN?
ORIGINALLY? YEAH, PROBABLY... BUT NOW IT'S BECAUSE I'VE GROWN VIOLENTLY INTOLERANT OF YOUR INTOLERANCE.
YOUR CASTLE IS BEAUTIFUL, BY THE WAY...
...VERY ROMANTIC.

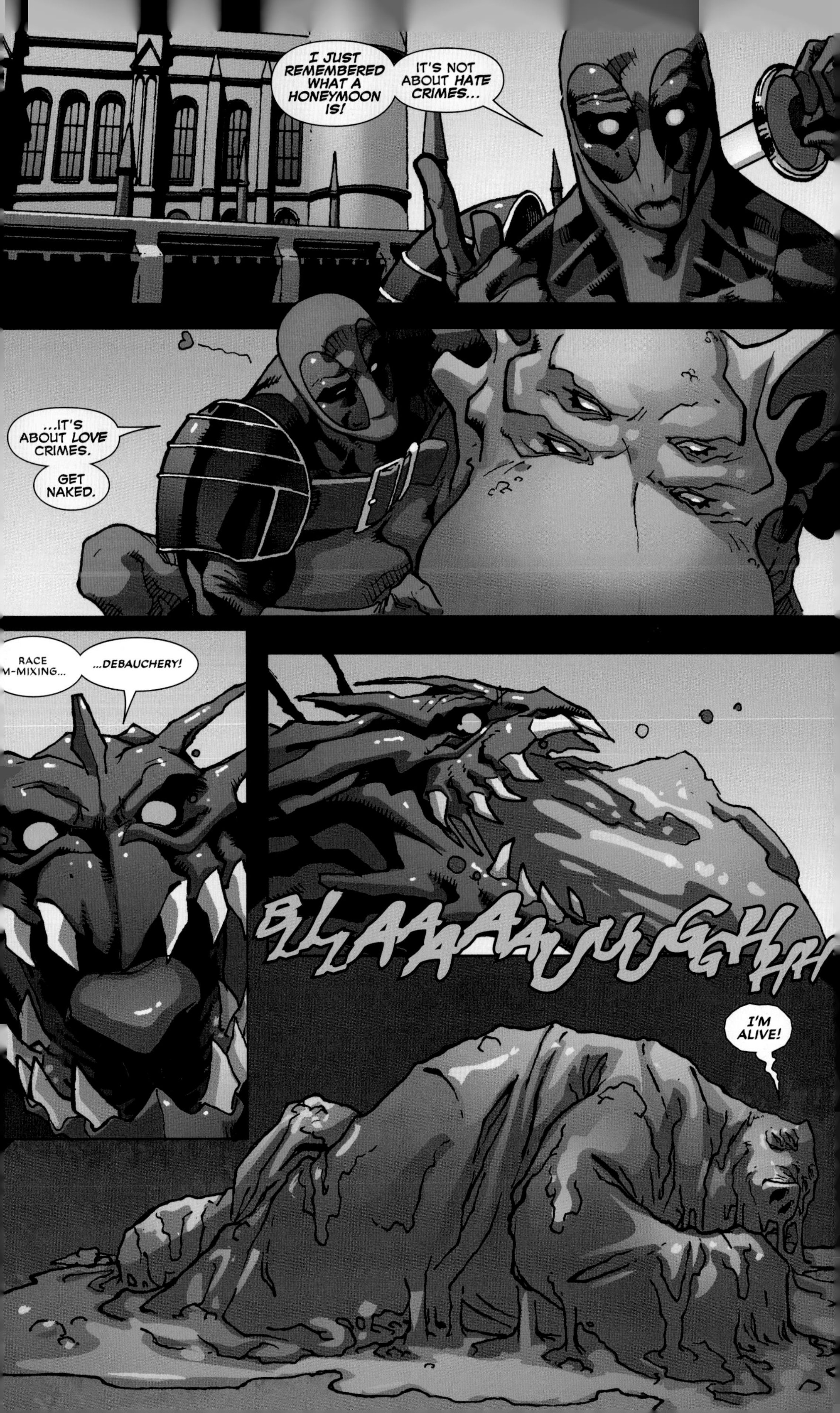
I JUST REMEMBERED WHAT A HONEYMOON IS!
IT'S NOT ABOUT HATE CRIMES...
...IT'S ABOUT LOVE CRIMES.
GET NAKED.
RACE M-MIXING...
...DEBAUCHERY!
BLLAAAAAUUUGHHH
I'M ALIVE!

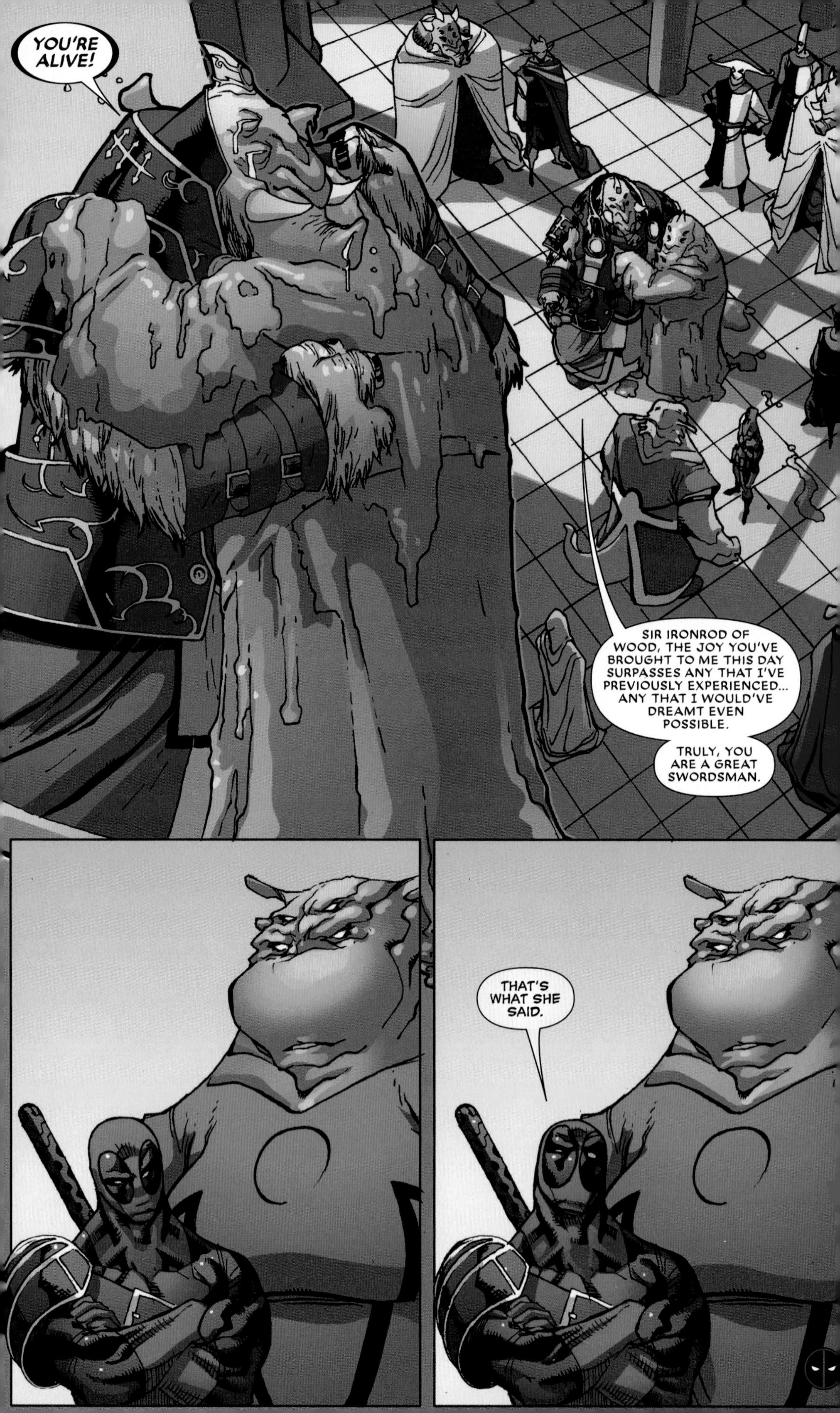
YOU'RE ALIVE!
SIR IRONROD OF WOOD, THE JOY YOU'VE BROUGHT TO ME THIS DAY SURPASSES ANY THAT I'VE PREVIOUSLY EXPERIENCED... ANY THAT I WOULD'VE DREAMT EVEN POSSIBLE.
TRULY, YOU ARE A GREAT SWORDSMAN.
THAT'S WHAT SHE SAID.

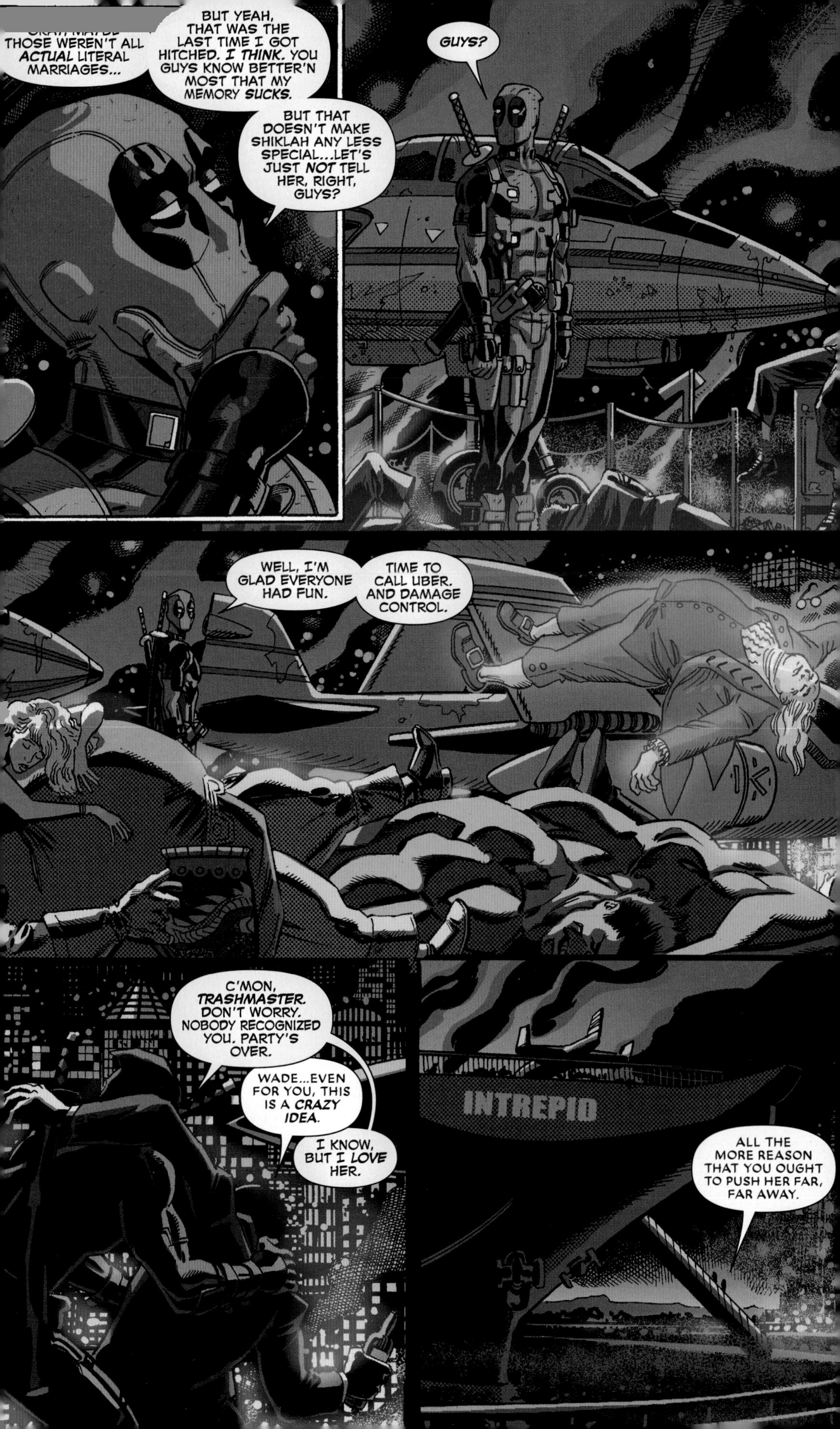
THOSE WEREN'T ALL *ACTUAL* LITERAL MARRIAGES...
BUT YEAH, THAT WAS THE LAST TIME I GOT HITCHED. *I THINK.* YOU GUYS KNOW BETTER'N MOST THAT MY MEMORY *SUCKS.*
BUT THAT DOESN'T MAKE SHIKLAH ANY LESS SPECIAL...LET'S JUST *NOT* TELL HER, RIGHT, GUYS?
GUYS?
WELL, I'M GLAD EVERYONE HAD FUN.
TIME TO CALL UBER. AND DAMAGE CONTROL.
C'MON, *TRASHMASTER.* DON'T WORRY. NOBODY RECOGNIZED YOU. PARTY'S OVER.
WADE...EVEN FOR YOU, THIS IS A *CRAZY IDEA.*
I KNOW, BUT I *LOVE* HER.
INTREPID
ALL THE MORE REASON THAT YOU OUGHT TO PUSH HER FAR, FAR AWAY.

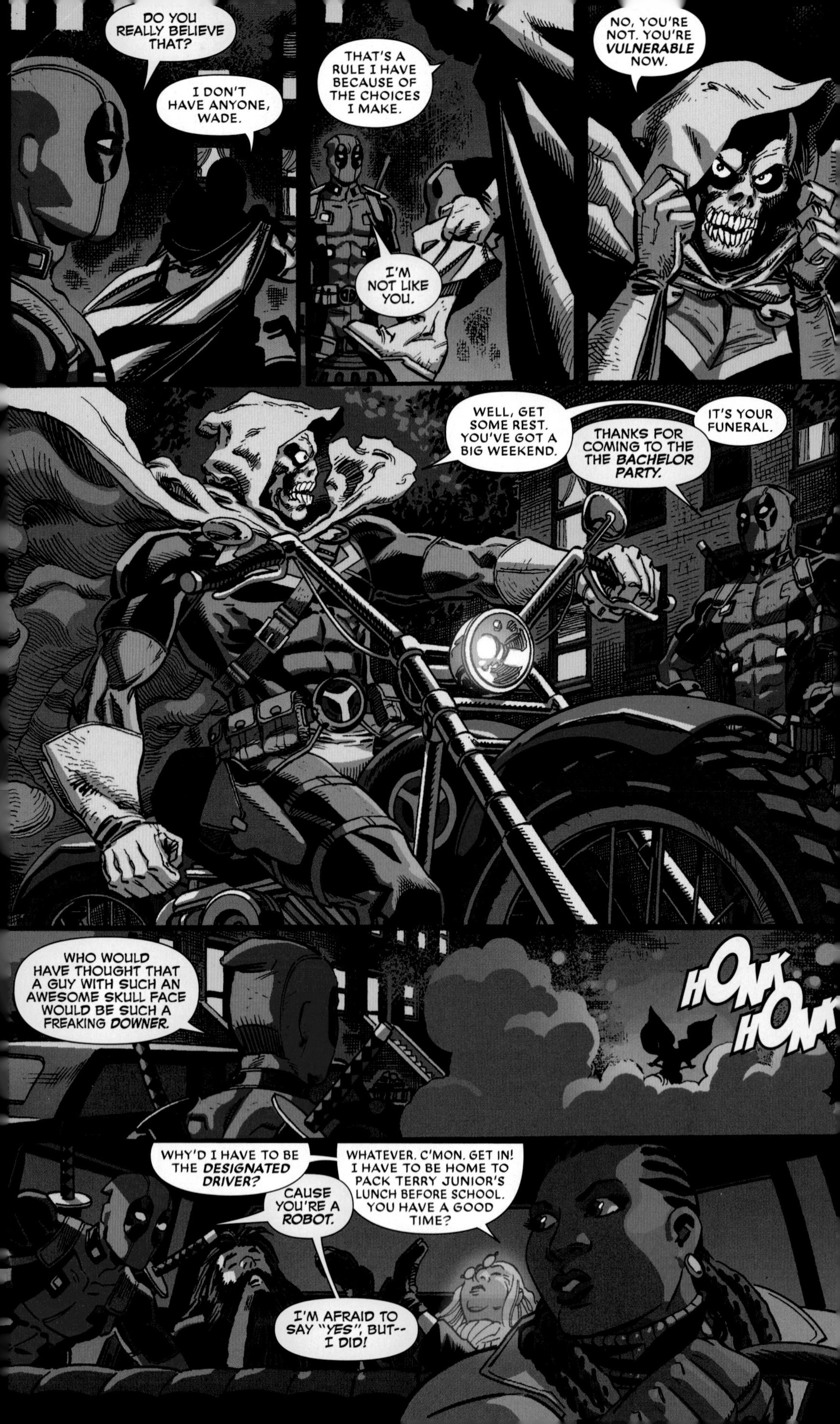
DO YOU REALLY BELIEVE THAT?
I DON'T HAVE ANYONE, WADE.
THAT'S A RULE I HAVE BECAUSE OF THE CHOICES I MAKE.
I'M NOT LIKE YOU.
NO, YOU'RE NOT. YOU'RE VULNERABLE NOW.
WELL, GET SOME REST. YOU'VE GOT A BIG WEEKEND.
IT'S YOUR FUNERAL.
THANKS FOR COMING TO THE THE BACHELOR PARTY.
WHO WOULD HAVE THOUGHT THAT A GUY WITH SUCH AN AWESOME SKULL FACE WOULD BE SUCH A FREAKING DOWNER.
HONK HONK
WHY'D I HAVE TO BE THE DESIGNATED DRIVER?
CAUSE YOU'RE A ROBOT.
WHATEVER. C'MON. GET IN! I HAVE TO BE HOME TO PACK TERRY JUNIOR'S LUNCH BEFORE SCHOOL. YOU HAVE A GOOD TIME?
I'M AFRAID TO SAY "YES", BUT-- I DID!

#27 VARIANT
BY CARLO BARBERI &
EDGAR DELGADO

No. 27
MAY, 1939
DEADPOOL
COMICS
$9.99
STARTING THIS ISSUE: THE AMAZING AND UNIQUE ADVENTURES OF THE DEADPOOL!

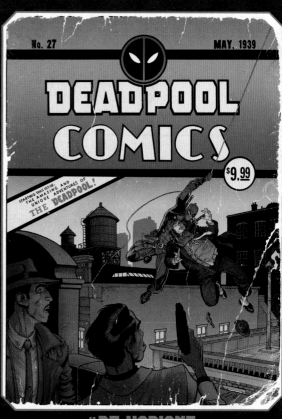

#27 VARIANT
BY ARTHUR ADAMS
& PETER STEIGERWALD

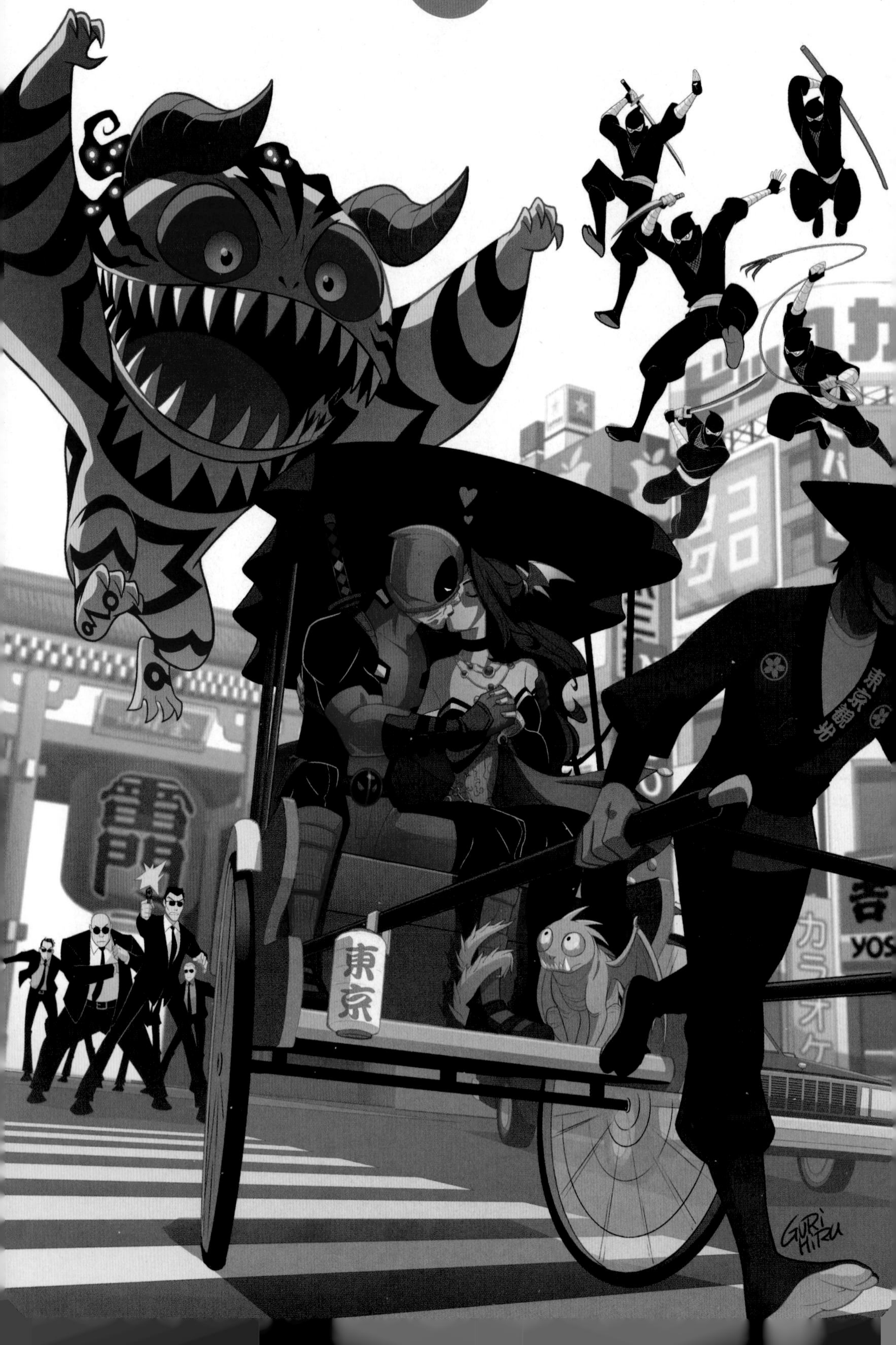
東京
カラオケ
GURI HIRU

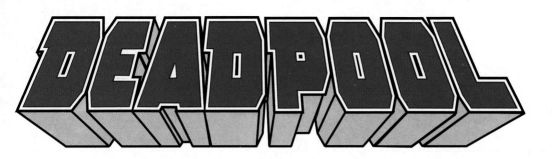

ssibly the world's most skilled mercenary, definitely the world's most annoying, Wade Wilson was osen for a top-secret government program that gave him a healing factor allowing him to heal from y wound. Now, Wade makes his way as a gun for hire, shooting his prey's faces off while talking his riends' ears off. Call him the Merc with the Mouth...call him the Regeneratin' Degenerate...call him...

DEADPOOL

HEY THERE, PALS! IT'S ME, DEADPOOL, THE MERC WITH THE MARRIAGE!
SO, YOU PROBABLY HEARD, BUT I RECENTLY GOT MARRIED. THIS HERE IS MY LADY-PAL, SHIKLAH. SHE'S THE QUEEN OF THE ENORMOUS MONSTER METROPOLIS HIDDEN UNDER NEW YORK CITY.
SHE'S ALSO SUPER DREAMY.
NOW, SOME PEOPLE HAVE SAID THAT MY MARRIAGE IS JUST ME DESPERATELY GRASPING AT SOMETHING CRAZY TO CHANGE MY LIFE AFTER A HORRIFYING ONE-TWO PUNCH OF ONE, A TRIP TO NORTH KOREA WHERE I LEARNED THAT I'VE BEEN EXPERIMENTED ON FOR YEARS, THAT THERE IS A WEIRD RACE OF SCREWED-UP X-MEN XEROXES BASED ON MY DNA, THAT A LADY WHO HAD THE DAUGHTER I DIDN'T KNOW I HAD IS DEAD, AND THAT THE DAUGHTER MAY OR MAY NOT BE DEAD, TOO...AND TWO, LOSING MY NEW BESTIE, AGENT PRESTON OF S.H.I.E.L.D., FROM INSIDE MY HEAD.
BUT THAT IS CRAZY. SHIKLAH AND I ARE HAPPY TOGETHER.

LI'L DEADPOOL ART BY
IRENE Y. LEE

HONEYMOON IN TOKYO

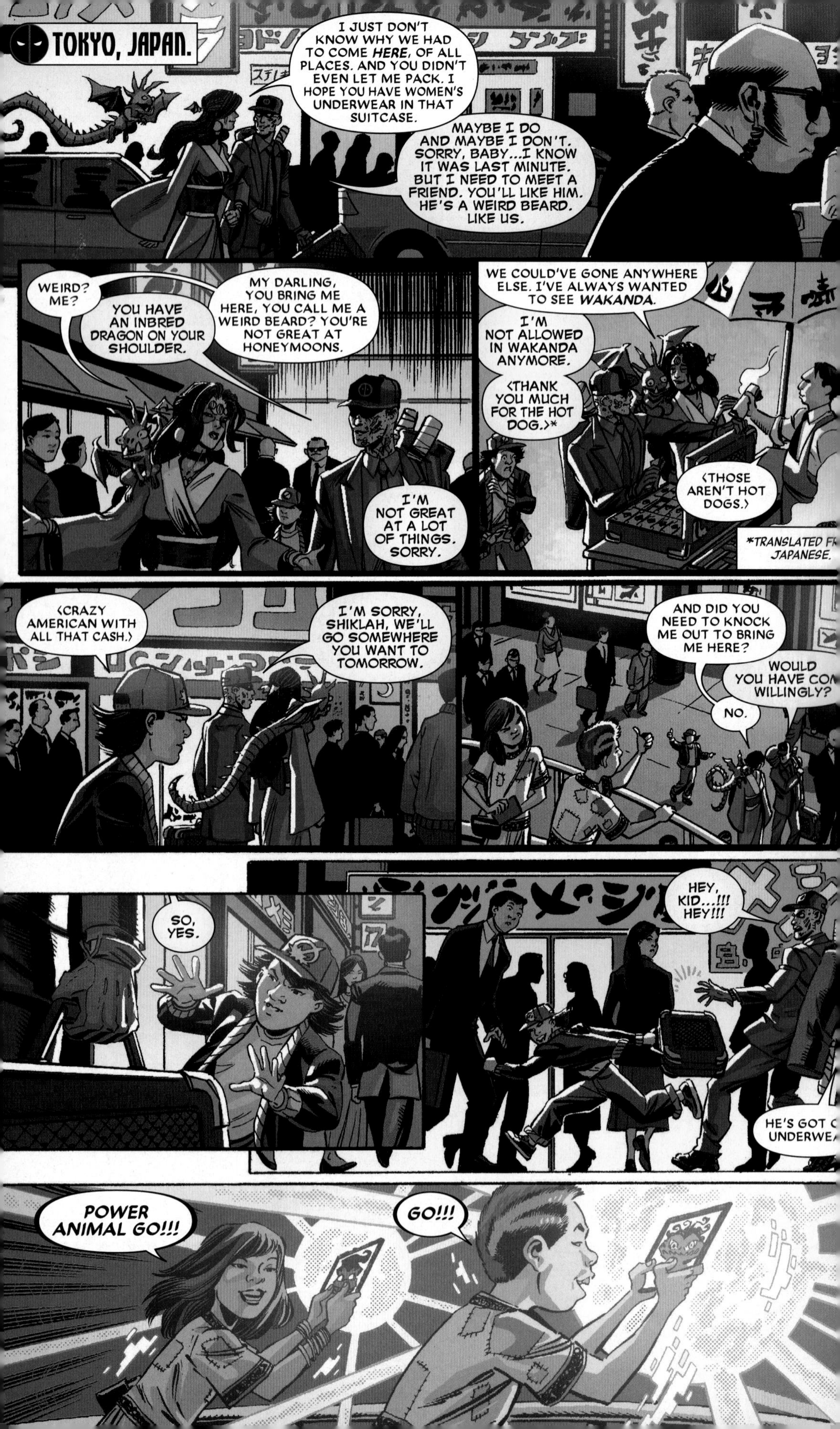

TOKYO, JAPAN.
I JUST DON'T KNOW WHY WE HAD TO COME HERE, OF ALL PLACES. AND YOU DIDN'T EVEN LET ME PACK. I HOPE YOU HAVE WOMEN'S UNDERWEAR IN THAT SUITCASE.
MAYBE I DO AND MAYBE I DON'T. SORRY, BABY...I KNOW IT WAS LAST MINUTE. BUT I NEED TO MEET A FRIEND. YOU'LL LIKE HIM. HE'S A WEIRD BEARD. LIKE US.
WEIRD? ME?
YOU HAVE AN INBRED DRAGON ON YOUR SHOULDER.
MY DARLING, YOU BRING ME HERE, YOU CALL ME A WEIRD BEARD? YOU'RE NOT GREAT AT HONEYMOONS.
I'M NOT GREAT AT A LOT OF THINGS. SORRY.
WE COULD'VE GONE ANYWHERE ELSE. I'VE ALWAYS WANTED TO SEE WAKANDA.
I'M NOT ALLOWED IN WAKANDA ANYMORE.
<THANK YOU MUCH FOR THE HOT DOG.>*
<THOSE AREN'T HOT DOGS.>
*TRANSLATED FR JAPANESE.
<CRAZY AMERICAN WITH ALL THAT CASH.>
I'M SORRY, SHIKLAH, WE'LL GO SOMEWHERE YOU WANT TO TOMORROW.
AND DID YOU NEED TO KNOCK ME OUT TO BRING ME HERE?
WOULD YOU HAVE COM WILLINGLY?
NO.
SO, YES.
HEY, KID...!!! HEY!!!
HE'S GOT UNDERWE
POWER ANIMAL GO!!!
GO!!!

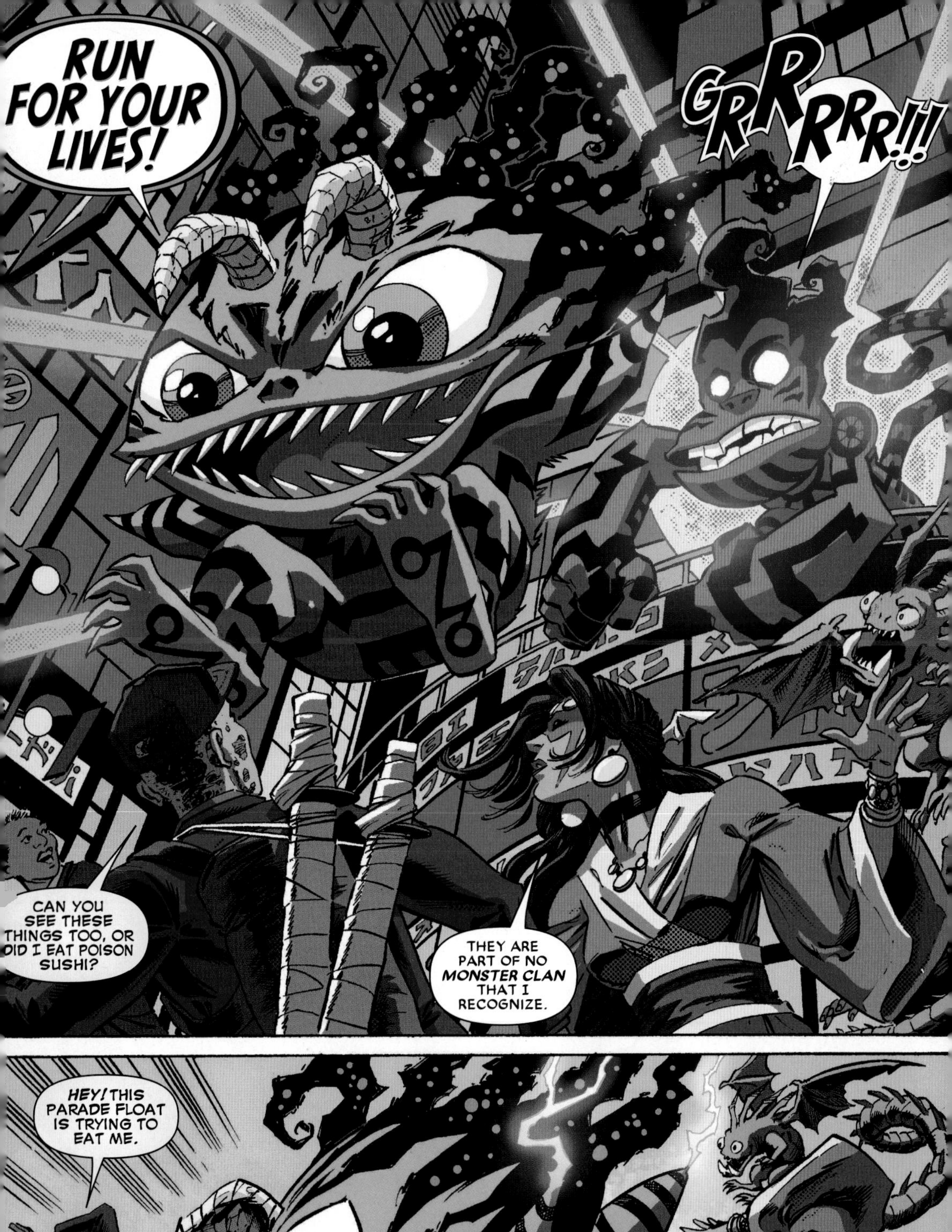
RUN FOR YOUR LIVES!
GRRRRR!!!
CAN YOU SEE THESE THINGS TOO, OR DID I EAT POISON SUSHI?
THEY ARE PART OF NO *MONSTER CLAN* THAT I RECOGNIZE.

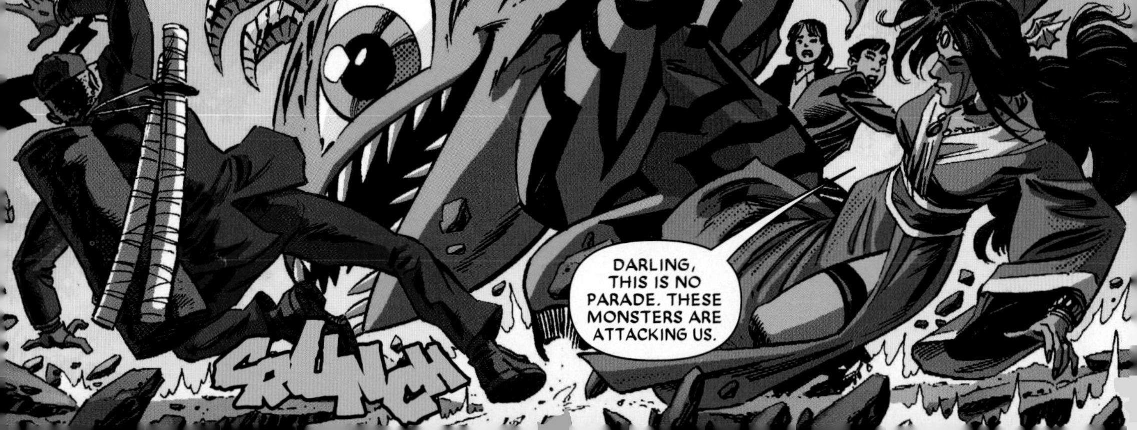
HEY! THIS PARADE FLOAT IS TRYING TO EAT ME.
DARLING, THIS IS NO PARADE. THESE MONSTERS ARE ATTACKING US.
SCRUNCH

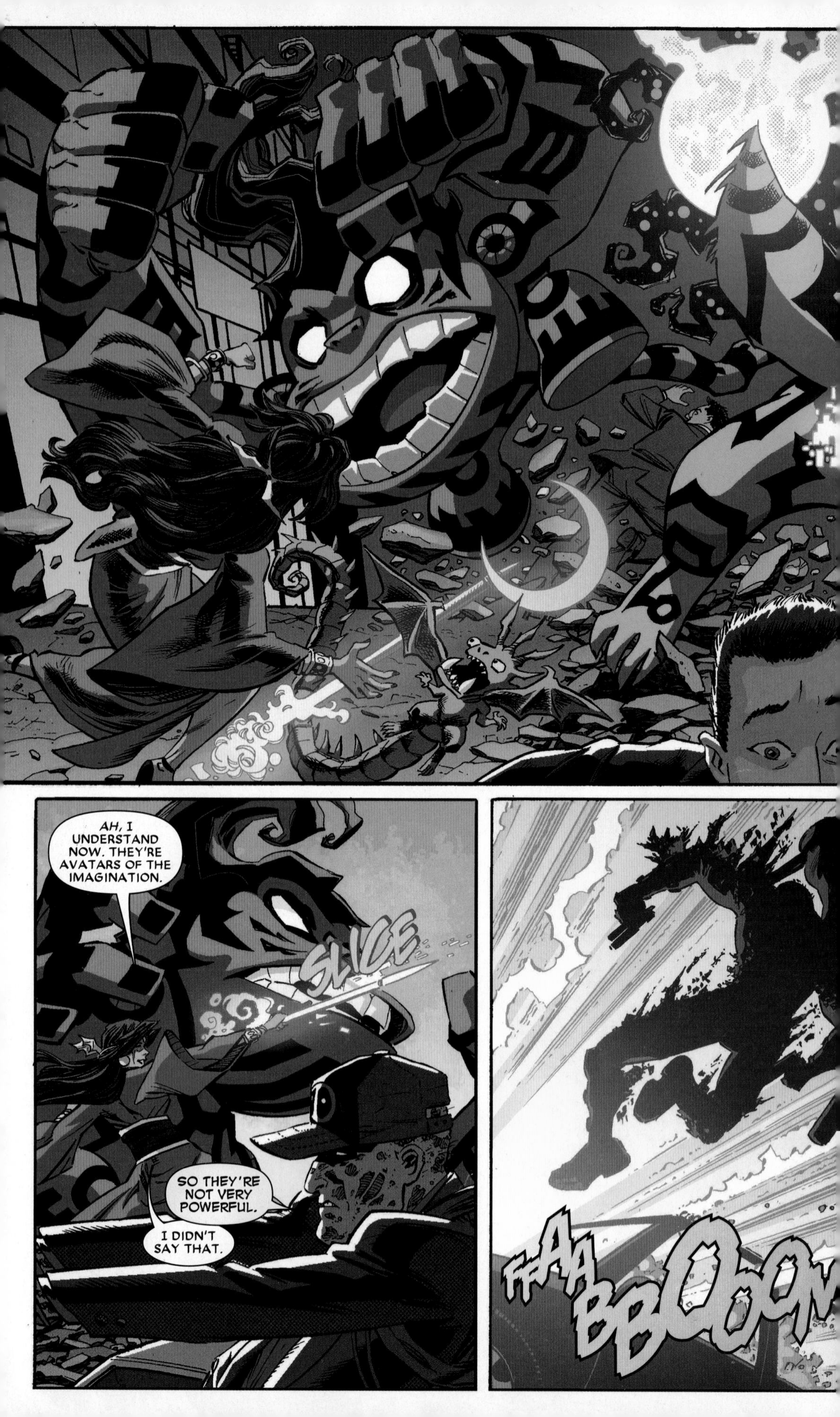
AH, I UNDERSTAND NOW. THEY'RE AVATARS OF THE IMAGINATION.
SLICE
SO THEY'RE NOT VERY POWERFUL.
I DIDN'T SAY THAT.
FFAABBOOOM

TAKE THAT, ADORABLE JAPANESE MONSTER!!!

WAIT, IF I STAB ONE OF THESE THINGS WHEN IT TRANSFORMS AM I GONNA HAVE A DEAD KID HANGING ON MY SWORD?

BLAM

SARK

BLAM BLAM

SARK SARK

ADIOS!

ᚦᚠᛉᛁ ᚼᛁᛈᚷᛝᚼ ᚠᛁᛁᛗᛦᚱᚱᛁᛉ ᚦᛁᛏ ᛏᚦᛅ ᛦᚾᛟᚷᛞᛁ ᛉᛁᚠᚱ

BUG, FOLLOW THAT BOY!!!

TRY ME, MONKEY MAN!

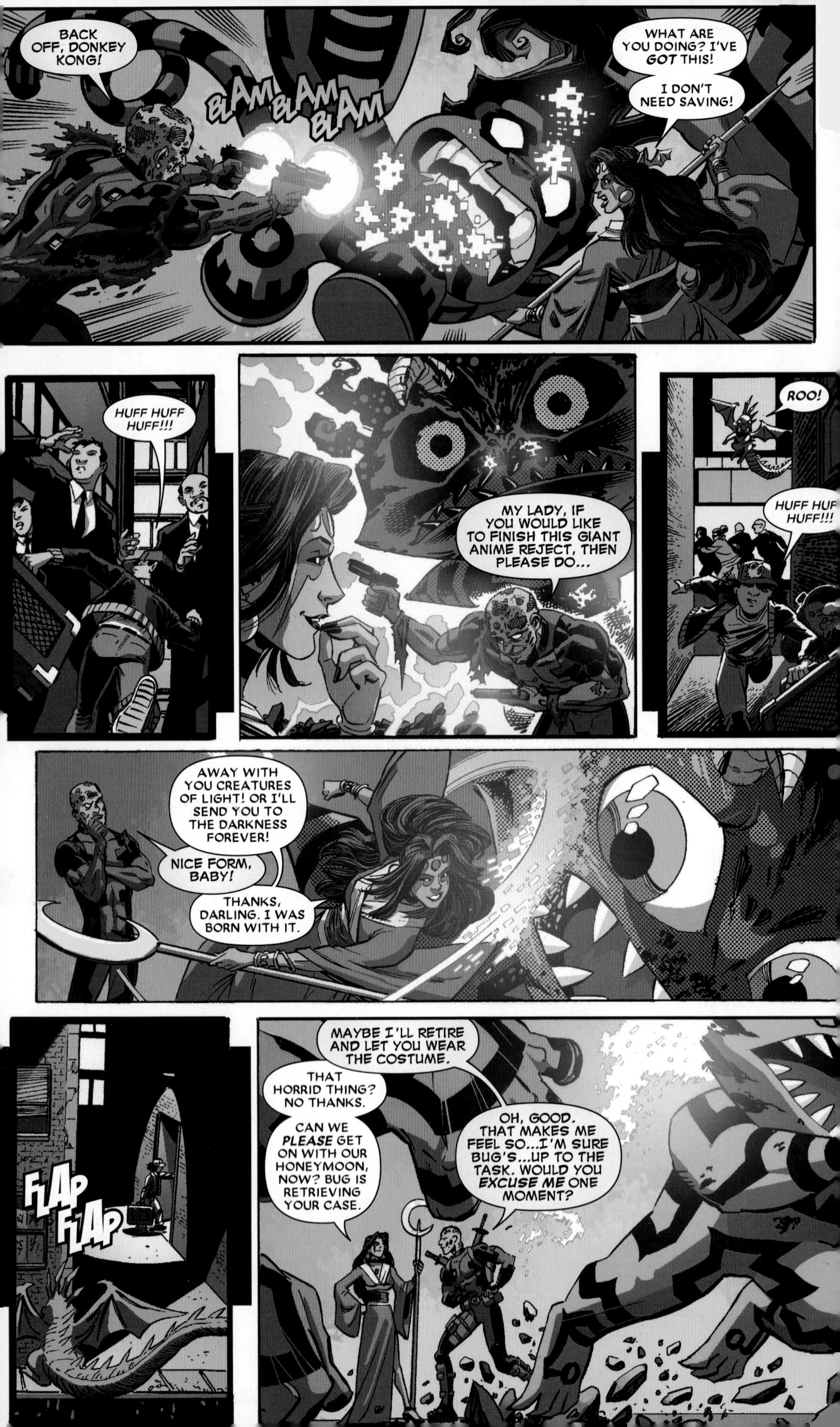
BACK OFF, DONKEY KONG!
BLAM BLAM BLAM
WHAT ARE YOU DOING? I'VE GOT THIS!
I DON'T NEED SAVING!
HUFF HUFF HUFF!!!
MY LADY, IF YOU WOULD LIKE TO FINISH THIS GIANT ANIME REJECT, THEN PLEASE DO...
ROO!
HUFF HUF HUFF!!!
AWAY WITH YOU CREATURES OF LIGHT! OR I'LL SEND YOU TO THE DARKNESS FOREVER!
NICE FORM, BABY!
THANKS, DARLING. I WAS BORN WITH IT.
FLAP FLAP
MAYBE I'LL RETIRE AND LET YOU WEAR THE COSTUME.
THAT HORRID THING? NO THANKS.
CAN WE PLEASE GET ON WITH OUR HONEYMOON, NOW? BUG IS RETRIEVING YOUR CASE.
OH, GOOD. THAT MAKES ME FEEL SO...I'M SURE BUG'S...UP TO THE TASK. WOULD YOU EXCUSE ME ONE MOMENT?

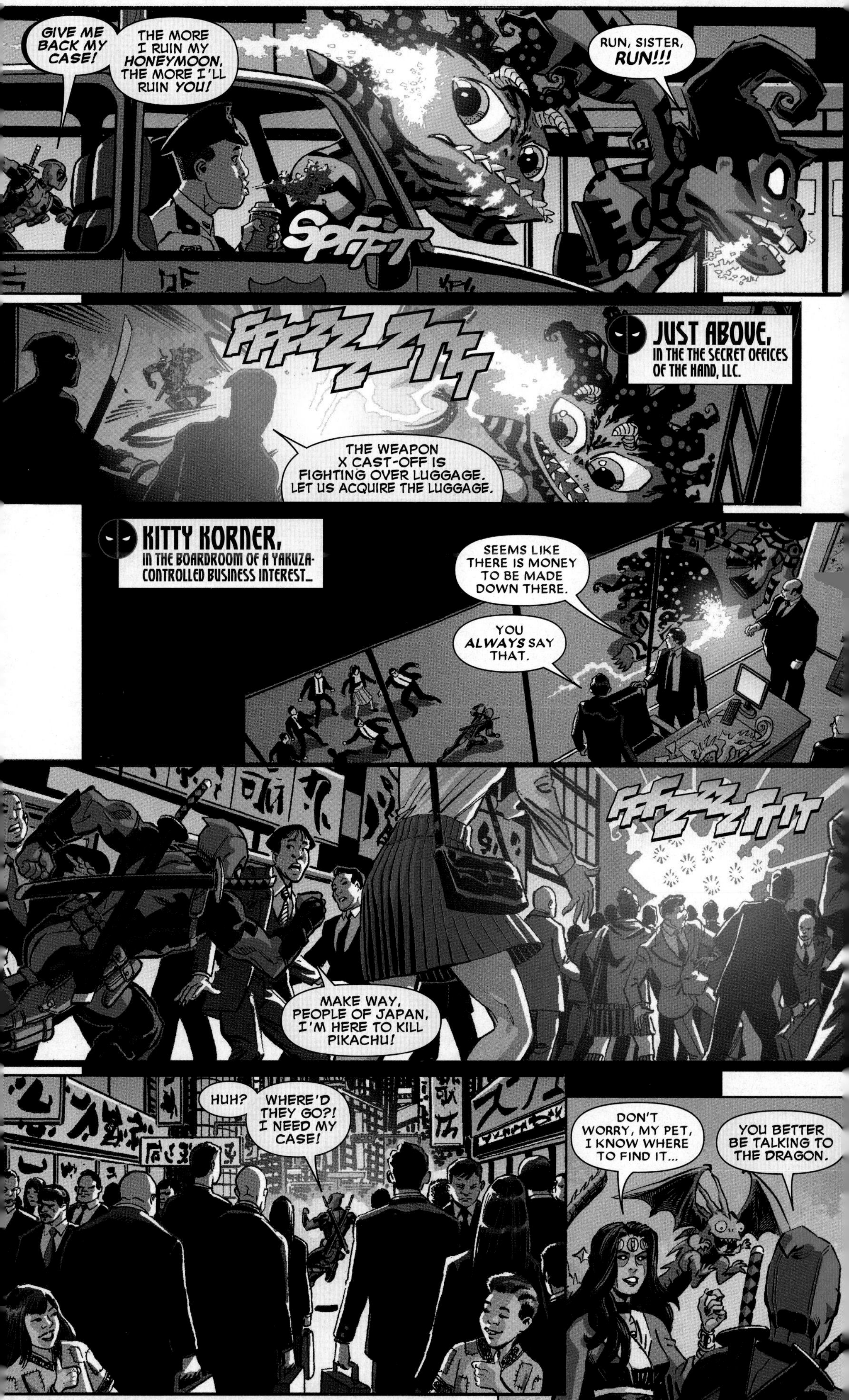

GIVE ME BACK MY CASE!
THE MORE I RUIN MY HONEYMOON, THE MORE I'LL RUIN YOU!
RUN, SISTER, RUN!!!
SPFFT
FFFZZZZZTTT
JUST ABOVE, IN THE THE SECRET OFFICES OF THE HAND, LLC.
THE WEAPON X CAST-OFF IS FIGHTING OVER LUGGAGE. LET US ACQUIRE THE LUGGAGE.
KITTY KORNER, IN THE BOARDROOM OF A YAKUZA-CONTROLLED BUSINESS INTEREST...
SEEMS LIKE THERE IS MONEY TO BE MADE DOWN THERE.
YOU ALWAYS SAY THAT.
FFFZZZZTTTT
MAKE WAY, PEOPLE OF JAPAN, I'M HERE TO KILL PIKACHU!
HUH?
WHERE'D THEY GO?! I NEED MY CASE!
DON'T WORRY, MY PET, I KNOW WHERE TO FIND IT...
YOU BETTER BE TALKING TO THE DRAGON.

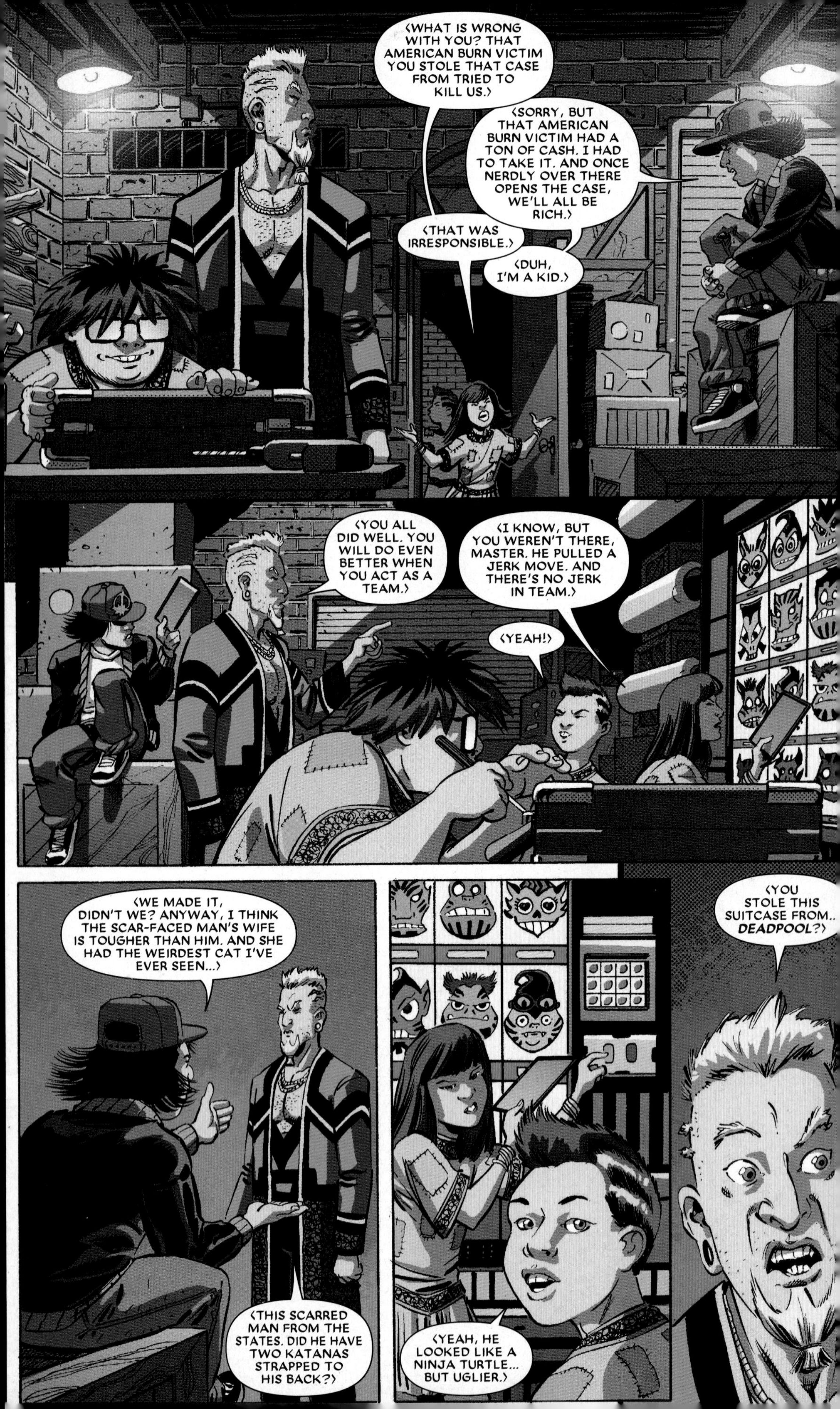

<WHAT IS WRONG WITH YOU? THAT AMERICAN BURN VICTIM YOU STOLE THAT CASE FROM TRIED TO KILL US.>
<SORRY, BUT THAT AMERICAN BURN VICTIM HAD A TON OF CASH. I HAD TO TAKE IT. AND ONCE NERDLY OVER THERE OPENS THE CASE, WE'LL ALL BE RICH.>
<THAT WAS IRRESPONSIBLE.>
<DUH, I'M A KID.>
<YOU ALL DID WELL. YOU WILL DO EVEN BETTER WHEN YOU ACT AS A TEAM.>
<I KNOW, BUT YOU WEREN'T THERE, MASTER. HE PULLED A JERK MOVE. AND THERE'S NO JERK IN TEAM.>
<YEAH!>
<WE MADE IT, DIDN'T WE? ANYWAY, I THINK THE SCAR-FACED MAN'S WIFE IS TOUGHER THAN HIM. AND SHE HAD THE WEIRDEST CAT I'VE EVER SEEN...>
<THIS SCARRED MAN FROM THE STATES. DID HE HAVE TWO KATANAS STRAPPED TO HIS BACK?>
<YEAH, HE LOOKED LIKE A NINJA TURTLE... BUT UGLIER.>
<YOU STOLE THIS SUITCASE FROM... DEADPOOL?>

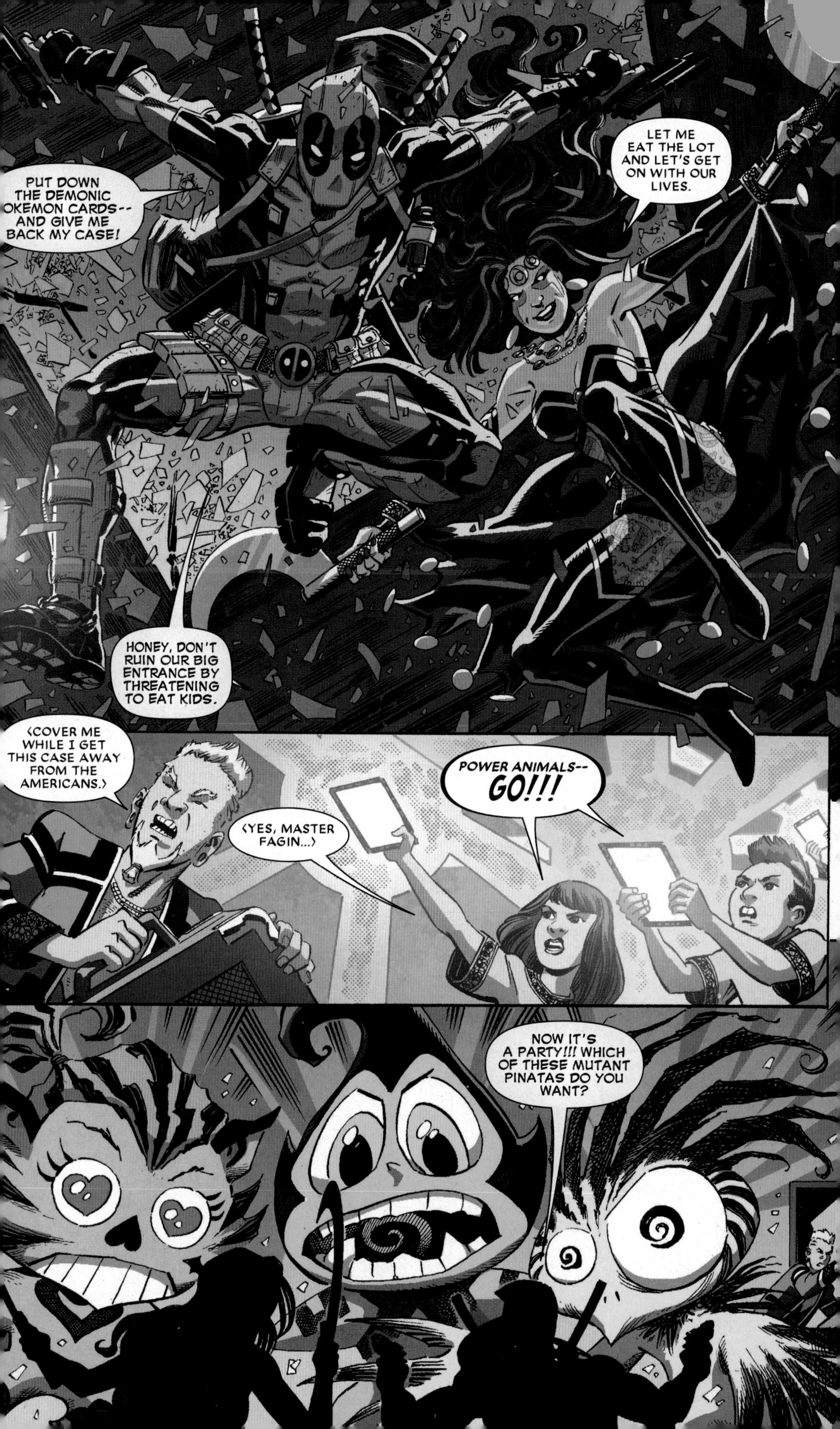
PUT DOWN THE DEMONIC OKEMON CARDS-- AND GIVE ME BACK MY CASE!
LET ME EAT THE LOT AND LET'S GET ON WITH OUR LIVES.
HONEY, DON'T RUIN OUR BIG ENTRANCE BY THREATENING TO EAT KIDS.
‹COVER ME WHILE I GET THIS CASE AWAY FROM THE AMERICANS.›
‹YES, MASTER FAGIN...›
POWER ANIMALS-- GO!!!
NOW IT'S A PARTY!!! WHICH OF THESE MUTANT PINATAS DO YOU WANT?

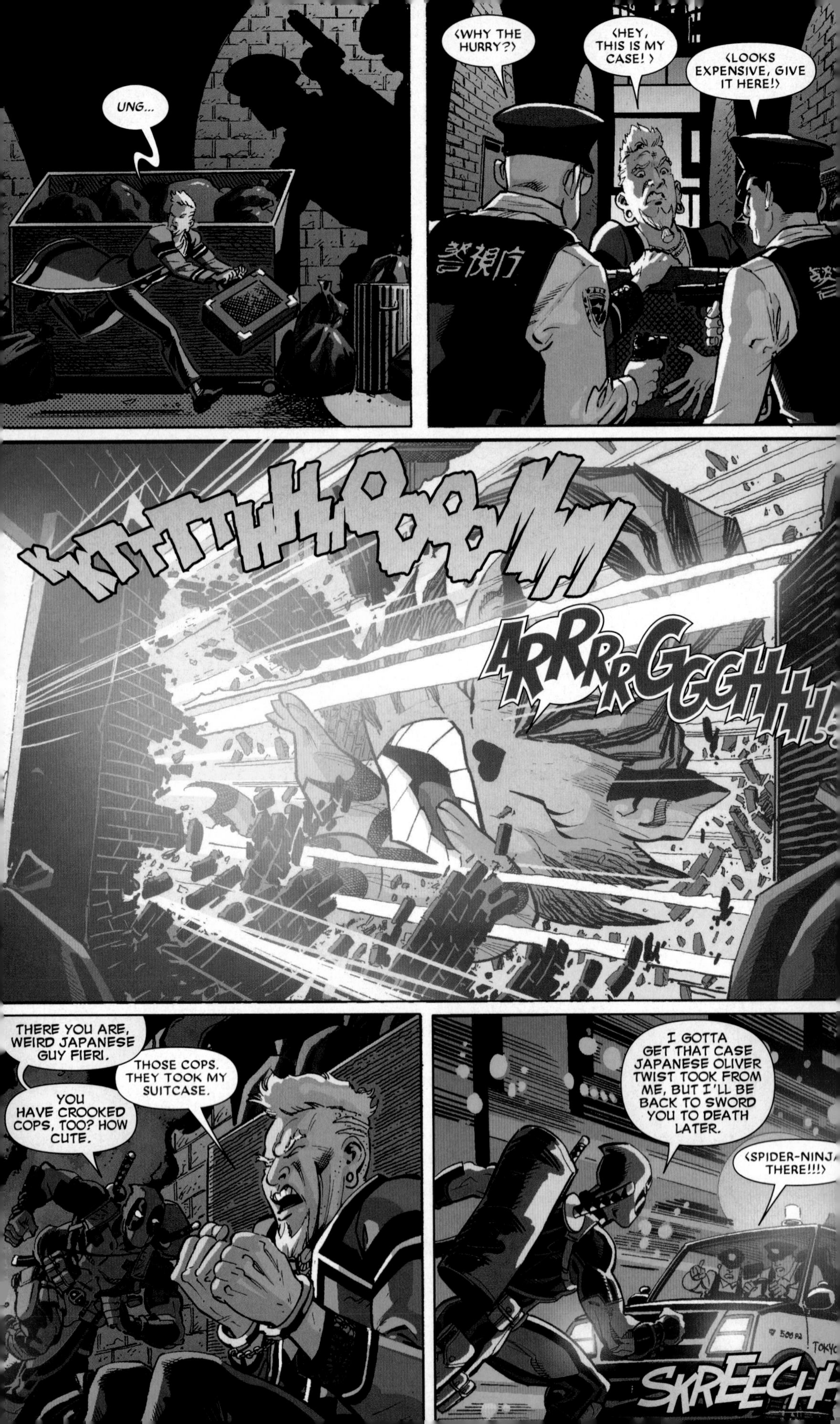
UNG...
‹WHY THE HURRY?›
‹HEY, THIS IS MY CASE! ›
‹LOOKS EXPENSIVE, GIVE IT HERE!›
KTTTTTHHHOOOOMM
ARRRRGGGHHH!
THERE YOU ARE, WEIRD JAPANESE GUY FIERI.
YOU HAVE CROOKED COPS, TOO? HOW CUTE.
THOSE COPS. THEY TOOK MY SUITCASE.
I GOTTA GET THAT CASE JAPANESE OLIVER TWIST TOOK FROM ME, BUT I'LL BE BACK TO SWORD YOU TO DEATH LATER.
‹SPIDER-NINJ THERE!!!›
SKREECH

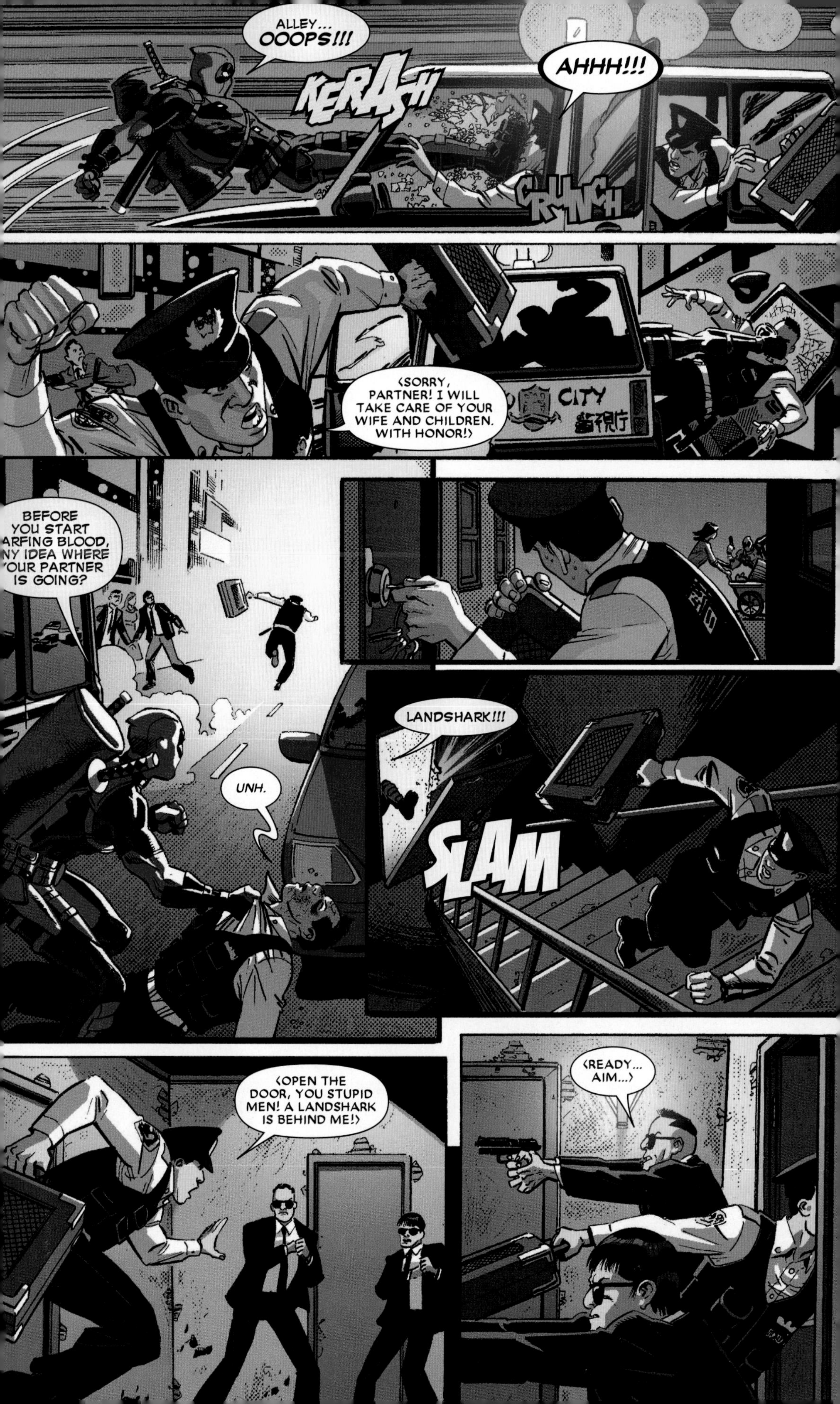

ALLEY... OOOPS!!!
KERASH
AHHH!!!
CRUNCH
‹SORRY, PARTNER! I WILL TAKE CARE OF YOUR WIFE AND CHILDREN. WITH HONOR!›
CITY
BEFORE YOU START ARFING BLOOD, NY IDEA WHERE YOUR PARTNER IS GOING?
LANDSHARK!!!
UNH.
SLAM
‹OPEN THE DOOR, YOU STUPID MEN! A LANDSHARK IS BEHIND ME!›
‹READY... AIM...›

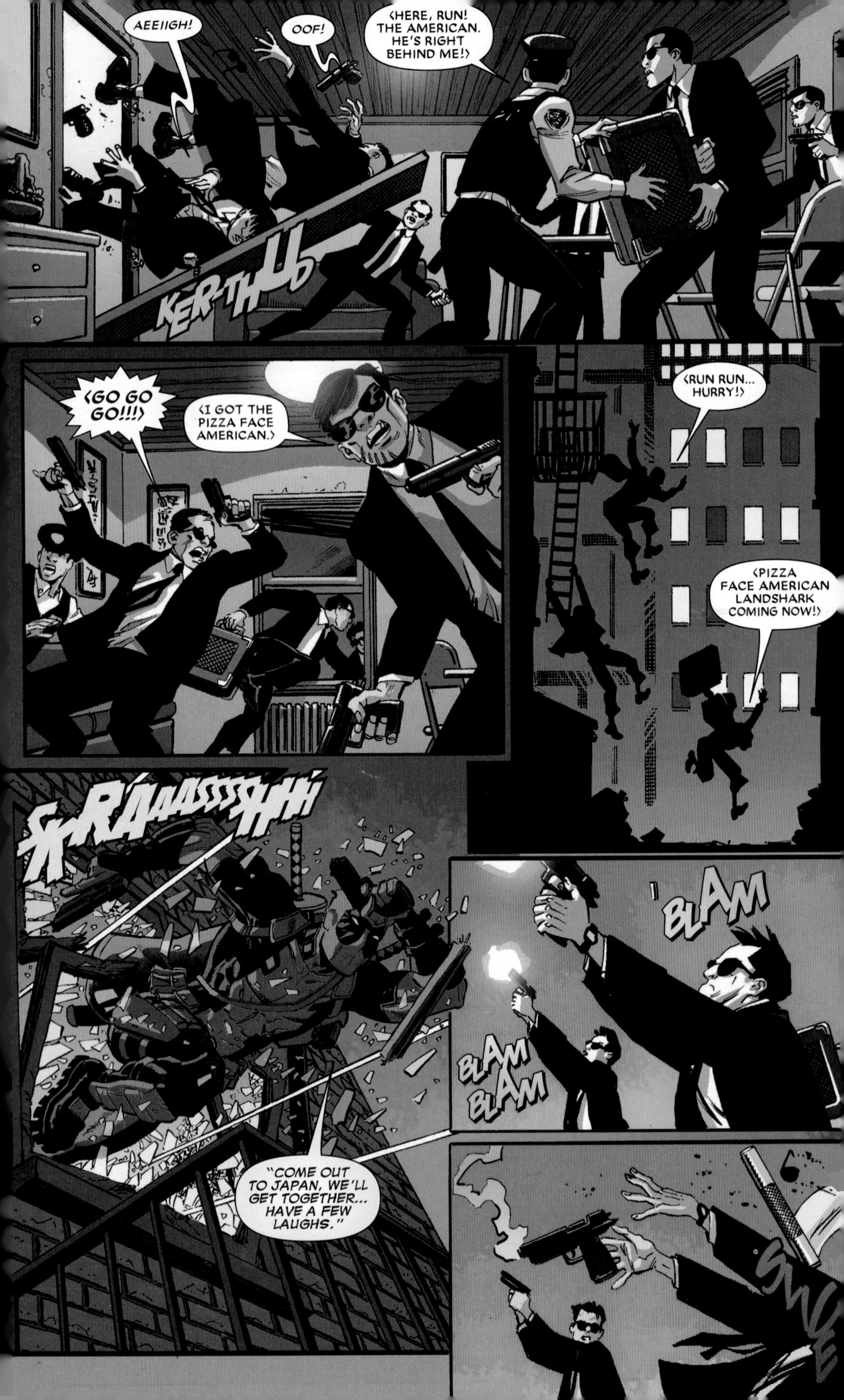
AEEIIGH!
OOF!
‹HERE, RUN! THE AMERICAN. HE'S RIGHT BEHIND ME!›
KERTHUD
‹GO GO GO!!!›
‹I GOT THE PIZZA FACE AMERICAN.›
‹RUN RUN... HURRY!›
‹PIZZA FACE AMERICAN LANDSHARK COMING NOW!›
SKRAAASSSHHH
"COME OUT TO JAPAN, WE'LL GET TOGETHER... HAVE A FEW LAUGHS."
BLAM
BLAM BLAM

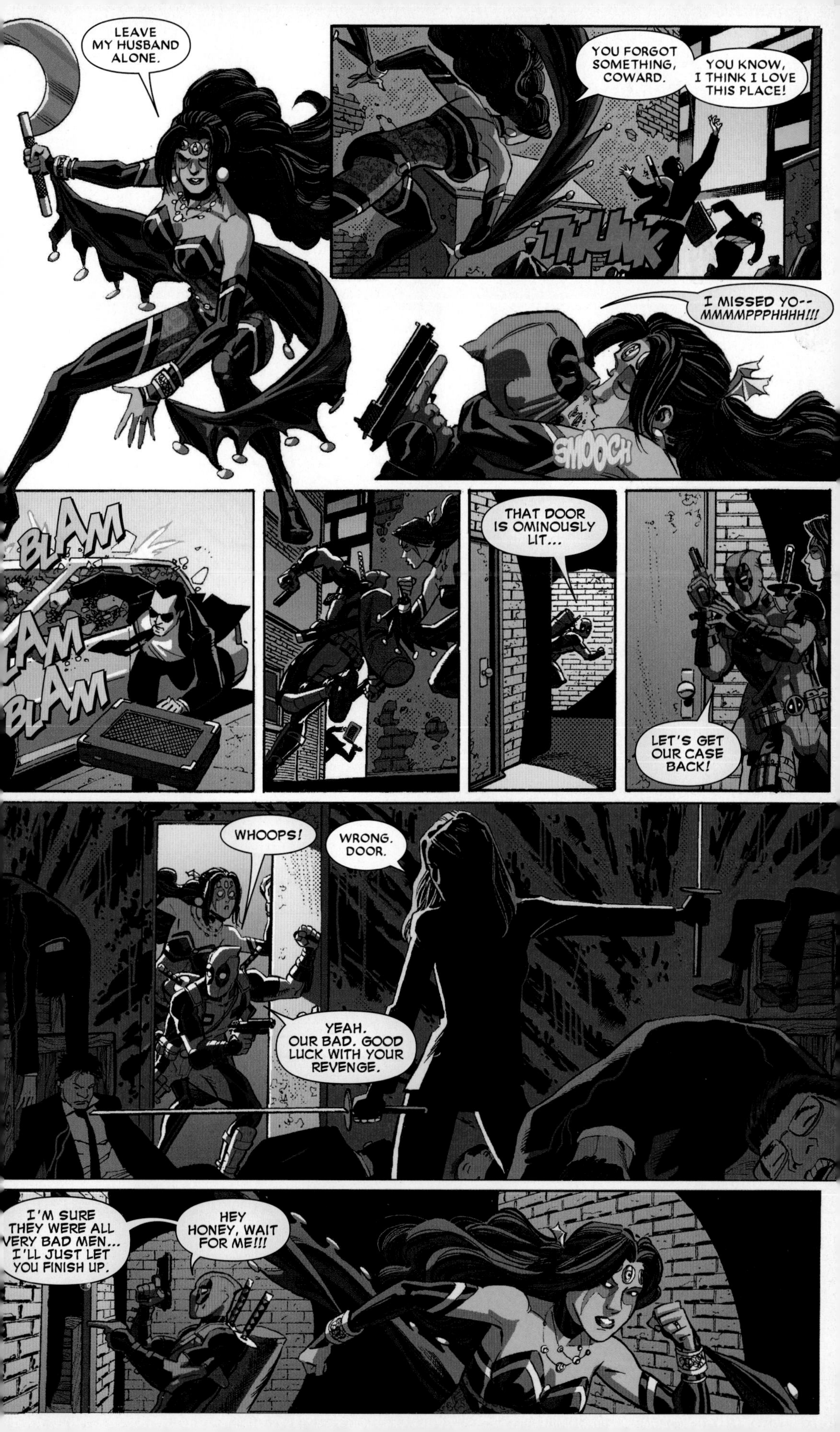
LEAVE MY HUSBAND ALONE.
YOU FORGOT SOMETHING, COWARD.
YOU KNOW, I THINK I LOVE THIS PLACE!
THUNK
I MISSED YO-- MMMMPPPHHHH!!!
SMOOCH
BLAM
BLAM
BLAM
THAT DOOR IS OMINOUSLY LIT...
LET'S GET OUR CASE BACK!
WHOOPS!
WRONG. DOOR.
YEAH. OUR BAD. GOOD LUCK WITH YOUR REVENGE.
I'M SURE THEY WERE ALL VERY BAD MEN... I'LL JUST LET YOU FINISH UP.
HEY HONEY, WAIT FOR ME!!!

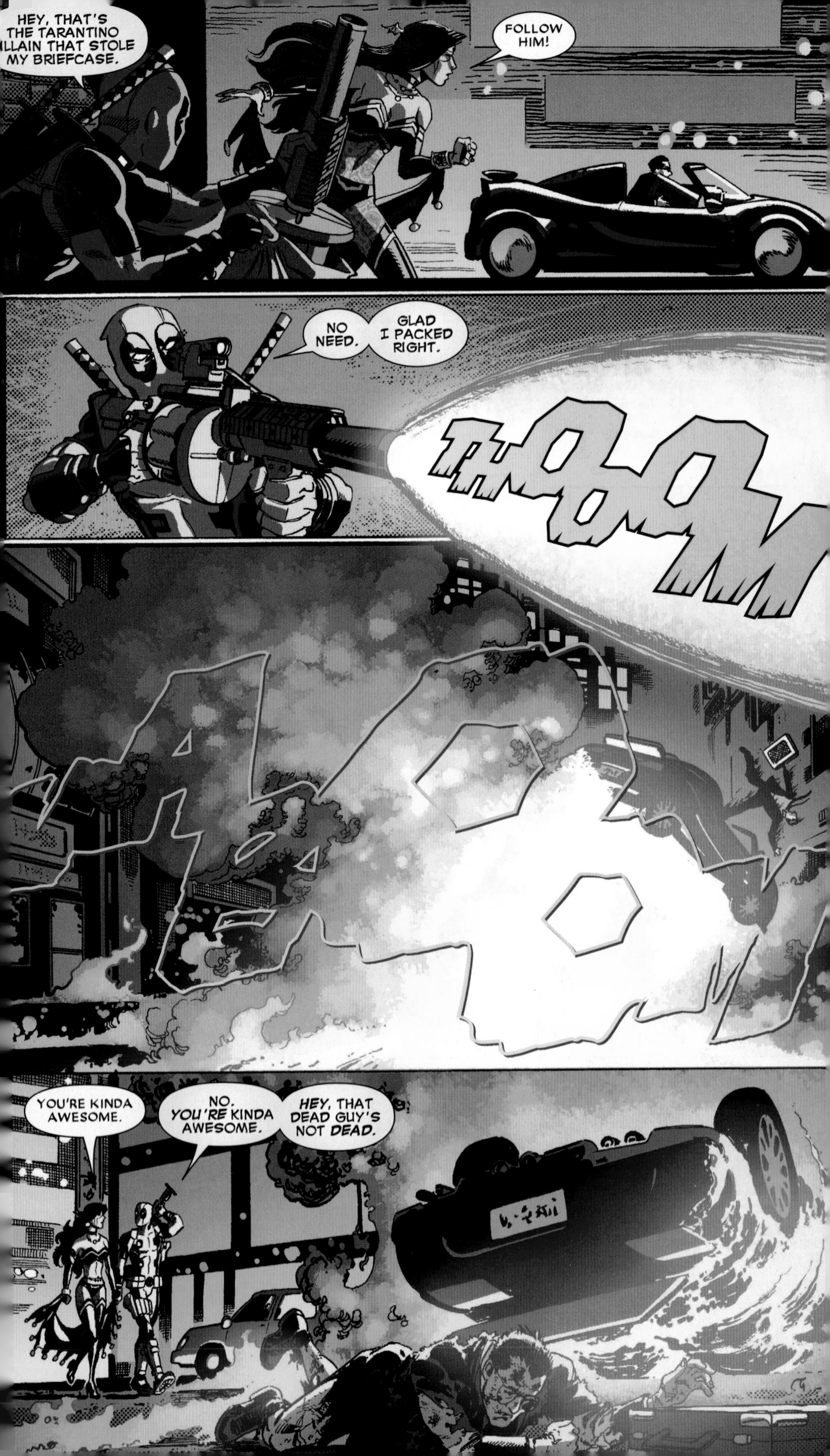
HEY, THAT'S THE TARANTINO ILLAIN THAT STOLE MY BRIEFCASE.
FOLLOW HIM!
NO NEED.
GLAD I PACKED RIGHT.
THOOM
YOU'RE KINDA AWESOME.
NO. *YOU'RE* KINDA AWESOME.
HEY, THAT DEAD GUY'S NOT *DEAD*.

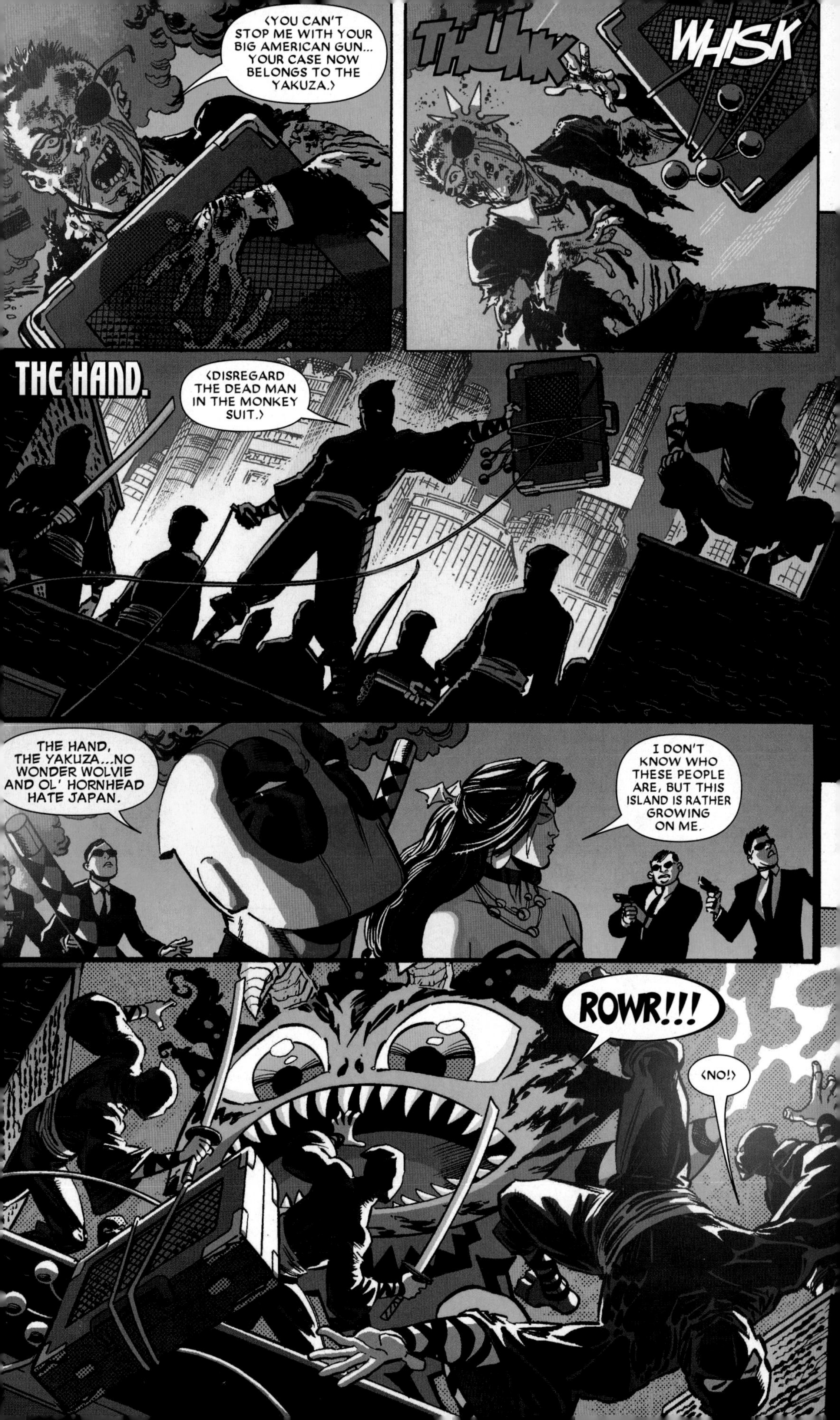
‹YOU CAN'T STOP ME WITH YOUR BIG AMERICAN GUN... YOUR CASE NOW BELONGS TO THE YAKUZA.›
THUNK
WHISK
THE HAND.
‹DISREGARD THE DEAD MAN IN THE MONKEY SUIT.›
THE HAND, THE YAKUZA...NO WONDER WOLVIE AND OL' HORNHEAD HATE JAPAN.
I DON'T KNOW WHO THESE PEOPLE ARE, BUT THIS ISLAND IS RATHER GROWING ON ME.
ROWR!!!
‹NO!›

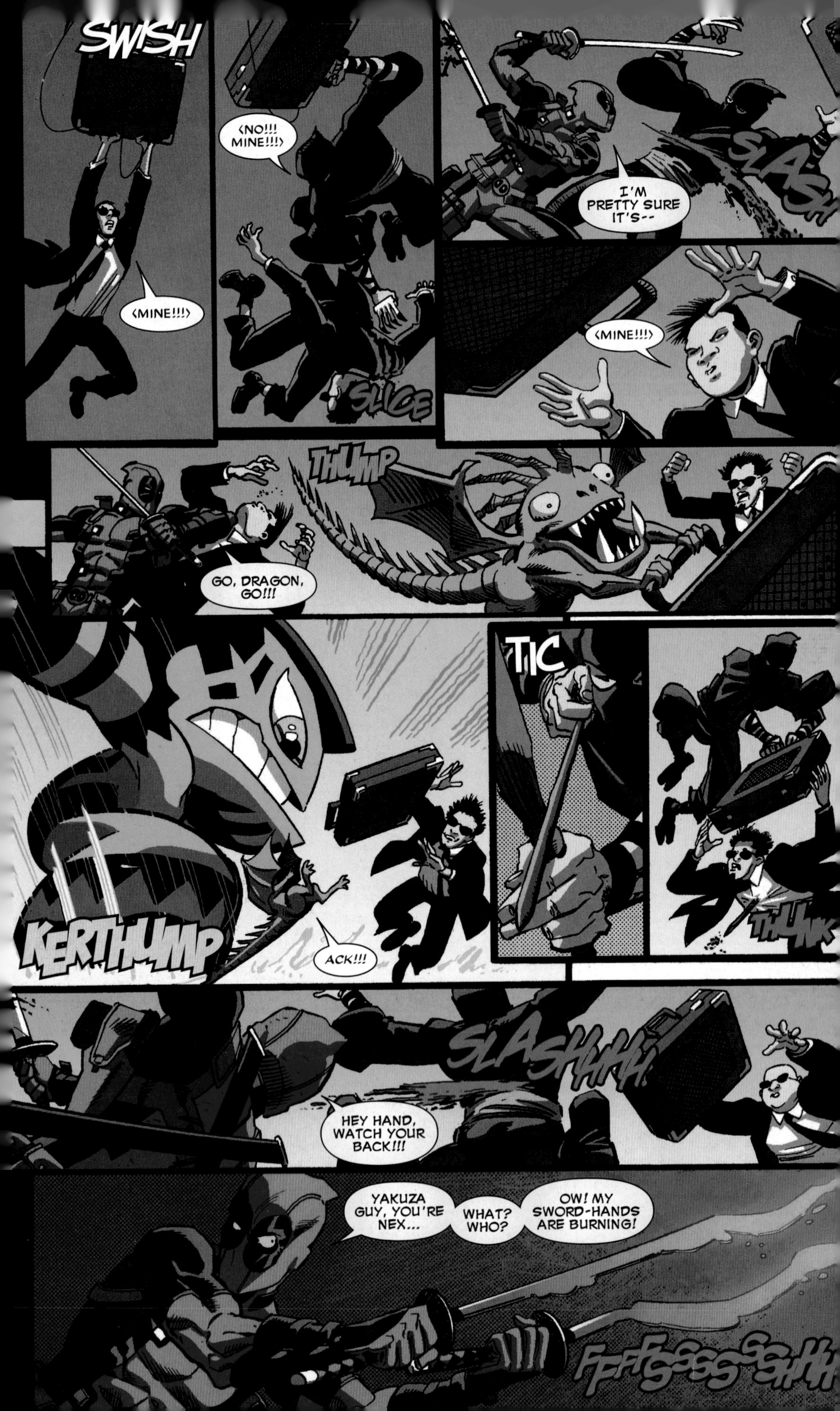
SWISH
‹MINE!!!›
‹NO!!! MINE!!!›
SLICE
I'M PRETTY SURE IT'S--
SLASH
‹MINE!!!›
THUMP
GO, DRAGON, GO!!!
KERTHUMP
ACK!!!
TIC
THUNK
SLASHHH
HEY HAND, WATCH YOUR BACK!!!
YAKUZA GUY, YOU'RE NEX...
WHAT? WHO?
OW! MY SWORD-HANDS ARE BURNING!
FFFSSSSSHHH

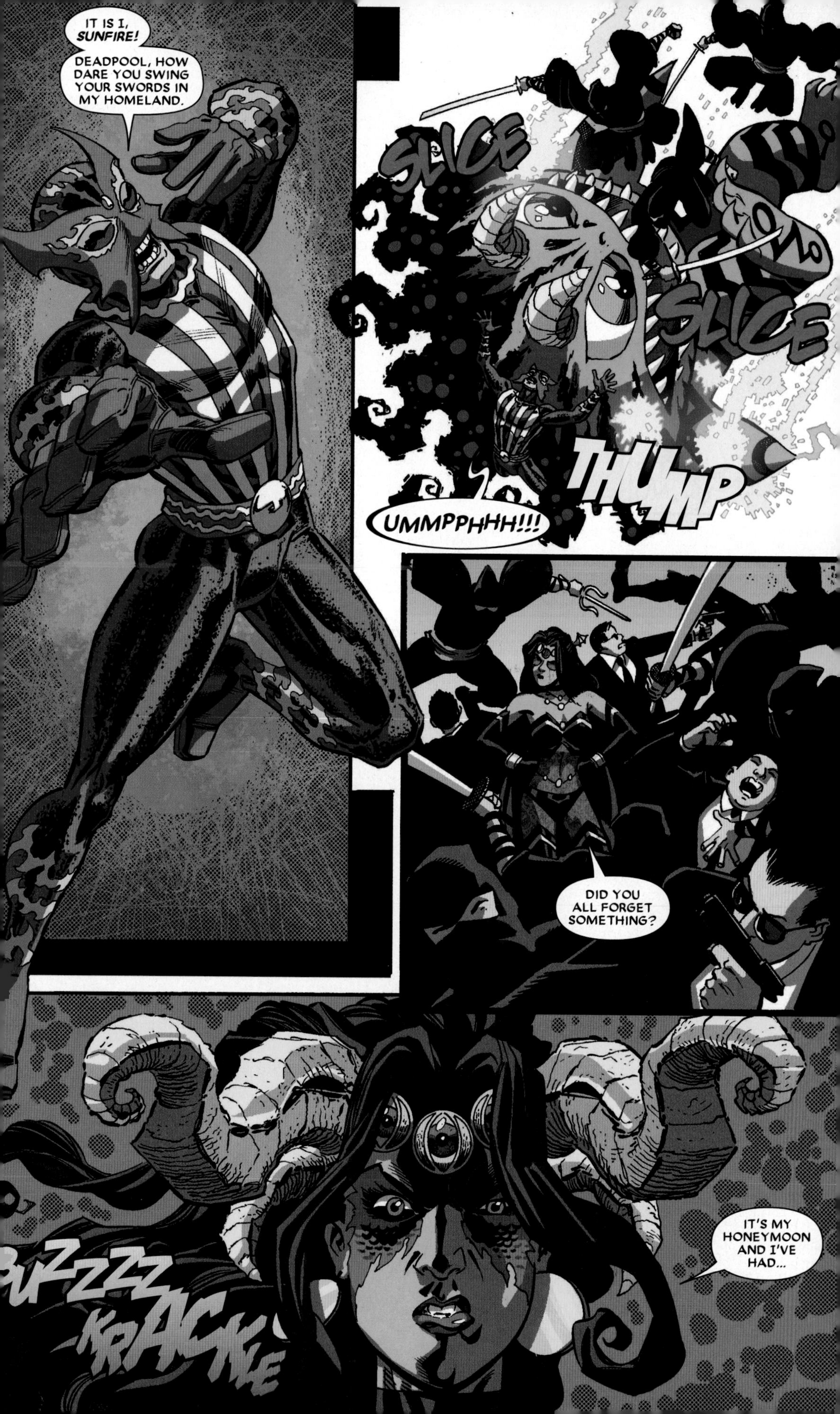
IT IS I, *SUNFIRE!*
DEADPOOL, HOW DARE YOU SWING YOUR SWORDS IN MY HOMELAND.
SLICE
SLICE
THUMP
UMMPPHHH!!!
DID YOU ALL FORGET SOMETHING?
IT'S MY HONEYMOON AND I'VE HAD...
BUZZZZ
KRACKLE

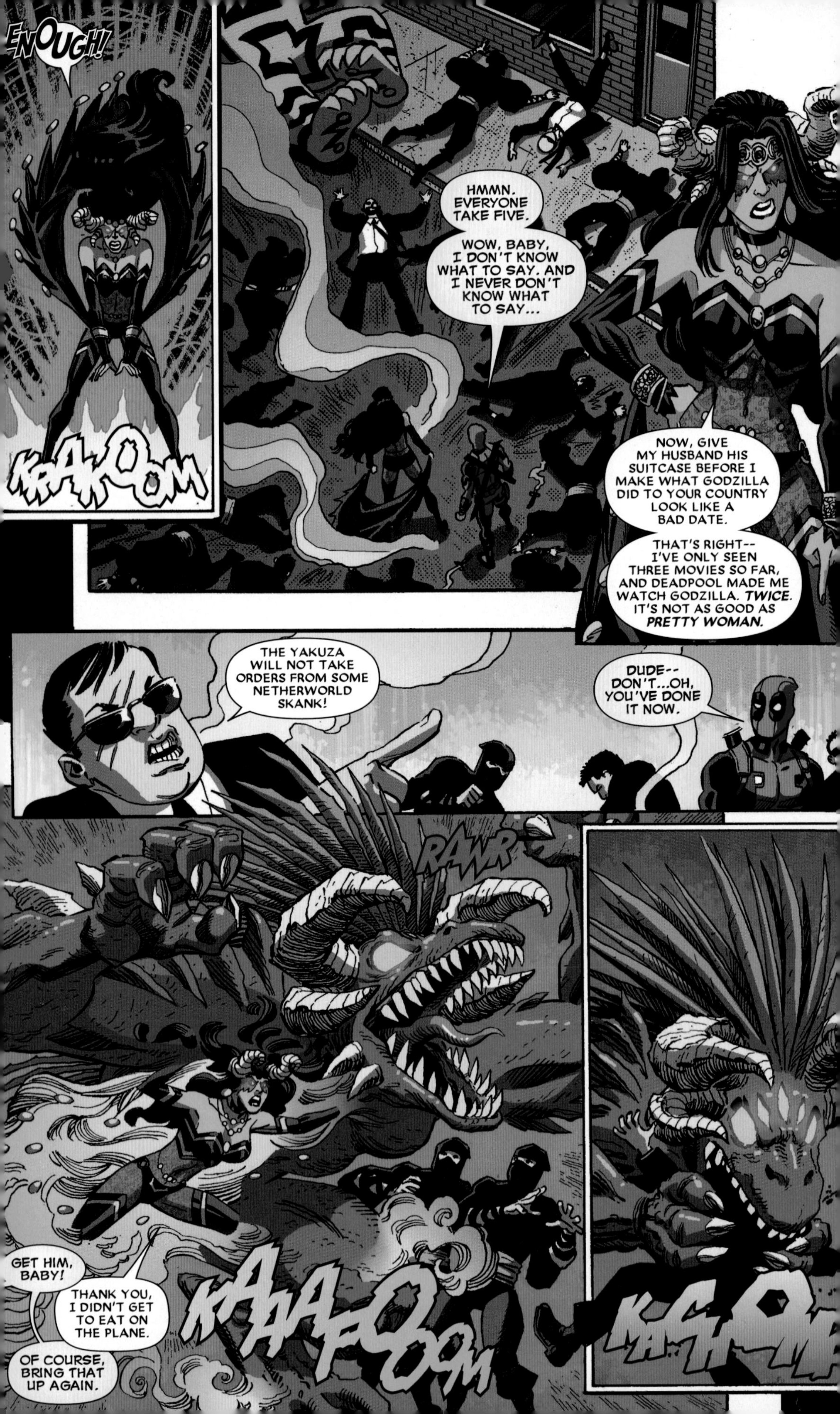
ENOUGH!
KRAKOOM
HMMN. EVERYONE TAKE FIVE.
WOW, BABY, I DON'T KNOW WHAT TO SAY. AND I NEVER DON'T KNOW WHAT TO SAY...
NOW, GIVE MY HUSBAND HIS SUITCASE BEFORE I MAKE WHAT GODZILLA DID TO YOUR COUNTRY LOOK LIKE A BAD DATE.
THAT'S RIGHT-- I'VE ONLY SEEN THREE MOVIES SO FAR, AND DEADPOOL MADE ME WATCH GODZILLA. *TWICE.* IT'S NOT AS GOOD AS *PRETTY WOMAN.*
THE YAKUZA WILL NOT TAKE ORDERS FROM SOME NETHERWORLD SKANK!
DUDE-- DON'T...OH, YOU'VE DONE IT NOW.
RAWR
GET HIM, BABY!
THANK YOU, I DIDN'T GET TO EAT ON THE PLANE.
OF COURSE, BRING THAT UP AGAIN.
KAAFOOM
KACHOMP

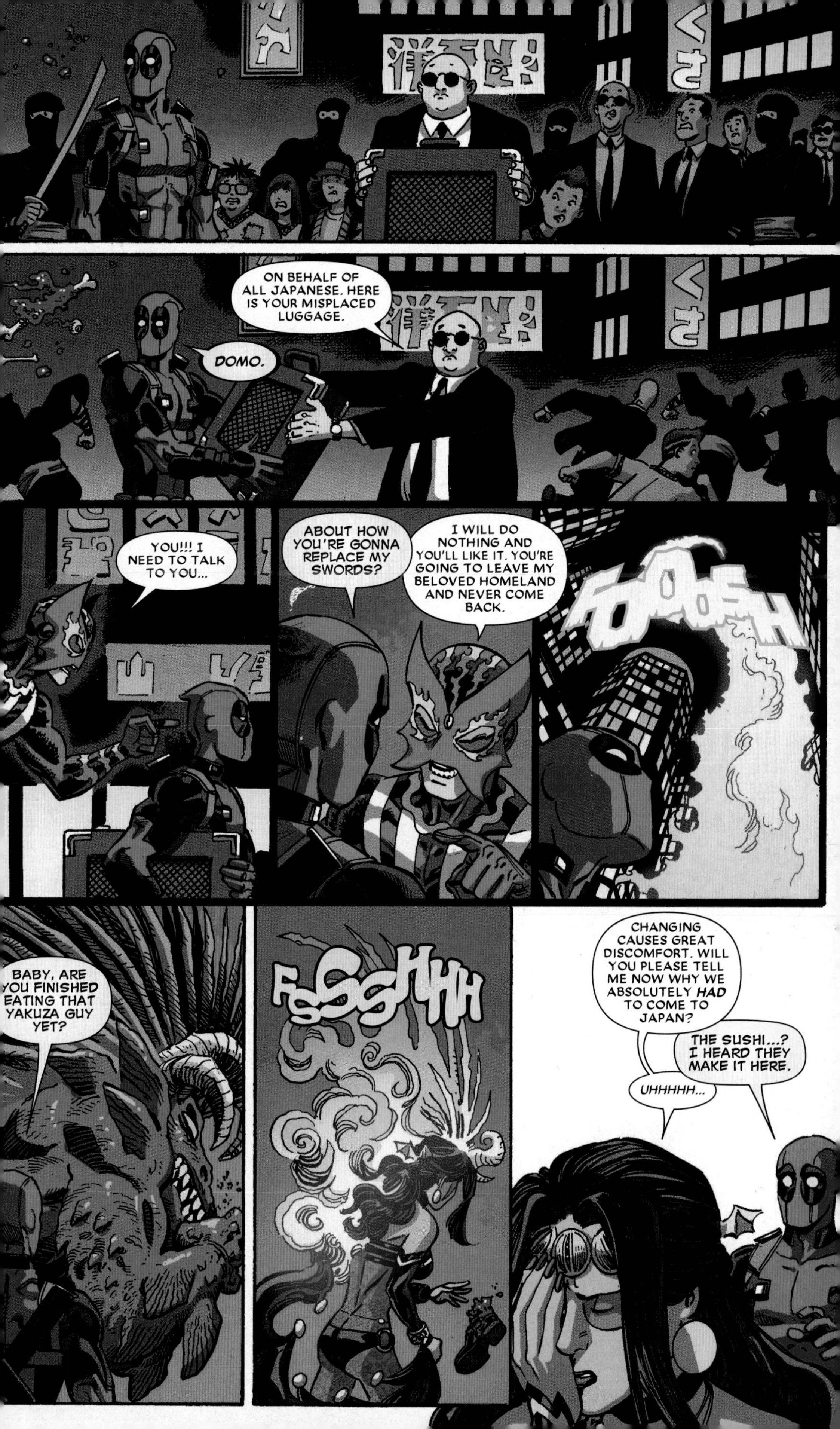
ON BEHALF OF ALL JAPANESE. HERE IS YOUR MISPLACED LUGGAGE.
DOMO.
YOU!!! I NEED TO TALK TO YOU...
ABOUT HOW YOU'RE GONNA REPLACE MY SWORDS?
I WILL DO NOTHING AND YOU'LL LIKE IT. YOU'RE GOING TO LEAVE MY BELOVED HOMELAND AND NEVER COME BACK.
FOOOOSH
BABY, ARE YOU FINISHED EATING THAT YAKUZA GUY YET?
FSSSHHH
CHANGING CAUSES GREAT DISCOMFORT. WILL YOU PLEASE TELL ME NOW WHY WE ABSOLUTELY HAD TO COME TO JAPAN?
UHHHHH...
THE SUSHI...? I HEARD THEY MAKE IT HERE.

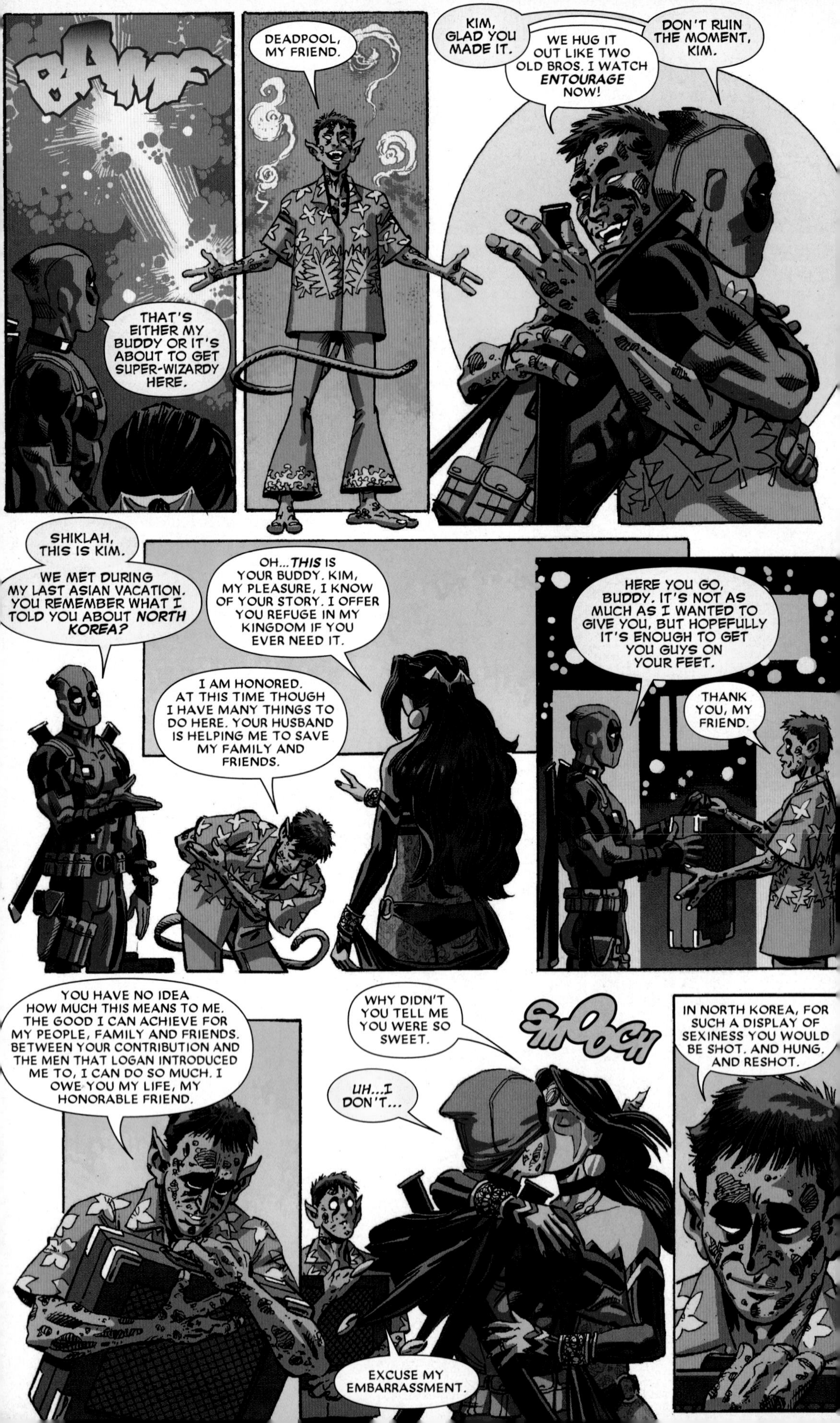
BAMF
THAT'S EITHER MY BUDDY OR IT'S ABOUT TO GET SUPER-WIZARDY HERE.
DEADPOOL, MY FRIEND.
KIM, GLAD YOU MADE IT.
WE HUG IT OUT LIKE TWO OLD BROS. I WATCH ENTOURAGE NOW!
DON'T RUIN THE MOMENT, KIM.
SHIKLAH, THIS IS KIM.
WE MET DURING MY LAST ASIAN VACATION. YOU REMEMBER WHAT I TOLD YOU ABOUT NORTH KOREA?
OH...THIS IS YOUR BUDDY. KIM, MY PLEASURE, I KNOW OF YOUR STORY. I OFFER YOU REFUGE IN MY KINGDOM IF YOU EVER NEED IT.
I AM HONORED. AT THIS TIME THOUGH I HAVE MANY THINGS TO DO HERE. YOUR HUSBAND IS HELPING ME TO SAVE MY FAMILY AND FRIENDS.
HERE YOU GO, BUDDY. IT'S NOT AS MUCH AS I WANTED TO GIVE YOU, BUT HOPEFULLY IT'S ENOUGH TO GET YOU GUYS ON YOUR FEET.
THANK YOU, MY FRIEND.
YOU HAVE NO IDEA HOW MUCH THIS MEANS TO ME. THE GOOD I CAN ACHIEVE FOR MY PEOPLE, FAMILY AND FRIENDS. BETWEEN YOUR CONTRIBUTION AND THE MEN THAT LOGAN INTRODUCED ME TO, I CAN DO SO MUCH. I OWE YOU MY LIFE, MY HONORABLE FRIEND.
WHY DIDN'T YOU TELL ME YOU WERE SO SWEET.
SMOOCH
UH...I DON'T...
EXCUSE MY EMBARRASSMENT.
IN NORTH KOREA, FOR SUCH A DISPLAY OF SEXINESS YOU WOULD BE SHOT. AND HUNG. AND RESHOT.

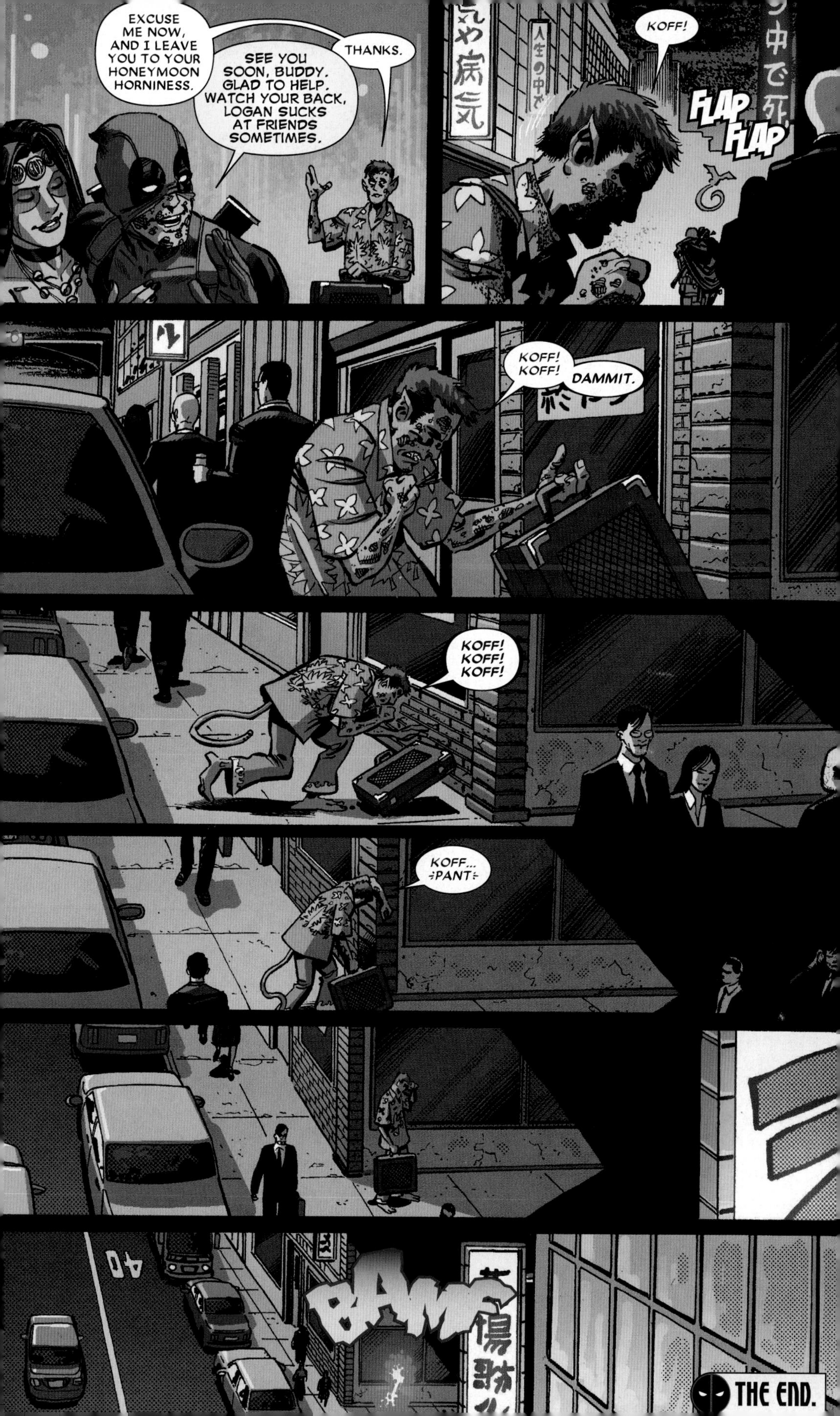
EXCUSE ME NOW, AND I LEAVE YOU TO YOUR HONEYMOON HORNINESS.
SEE YOU SOON, BUDDY. GLAD TO HELP. WATCH YOUR BACK, LOGAN SUCKS AT FRIENDS SOMETIMES.
THANKS.
KOFF!
FLAP FLAP
KOFF! KOFF!
DAMMIT.
KOFF! KOFF! KOFF!
KOFF... PANT
BAM
THE END.

**#26 VARIANT
BY HOWARD CHAYKIN &
EDGAR DELGADO**

**#26 CAPTAIN AMERICA
TEAM-UP VARIANT
BY MIKE PERKINS & ANDY TROY**

26

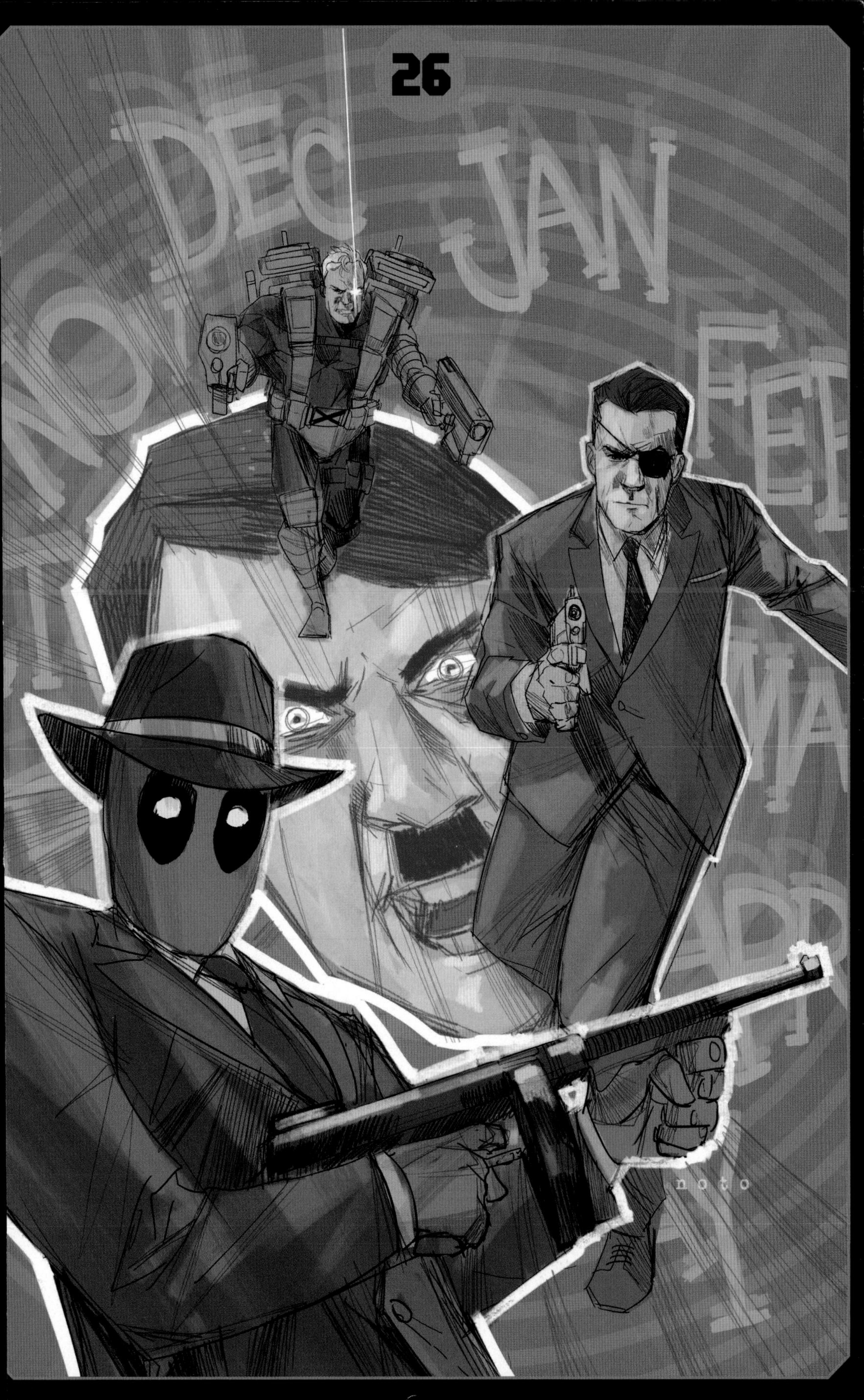
DEC
JAN
noto

DEATH COMES TO TINSELTOWN

Possibly the world's most skilled mercenary, definitely the world's most annoying, Wade Wilson was chosen for a top-secret government program that gave him a healing factor allowing him to heal from any wound. Now, Wade makes his way as a gun for hire, shooting his prey's faces off while talking his friends' ears off. Call him the Merc with the Mouth…call him the Regeneratin' Degenerate…call him…DEADPOOL.

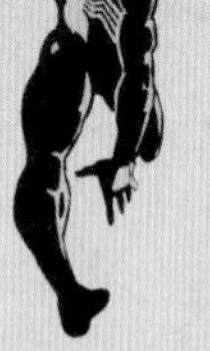

OK, this is a weird one.

Just when I thought we had completely run out of old inventory issues of Deadpool we could run, we stumbled upon this crazy gem.

It was intended to be an issue of SERGEANT FURY AND HIS HOWLING COMMANDOS. The notes from the editor at the time seem to suggest the two writers were stinking drunk when they came up with the idea for the issue, and in his opinion, it showed. He couldn't make heads or tails of the mess, fired the pair of them on the spot, and slipped the pages into a file marked "Last resort—run only in the direst of deadline crunches."

As you might have heard, we've got a pretty massive issue planned for issue 27. I don't want to spoil it for you…but suffice to say there are HUGE developments in Wade's life, in addition to there just being a MASSIVE amount of story jam-packed into the issue. It should come as no surprise to you that that means Gerry, Brian, and artist Mike Hawthorne have all fallen WAY behind. I think they got so caught up in celebrating what a great idea issue 27 was that they never got around to actually MAKING the epic, record breaking masterpiece.

I'd say that qualifies as the direst of deadline crunches.

Don't think of it as having a terrible, old, rejected story foisted-off on you…think of it as giving the creative team that little bit of extra time to REALLY knock your socks off next issue.

Be seeing you!

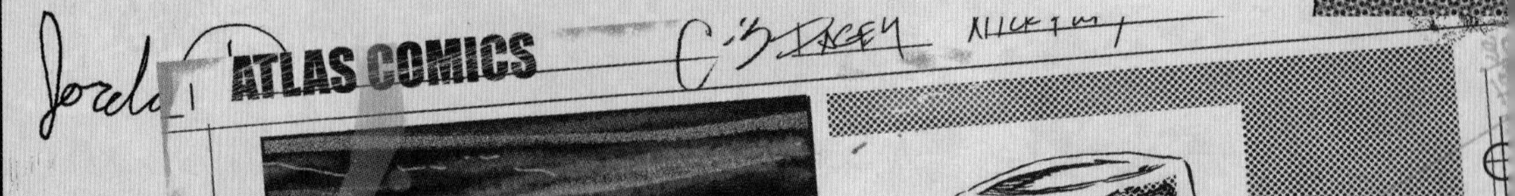
ATLAS COMICS

DEATH COMES TO TINSELTOWN (OR THE LAST HITLER)

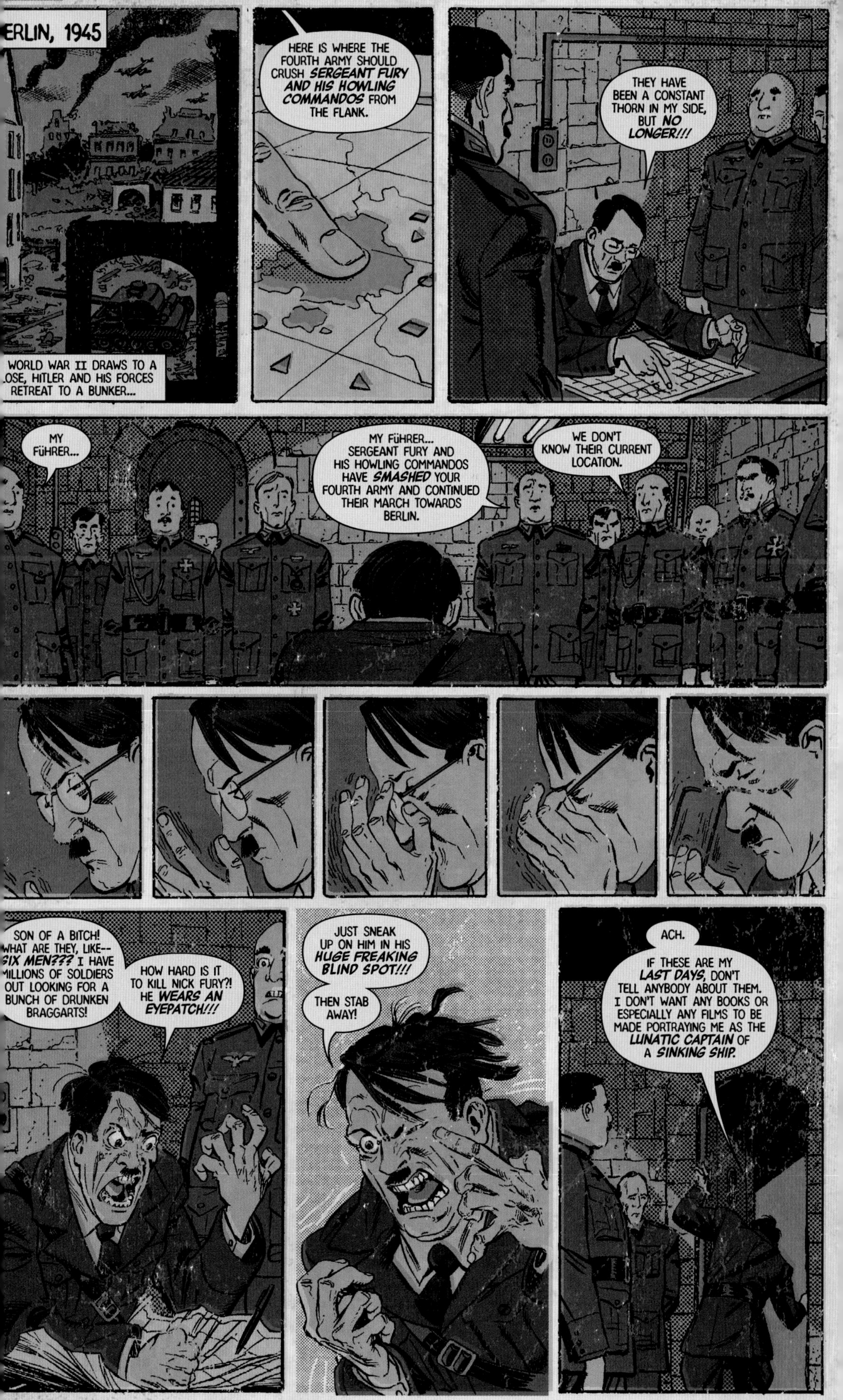
ERLIN, 1945
WORLD WAR II DRAWS TO A
LOSE, HITLER AND HIS FORCES
RETREAT TO A BUNKER...
HERE IS WHERE THE FOURTH ARMY SHOULD CRUSH SERGEANT FURY AND HIS HOWLING COMMANDOS FROM THE FLANK.
THEY HAVE BEEN A CONSTANT THORN IN MY SIDE, BUT NO LONGER!!!
MY FüHRER...
MY FüHRER... SERGEANT FURY AND HIS HOWLING COMMANDOS HAVE SMASHED YOUR FOURTH ARMY AND CONTINUED THEIR MARCH TOWARDS BERLIN.
WE DON'T KNOW THEIR CURRENT LOCATION.
SON OF A BITCH! WHAT ARE THEY, LIKE-- SIX MEN??? I HAVE MILLIONS OF SOLDIERS OUT LOOKING FOR A BUNCH OF DRUNKEN BRAGGARTS!
HOW HARD IS IT TO KILL NICK FURY?! HE WEARS AN EYEPATCH!!!
JUST SNEAK UP ON HIM IN HIS HUGE FREAKING BLIND SPOT!!!
THEN STAB AWAY!
ACH.
IF THESE ARE MY LAST DAYS, DON'T TELL ANYBODY ABOUT THEM. I DON'T WANT ANY BOOKS OR ESPECIALLY ANY FILMS TO BE MADE PORTRAYING ME AS THE LUNATIC CAPTAIN OF A SINKING SHIP.

BUT EVEN AS THE FÜHRER FURROWS INTO HIS FUROR OVER FURY...

ONE OF THEM IS EVEN CALLED "DUM DUM"--MY FINEST CANNOT DEFEAT A MAN NAMED "DUM DUM"?!

OH, DO I WISH DUM DUM WAS HERE FOR THIS. HE'D GIVE HITLER THE "WHAT FOR"!

BZWANG

GET A LOAD OF THIS GUY!

HITLER, HISTORY HAS JUDGED YOU!

--VAT IS ZIS?!

NOT ANOTHER TIME TRAVELER!

NEVER THOUGHT I'D SAY IT, BUT LOOK OUT, HITLER!

I MUST TAKE ONE LIFE TO SAVE MANY!

NOW DI-IIIIEEEEEEEEEEAAAH!

YOU CRAZY TIME TRAVELERS WILL NEVER KILL ADOLF HITLER!

UHN!!!

KRAK

GET HIM, HITLE

OH NO! I ONLY WANTED TO KILL HITLER, BUT NOW I'VE BEEN DEFEATED...

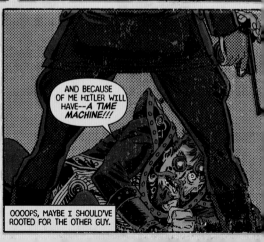

AND BECAUSE OF ME HITLER WILL HAVE--A TIME MACHINE!!!

OOOOPS, MAYBE I SHOULD'VE ROOTED FOR THE OTHER GUY.

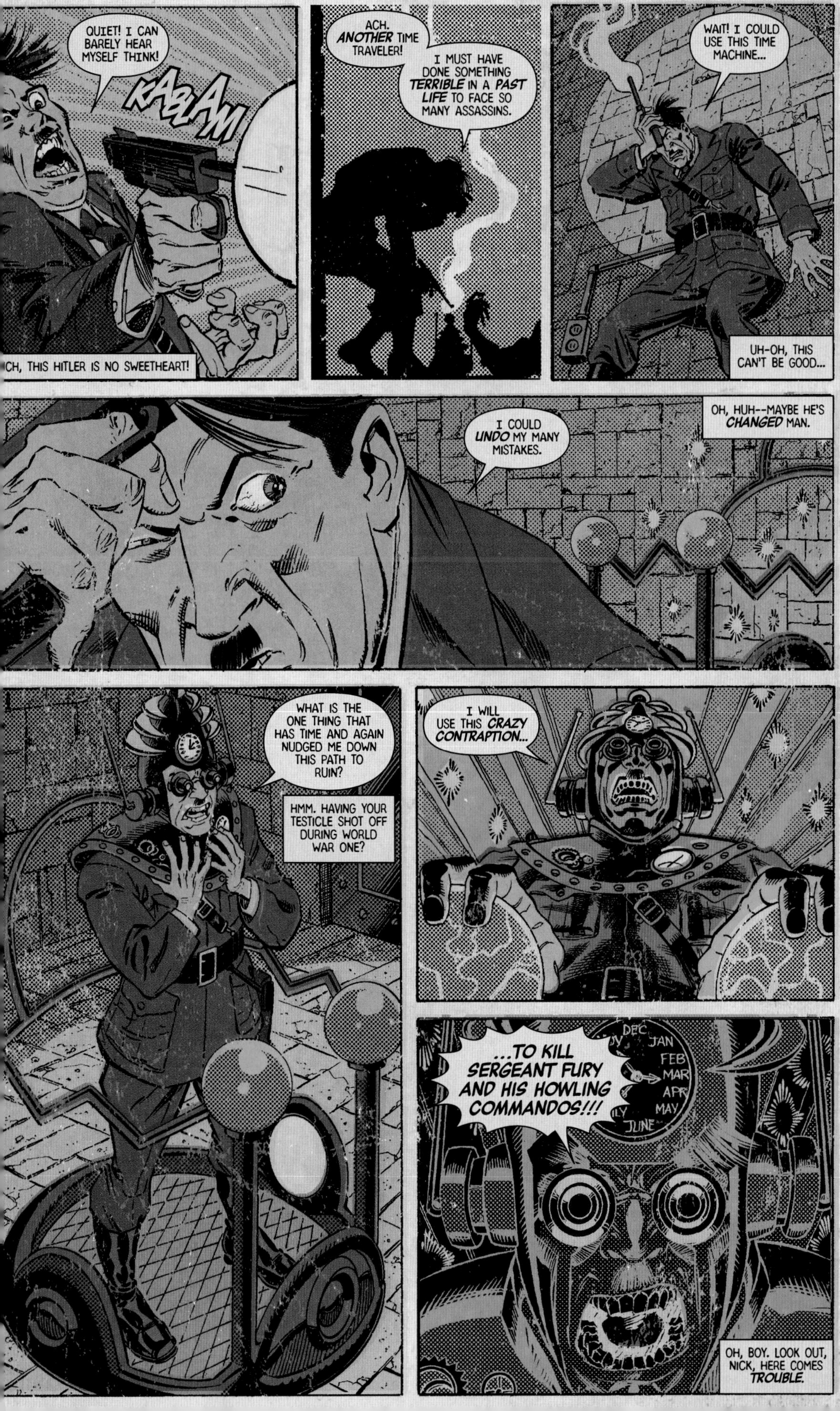
QUIET! I CAN BARELY HEAR MYSELF THINK!
KABLAM
CH, THIS HITLER IS NO SWEETHEART!
ACH. ANOTHER TIME TRAVELER!
I MUST HAVE DONE SOMETHING TERRIBLE IN A PAST LIFE TO FACE SO MANY ASSASSINS.
WAIT! I COULD USE THIS TIME MACHINE...
UH-OH, THIS CAN'T BE GOOD...
I COULD UNDO MY MANY MISTAKES.
OH, HUH--MAYBE HE'S CHANGED MAN.
WHAT IS THE ONE THING THAT HAS TIME AND AGAIN NUDGED ME DOWN THIS PATH TO RUIN?
HMM. HAVING YOUR TESTICLE SHOT OFF DURING WORLD WAR ONE?
I WILL USE THIS CRAZY CONTRAPTION...
...TO KILL SERGEANT FURY AND HIS HOWLING COMMANDOS!!!
DEC JAN FEB MAR APR MAY JUNE
OH, BOY. LOOK OUT, NICK, HERE COMES TROUBLE.

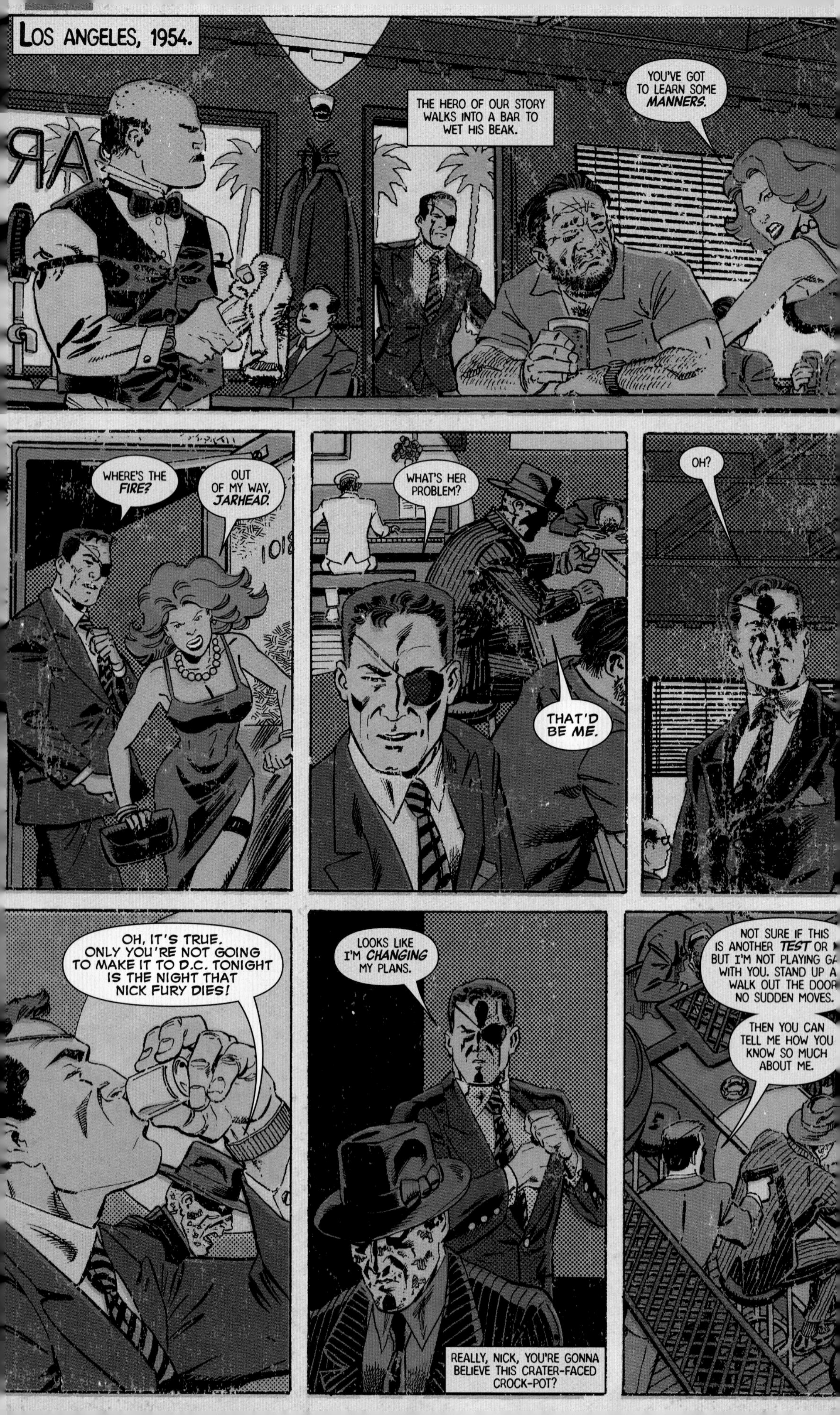
LOS ANGELES, 1954.
THE HERO OF OUR STORY WALKS INTO A BAR TO WET HIS BEAK.
YOU'VE GOT TO LEARN SOME MANNERS.
WHERE'S THE FIRE?
OUT OF MY WAY, JARHEAD.
WHAT'S HER PROBLEM?
THAT'D BE ME.
OH?
OH, IT'S TRUE. ONLY YOU'RE NOT GOING TO MAKE IT TO D.C. TONIGHT IS THE NIGHT THAT NICK FURY DIES!
LOOKS LIKE I'M CHANGING MY PLANS.
REALLY, NICK, YOU'RE GONNA BELIEVE THIS CRATER-FACED CROCK-POT?
NOT SURE IF THIS IS ANOTHER TEST OR
BUT I'M NOT PLAYING
WITH YOU. STAND UP
WALK OUT THE DOOR
NO SUDDEN MOVES.
THEN YOU CAN TELL ME HOW YOU KNOW SO MUCH ABOUT ME.

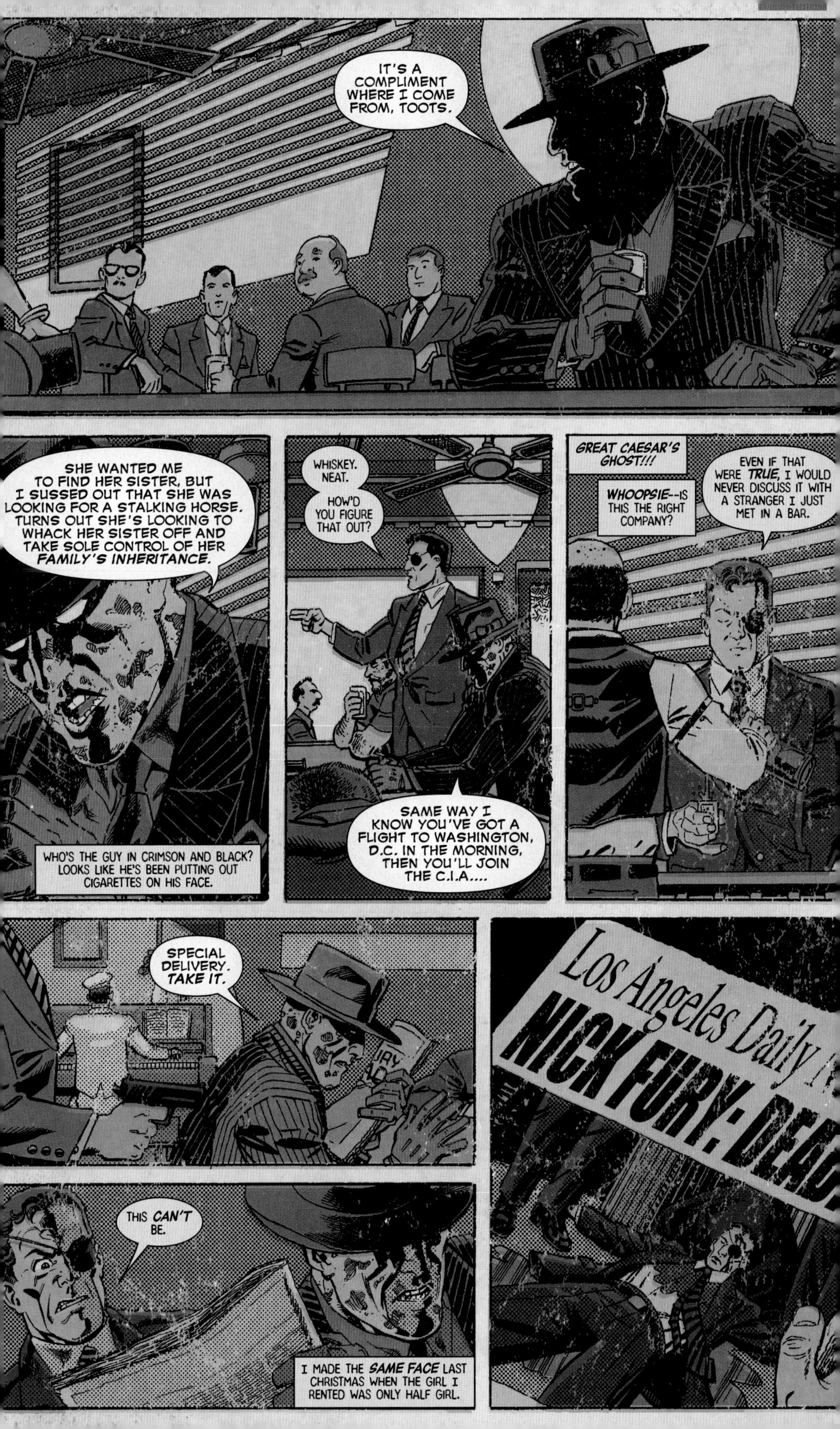
IT'S A COMPLIMENT WHERE I COME FROM, TOOTS.
SHE WANTED ME TO FIND HER SISTER, BUT I SUSSED OUT THAT SHE WAS LOOKING FOR A STALKING HORSE. TURNS OUT SHE'S LOOKING TO WHACK HER SISTER OFF AND TAKE SOLE CONTROL OF HER FAMILY'S INHERITANCE.
WHO'S THE GUY IN CRIMSON AND BLACK? LOOKS LIKE HE'S BEEN PUTTING OUT CIGARETTES ON HIS FACE.
WHISKEY. NEAT.
HOW'D YOU FIGURE THAT OUT?
SAME WAY I KNOW YOU'VE GOT A FLIGHT TO WASHINGTON, D.C. IN THE MORNING, THEN YOU'LL JOIN THE C.I.A....
GREAT CAESAR'S GHOST!!!
WHOOPSIE--IS THIS THE RIGHT COMPANY?
EVEN IF THAT WERE TRUE, I WOULD NEVER DISCUSS IT WITH A STRANGER I JUST MET IN A BAR.
SPECIAL DELIVERY. TAKE IT.
THIS CAN'T BE.
I MADE THE SAME FACE LAST CHRISTMAS WHEN THE GIRL I RENTED WAS ONLY HALF GIRL.
Los Angeles Daily
NICK FURY: DEAD

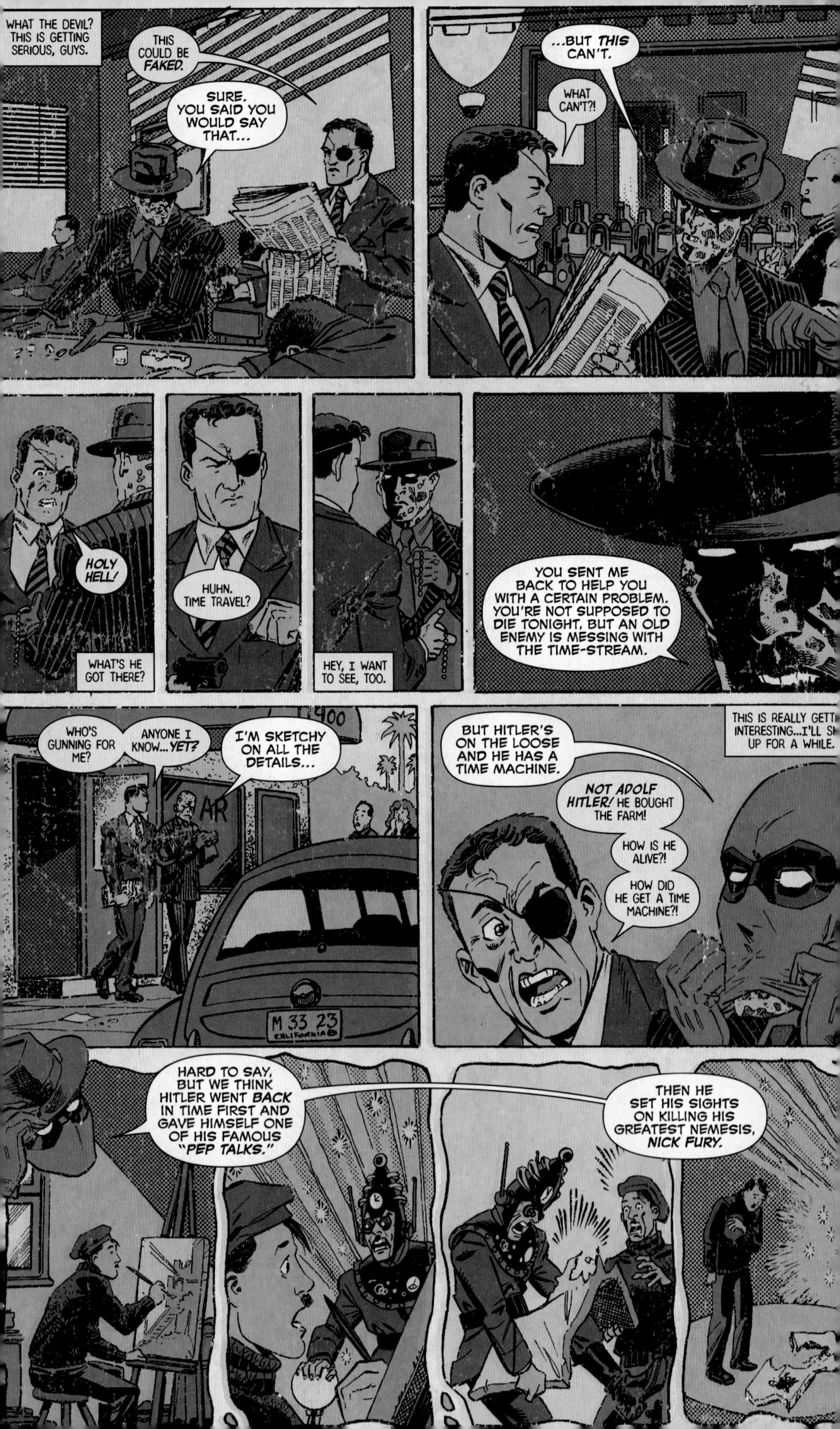
WHAT THE DEVIL? THIS IS GETTING SERIOUS, GUYS.
THIS COULD BE FAKED.
SURE. YOU SAID YOU WOULD SAY THAT...
...BUT THIS CAN'T.
WHAT CAN'T?!
HOLY HELL!
WHAT'S HE GOT THERE?
HUHN. TIME TRAVEL?
HEY, I WANT TO SEE, TOO.
YOU SENT ME BACK TO HELP YOU WITH A CERTAIN PROBLEM. YOU'RE NOT SUPPOSED TO DIE TONIGHT, BUT AN OLD ENEMY IS MESSING WITH THE TIME-STREAM.
WHO'S GUNNING FOR ME?
ANYONE I KNOW...YET?
I'M SKETCHY ON ALL THE DETAILS...
M 33 23
THIS IS REALLY GETT INTERESTING...I'LL S UP FOR A WHILE.
BUT HITLER'S ON THE LOOSE AND HE HAS A TIME MACHINE.
NOT ADOLF HITLER! HE BOUGHT THE FARM!
HOW IS HE ALIVE?!
HOW DID HE GET A TIME MACHINE?!
HARD TO SAY, BUT WE THINK HITLER WENT BACK IN TIME FIRST AND GAVE HIMSELF ONE OF HIS FAMOUS "PEP TALKS."
THEN HE SET HIS SIGHTS ON KILLING HIS GREATEST NEMESIS, NICK FURY.

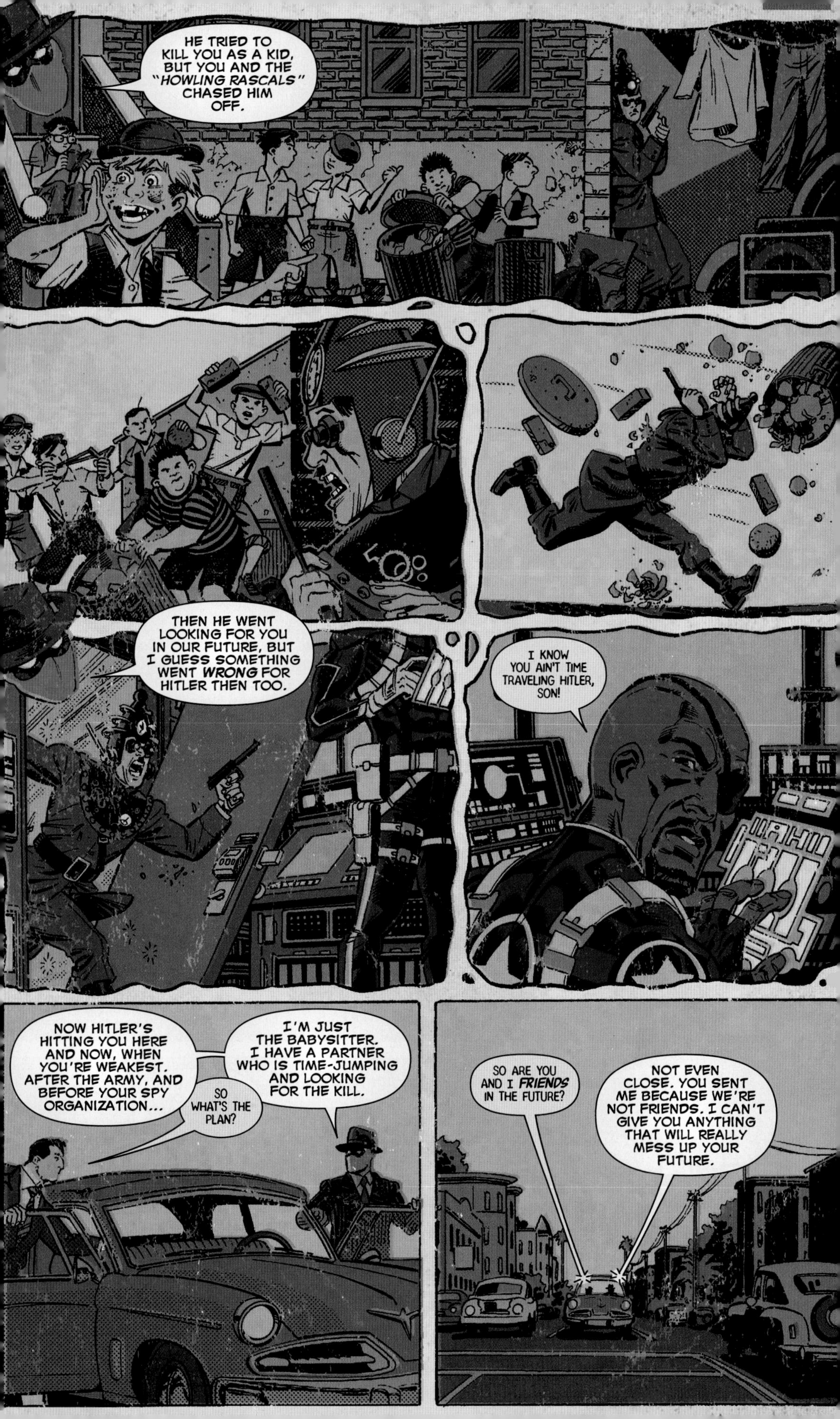

HE TRIED TO KILL YOU AS A KID, BUT YOU AND THE "*HOWLING RASCALS*" CHASED HIM OFF.
THEN HE WENT LOOKING FOR YOU IN OUR FUTURE, BUT I GUESS SOMETHING WENT *WRONG* FOR HITLER THEN TOO.
I KNOW YOU AIN'T TIME TRAVELING HITLER, SON!
NOW HITLER'S HITTING YOU HERE AND NOW, WHEN YOU'RE WEAKEST. AFTER THE ARMY, AND BEFORE YOUR SPY ORGANIZATION...
SO WHAT'S THE PLAN?
I'M JUST THE BABYSITTER. I HAVE A PARTNER WHO IS TIME-JUMPING AND LOOKING FOR THE KILL.
SO ARE YOU AND I *FRIENDS* IN THE FUTURE?
NOT EVEN CLOSE. YOU SENT ME BECAUSE WE'RE NOT FRIENDS. I CAN'T GIVE YOU ANYTHING THAT WILL REALLY MESS UP YOUR FUTURE.

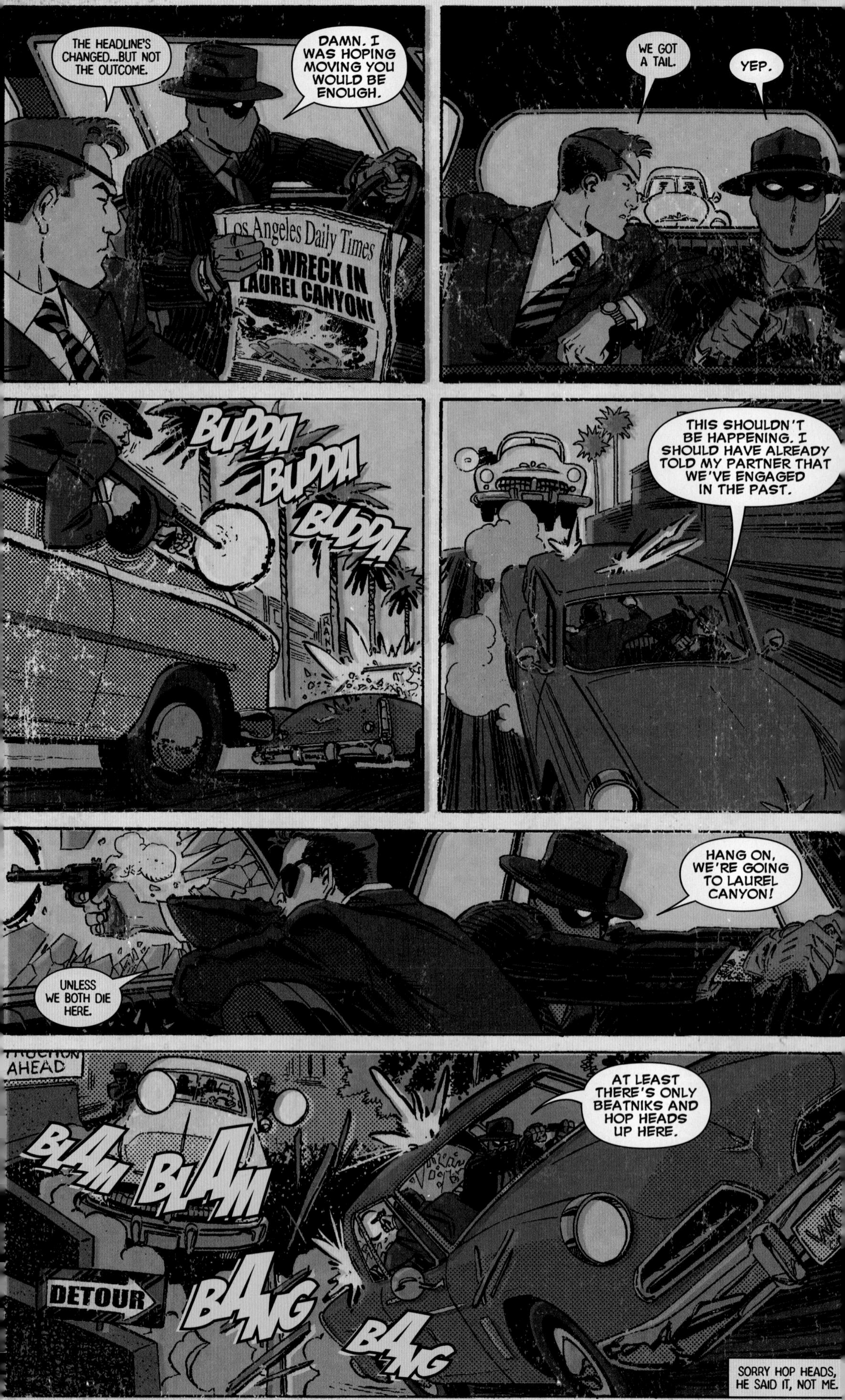
THE HEADLINE'S CHANGED...BUT NOT THE OUTCOME.
DAMN. I WAS HOPING MOVING YOU WOULD BE ENOUGH.
Los Angeles Daily Times
LAUREL CANYON!
WE GOT A TAIL.
YEP.
BUDDA
BUDDA
BUDDA
THIS SHOULDN'T BE HAPPENING. I SHOULD HAVE ALREADY TOLD MY PARTNER THAT WE'VE ENGAGED IN THE PAST.
HANG ON, WE'RE GOING TO LAUREL CANYON!
UNLESS WE BOTH DIE HERE.
AHEAD
AT LEAST THERE'S ONLY BEATNIKS AND HOP HEADS UP HERE.
BLAM
BLAM
DETOUR
BANG
BANG
SORRY HOP HEADS, HE SAID IT, NOT ME.

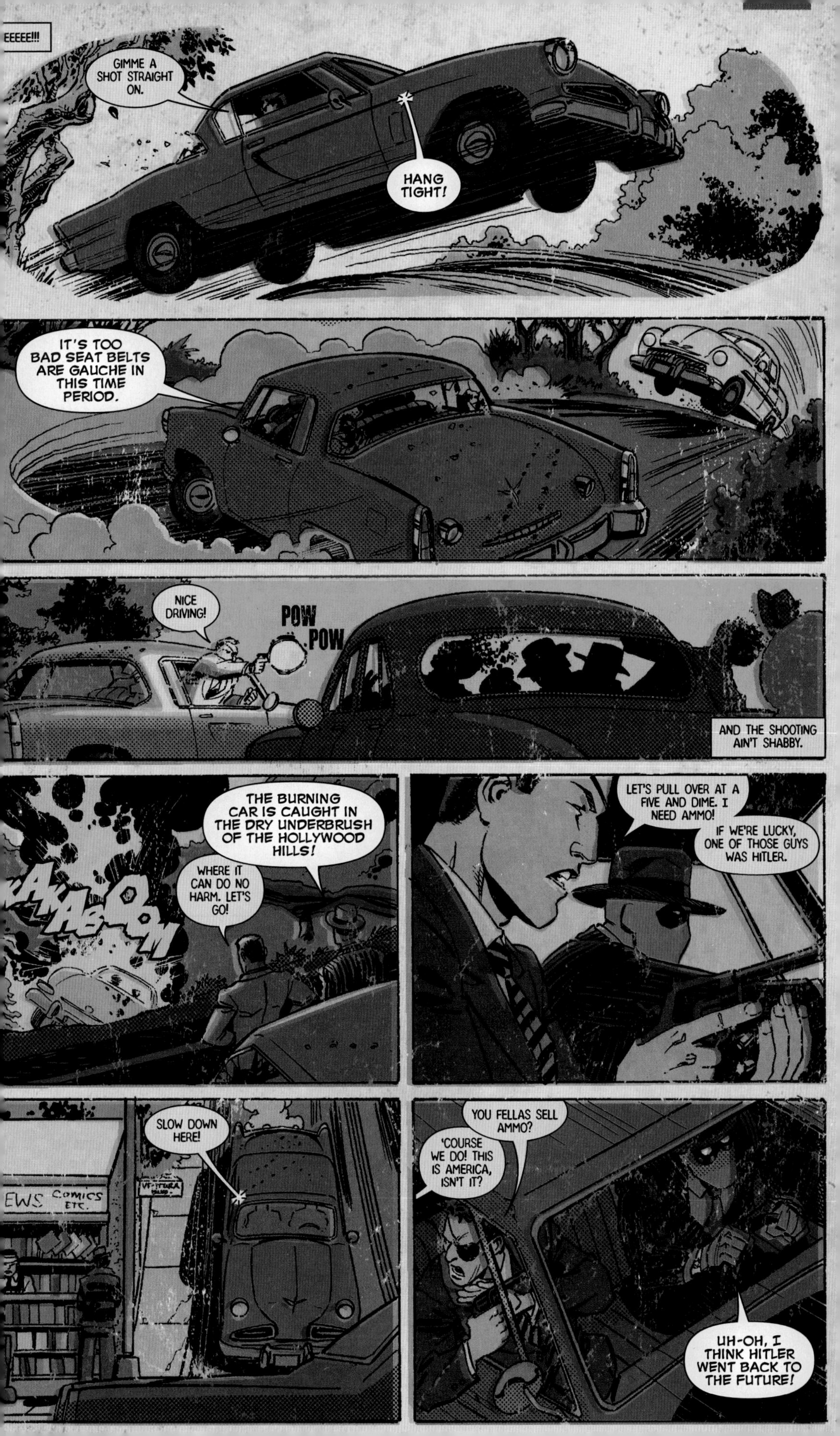
EEEEE!!!
GIMME A SHOT STRAIGHT ON.
HANG TIGHT!
IT'S TOO BAD SEAT BELTS ARE GAUCHE IN THIS TIME PERIOD.
NICE DRIVING!
POW
POW
AND THE SHOOTING AIN'T SHABBY.
THE BURNING CAR IS CAUGHT IN THE DRY UNDERBRUSH OF THE HOLLYWOOD HILLS!
WHERE IT CAN DO NO HARM. LET'S GO!
LET'S PULL OVER AT A FIVE AND DIME. I NEED AMMO!
IF WE'RE LUCKY, ONE OF THOSE GUYS WAS HITLER.
SLOW DOWN HERE!
EWS COMICS ETC.
YOU FELLAS SELL AMMO?
'COURSE WE DO! THIS IS AMERICA, ISN'T IT?
UH-OH, I THINK HITLER WENT BACK TO THE FUTURE!

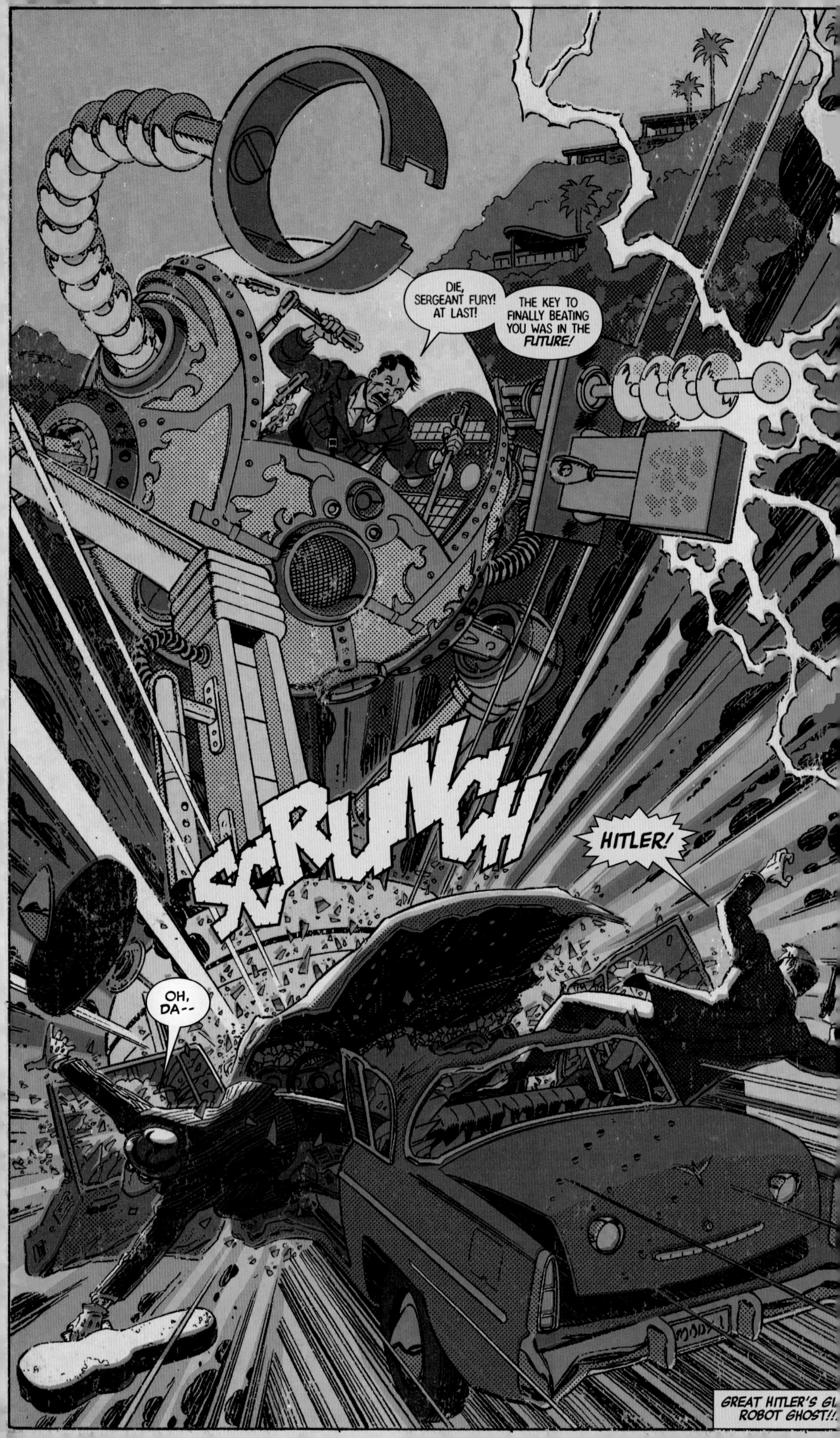
DIE, SERGEANT FURY! AT LAST!
THE KEY TO FINALLY BEATING YOU WAS IN THE FUTURE!
SCRUNCH
HITLER!
OH, DA--
GREAT HITLER'S GI
ROBOT GHOST!!

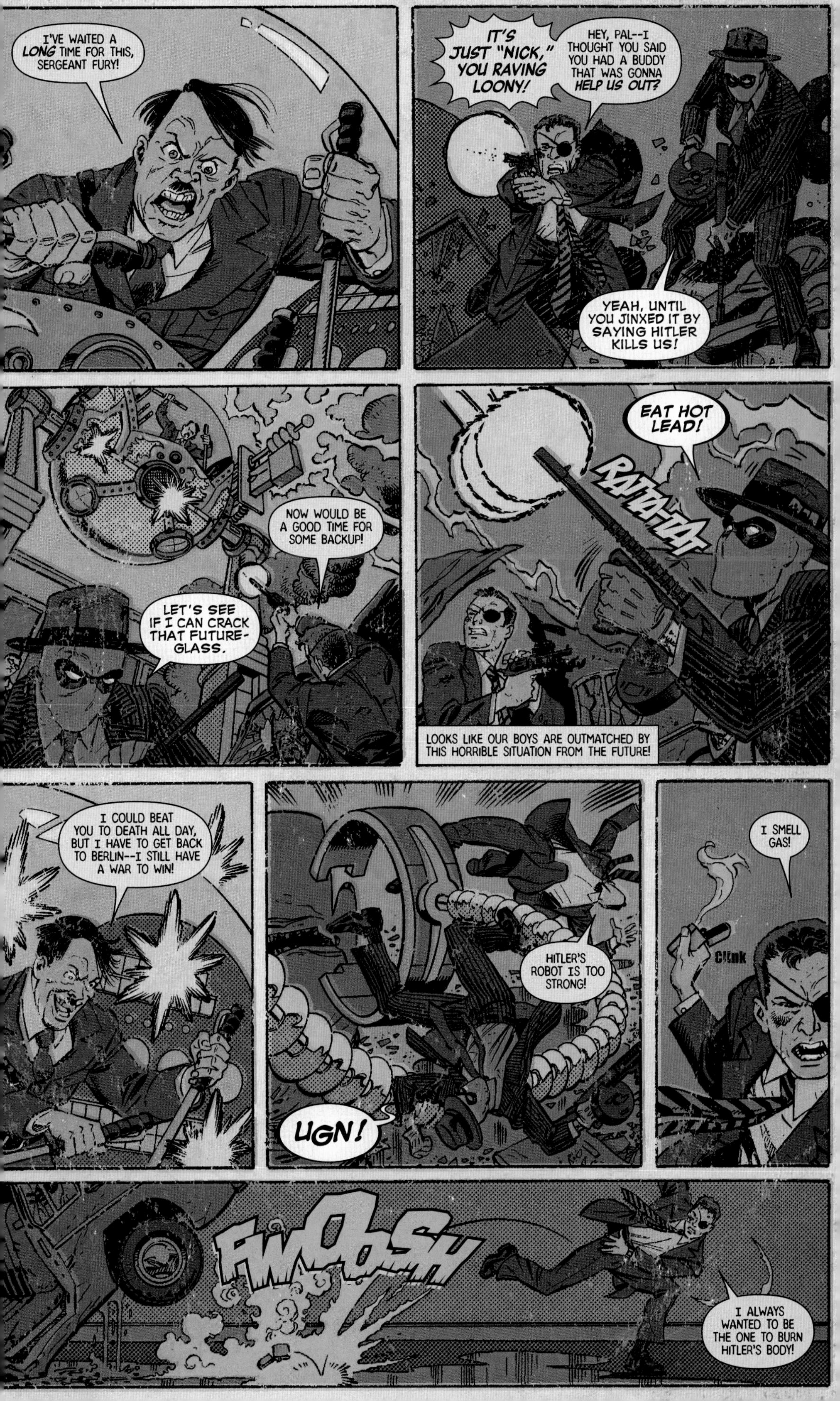

I'VE WAITED A LONG TIME FOR THIS, SERGEANT FURY!
IT'S JUST "NICK," YOU RAVING LOONY!
HEY, PAL--I THOUGHT YOU SAID YOU HAD A BUDDY THAT WAS GONNA HELP US OUT?
YEAH, UNTIL YOU JINXED IT BY SAYING HITLER KILLS US!
NOW WOULD BE A GOOD TIME FOR SOME BACKUP!
LET'S SEE IF I CAN CRACK THAT FUTURE-GLASS.
EAT HOT LEAD!
RATATAT
LOOKS LIKE OUR BOYS ARE OUTMATCHED BY THIS HORRIBLE SITUATION FROM THE FUTURE!
I COULD BEAT YOU TO DEATH ALL DAY, BUT I HAVE TO GET BACK TO BERLIN--I STILL HAVE A WAR TO WIN!
HITLER'S ROBOT IS TOO STRONG!
UGN!
I SMELL GAS!
Clink
FWOOSH
I ALWAYS WANTED TO BE THE ONE TO BURN HITLER'S BODY!

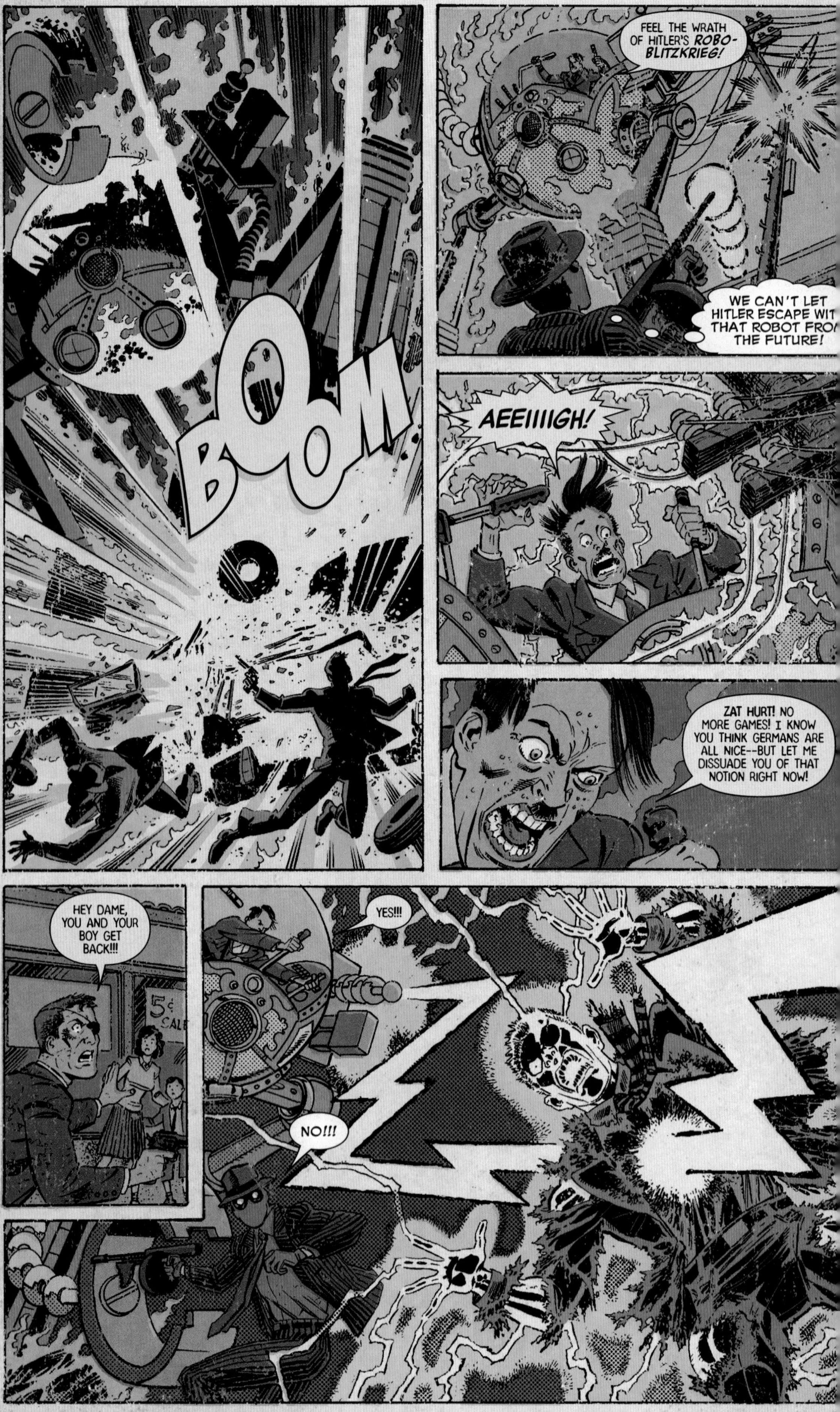
BOOM
FEEL THE WRATH OF HITLER'S ROBO-BLITZKRIEG!
WE CAN'T LET HITLER ESCAPE WIT THAT ROBOT FRO THE FUTURE!
AEEIIIIGH!
ZAT HURT! NO MORE GAMES! I KNOW YOU THINK GERMANS ARE ALL NICE--BUT LET ME DISSUADE YOU OF THAT NOTION RIGHT NOW!
HEY DAME, YOU AND YOUR BOY GET BACK!!!
5¢ SALE
YES!!!
NO!!!

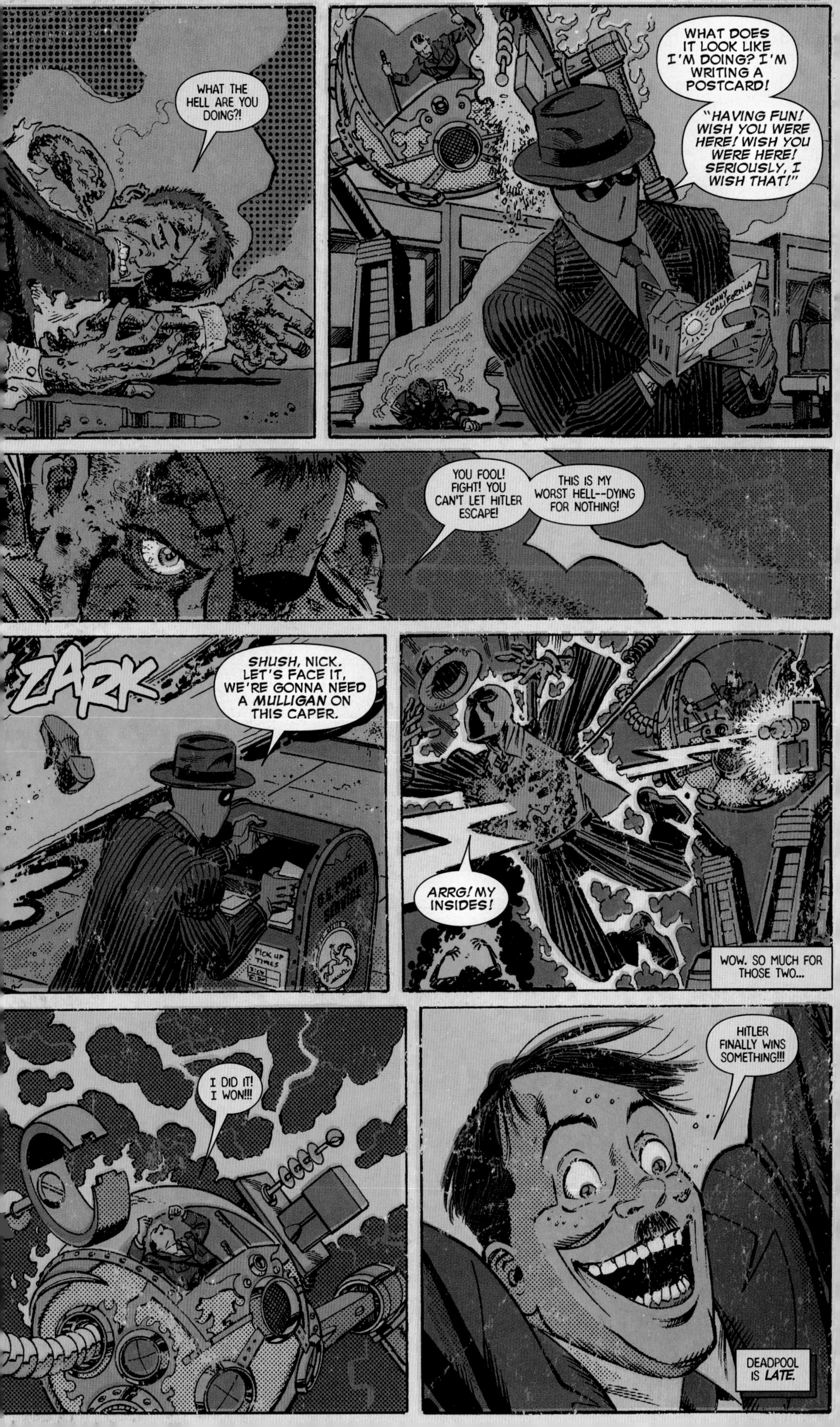
WHAT THE HELL ARE YOU DOING?!
WHAT DOES IT LOOK LIKE I'M DOING? I'M WRITING A POSTCARD!
"HAVING FUN! WISH YOU WERE HERE! WISH YOU WERE HERE! SERIOUSLY, I WISH THAT!"
SUNNY CALIFORNIA
YOU FOOL! FIGHT! YOU CAN'T LET HITLER ESCAPE!
THIS IS MY WORST HELL--DYING FOR NOTHING!
ZARK
SHUSH, NICK. LET'S FACE IT, WE'RE GONNA NEED A MULLIGAN ON THIS CAPER.
PICK UP TIMES
ARRG! MY INSIDES!
WOW. SO MUCH FOR THOSE TWO...
I DID IT! I WON!!!
HITLER FINALLY WINS SOMETHING!!!
DEADPOOL IS LATE.

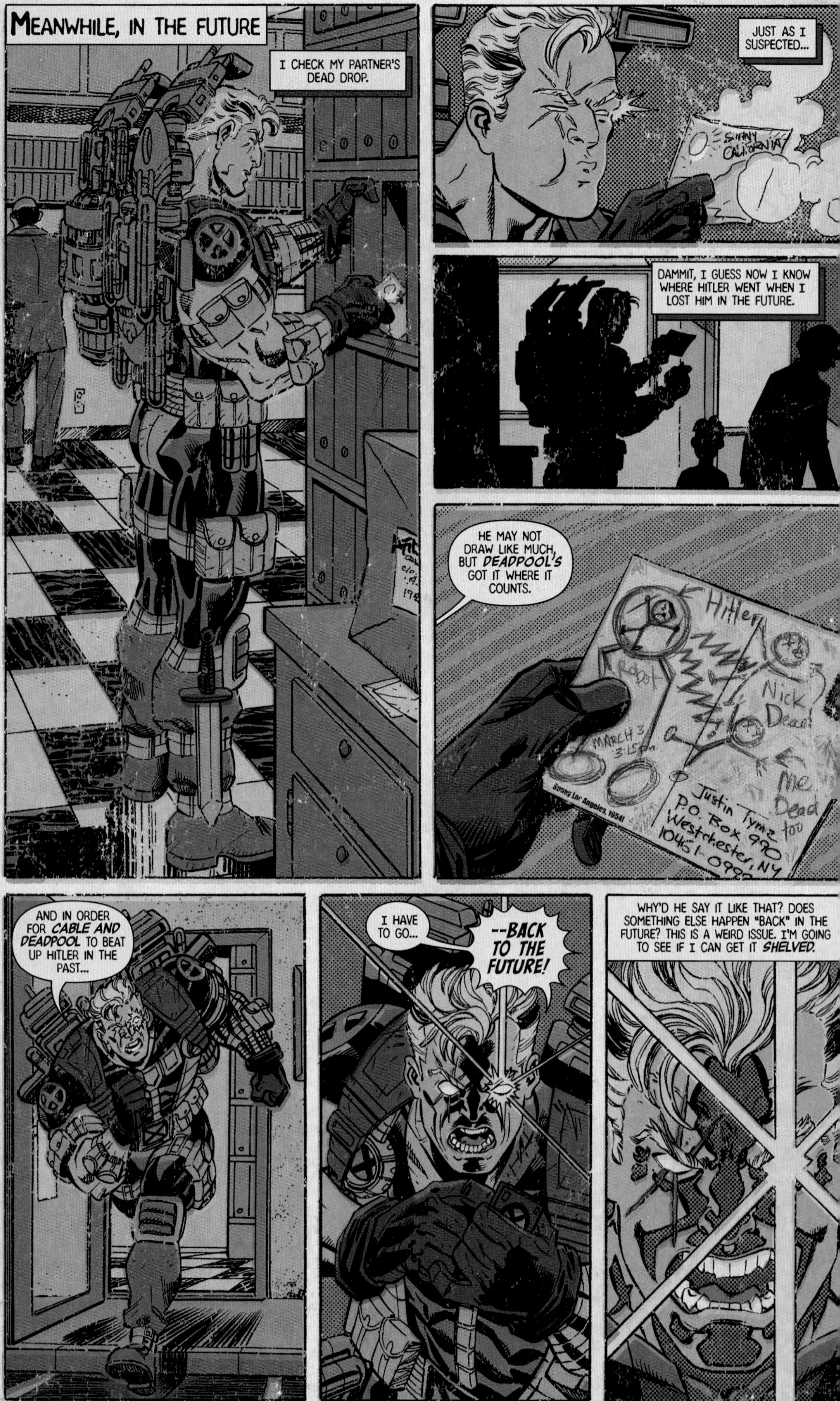
MEANWHILE, IN THE FUTURE
I CHECK MY PARTNER'S DEAD DROP.
JUST AS I SUSPECTED...
DAMMIT, I GUESS NOW I KNOW WHERE HITLER WENT WHEN I LOST HIM IN THE FUTURE.
HE MAY NOT DRAW LIKE MUCH, BUT DEADPOOL'S GOT IT WHERE IT COUNTS.
AND IN ORDER FOR CABLE AND DEADPOOL TO BEAT UP HITLER IN THE PAST...
I HAVE TO GO...
--BACK TO THE FUTURE!
WHY'D HE SAY IT LIKE THAT? DOES SOMETHING ELSE HAPPEN "BACK" IN THE FUTURE? THIS IS A WEIRD ISSUE. I'M GOING TO SEE IF I CAN GET IT SHELVED.

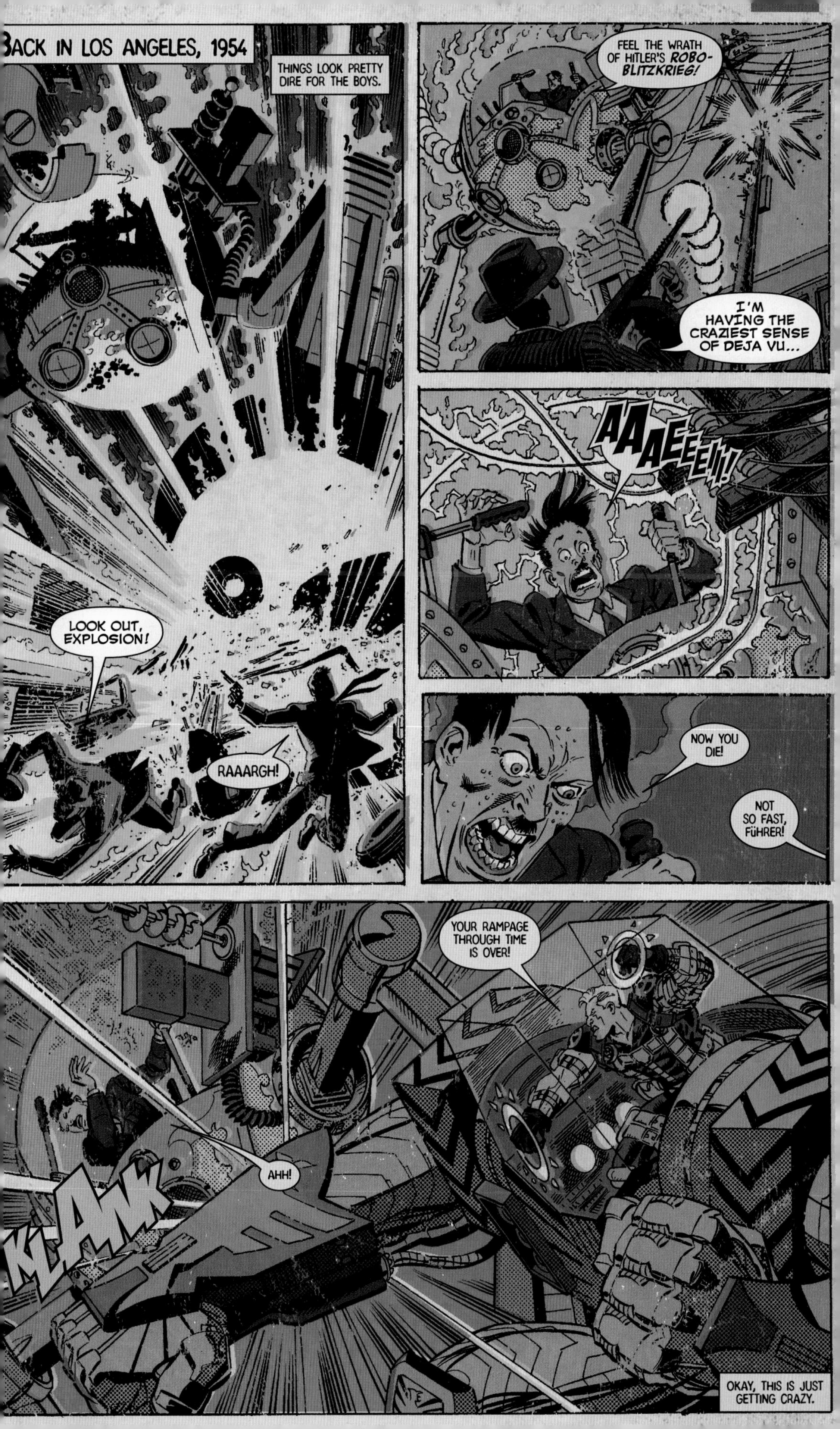
BACK IN LOS ANGELES, 1954
THINGS LOOK PRETTY DIRE FOR THE BOYS.
LOOK OUT, EXPLOSION!
RAAARGH!
FEEL THE WRATH OF HITLER'S ROBO-BLITZKRIEG!
I'M HAVING THE CRAZIEST SENSE OF DEJA VU...
AAAEEE!!!
NOW YOU DIE!
NOT SO FAST, FÜHRER!
YOUR RAMPAGE THROUGH TIME IS OVER!
AHH!
KLANK
OKAY, THIS IS JUST GETTING CRAZY.

GOOD TO SEE YOU, SERGEANT!

I GOT YOUR POSTCARD, WADE!

NICE TO SEE YOU, CABLE.

AMAZING! THESE CONTRAPTIONS MUST REPLACE CARS IN THE FUTURE.

I DON'T KNOW WHO YOU ARE, BUT I DON'T CARE, I WON'T LET YOU STOP ME FROM KILLING SERGEANT FURY!

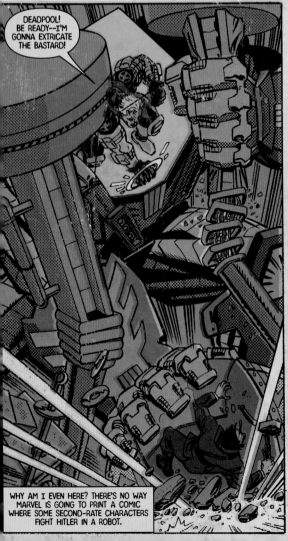

DEADPOOL! BE READY--I'M GONNA EXTRICATE THE BASTARD!

WHY AM I EVEN HERE? THERE'S NO WAY MARVEL IS GOING TO PRINT A COMIC WHERE SOME SECOND-RATE CHARACTERS FIGHT HITLER IN A ROBOT.

MY ROBOTIC MACHINE IS UNBREAKABLE! I GOT IT IN THE FUTURE!

I KNOW...BUT I GOT THIS SUIT IN YOUR FUTURE'S FUTURE! SO IT CAN BREAK UNBREAKABLE ROBOTS!

ACTUALLY, THAT'S NOT A B[?] 1950S' SCI-FI TWIST RIG[HT] THERE...LET'S SEE IF OU[R] BOYS STRIKE PAY DIRT!

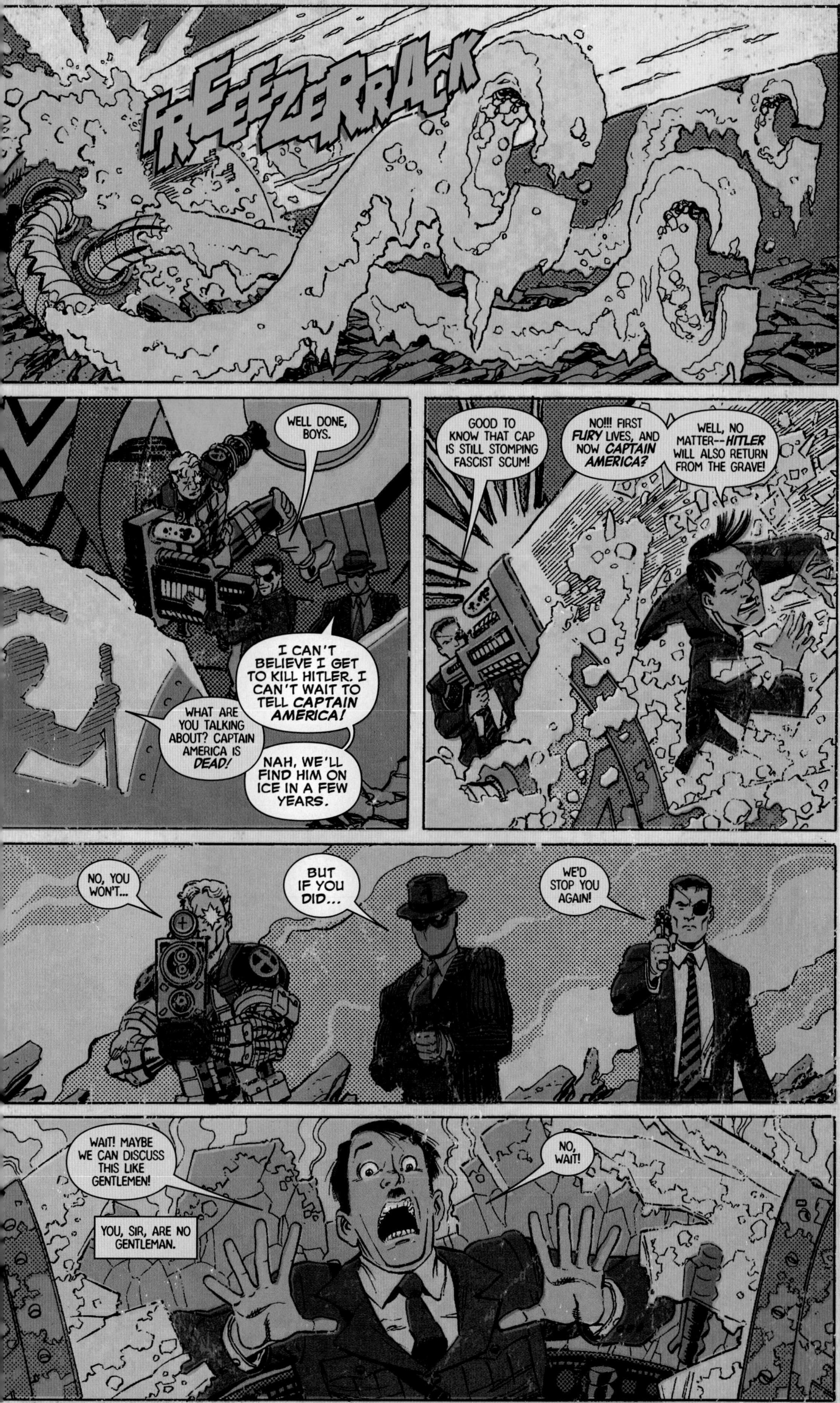
FREEEZERRACK
WELL DONE, BOYS.
I CAN'T BELIEVE I GET TO KILL HITLER. I CAN'T WAIT TO TELL *CAPTAIN AMERICA!*
WHAT ARE YOU TALKING ABOUT? CAPTAIN AMERICA IS *DEAD!*
NAH, WE'LL FIND HIM ON ICE IN A FEW YEARS.
GOOD TO KNOW THAT CAP IS STILL STOMPING FASCIST SCUM!
NO!!! FIRST *FURY* LIVES, AND NOW *CAPTAIN AMERICA?*
WELL, NO MATTER--*HITLER* WILL ALSO RETURN FROM THE GRAVE!
NO, YOU WON'T...
BUT IF YOU DID...
WE'D STOP YOU AGAIN!
WAIT! MAYBE WE CAN DISCUSS THIS LIKE GENTLEMEN!
NO, WAIT!
YOU, SIR, ARE NO GENTLEMAN.

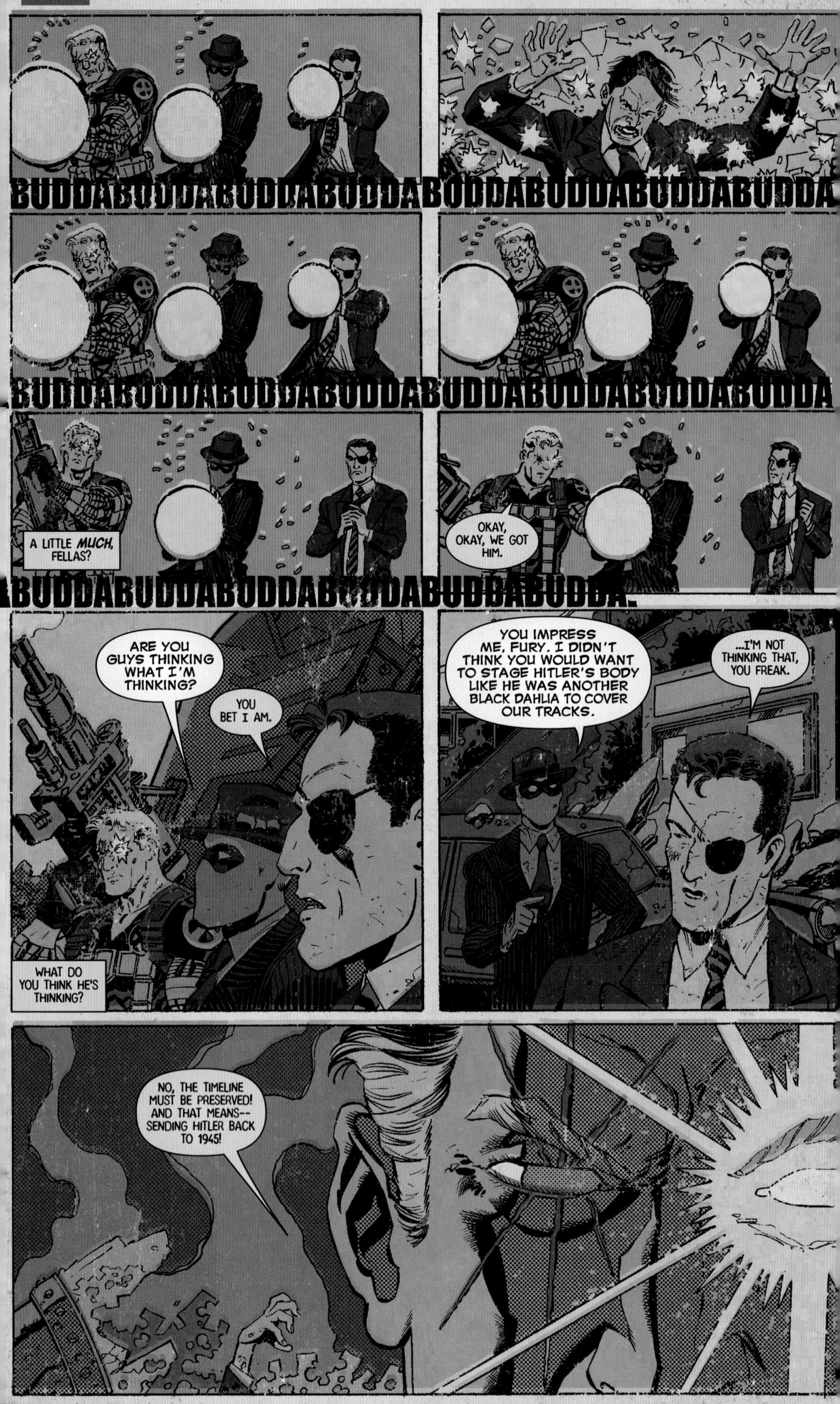

BUDDABUDDABUDDABUDDABUDDABUDDABUDDABUDDA
BUDDABUDDABUDDABUDDABUDDABUDDABUDDABUDDA
A LITTLE *MUCH*, FELLAS?
OKAY, OKAY, WE GOT HIM.
BUDDABUDDABUDDABUDDABUDDABUDDA.
ARE YOU GUYS THINKING WHAT I'M THINKING?
YOU BET I AM.
WHAT DO YOU THINK HE'S THINKING?
YOU IMPRESS ME, FURY. I DIDN'T THINK YOU WOULD WANT TO STAGE HITLER'S BODY LIKE HE WAS ANOTHER BLACK DAHLIA TO COVER OUR TRACKS.
...I'M NOT THINKING THAT, YOU FREAK.
NO, THE TIMELINE MUST BE PRESERVED! AND THAT MEANS-- SENDING HITLER BACK TO 1945!

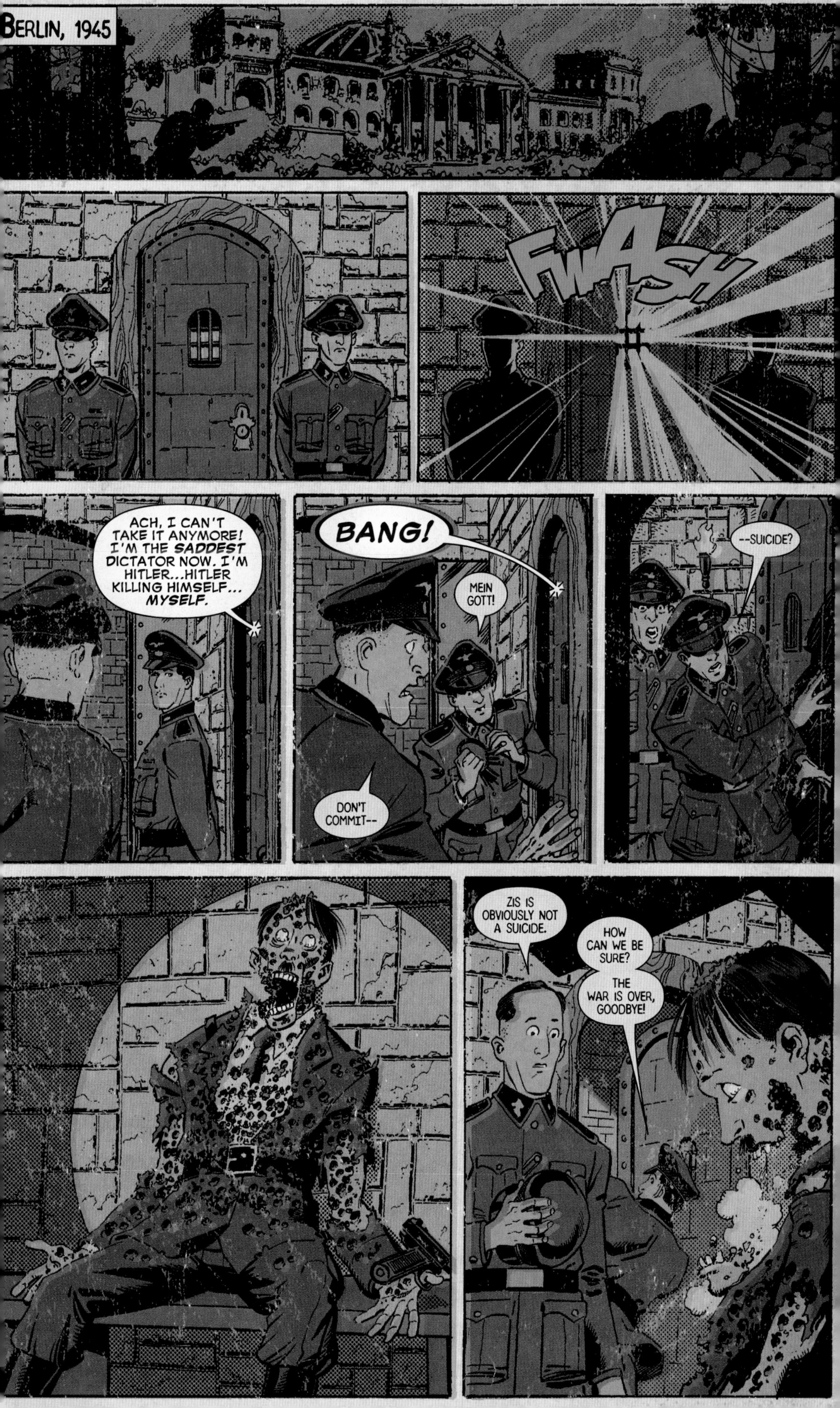
BERLIN, 1945
FWASH
ACH, I CAN'T TAKE IT ANYMORE! I'M THE SADDEST DICTATOR NOW. I'M HITLER...HITLER KILLING HIMSELF... MYSELF.
BANG!
MEIN GOTT!
DON'T COMMIT--
--SUICIDE?
ZIS IS OBVIOUSLY NOT A SUICIDE.
HOW CAN WE BE SURE?
THE WAR IS OVER, GOODBYE!

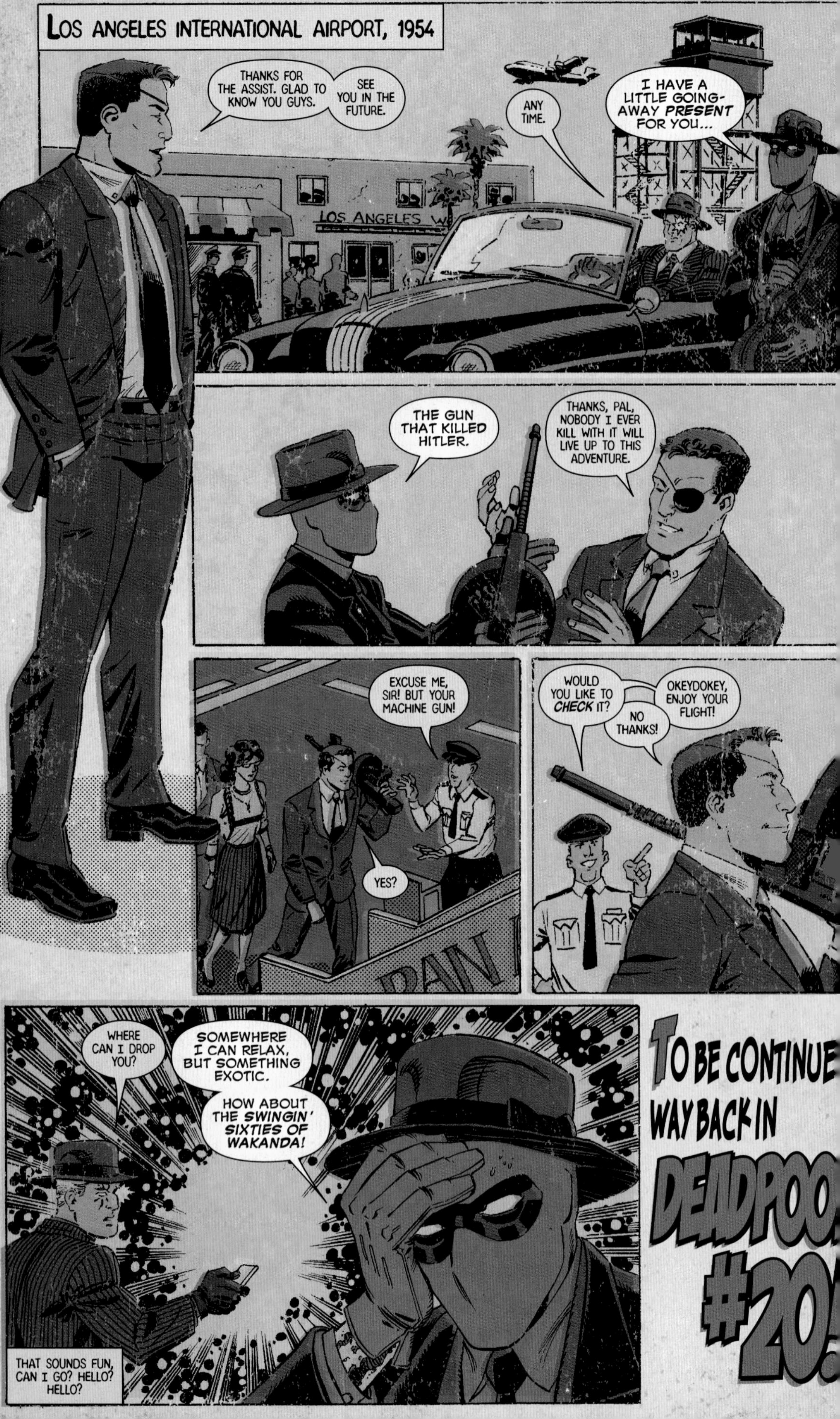
LOS ANGELES INTERNATIONAL AIRPORT, 1954
THANKS FOR THE ASSIST. GLAD TO KNOW YOU GUYS.
SEE YOU IN THE FUTURE.
ANY TIME.
I HAVE A LITTLE GOING-AWAY PRESENT FOR YOU...
LOS ANGELES
THE GUN THAT KILLED HITLER.
THANKS, PAL, NOBODY I EVER KILL WITH IT WILL LIVE UP TO THIS ADVENTURE.
EXCUSE ME, SIR! BUT YOUR MACHINE GUN!
YES?
WOULD YOU LIKE TO CHECK IT?
NO THANKS!
OKEYDOKEY, ENJOY YOUR FLIGHT!
WHERE CAN I DROP YOU?
SOMEWHERE I CAN RELAX, BUT SOMETHING EXOTIC.
HOW ABOUT THE SWINGIN' SIXTIES OF WAKANDA!
THAT SOUNDS FUN, CAN I GO? HELLO? HELLO?
TO BE CONTINUE
WAY BACK IN
DEADPOO
#20

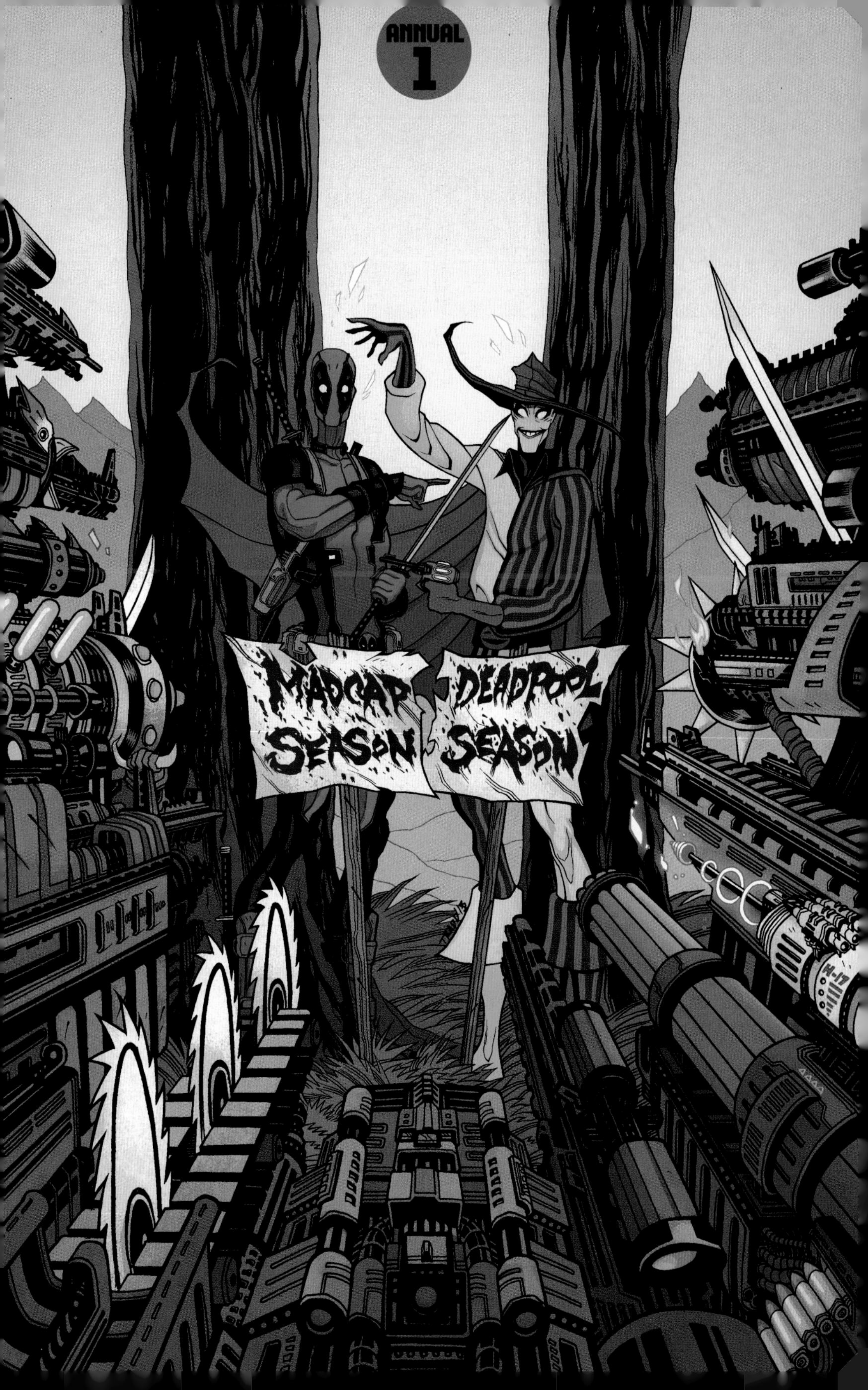
ANNUAL
1
MADCAP SEASON
DEADPOOL SEASON

Possibly the world's most skilled mercenary, definitely the world's most annoying, Wade Wilson w
chosen for a top-secret government program that gave him a healing factor allowing him to heal fr
any wound. Now, Wade makes his way as a gun for hire, shooting his prey's faces off while talking
friends' ears off. Call him the Merc with the Mouth...call him the Regeneratin' Degenerate...call him..

DEADPOOL

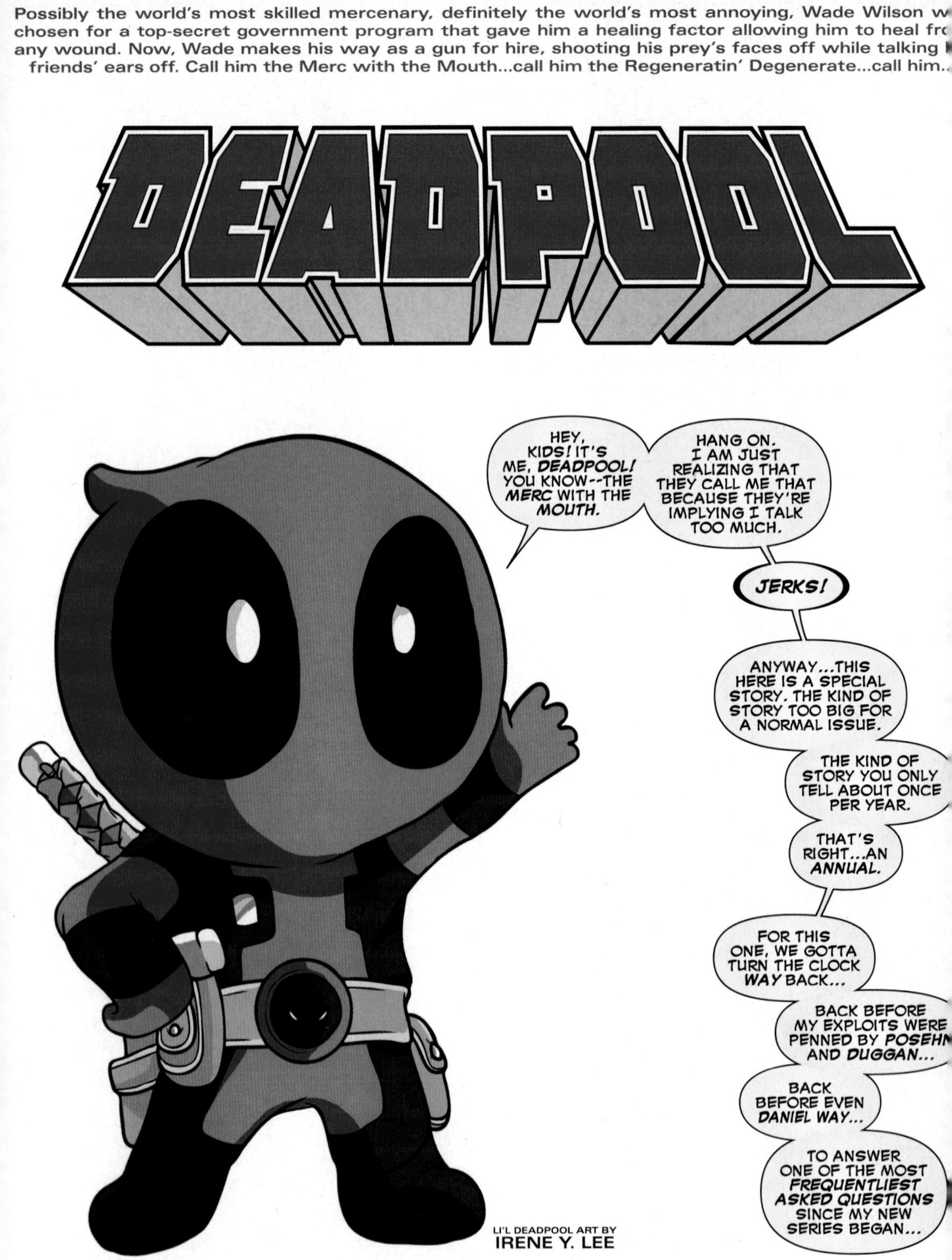
HEY, KIDS! IT'S ME, DEADPOOL! YOU KNOW--THE MERC WITH THE MOUTH.
HANG ON. I AM JUST REALIZING THAT THEY CALL ME THAT BECAUSE THEY'RE IMPLYING I TALK TOO MUCH.
JERKS!
ANYWAY...THIS HERE IS A SPECIAL STORY. THE KIND OF STORY TOO BIG FOR A NORMAL ISSUE.
THE KIND OF STORY YOU ONLY TELL ABOUT ONCE PER YEAR.
THAT'S RIGHT...AN ANNUAL.
FOR THIS ONE, WE GOTTA TURN THE CLOCK WAY BACK...
BACK BEFORE MY EXPLOITS WERE PENNED BY POSEH AND DUGGAN...
BACK BEFORE EVEN DANIEL WAY...
TO ANSWER ONE OF THE MOST FREQUENTLIEST ASKED QUESTIONS SINCE MY NEW SERIES BEGAN...

LI'L DEADPOOL ART BY
IRENE Y. LEE

MADCAPPED!

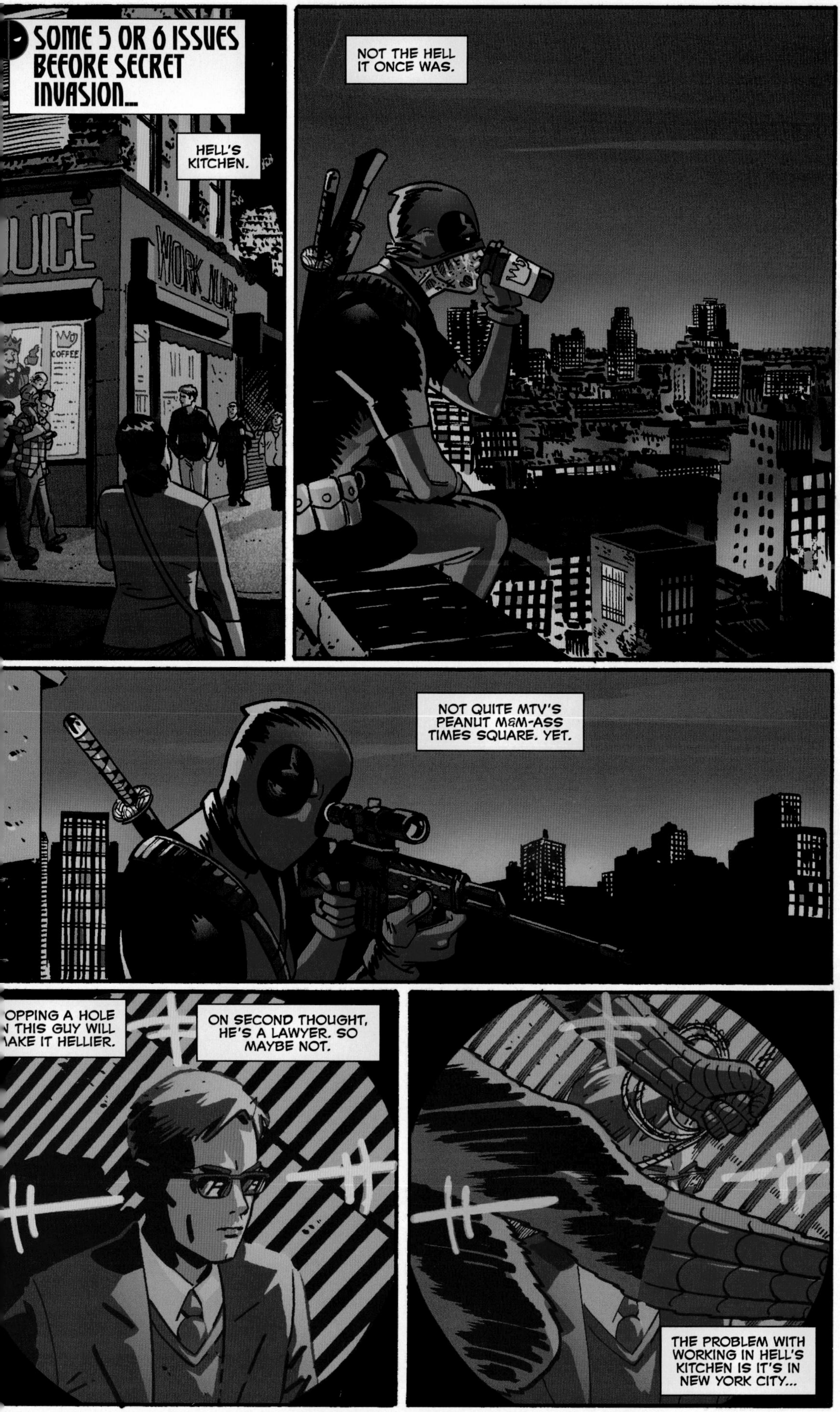
SOME 5 OR 6 ISSUES BEFORE SECRET INVASION...
HELL'S KITCHEN.
WORK JUICE
COFFEE
NOT THE HELL IT ONCE WAS.
NOT QUITE MTV'S PEANUT M&M-ASS TIMES SQUARE. YET.
OPPING A HOLE N THIS GUY WILL AKE IT HELLIER.
ON SECOND THOUGHT, HE'S A LAWYER. SO MAYBE NOT.
THE PROBLEM WITH WORKING IN HELL'S KITCHEN IS IT'S IN NEW YORK CITY...

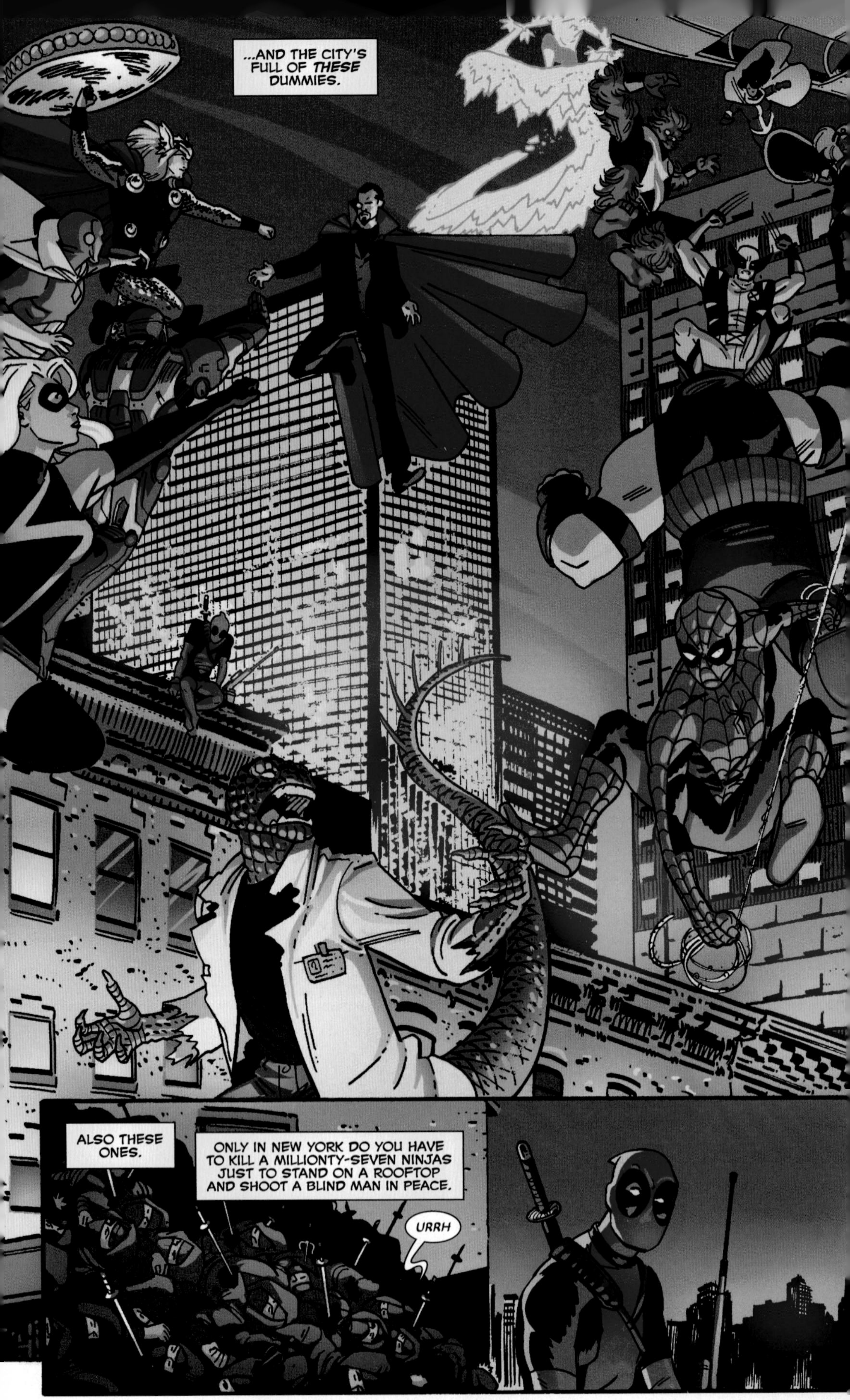
...AND THE CITY'S FULL OF *THESE* DUMMIES.
ALSO THESE ONES.
ONLY IN NEW YORK DO YOU HAVE TO KILL A MILLIONTY-SEVEN NINJAS JUST TO STAND ON A ROOFTOP AND SHOOT A BLIND MAN IN PEACE.
URRH

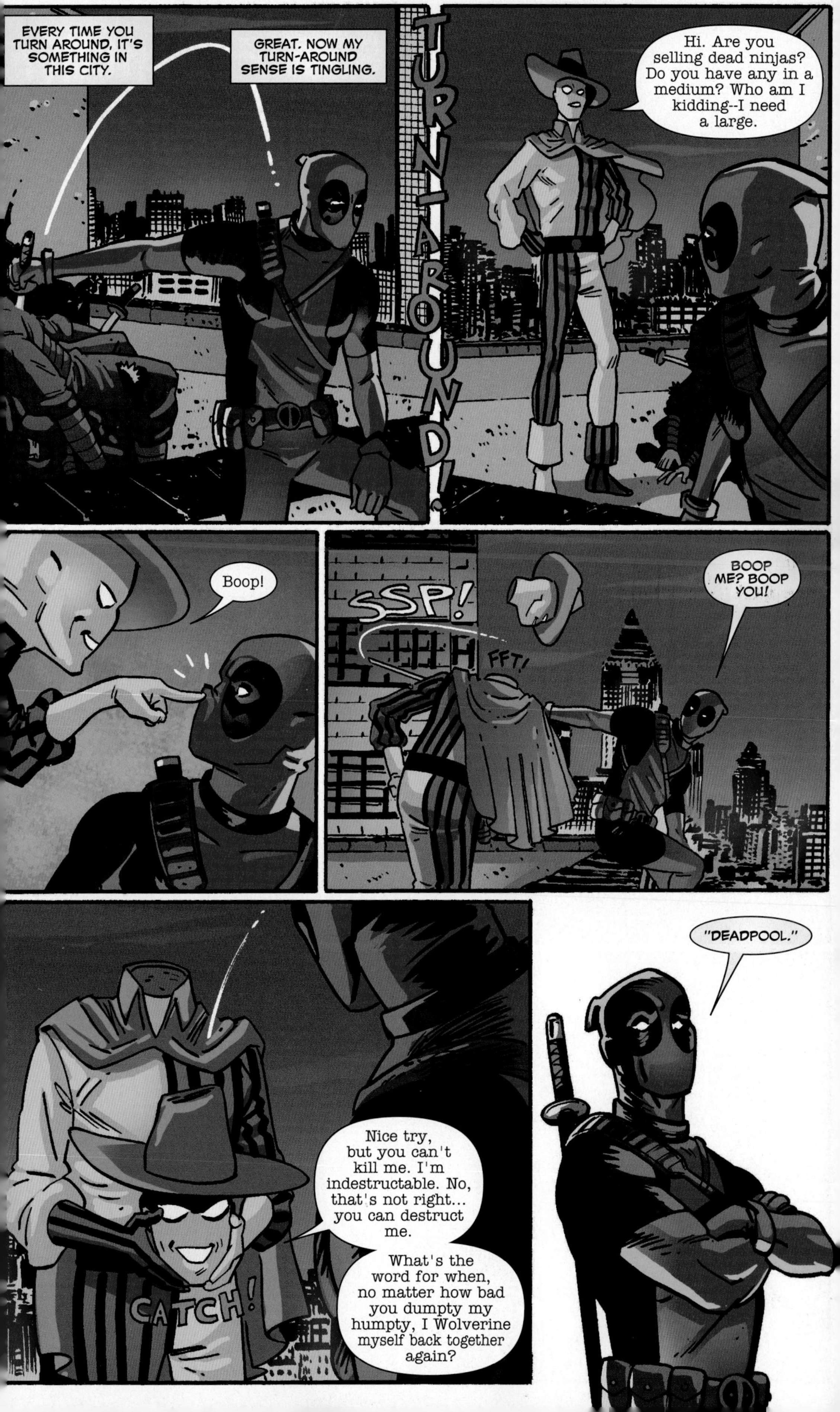
EVERY TIME YOU TURN AROUND, IT'S SOMETHING IN THIS CITY.
GREAT. NOW MY TURN-AROUND SENSE IS TINGLING.
TURNIAROUND!
Hi. Are you selling dead ninjas? Do you have any in a medium? Who am I kidding--I need a large.
Boop!
SSP!
FFT!
BOOP ME? BOOP YOU!
CATCH!
Nice try, but you can't kill me. I'm indestructable. No, that's not right... you can destruct me.
What's the word for when, no matter how bad you dumpty my humpty, I Wolverine myself back together again?
"DEADPOOL."

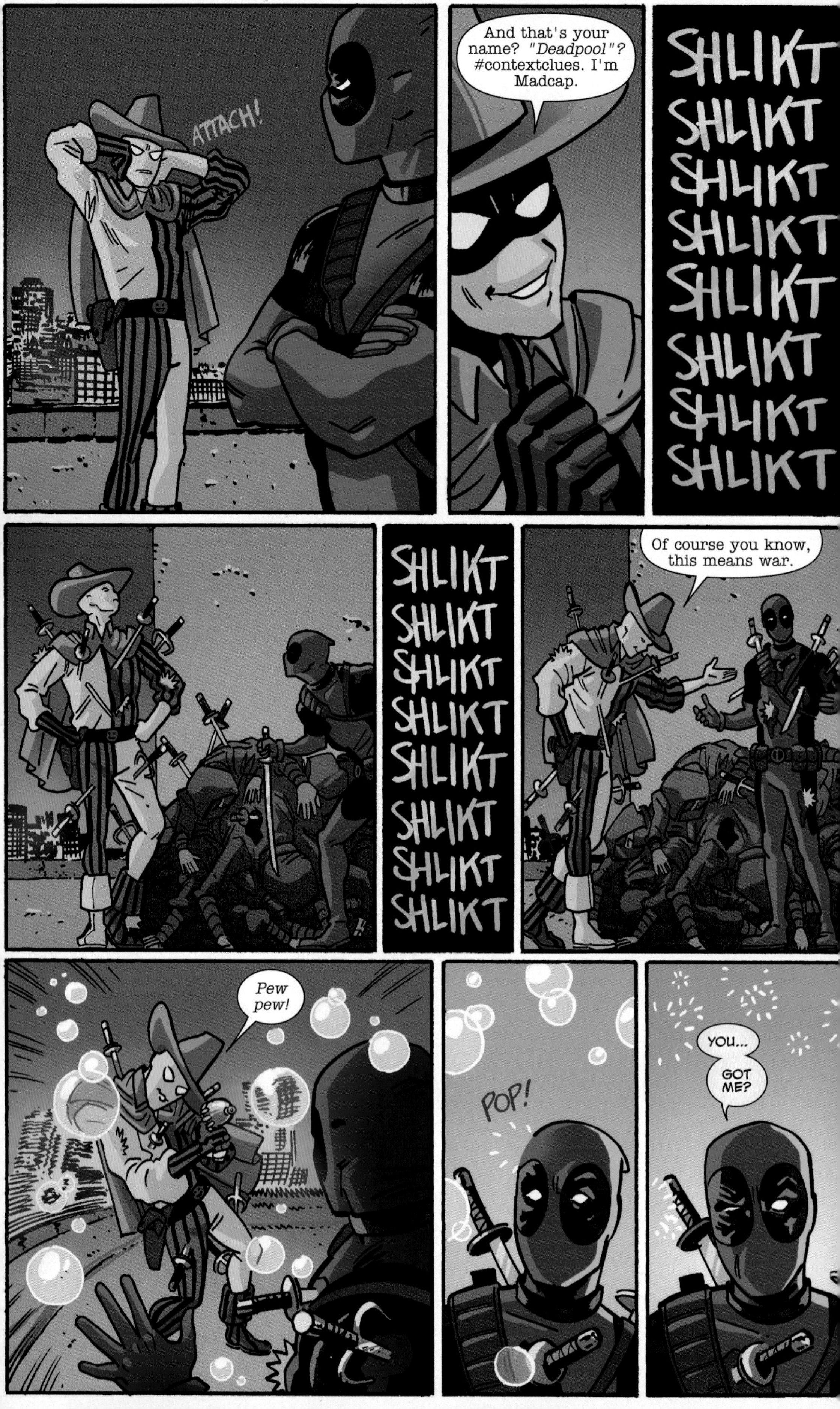
ATTACH!
And that's your name? *"Deadpool"*? #contextclues. I'm Madcap.
SHLIKT SHLIKT SHLIKT SHLIKT SHLIKT SHLIKT SHLIKT SHLIKT
SHLIKT SHLIKT SHLIKT SHLIKT SHLIKT SHLIKT SHLIKT SHLIKT
Of course you know, this means war.
Pew pew!
POP!
YOU...
GOT ME?

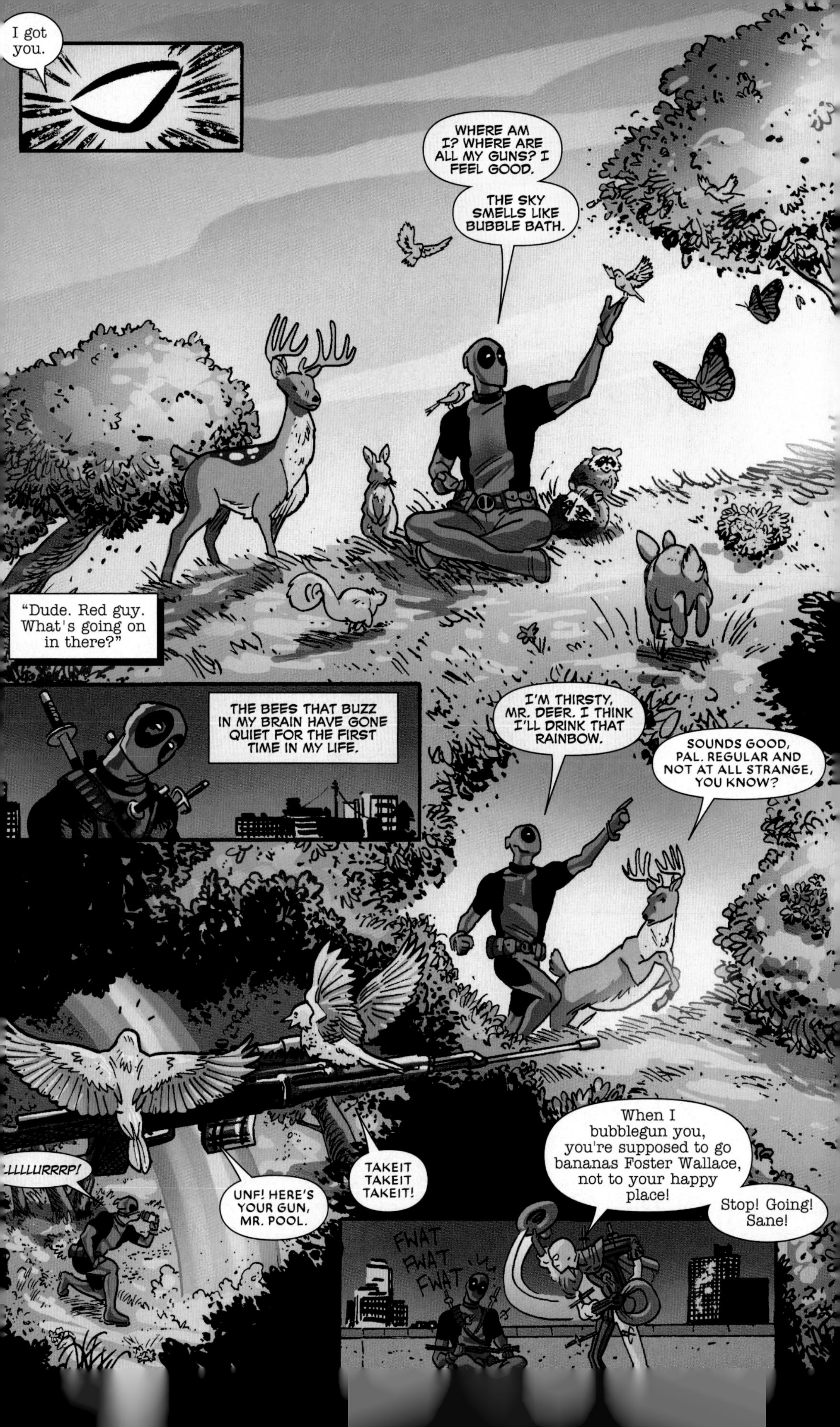
I got you.
WHERE AM I? WHERE ARE ALL MY GUNS? I FEEL GOOD.
THE SKY SMELLS LIKE BUBBLE BATH.
"Dude. Red guy. What's going on in there?"
THE BEES THAT BUZZ IN MY BRAIN HAVE GONE QUIET FOR THE FIRST TIME IN MY LIFE.
I'M THIRSTY, MR. DEER. I THINK I'LL DRINK THAT RAINBOW.
SOUNDS GOOD, PAL. REGULAR AND NOT AT ALL STRANGE, YOU KNOW?
LLLLLURRRP!
UNF! HERE'S YOUR GUN, MR. POOL.
TAKEIT TAKEIT TAKEIT!
When I bubblegun you, you're supposed to go bananas Foster Wallace, not to your happy place!
Stop! Going! Sane!
FWAT FWAT FWAT

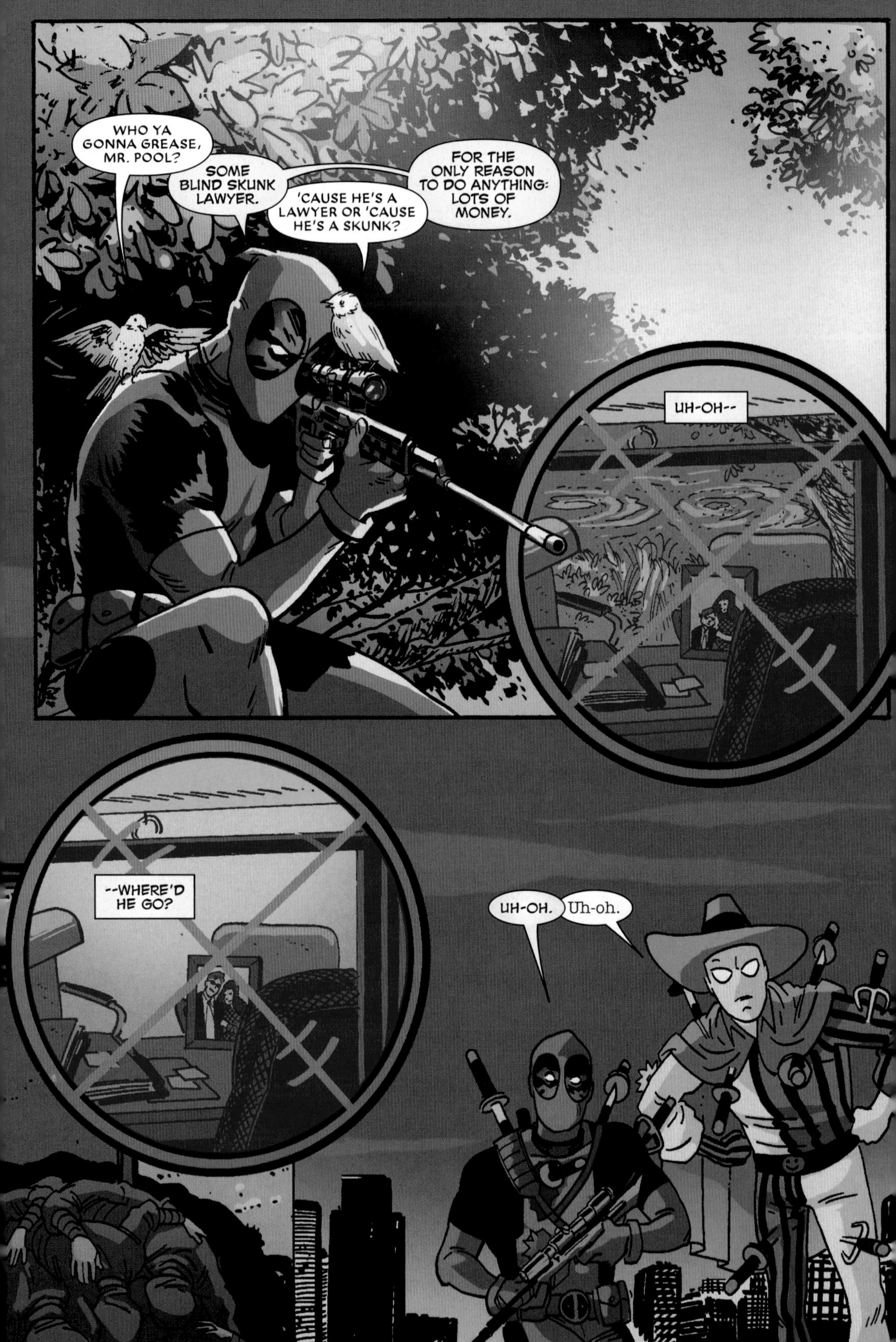

WHO YA GONNA GREASE, MR. POOL?
SOME BLIND SKUNK LAWYER.
'CAUSE HE'S A LAWYER OR 'CAUSE HE'S A SKUNK?
FOR THE ONLY REASON TO DO ANYTHING: LOTS OF MONEY.
UH-OH--
--WHERE'D HE GO?
UH-OH.
Uh-oh.

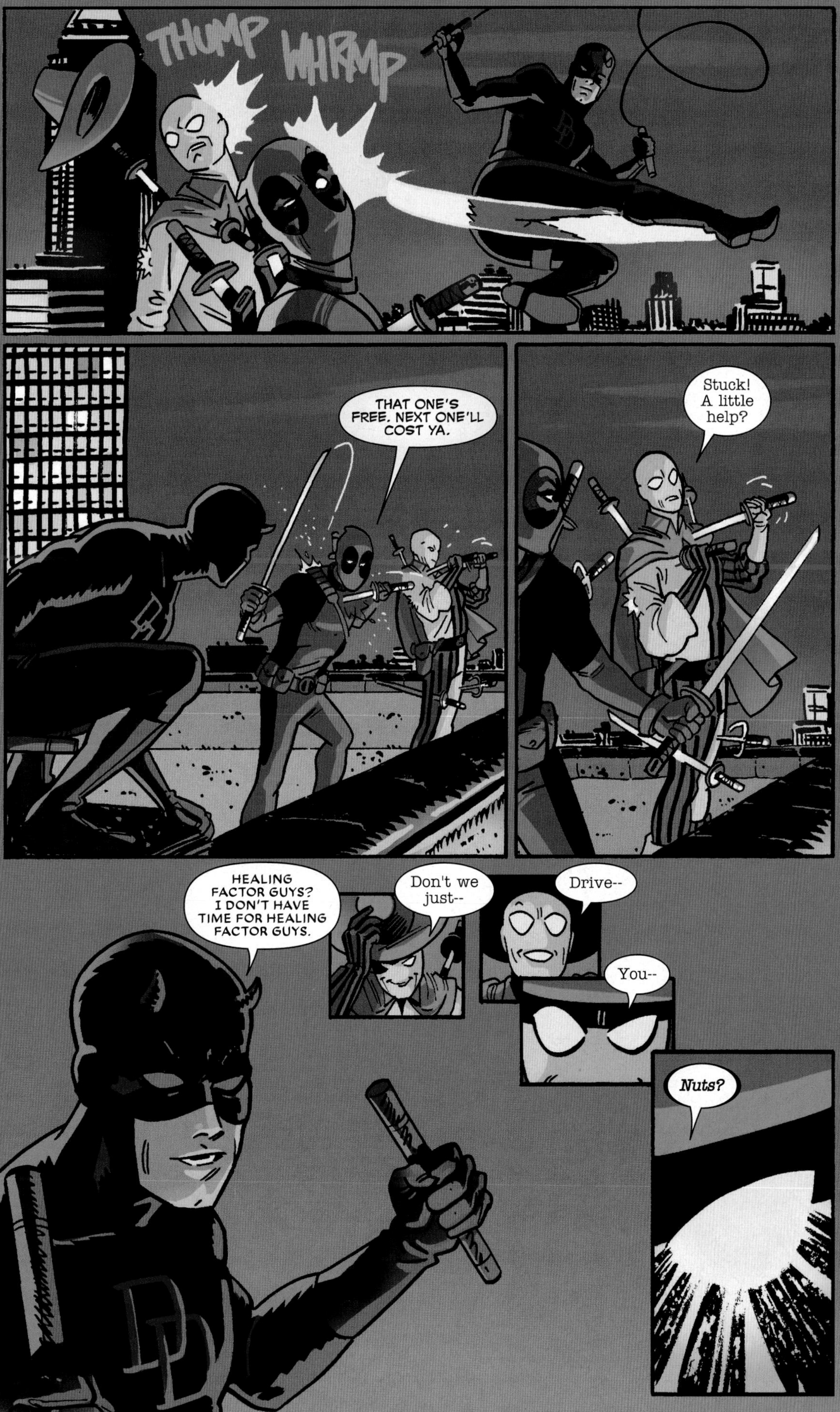
THUMP
WHRMP
THAT ONE'S FREE. NEXT ONE'LL COST YA.
Stuck! A little help?
HEALING FACTOR GUYS? I DON'T HAVE TIME FOR HEALING FACTOR GUYS.
Don't we just--
Drive--
You--
Nuts?

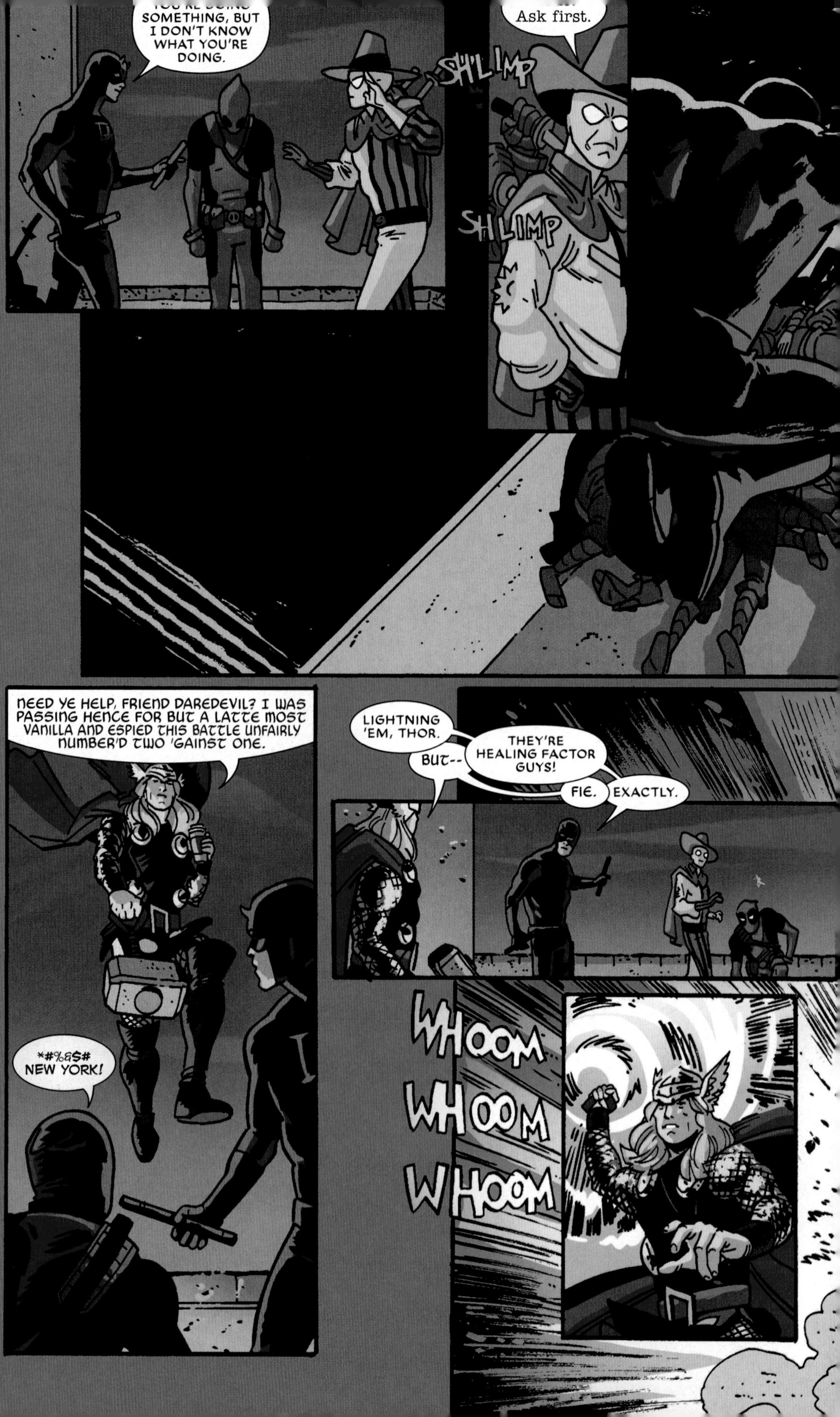
SOMETHING, BUT I DON'T KNOW WHAT YOU'RE DOING.
Ask first.
SH'LIMP
SH'LIMP
NEED YE HELP, FRIEND DAREDEVIL? I WAS PASSING HENCE FOR BUT A LATTE MOST VANILLA AND ESPIED THIS BATTLE UNFAIRLY NUMBER'D TWO 'GAINST ONE.
*#%&$# NEW YORK!
LIGHTNING 'EM, THOR.
BUT--
THEY'RE HEALING FACTOR GUYS!
FIE.
EXACTLY.
WHOOM
WHOOM
WHOOM

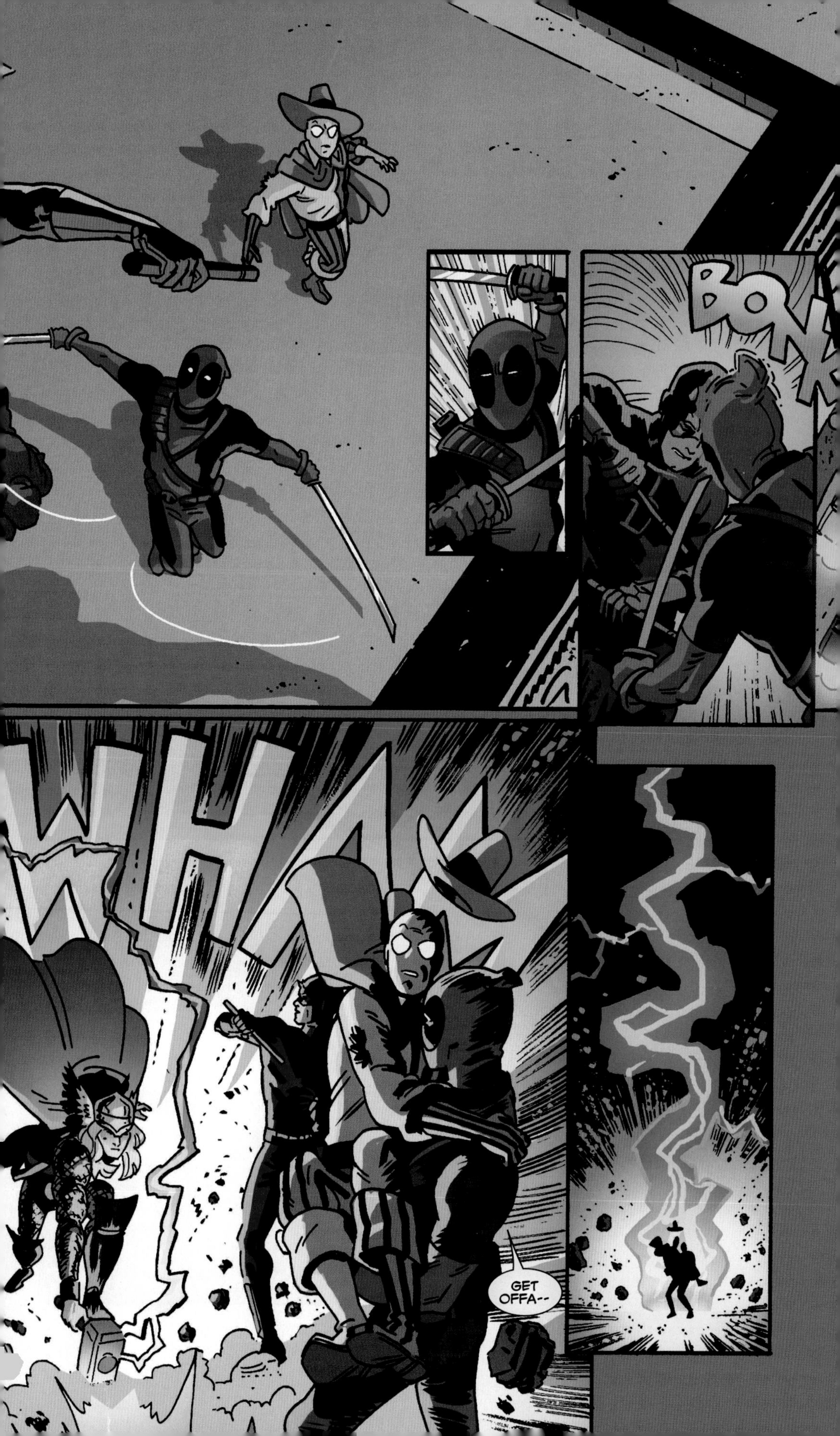
GET OFFA--

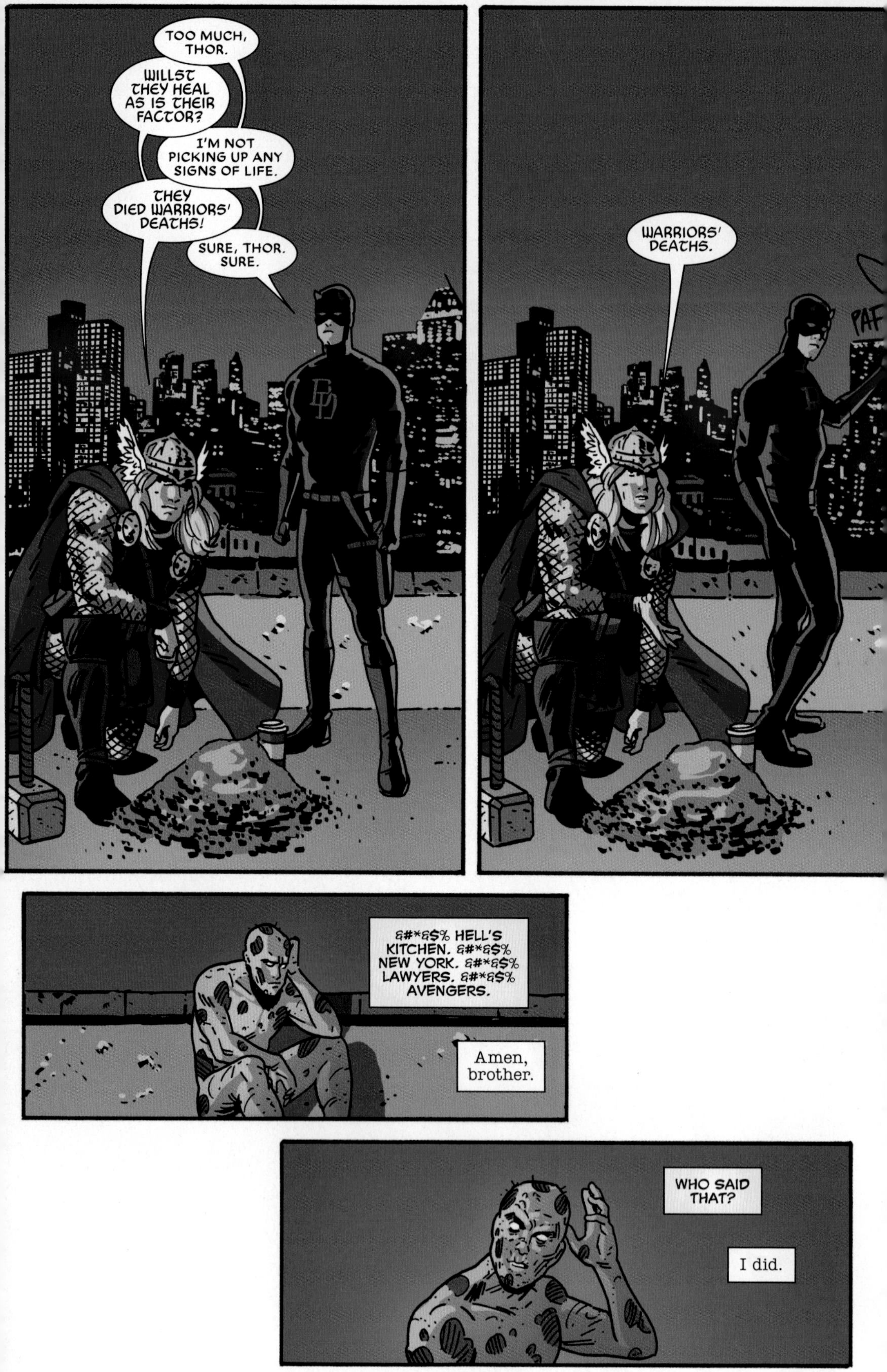

TOO MUCH, THOR.
WILLST THEY HEAL AS IS THEIR FACTOR?
I'M NOT PICKING UP ANY SIGNS OF LIFE.
THEY DIED WARRIORS' DEATHS!
SURE, THOR. SURE.
WARRIORS' DEATHS.
&#*&$% HELL'S KITCHEN. &#*&$% NEW YORK. &#*&$% LAWYERS. &#*&$% AVENGERS.
Amen, brother.
WHO SAID THAT?
I did.

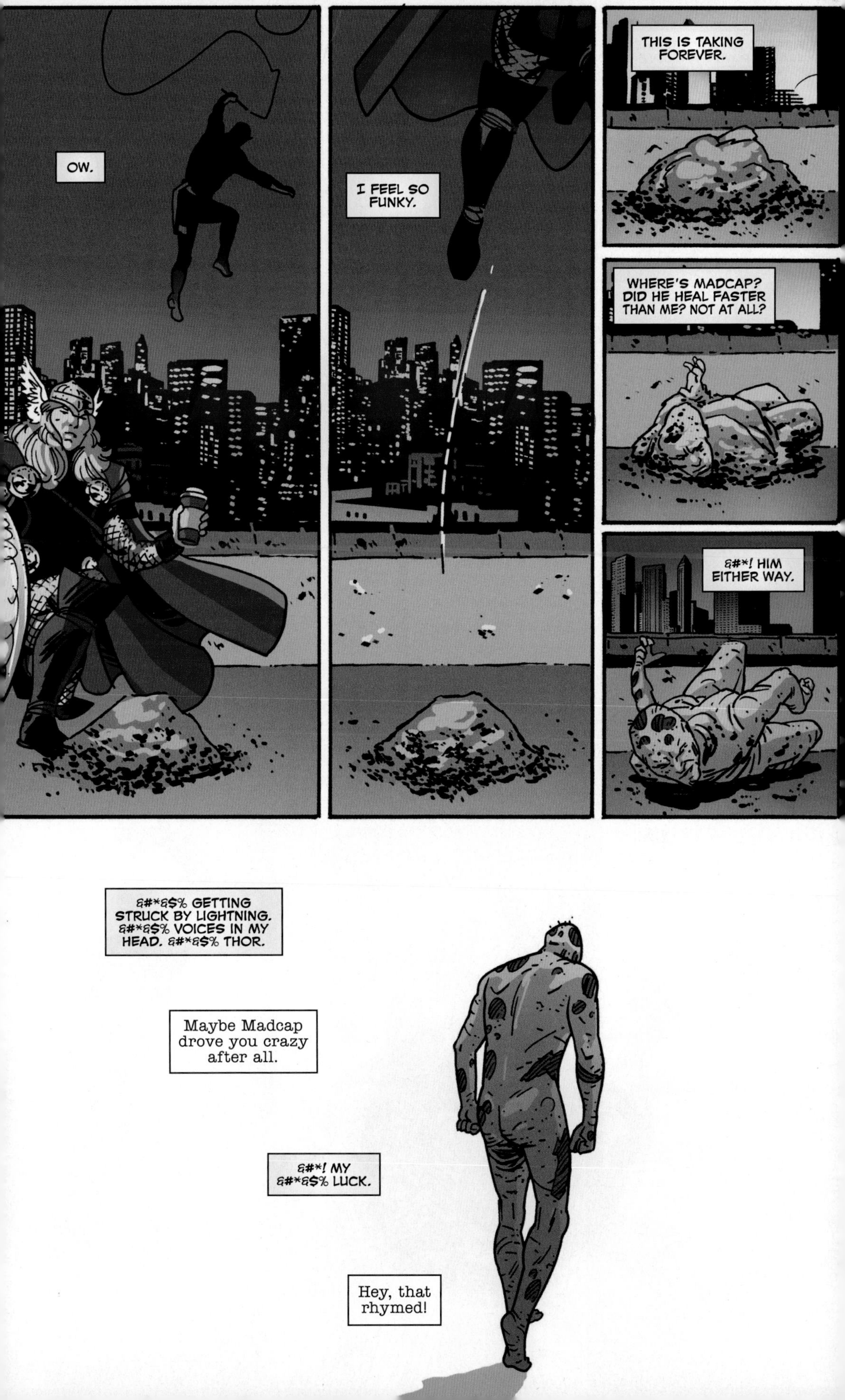
OW.
I FEEL SO FUNKY.
THIS IS TAKING FOREVER.
WHERE'S MADCAP? DID HE HEAL FASTER THAN ME? NOT AT ALL?
&#*! HIM EITHER WAY.
&#*&$% GETTING STRUCK BY LIGHTNING. &#*&$% VOICES IN MY HEAD. &#*&$% THOR.
Maybe Madcap drove you crazy after all.
&#*! MY &#*&$% LUCK.
Hey, that rhymed!

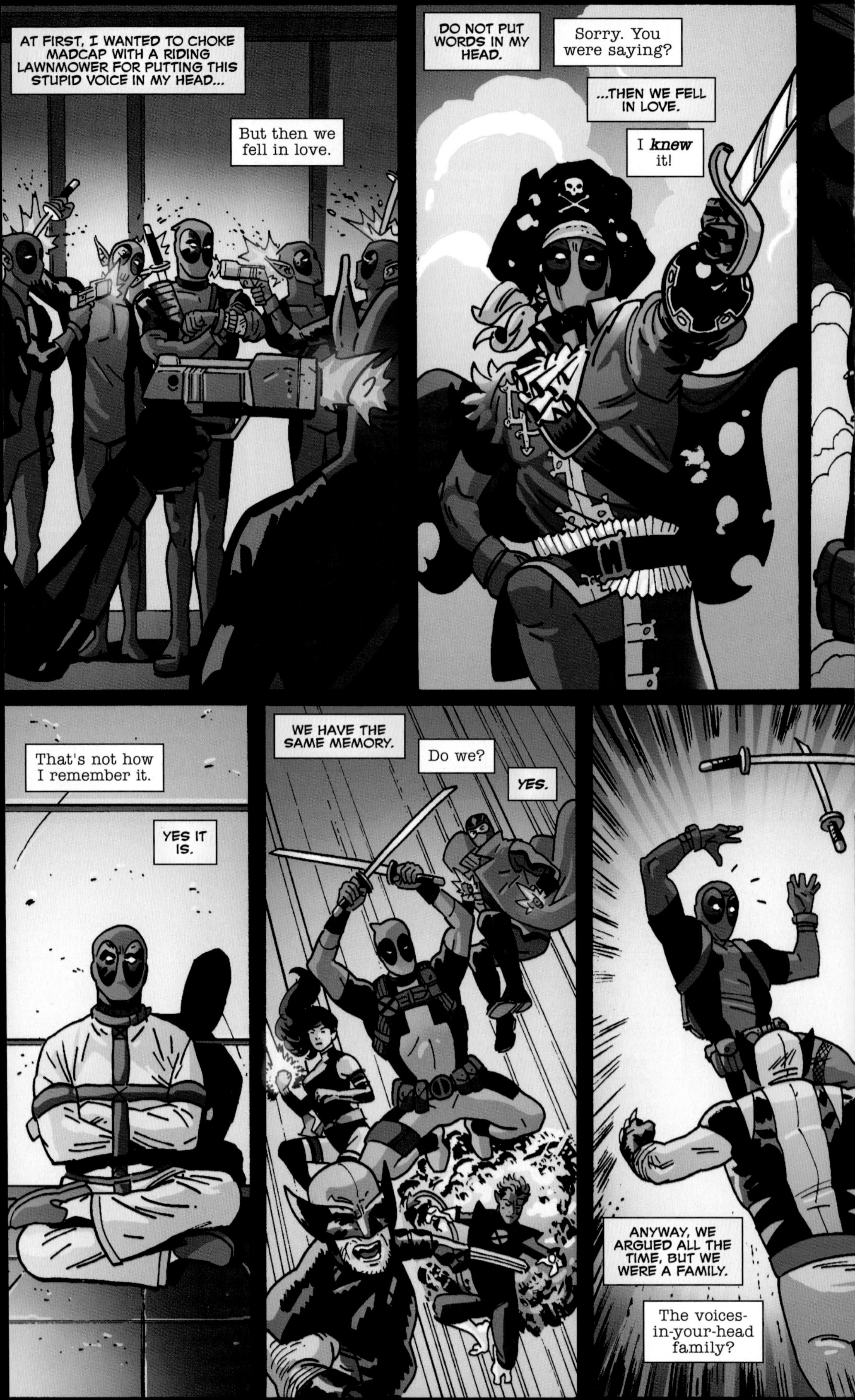
AT FIRST, I WANTED TO CHOKE MADCAP WITH A RIDING LAWNMOWER FOR PUTTING THIS STUPID VOICE IN MY HEAD...
But then we fell in love.
DO NOT PUT WORDS IN MY HEAD.
Sorry. You were saying?
...THEN WE FELL IN LOVE.
I *knew* it!
That's not how I remember it.
YES IT IS.
WE HAVE THE SAME MEMORY.
Do we?
YES.
ANYWAY, WE ARGUED ALL THE TIME, BUT WE WERE A FAMILY.
The voices-in-your-head family?

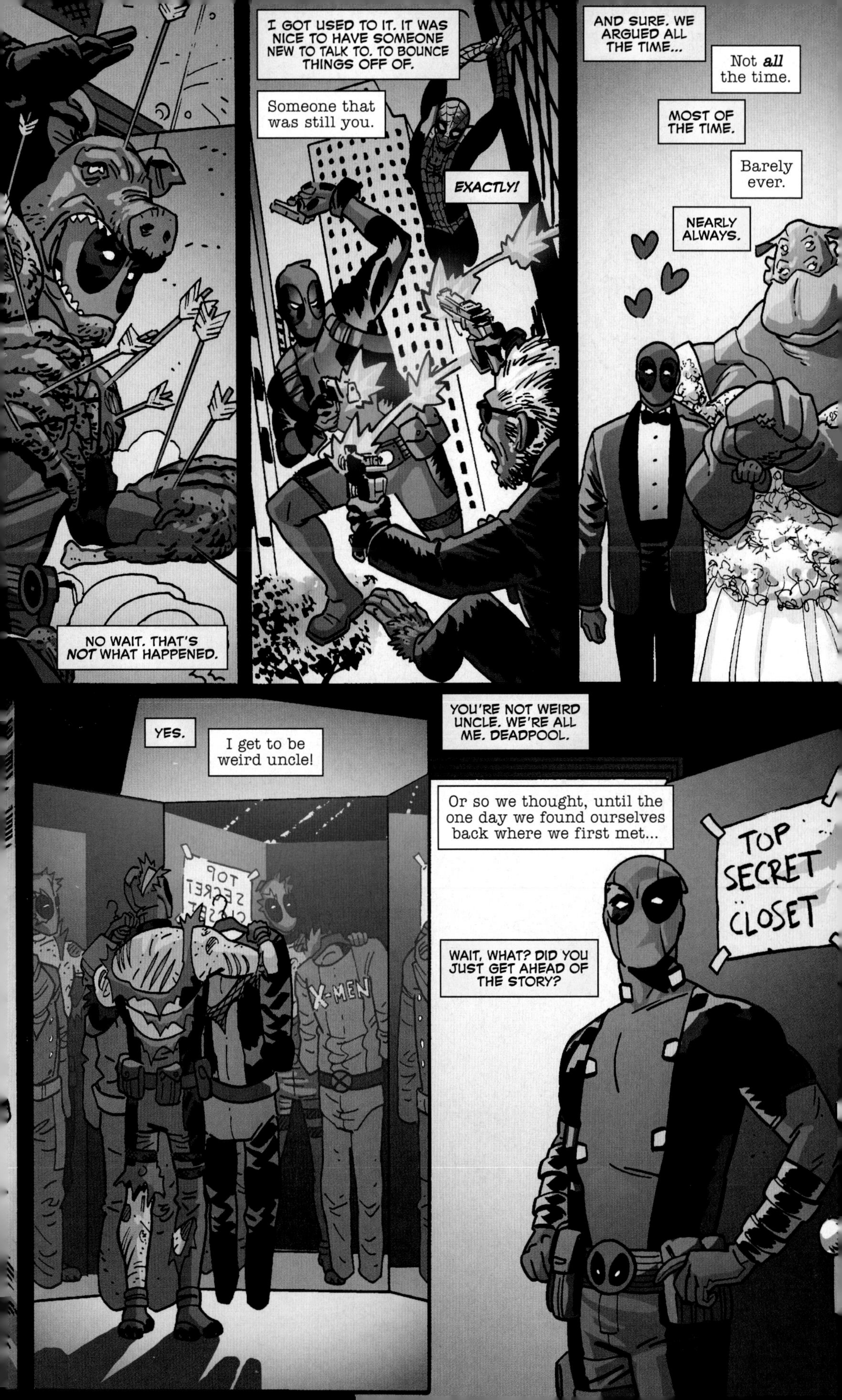
NO WAIT. THAT'S *NOT* WHAT HAPPENED.
I GOT USED TO IT. IT WAS NICE TO HAVE SOMEONE NEW TO TALK TO. TO BOUNCE THINGS OFF OF.
Someone that was still you.
EXACTLY!
AND SURE. WE ARGUED ALL THE TIME...
Not ***all*** the time.
MOST OF THE TIME.
Barely ever.
NEARLY ALWAYS.
YES.
I get to be weird uncle!
TOP SECRET CLOSET
X-MEN
YOU'RE NOT WEIRD UNCLE. WE'RE ALL ME. DEADPOOL.
Or so we thought, until the one day we found ourselves back where we first met...
TOP SECRET CLOSET
WAIT, WHAT? DID YOU JUST GET AHEAD OF THE STORY?

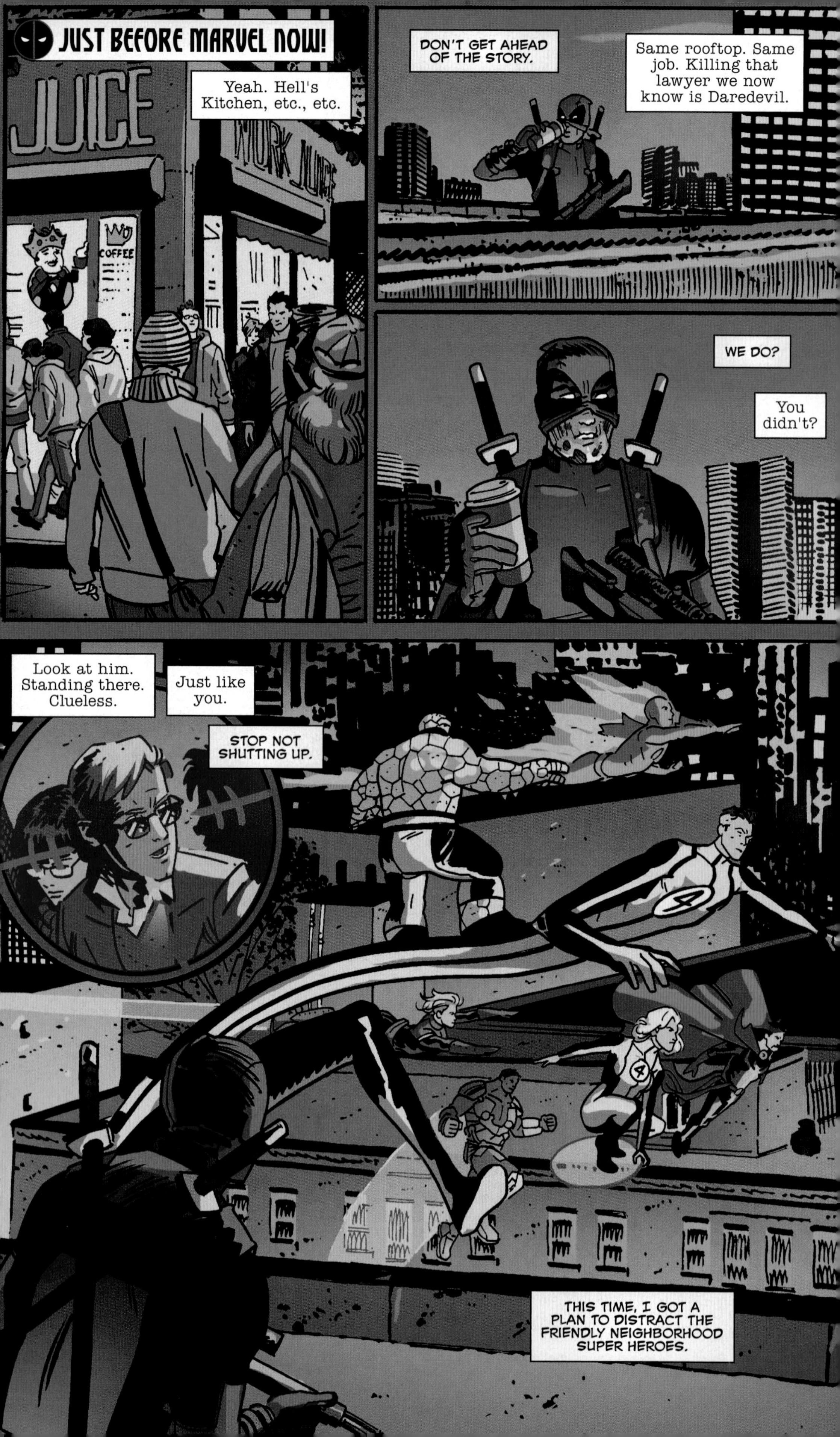
JUST BEFORE MARVEL NOW!
JUICE
Yeah. Hell's Kitchen, etc., etc.
COFFEE
DON'T GET AHEAD OF THE STORY.
Same rooftop. Same job. Killing that lawyer we now know is Daredevil.
WE DO?
You didn't?
Look at him. Standing there. Clueless.
Just like you.
STOP NOT SHUTTING UP.
THIS TIME, I GOT A PLAN TO DISTRACT THE FRIENDLY NEIGHBORHOOD SUPER HEROES.

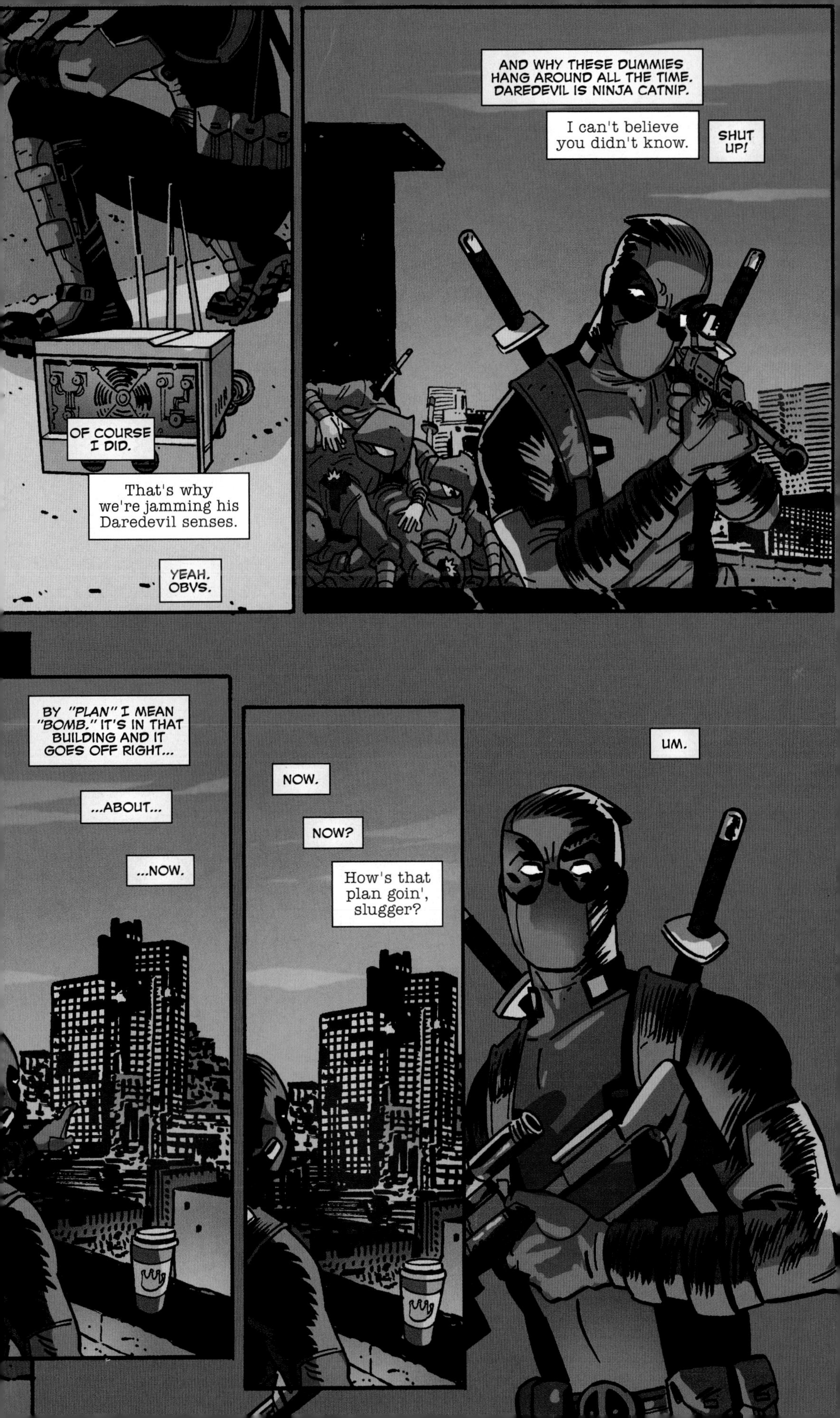
OF COURSE I DID.
That's why we're jamming his Daredevil senses.
YEAH. OBVS.
AND WHY THESE DUMMIES HANG AROUND ALL THE TIME. DAREDEVIL IS NINJA CATNIP.
I can't believe you didn't know.
SHUT UP!
BY "PLAN" I MEAN "BOMB." IT'S IN THAT BUILDING AND IT GOES OFF RIGHT...
...ABOUT...
...NOW.
NOW.
NOW?
How's that plan goin', slugger?
UM.

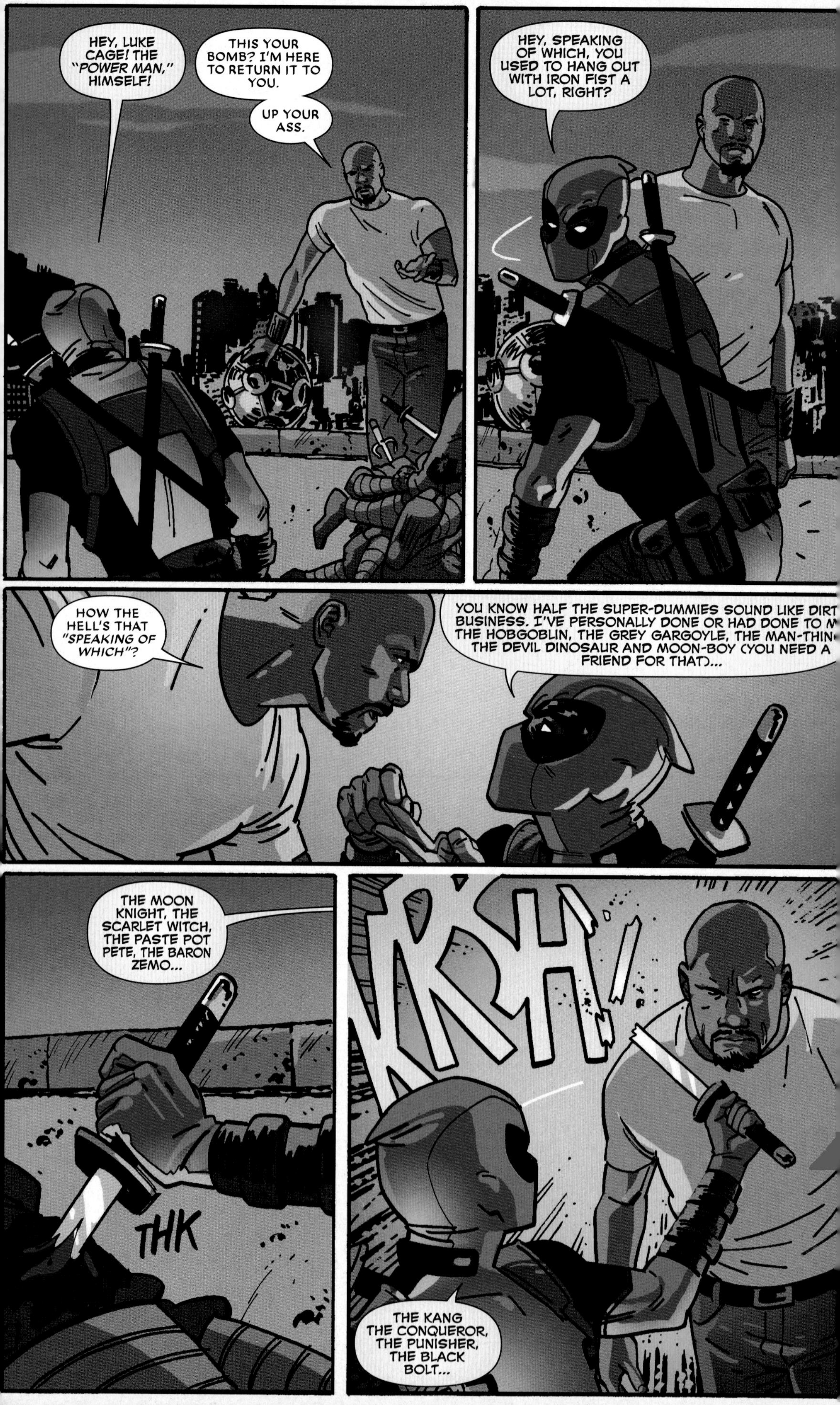

HEY, LUKE CAGE! THE "POWER MAN," HIMSELF!
THIS YOUR BOMB? I'M HERE TO RETURN IT TO YOU.
UP YOUR ASS.
HEY, SPEAKING OF WHICH, YOU USED TO HANG OUT WITH IRON FIST A LOT, RIGHT?
HOW THE HELL'S THAT "SPEAKING OF WHICH"?
YOU KNOW HALF THE SUPER-DUMMIES SOUND LIKE DIRT BUSINESS. I'VE PERSONALLY DONE OR HAD DONE TO THE HOBGOBLIN, THE GREY GARGOYLE, THE MAN-THIN THE DEVIL DINOSAUR AND MOON-BOY (YOU NEED A FRIEND FOR THAT)...
THE MOON KNIGHT, THE SCARLET WITCH, THE PASTE POT PETE, THE BARON ZEMO...
THK
KRRH!
THE KANG THE CONQUEROR, THE PUNISHER, THE BLACK BOLT...

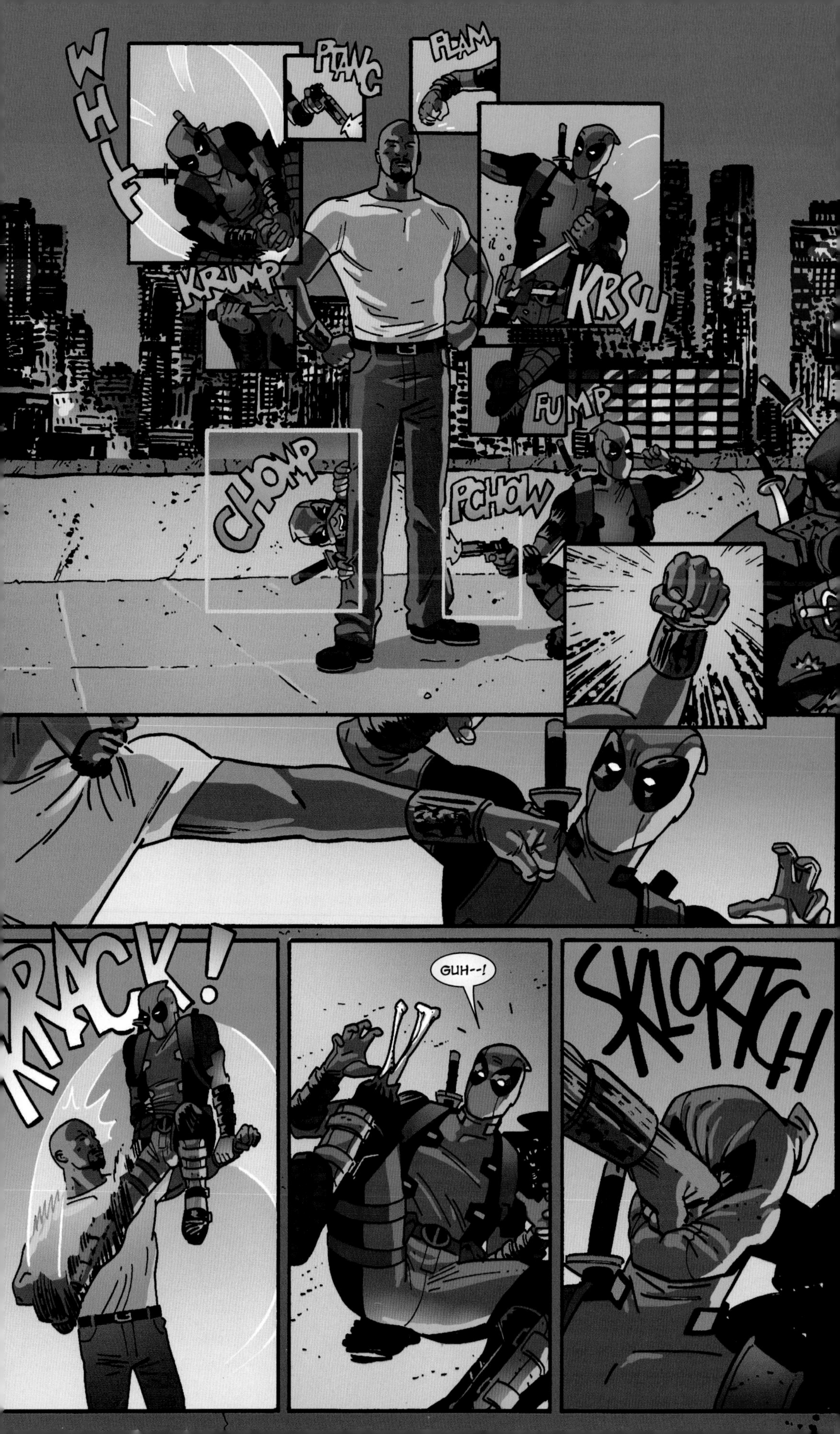
WHIFF
PTANG
PLAM
KRUMP
KRSH
FUMP
CHOMP
PCHOW
KRACK!
GUH--!
SKLORTCH

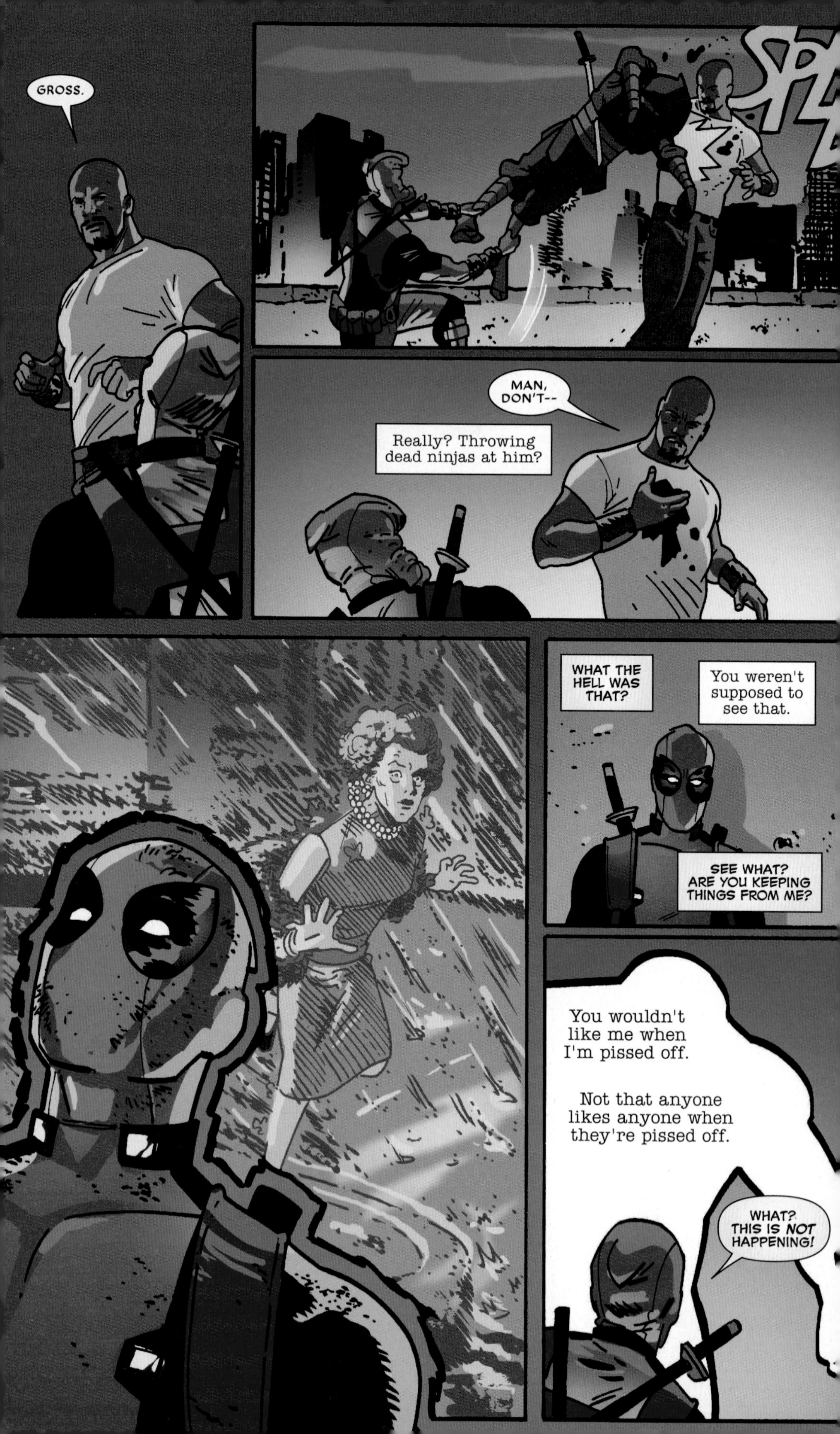
GROSS.
MAN, DON'T--
Really? Throwing dead ninjas at him?
WHAT THE HELL WAS THAT?
You weren't supposed to see that.
SEE WHAT? ARE YOU KEEPING THINGS FROM ME?
You wouldn't like me when I'm pissed off.
Not that anyone likes anyone when they're pissed off.
WHAT? THIS IS *NOT* HAPPENING!

ONE OF THESE DUMMIES HAS TO HAVE A SMOKE BOMB ON HIM SO I CAN ESCAPE.

AND THE PLURAL OF NINJA IS NINJA.

STOP THROWING NINJA AT ME.

SEE?

DON'T BLAME ME! I DIDN'T KNOW ABOUT IT.

Don't yell at me. Or else.

OR ELSE WHAT?

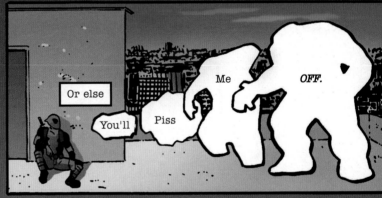

Or else

You'll

Piss

Me

OFF.

This is absolutely happening, True Believer!

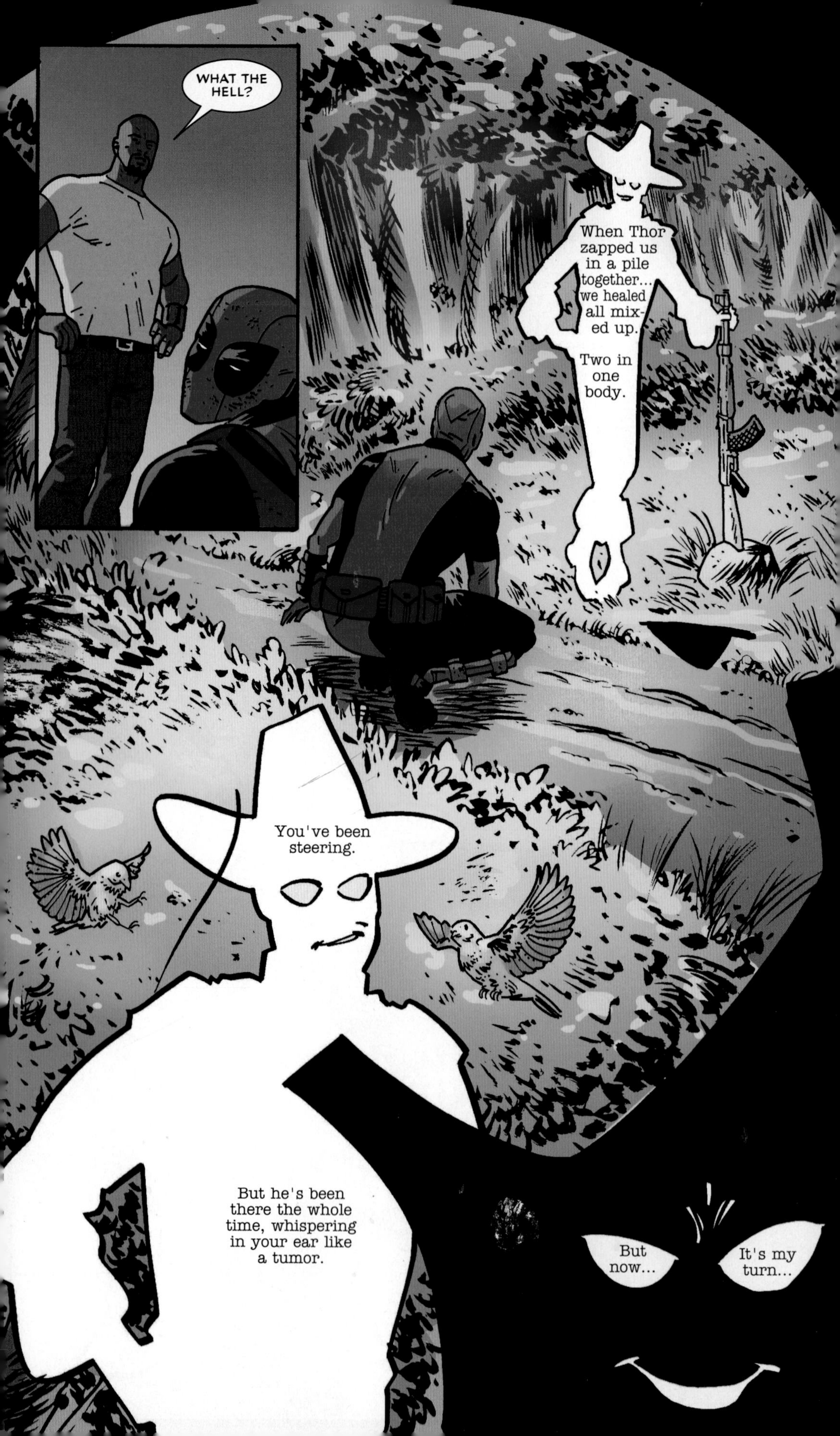
WHAT THE HELL?
When Thor zapped us in a pile together... we healed all mix-ed up.
Two in one body.
You've been steering.
But he's been there the whole time, whispering in your ear like a tumor.
But now...
It's my turn...

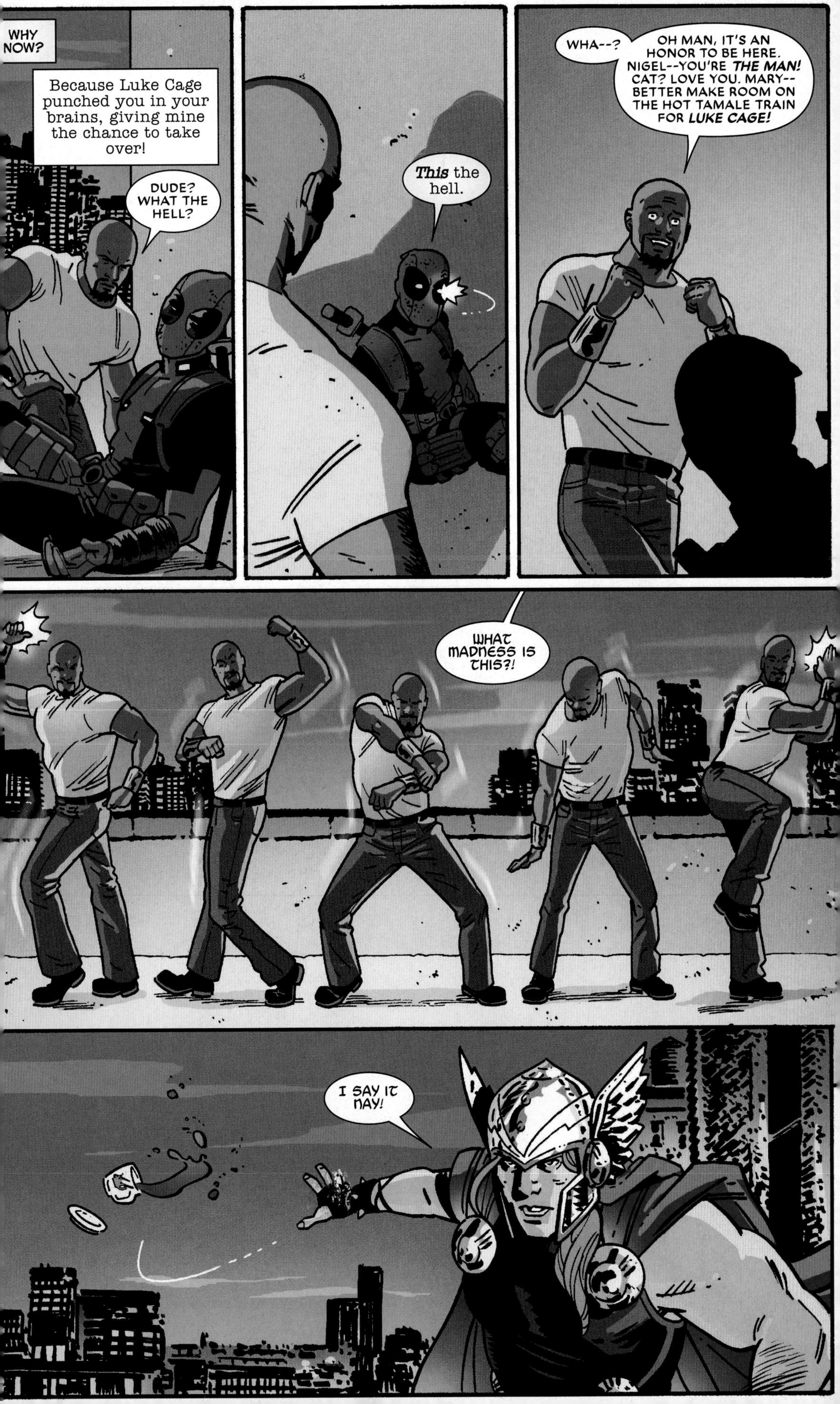

WHY NOW?
Because Luke Cage punched you in your brains, giving mine the chance to take over!
DUDE? WHAT THE HELL?
This the hell.
WHA--?
OH MAN, IT'S AN HONOR TO BE HERE. NIGEL--YOU'RE THE MAN! CAT? LOVE YOU. MARY--BETTER MAKE ROOM ON THE HOT TAMALE TRAIN FOR LUKE CAGE!
WHAT MADNESS IS THIS?!
I SAY IT NAY!

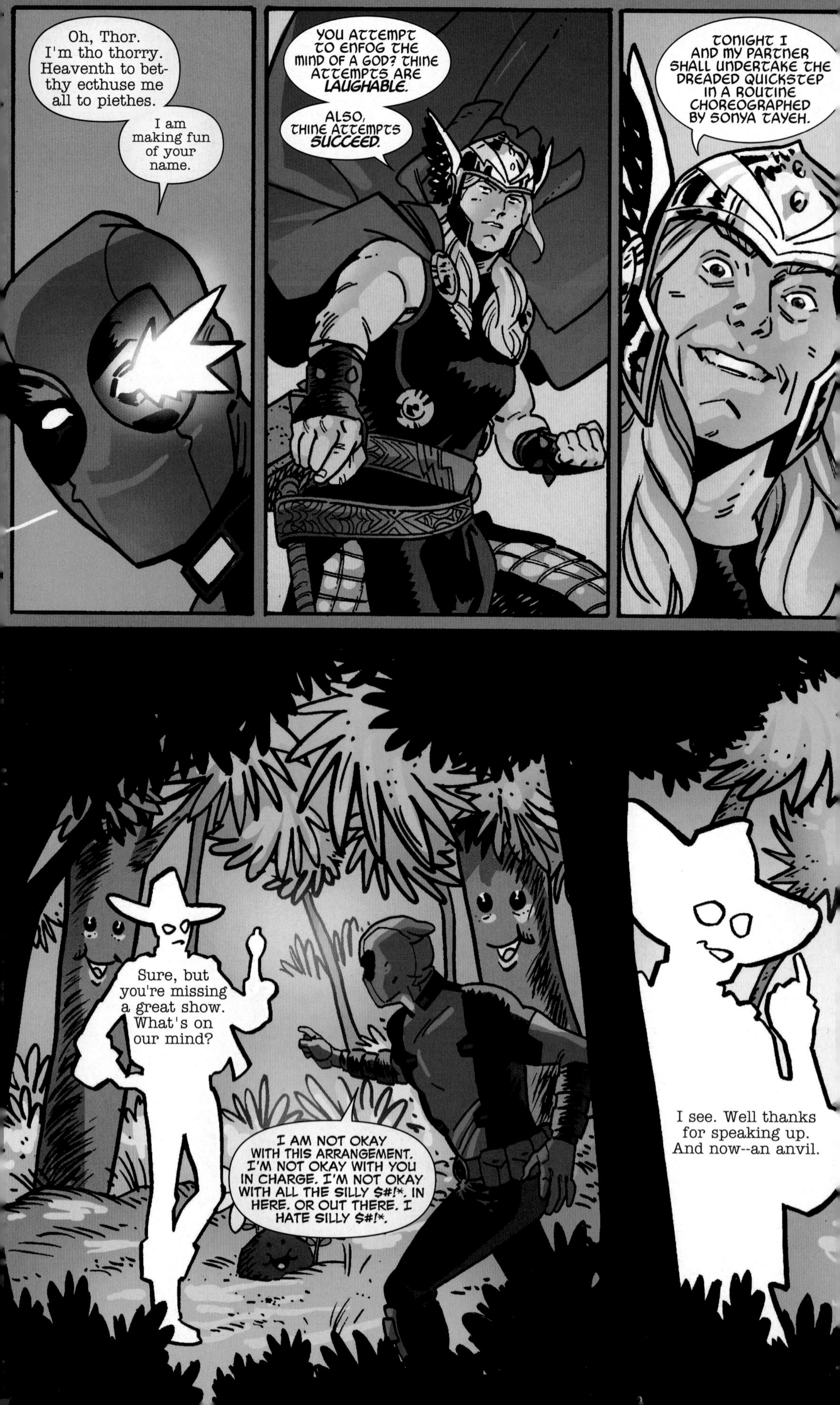
Oh, Thor. I'm tho thorry. Heaventh to bet-thy ecthuse me all to piethes.
I am making fun of your name.
YOU ATTEMPT TO ENFOG THE MIND OF A GOD? THINE ATTEMPTS ARE LAUGHABLE.
ALSO, THINE ATTEMPTS SUCCEED.
TONIGHT I AND MY PARTNER SHALL UNDERTAKE THE DREADED QUICKSTEP IN A ROUTINE CHOREOGRAPHED BY SONYA TAYEH.
Sure, but you're missing a great show. What's on our mind?
I AM NOT OKAY WITH THIS ARRANGEMENT. I'M NOT OKAY WITH YOU IN CHARGE. I'M NOT OKAY WITH ALL THE SILLY $#!*. IN HERE. OR OUT THERE. I HATE SILLY $#!*.
I see. Well thanks for speaking up. And now--an anvil.

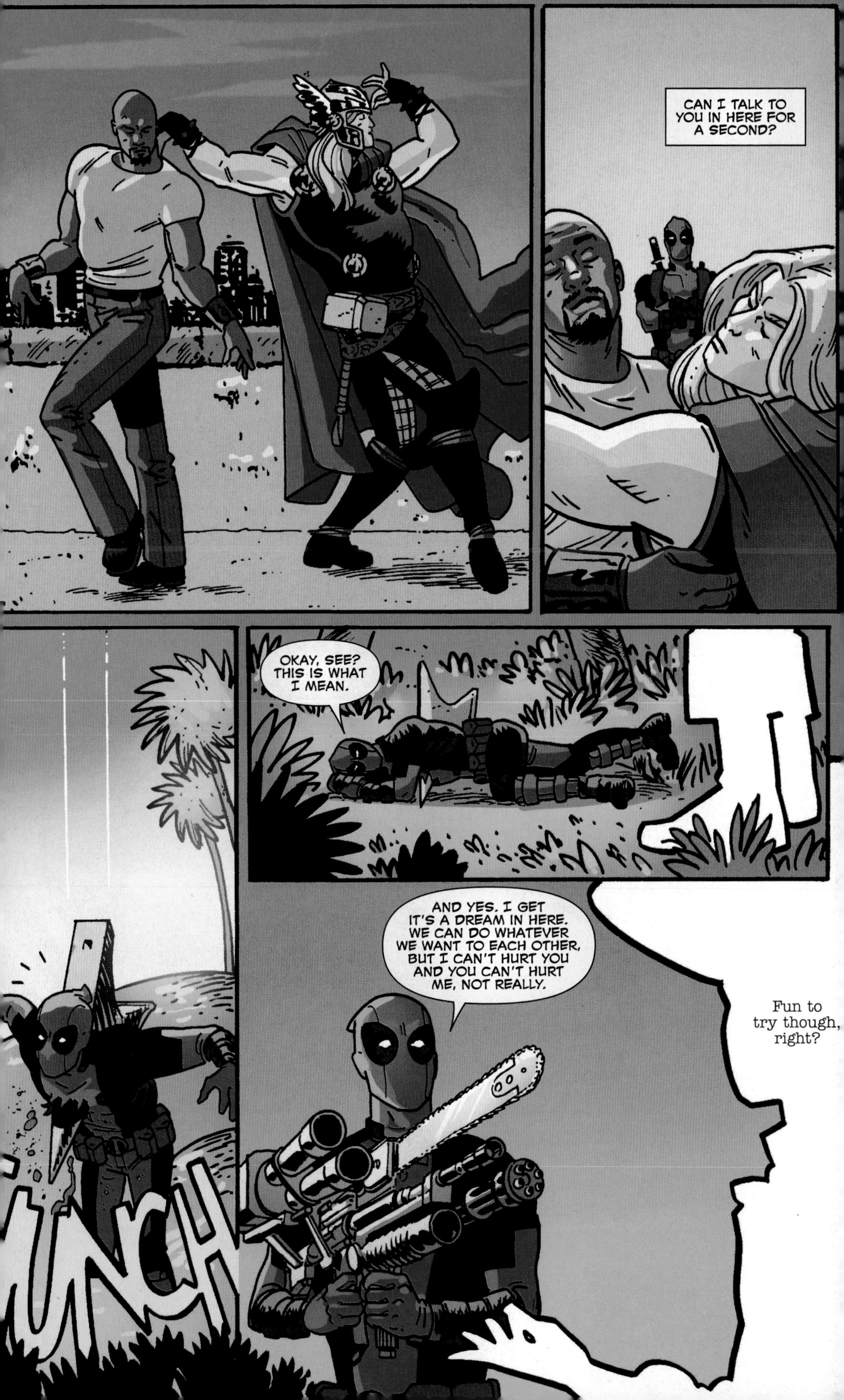
CAN I TALK TO YOU IN HERE FOR A SECOND?
OKAY, SEE? THIS IS WHAT I MEAN.
UNCH
AND YES. I GET IT'S A DREAM IN HERE. WE CAN DO WHATEVER WE WANT TO EACH OTHER, BUT I CAN'T HURT YOU AND YOU CAN'T HURT ME, NOT REALLY.
Fun to try though, right?

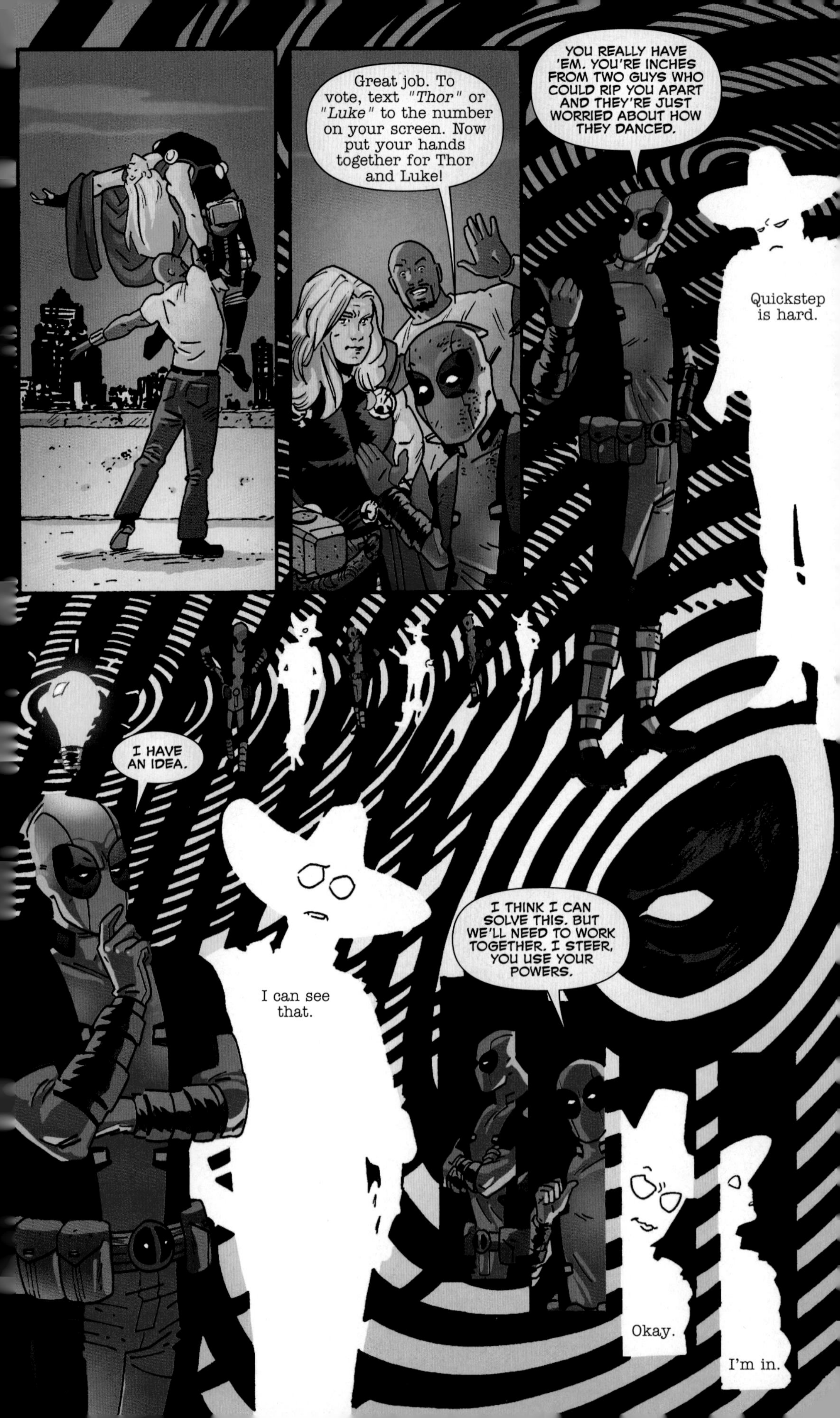

Great job. To vote, text "Thor" or "Luke" to the number on your screen. Now put your hands together for Thor and Luke!
YOU REALLY HAVE 'EM. YOU'RE INCHES FROM TWO GUYS WHO COULD RIP YOU APART AND THEY'RE JUST WORRIED ABOUT HOW THEY DANCED.
Quickstep is hard.
I HAVE AN IDEA.
I can see that.
I THINK I CAN SOLVE THIS. BUT WE'LL NEED TO WORK TOGETHER. I STEER, YOU USE YOUR POWERS.
Okay.
I'm in.

I think I'm thinking what
you're thinking. And it's
crazy enough to work.

Or else, maybe
just crazy. Which
is fine by me.

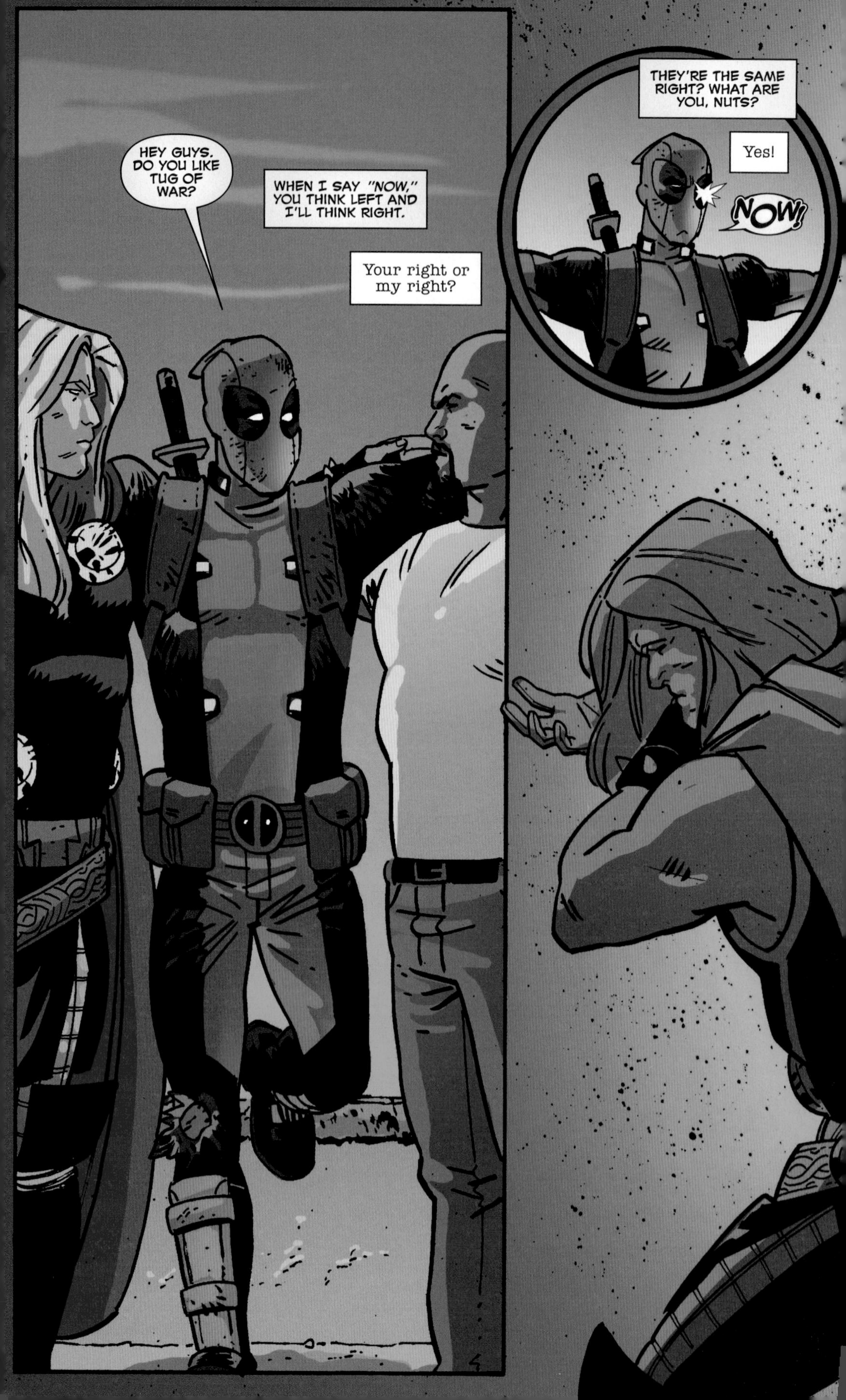
HEY GUYS. DO YOU LIKE TUG OF WAR?
WHEN I SAY "NOW," YOU THINK LEFT AND I'LL THINK RIGHT.
Your right or my right?
THEY'RE THE SAME RIGHT? WHAT ARE YOU, NUTS?
Yes!
NOW!

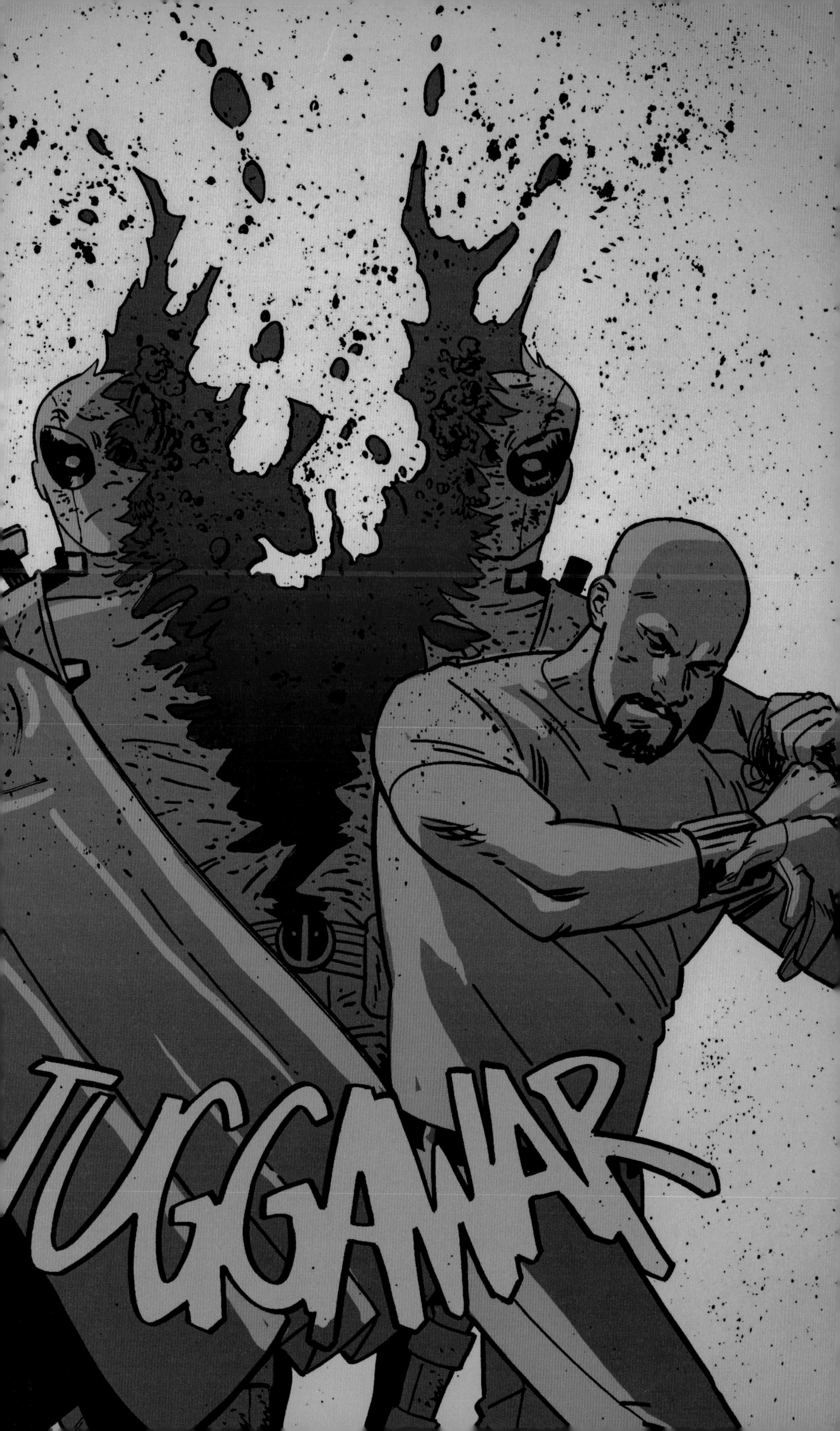
TUGGAWR

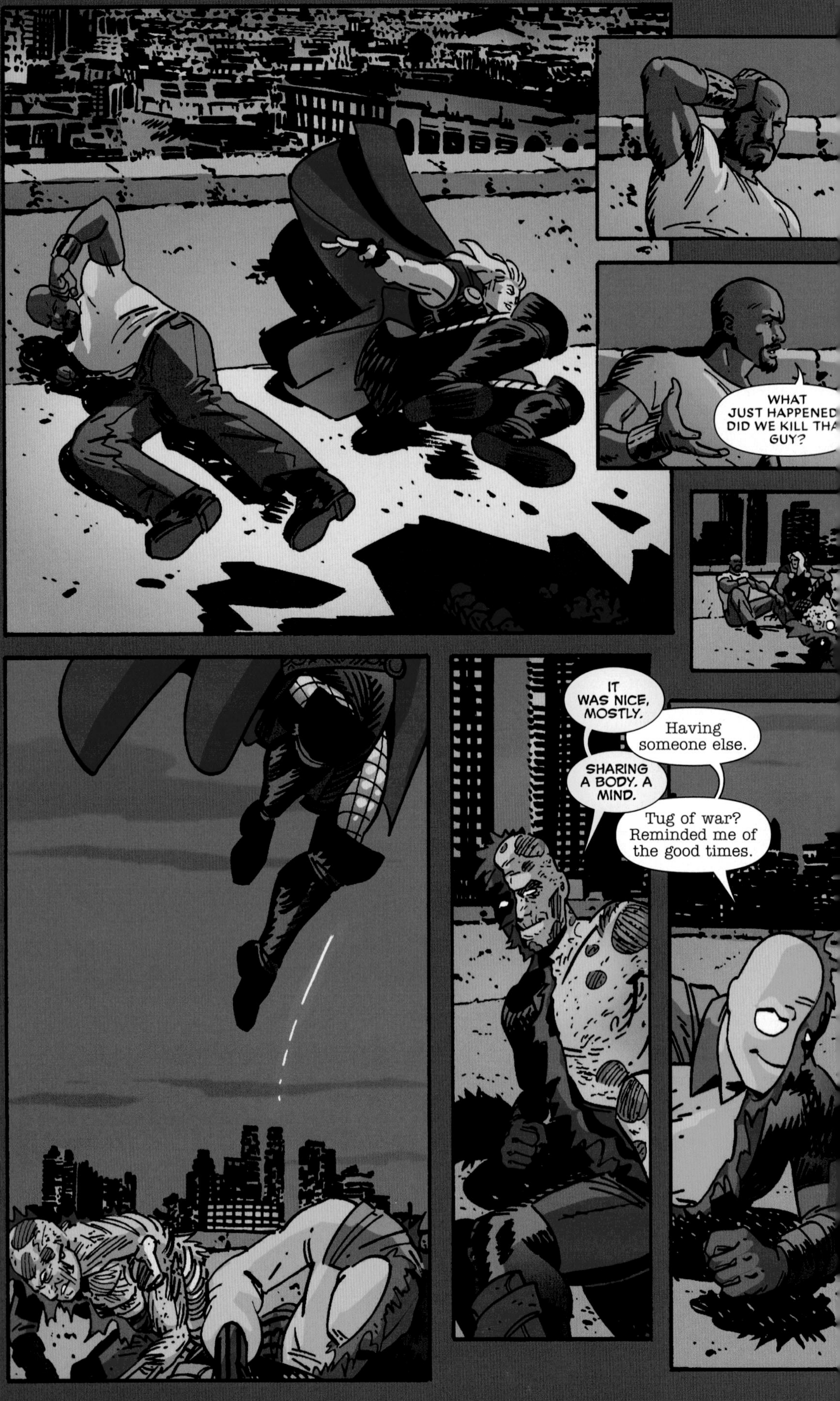
WHAT JUST HAPPENED DID WE KILL THA GUY?
IT WAS NICE, MOSTLY.
Having someone else.
SHARING A BODY. A MIND.
Tug of war? Reminded me of the good times.

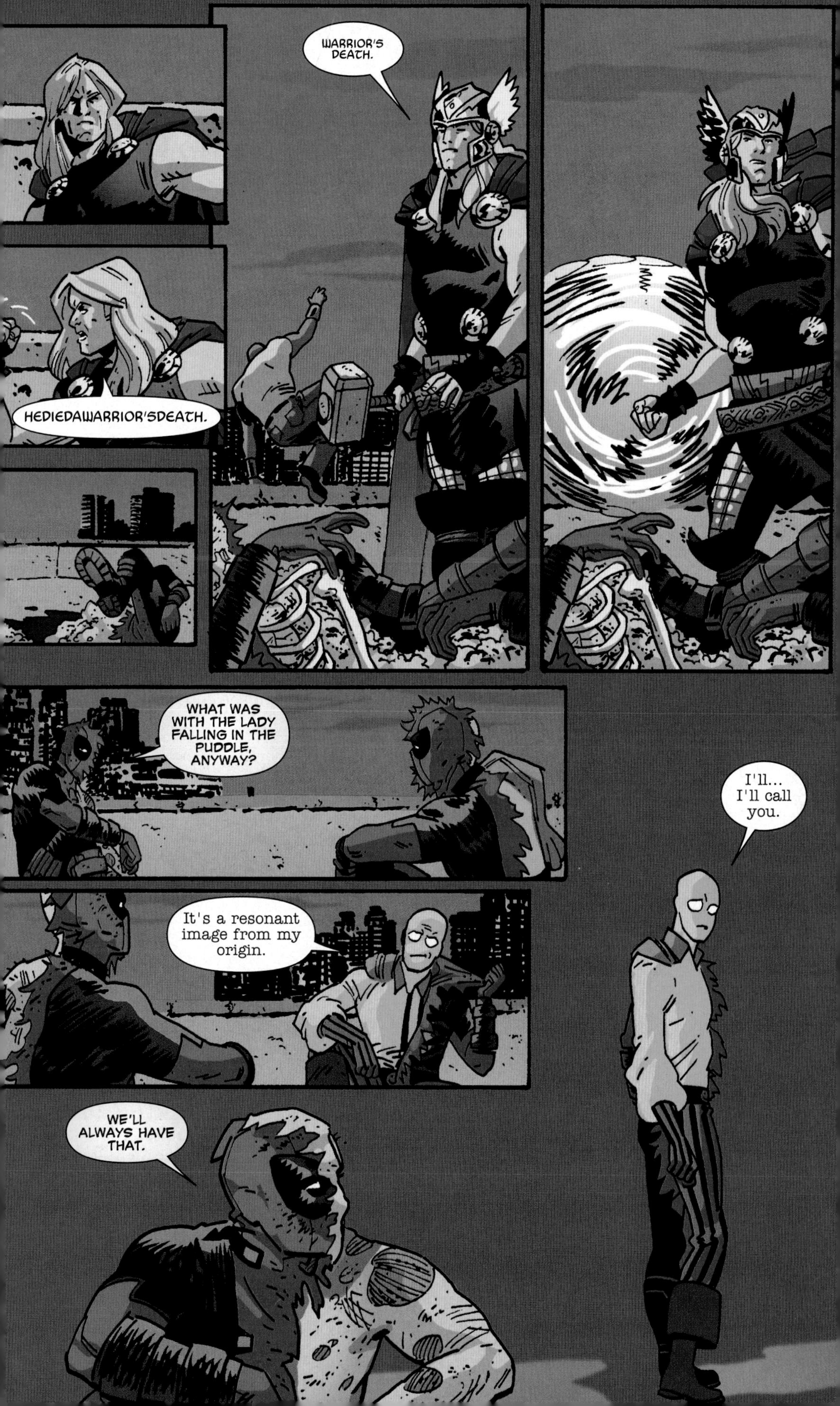
HEDIEDAWARRIOR'SDEATH.
WARRIOR'S DEATH.
WHAT WAS WITH THE LADY FALLING IN THE PUDDLE, ANYWAY?
It's a resonant image from my origin.
WE'LL ALWAYS HAVE THAT.
I'll... I'll call you.

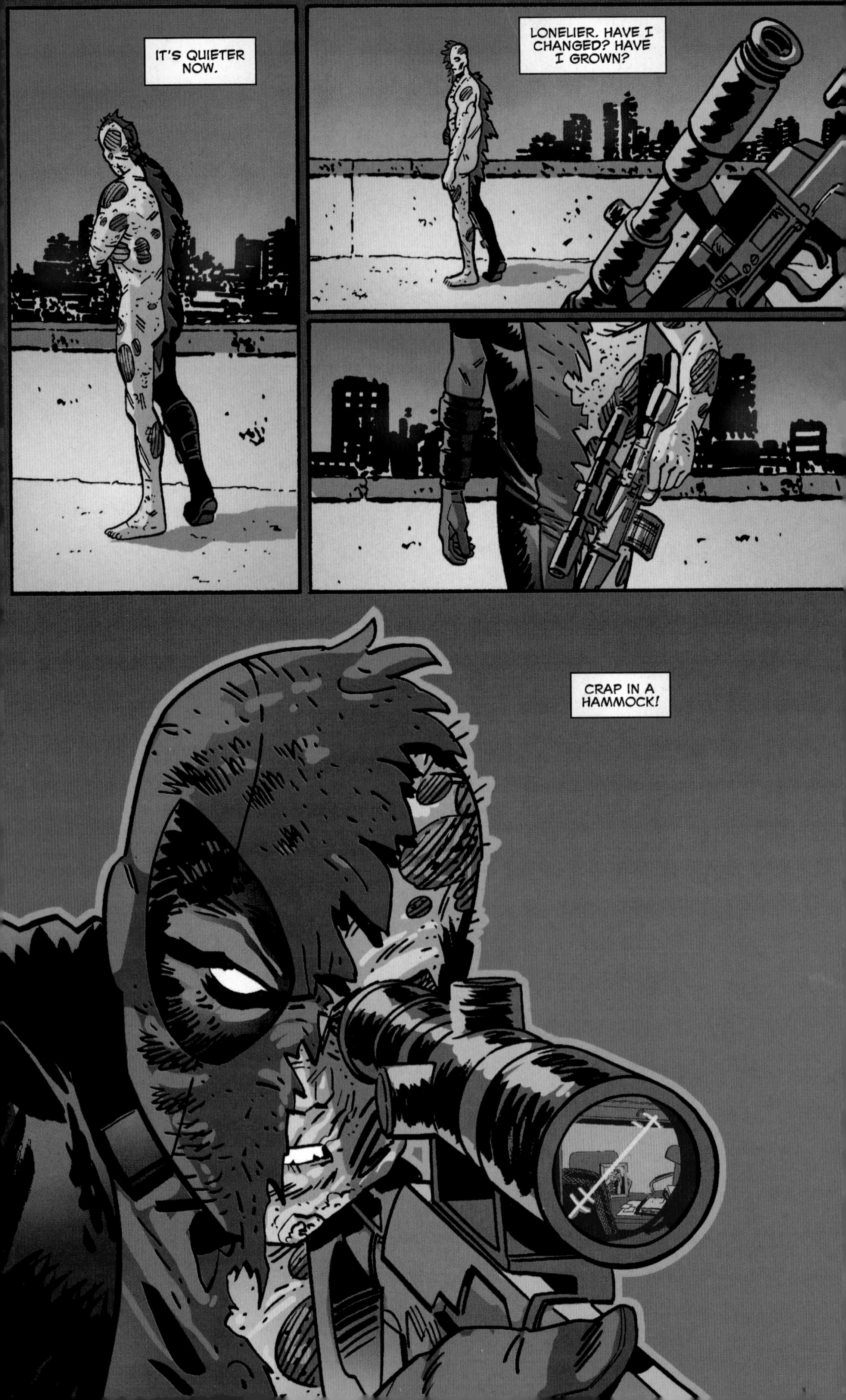
IT'S QUIETER NOW.
LONELIER. HAVE I CHANGED? HAVE I GROWN?
CRAP IN A HAMMOCK!

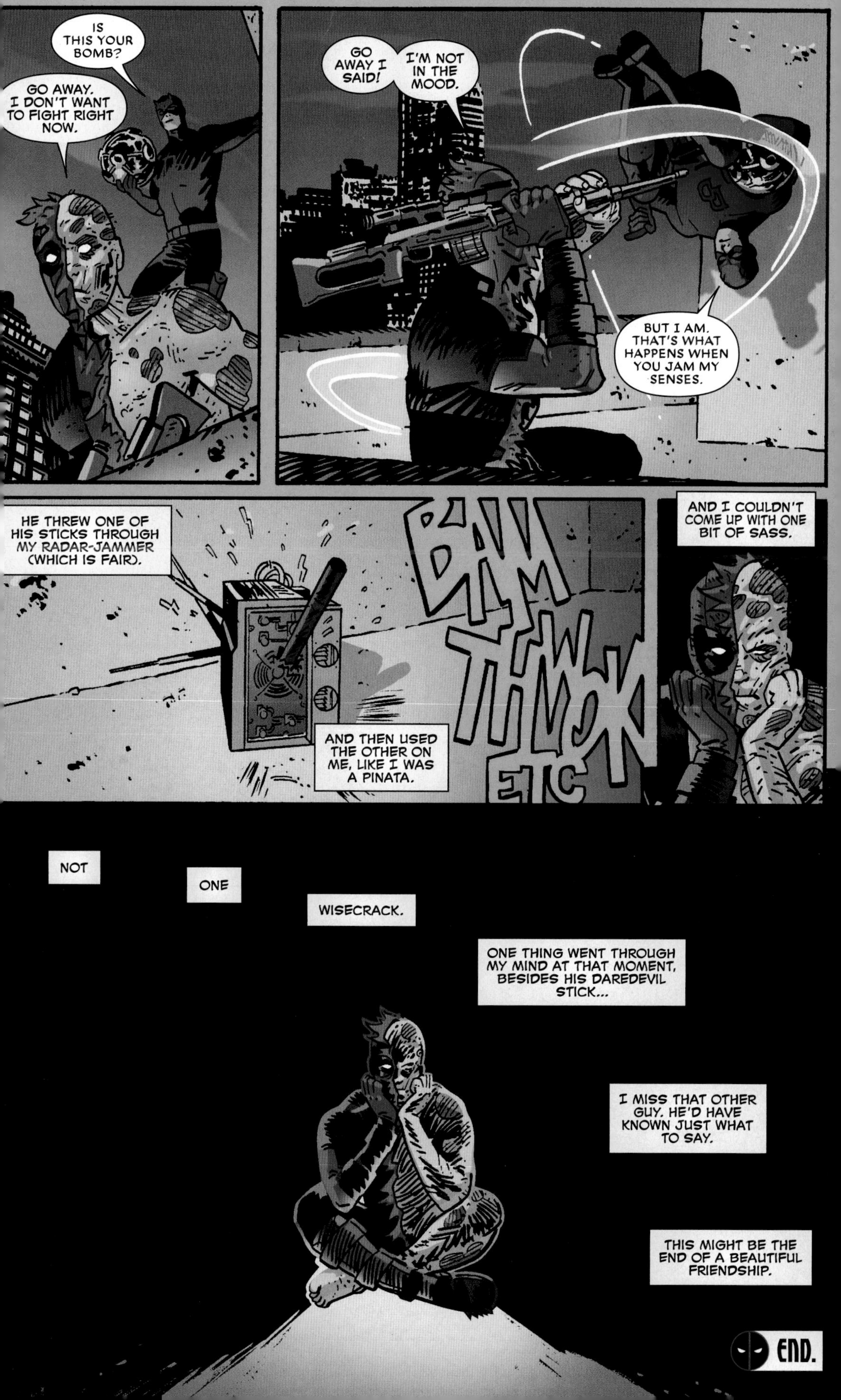
IS THIS YOUR BOMB?
GO AWAY. I DON'T WANT TO FIGHT RIGHT NOW.
GO AWAY I SAID!
I'M NOT IN THE MOOD.
BUT I AM. THAT'S WHAT HAPPENS WHEN YOU JAM MY SENSES.
HE THREW ONE OF HIS STICKS THROUGH MY RADAR-JAMMER (WHICH IS FAIR).
AND THEN USED THE OTHER ON ME, LIKE I WAS A PINATA.
BAM
THWAK
ETC
AND I COULDN'T COME UP WITH ONE BIT OF SASS.
NOT
ONE
WISECRACK.
ONE THING WENT THROUGH MY MIND AT THAT MOMENT, BESIDES HIS DAREDEVIL STICK...
I MISS THAT OTHER GUY. HE'D HAVE KNOWN JUST WHAT TO SAY.
THIS MIGHT BE THE END OF A BEAUTIFUL FRIENDSHIP.
END.

Deadpool #27 Cover Guide

On the next pages, you can see the cover for this issue in all its "naked" glor uncovered by logo, UPC or trade dress. As you can see…there are an INSANE numb of characters there — so many, in fact, that it currently holds the Guinne Book of World Records certified world record for the most characters on single issue's cover. Check out the full list of characters below! Although ou guide counts the characters at a whopping 236 characters, the Guinness judg have it pegged at 224, deciding that the creators and editors don't count "characters" (plus Multiple Man and Collective Man only count once each thanks for trying, guys).

The idea for the cover actually came from artist Scott Koblish. Upon hearing the wedding issue, Scott proposed the cover concept along with a very roug layout, saying "I'm feeling insane enough to try it." If Scott himself didn't com to regret those words, surely we can guess colorist Val Staples did, after takin on the herculean task of coloring each individual character in the recor setting piece. Now, months after finishing the cover, both artists are almo entirely recovered…although both are still known to give a startled yelp whe they hear the word "wedding." We are 94% sure that is because of this cover.

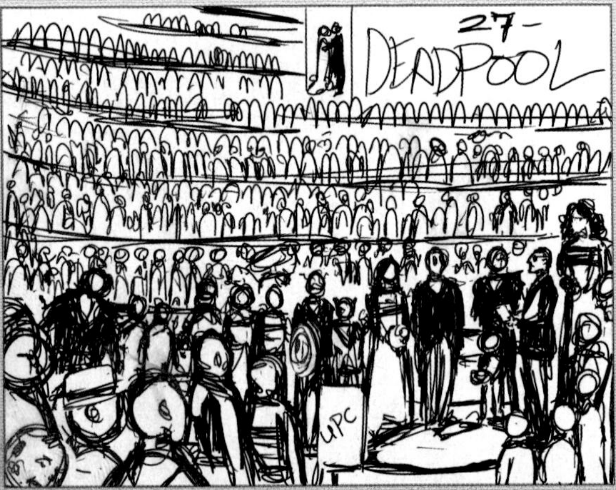
27-
DEADPOOL
UPC

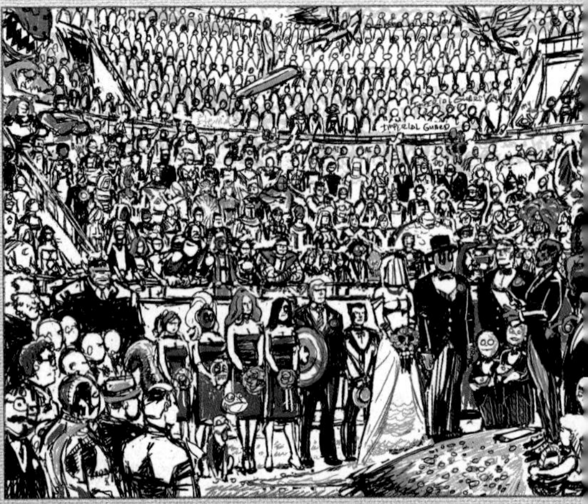

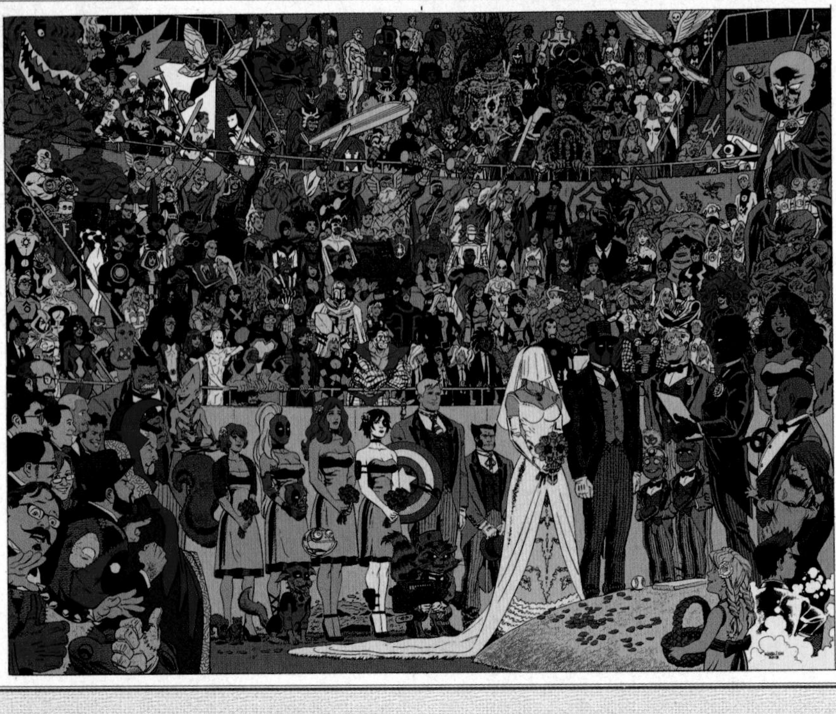

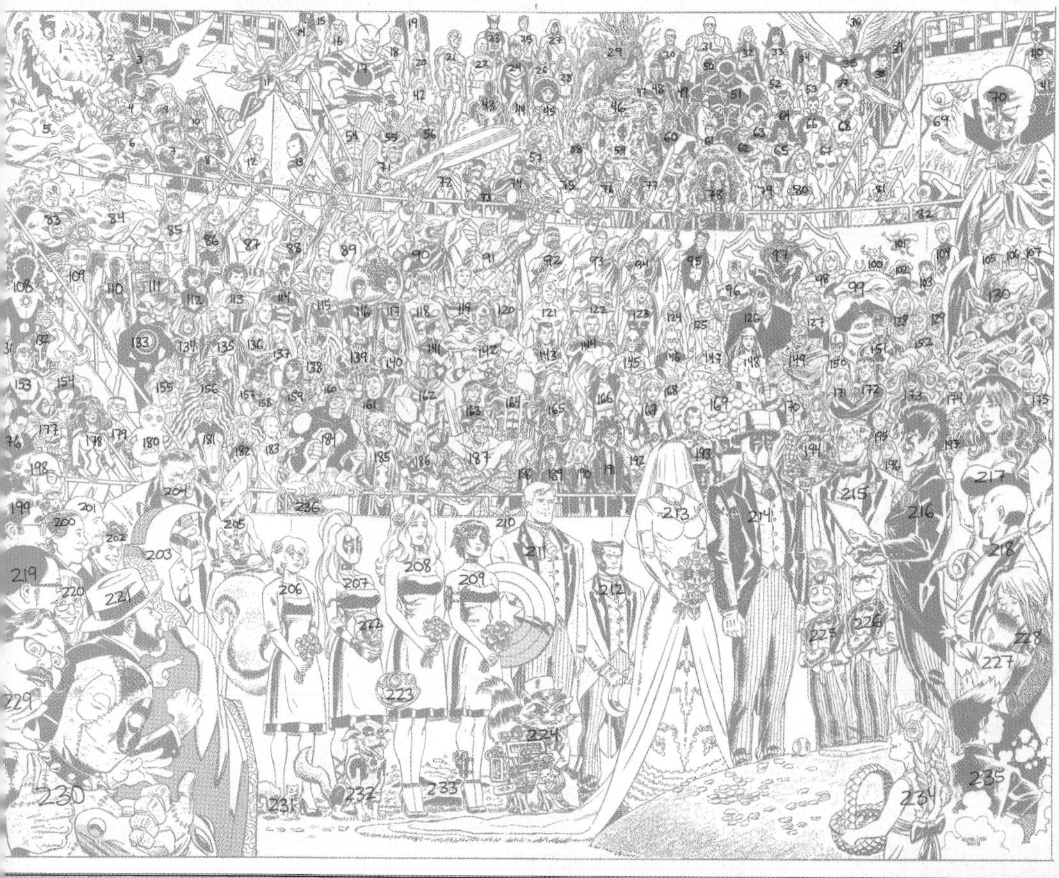

EVIL DINOSAUR
NOWBIRD
OON-BOY
HAMAN
ASQUATCH
UARDIAN
ORTHSTAR
URORA
NDICATOR
MARRINA
PIXIE
TARFOX
THE WHITE
TIGER
UNION JACK
THE COLLECTIVE
MAN
SPITFIRE
GIANT-MAN
THE VISION
THE COLLECTIVE
MAN
ALEXIS
THE SILVER
URFER
THE RED
GUARDIAN
D-MAN
VELOCIDAD
QUICKSILVER
TRANSONIC
WICCAN
LUCY IN THE SKY
GROOT
PRODIGY
DRAX
GAMORA
MANTIS
THE COLLECTIVE
MAN
THE ORIGINAL
ANGEL
GHOST RIDER
MADROX THE
MULTIPLE MAN
MADROX THE
MULTIPLE MAN

39. MADROX THE MULTIPLE MAN
40. SCARLET SPIDER
41. QUASAR
42. JIM HAMMOND, THE ORIGINAL HUMAN TORCH
43. VENOM
44. COLLEEN WING
45. MISTY KNIGHT
46. CH'OD
47. CR'EEE
48. DARKHAWK
49. STAR-LORD
50. B'NEE (WARSTAR)
51. C'CIL (WARSTAR)
52. GRAVITY
53. THE FIN
54. 3-D MAN
55. NIGHTHAWK
56. RAGE
57. TIGRA
58. SCINTILLA
59. STARBOLT
60. NEURON
61. ORACLE
62. MENTOR
63. EARTHQUAKE
64. FANG
65. ELECTRON
66. MANTA
67. HUSSAR
68. PULSAR (ALSO KNOWN AS IMPULSE)
69. FIN FANG FOOM
70. THE WATCHER
71. RED RAVEN
72. STINGRAY
73. DUST
74. THE SHROUD
75. HOBGOBLIN
76. ASTRA
77. GLADIATOR
78. THE MAN-THING
79. AMADEUS CHO
80. SHANNA THE SHE-DEVIL
81. SON OF SATAN
82. EYE-ROBOT
83. THE CHAMPION
84. RED HULK
85. SIF
86. VALKYRIE
87. FANDRALL
88. HOGUN
89. VOLSTAGG
90. BETA RAY BILL
91. ODIN
92. HERCULES
93. BALDER
94. THOR-GIRL
95. MACHINE MAN
96. DAREDEVIL
97. SUPERIOR SPIDER-MAN
98. DARLA DEERING
99. LOCKJAW
100. HAIRBALL
101. THOR FROG
102. MS. LION
103. ONOME
104. ALEX POWER
105. TONG
106. KORR
107. MIK
108. SUNSPOT
109. FORBUSH MAN
110. CAPTAIN UNIVERSE
111. HAWKEYE
112. PHOTON
113. MANIFOLD
114. BLACK PANTHER
115. CAPTAIN MARVEL
116. SMASHER
117. ABYSS
118. FALCON
119. HYPERION
120. STARBRAND
121. NIGHTMASK
122. M-11
123. NAMORA
124. VENUS
125. JIMMY WOO
126. GORILLA-MAN
127. BLACK SWAN
128. WU
129. VIL
130. DRAGON MAN
131. ICEMAN
132. NOVA
133. HAVOK
134. ROGUE
135. STORM
136. CAPTAIN BRITAIN
137. MEGGAN
138. GARGOYLE
139. SUNFIRE
140. THE SCARLET WITCH
141. WONDER MAN
142. THE BEAST
143. NAMOR
144. BLUE MARVEL
145. IRON FIST
146. QUENTIN QUIRE
147. KID GLADIATOR
148. ELEKTRA
149. GORGON
150. KARNAK
151. BLACK BOLT
152. TRITON
153. CANNONBALL
154. EX NIHILO
155. DAGGER
156. CLOAK
157. JUBILEE
158. SHOGO
159. PSYLOCKE
160. BENJAMIN DEEDS
161. FABIO MEDINA
162. MAGNETO
163. EVA BELL
164. CYCLOPS
165. EMMA FROST
166. ELSA BLOODSTONE
167. KITTY PRYDE
168. LOCKHEED
169. THE THING
170. HUMAN TORCH
171. INVISIBLE WOMAN
172. MR. FANTASTIC
173. MEDUSA
174. CRYSTAL
175. YONDU
176. RAUNAK
177. MOON KNIGHT
178. SPIDER-WOMAN
179. ANARCHIST
180. DOOP
181. THE ORIGINAL CYCLOPS
182. THE ORIGINAL MARVEL GIRL
183. THE ORIGINAL ICEMAN
184. THE ORIGINAL BEAST
185. RACHEL SUMMERS
186. MAGIC
187. COLOSSUS
188-190. EMMA FROST'S CUCKOOS
191. TRIAGE
192. BROO
193. IRON MAN
194. THOR
195. FRANKLIN RICHARDS
196. VAL RICHARDS
197. ANT-MAN (SCOTT LANG)
198. BRIAN POSEHN
199. SCOTT KOBLISH
200. VAL STAPLES
201. AXEL ALONSO
202. MIKE HAWTHORNE
203. DR. STRANGE
204. THE INCREDIBLE HULK
205. THE IMPOSSIBLE MAN
206. SQUIRREL GIRL
207. LADY DEADPOOL
208. SIRYN
209. DOMINO
210. THE WASP
211. CAPTAIN AMERICA
212. WOLVERINE
213. THE BRIDE
214. DEADPOOL
215. CABLE
216. NIGHTCRAWLER
217. SHE-HULK
218. LUKE CAGE
219. DECLAN SHALVEY
220. JORDIE BELLAIRE
221. GERRY DUGGAN
222. ZOMBIE HEADPOOL
223. WIDGET
224. ROCKET RACCOON
225. ARTIE
226. LEECH
227. DANIELLE JONES-CAGE
228. JESSICA JONES
229. JORDAN D. WHITE
230. EVIL DEADPOOL
231. MONKEY JOE
232. DEADPOOL DOG
233. KRAKOA
234. KATIE POWER
235. JACK POWER
236. PUCK

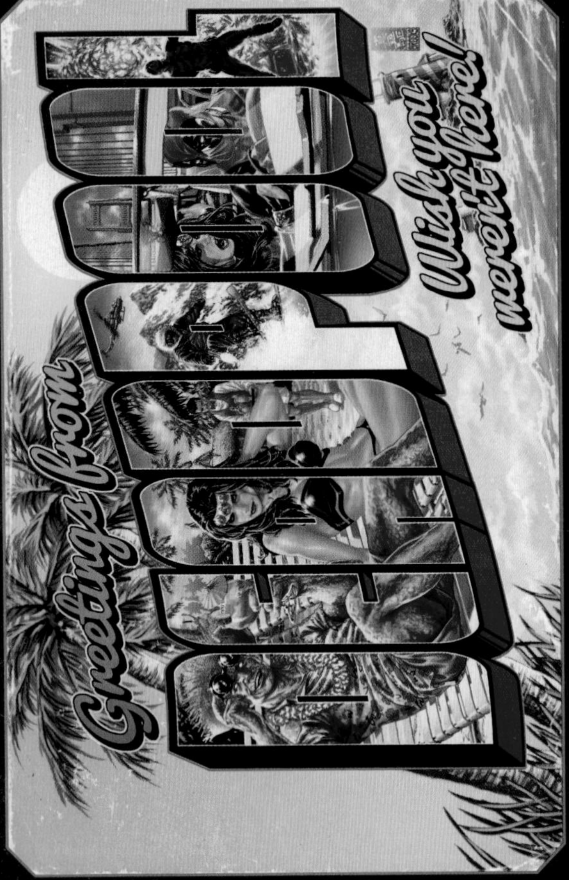

Greetings from
DEADPOOL
Wish you weren't here!

#28 VARIANT
BY MARK BROOKS

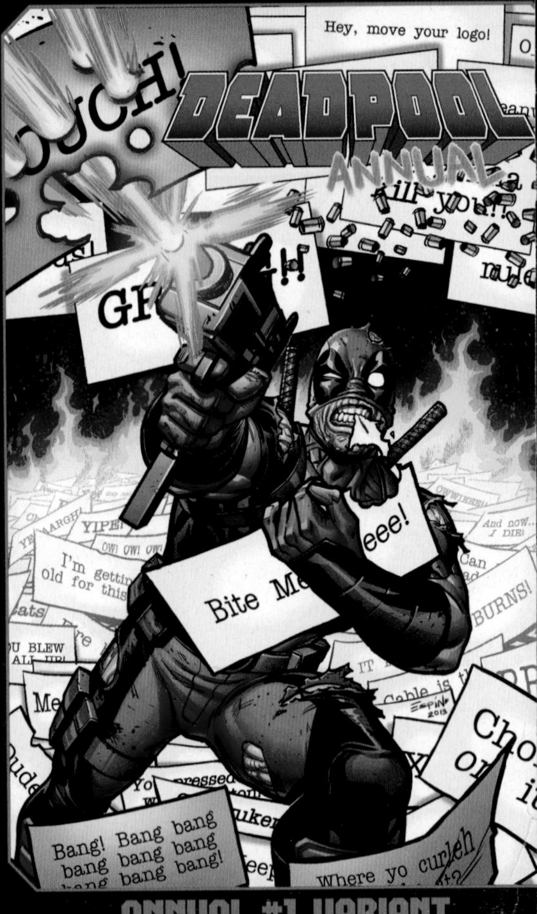

Hey, move your logo!
DEADPOOL
ANNUAL
Bite Me
And now... I DIE!
BURNS!
Bang! Bang bang
bang bang bang
bang bang!

ANNUAL #1 VARIANT
BY SALVA ESPIN & GURU-EFX